Tenants' Rights

11th California Edition

**BY CALIFORNIA ATTORNEYS
MYRON MOSKOVITZ & RALPH WARNER**

EDITED BY STEPHEN ELIAS, MARY RANDOLPH,
MARCIA STEWART & PATRICIA GIMA

ILLUSTRATIONS BY LINDA ALLISON

NOLO PRESS   BERKELEY, CALIFORNIA

your responsibility when using a self-help law book

We've done our best to give you useful and accurate information in this book. But laws and procedures change frequently and are subject to differing interpretations. If you want legal advice backed by a guarantee, see a lawyer. If you use this book, it's your responsibility to make sure that the facts and general advice contained in it are applicable to your situation.

keeping up-to-date

To keep its books up to date, Nolo Press issues new printings and new editions periodically. New printings reflect minor legal changes and technical corrections. New editions contain major legal changes, major text additions or major reorganizations. To find out if a later printing or edition of any Nolo book is available, call Nolo Press at (510) 549-1976 or check the catalog in the *Nolo News,* our quarterly newspaper.

To stay current, follow the "Update" service in the *Nolo News.* You can get the paper free by sending us the registration card in the back of the book. In another effort to help you use Nolo's latest materials, we offer a 25% discount off the purchase of any new Nolo book if you turn in any earlier printing or edition. (See the "Recycle Offer" in the back of the book.)

This book was last revised in: **JUNE 1993.**

ELEVENTH EDITION	
THIRD PRINTING	June 1993
BOOK DESIGN	Jackie Mancuso
PROOFREADING	David Freund
INDEX	Sayre van Young
PRINTING	Delta Lithograph

Moskovitz, Myron.
    Tenants' rights / by Myron Moskovitz & Ralph Warner : edited by Toni Ihara & Stephen Elias : illustrations by Linda Allison. -- 11th Calif. ed.
      p. cm
    Rev. ed. of : California tenants' handbook. c1989.
    Includes index.
    ISBN 0-87337-170-4 : $15.95
    1. Landlord and tenant--California--Popular works. I. Warner, Ralph E. II. Randolph, Mary. III. Elias, Stephen. IV. Stewart, Marcia. V. Moskovitz, Myron. California tenants' handbook. V. Title.
KFC145.Z9M68 1991
346.79404'34--dc20   91-22853
[347.9406434]   CIP

Copyright © 1972, 1981, 1982, 1984, 1985, 1986, 1987, 1989, 1991
by Myron Moskovitz & Ralph Warner
All Rights Reserved
Printed on paper with recycled content. Cover coating is water-based.

recycled paper

thank you

We wish to thank the following people associated with the first Moskovitz manuscript: Pedro Echeverria and Ronald Vera for their research assistance, Mary Durant and Madeline Finlay for their secretarial assistance, Allan David Heskin for his editorial assistance, and Ann Curtis for her art work.

We also wish to express our gratitude to some friends who helped make this a better book: Lucretia Edwards, Jeffrey Carter, David Brown, Patricia Gima, Marcia Stewart, M: Randolph, Mady Shumofsky, Barbara Kaufman, Steve Elias and J. Wallace Oman.

We would also like to acknowledge the many excellent contributions of our original c author Charles Sherman, many of whose original words still appear 19 years (and ten editions) after his valuable contributions to the first edition.

contents

INTRODUCTION

1

SOME GENERAL THINGS YOU SHOULD KNOW

A.	Who Is Your Landlord?	1/2
B.	The Landlord Business	1/4
C.	Renters' Tax Credit—California Income Tax	1/5
D.	Lawyers	1/5
E.	Typing Services	1/9
F.	Legal Research Notes	1/9
G.	Mediation	1/12

2

LOOKING FOR A PLACE AND RENTING IT

A.	Get Organized	2/2
B.	Learn About Rental Agreements	2/2
C.	Fees and Deposits	2/9
D.	Credit Reports	2/11
E.	How To Check a Place Over	2/12
F.	How to Bargain for the Best Deal	2/15
G.	Get All Promises In Writing	2/16
H.	The Landlord-Tenant Checklist	2/18
I.	Your Responsibilities as a Tenant	2/18
J.	Co-Signing Leases	2/20

3

SHARING A HOME

- A. Is It Legal to Live Together? .... 3 / 2
- B. The Legal Obligations of Roommates to the Landlord .... 3 / 2
- C. The Legal Obligations of Roommates to Each Other .... 3 / 3
- D. Having a Friend Move In .... 3 / 5
- E. Guests .... 3 / 10

4

ALL ABOUT RENT

- A. When Is Rent Due? .... 4 / 2
- B. Late Charges .... 4 / 2
- C. Partial Rent Payments .... 4 / 3
- D. Rent Increases: General Law .... 4 / 4
- E. Rent Increase Notices .... 4 / 4
- F. Rent Control .... 4 / 5
- G. General Types of Rent Control Laws .... 4 / 9
- H. Rent Control Board Hearings .... 4 / 10
- I. What to Do If the Landlord Violates Rent Control Rules .... 4 / 14
- J. Rent Control Chart: Specific Provisions of Rent Control .... 4 / 14

5

DISCRIMINATION

- A. Forbidden Types of Discrimination .... 5 / 2
- B. Legal Reasons to Discriminate .... 5 / 4
- C. How to Tell If a Landlord Is Discriminating .... 5 / 7
- D. What to Do About Discrimination .... 5 / 7
- E. Sexual Harassment by Landlords or Managers .... 5 / 9

6

THE OBNOXIOUS LANDLORD AND YOUR RIGHT TO PRIVACY

- A. Your Landlord's Right of Entry .... 6 / 2
- B. What to Do About a Landlord's Improper Entry .... 6 / 4
- C. Other Types of Invasions of Privacy .... 6 / 6

7

REPAIRS AND MAINTENANCE

    A. The Landlord's Duties .... 7 / 2
    B. Remedies .... 7 / 3

8

INJURIES TO A TENANT DUE TO SUBSTANDARD HOUSING CONDITIONS

    A. Standard of Care Imposed on Landlords .... 8 / 2
    B. Landlord Liability for Defects in the Premises .... 8 / 2
    C. Landlord's Duty To Protect Tenant from Injury Caused by Others ... 8 / 3
    D. Landlord Liability for Damage to Your Property .... 8 / 5

9

BREAKING A LEASE, SUBLEASING, AND OTHER LEASING PROBLEMS

    A. What Happens When the Lease Runs Out .... 9 / 2
    B. Subleases and Assignments .... 9 / 2
    C. Subleasing With the Idea of Returning Later .... 9 / 3
    D. How to Break a Lease .... 9 / 3
    E. Belongings You Leave Behind .... 9 / 8

10

SECURITY DEPOSITS AND LAST MONTH'S RENT

    A. Amount of Deposit .... 10 / 2
    B. Non-Refundable Deposits .... 10 / 3
    C. What the Deposits May Be Used For .... 10 / 3
    D. Landlord's Duty to Return Deposit .... 10 / 4
    E. Effect of Sale of Premises on Security Deposits .... 10 / 4
    F. May the Landlord Increase the Security Deposit? .... 10 / 5
    G. Avoiding Deposit Problems .... 10 / 5
    H. If the Landlord Won't Return Your Deposit .... 10 / 6
    I. Rent Withholding as a Way to Get Deposits Back In Advance ...... 10 / 9
    J. Interest on Security Deposits .... 10 / 10
    K. Last Month's Rent .... 10 / 10

11

EVICTIONS

A.	Illegal Self-Help Evictions	11 / 3
B.	Illegal Retaliatory Evictions	11 / 4
C.	Overview of Eviction Procedure	11 / 5
D.	Termination of Tenancy Notices	11 / 8
E.	Your Options After a Three-Day or 30-Day Notice Is Served	11 / 12
F.	The Eviction Lawsuit	11 / 13
G.	Stopping an Eviction	11 / 46
H.	Postponing an Eviction	11 / 48
I.	Appeal From an Eviction	11 / 50
J.	After the Lawsuit—Eviction by the Sheriff	11 / 50
K.	Small Claims Court Evictions	11 / 55

12

TENANTS ACTING TOGETHER

A.	Tenant Organizing	12 / 2
B.	Setting Up a Tenants' Organization	12 / 3
C.	Getting Information on the Landlord	12 / 6
D.	Tactics	12 / 8
E.	Negotiations	12 / 12
F.	The Agreement	12 / 13

13

RENTER'S INSURANCE

14

CONDOMINIUM CONVERSION

A.	Legal Protection for Tenants	14 / 2
B.	Changing the Law	14 / 2

APPENDIX

introduction

Here is a detailed legal guide designed for use by California residential tenants. Our purpose in writing it is twofold. First, we explain California landlord-tenant law in as straightforward a manner as possible. Second, we focus on how you can use this knowledge to anticipate and, where possible, avoid legal problems. In this latter regard, particularly, ours is a result-oriented approach. We have specifically designed this book so that a tenant who believes that his or her rights have been violated can quickly understand the relevant law that covers the area, as well as the remedies available to deal with the problem.

Since the first edition of *Tenants' Rights*, landlord-tenant law has experienced so many changes that little of the original book remains. Of far more importance to you, however, is the fact that today the legal and practical strategies necessary to be a successful tenant are far different than they were just a few years ago.

The reasons for this have to do with two major changes in the California landlord-tenant scene. The first big change is that in the last decade, the legal rights available to tenants to protect themselves from outrageous landlord conduct have greatly improved. For example, today a tenant has a number of fairly powerful weapons when it comes to dealing with a landlord who does any one of a number of obnoxious things, including discriminating against her for almost any reason not directly related to her being a bad tenant, invading her privacy, refusing to fix dangerous conditions on the rental premises, or failing to return a security deposit when a unit has been left clean and undamaged.

So far, so good, but unfortunately, the other major change in the landlord-tenant relationship is not beneficial to tenants. This is simply that, in the great majority of California cities and counties, there is not enough rental housing to go around. The fact that there are too many tenants chasing not enough rental units is, of course, not lost on landlords, many of whom have taken advantage of it to raise rents, reduce services and adopt all sorts of other strategies to maximize their economic return. And sadly, it has also made a deep impact on many tenants who have become so worried about not having a place to live that they are reluctant to assert their obvious legal rights, for fear the landlord will ask them to leave.

Our job is to explain your rights as a tenant and the remedies available to you should any of these rights be violated. But we do so with emphasis on how you can both take advantage of your legal rights and feel as secure as possible in doing so. In other words, we want you to know how to improve the condition of your tenancy, while at the same time you don't risk losing it.

Here at the beginning, let us confess an important bias. We believe that in the long run a tenant is best served if he establishes a positive relationship with his landlord (or property manager, if the landlord is not on the scene). Why? First, because it's our view that adherence to the law and principles of fairness is a good way to live. Second, because your landlord is intimately involved with providing you one of your most important services, the roof over your head, you want your relationship with this person or corporation to be free of paranoia and hostility. For these reasons, we present your legal rights and remedies in the context of using them to arrive at solutions both you and your landlord can feel good about.

Occasionally, however, tenants must deal with a landlord (or manager) so neglectful, hostile, or just plain difficult that a positive approach is impossible, and perhaps even counter-productive. If you find yourself in this unpleasant situation, there is little that you can do except assert your legal rights early and often. We are mindful of this possibility and provide detailed information as to how to cope with the obnoxious landlord.

Now, here are a few tips about using this book. Landlord-tenant law is a complicated and intertwined subject. Necessarily, when laying it out in a linear fashion on the pages of this book, we have had to make dozens of organizational decisions. Thus, because getting deposits returned is principally of interest when you move out, we deal with the law on this subject in Chapter 10, in the context of ending a tenancy. However, we discuss the process of renting a place in Chapter 2, another time when understanding the law as it applies to deposits is important. The point is that unless you are very knowledgeable about California landlord-tenant law to begin with, your best bet is to read this entire book at least once. You will then have the perspective and background necessary to be able to focus on those specific legal areas which concern you.

A special word is appropriate for those of you who live in areas covered by rent control ordinances. These laws generally establish how much your rent can be increased for most residential living spaces. It is also of great importance, however, that they can, and often do, override general California law in a number of other ways. For example, in many cities (including San Francisco and Los Angeles) rent-control ordinances restrict a landlord's ability to terminate month-to-month tenancies: these laws require "just cause" to evict. We handle rent control in two ways. First, throughout this book, as part of explaining tenants' rights and responsibilities under general state law, we indicate those areas in which rent control laws are likely to modify or change these rules. Second, we provide a detailed discussion of rent control in Chapters 4 and 11. These chapters are designed to be used along with a careful reading of a current copy of your local rent control ordinance.

Finally, may we wish you nothing but good landlords, understanding managers and, above all else, good luck.

Guide to Abbreviations Used in This Book

We use these standard abbreviations throughout this book for important statutes and court cases covering tenants' rights.

CALIFORNIA CODES

CC	Civil
CCP	Civil Procedure
UHC	Uniform Housing Code

FEDERAL LAWS

U.S.C.	United States Code

CASES

Cal. App.	California Court of Appeal
Cal. Rptr.	California Court of Appeal and California Supreme Court
Cal.	California Supreme Court
N.J. Spr.	New Jersey Superior Court Reports
A. or A.2d	Atlantic Reporter
S.E. or S.E. 2d	South Eastern Reporter
F. Supp.	United States District Court
F.2d	United States Court of Appeal
U.S.	United States Supreme Court

OPINIONS

Ops. Cal. Atty. Gen.	California Attorney General Opinions

chapter 1

Some General Things You Should Know

A. Who Is Your Landlord?	1/2
1. Finding Out the Name of the Owner	1/2
2. Effect of Sale of Premises on Tenant's Rights	1/2
3. Know Your Manager	1/3
B. The Landlord Business	1/4
C. Renters' Tax Credit—California Income Tax	1/5
D. Lawyers	1/5
1. When Do You Need a Lawyer?	1/6
2. What Lawyers Can Do For You	1/6
3. Finding a Lawyer	1/7
4. Legal Advice over the Phone	1/8
E. Typing Services	1/9
F. Legal Research Notes	1/9
G. Mediation	1/12

A. Who Is Your Landlord?

There is no typical landlord. Your landlord may be a little old man with a Siamese cat and a bad head for arithmetic or you may rent from a large corporation. It is extremely important that you find out what kind of person your landlord is, because having complete knowledge of your legal rights will help you very little if you lack a good human understanding of the person with whom you are dealing. Coupled with such an understanding this book can be of great value.

Along with understanding the personality of your landlord, it is important to know his problems, circumstances and style of operating. Dealing with a retired schoolteacher managing her late uncle's duplex will obviously be a lot different from dealing with an institution with 500 units, managers, rules and red tape. Still, the law remains the same for all landlords—with the exception of some landlord-occupied premises. (See Chapter 5.B.)

1. Finding Out the Name of the Owner

In the past, some owners have instructed their managers not to tell the tenants who they were or where they could be located, so the tenant could not "bother" them. State law tries to solve this problem.[1] It provides that:

a. The rental agreement must state the name and address of both the manager and the owner (or person authorized by him to receive notices, demands and lawsuits against the owner). This information must be kept current with the tenant being informed of all changes,

or,

b. Instead of putting this information in each rental agreement, the owner may choose to post notices containing the same information in the building. A notice must be posted in at least two easy-to-see places (including all elevators).

If the owner fails to follow this law, then the person who rented the dwelling for the owner automatically becomes his agent for receiving notices, demands and lawsuits.

2. Effect of Sale of Premises on Tenant's Rights

If your landlord sells the house or apartment building where you rent, your rights as a tenant remain the same. If you have a month-to-month agreement, the new landlord must give you 30 days' notice in order to raise your rent, change other terms of your tenancy, or have you move out. There may be further restrictions in communities with rent control laws requiring the landlord to show "just cause" to evict. (See Chapter 4 for the law on rent increases and details on rent control, and Chapter 11 for information on evictions.)

If you have a lease, the new landlord cannot evict you (unless you break the terms of the lease) or change the terms of your agreement until the lease runs out. (Landlord bankruptcy is an exception to this. See note below.) For example, the new landlord cannot make you give away your dog if your lease does not prohibit pets.

You still retain all your rights: to be free of arbitrary and discriminatory treatment on the basis of factors such as race or religion (Chapter 5), to privacy and peaceful occupancy (which may particularly be an issue while the rental house or building is being shown to prospective buyers—see Chapter 6), to repair and deduct the cost of repairs (Chapter 7), and to get a refund on your security deposit or a detailed itemization of charges within two weeks after you move out (Chapter 10).

Note on Landlord Bankruptcy: You may be evicted in the middle of a fixed-term lease if your landlord's mortgage has been foreclosed upon and the lender who has obtained title to the property wants you out

---

[1] CC § 1962.

in order to sell it.[2] This seems unfair, but it is your landlord's fault for not making her payments, and the bank is legally allowed to protect its interests in this fashion. If you're having a difficult time finding another place, the bank may give you some extra time to move out. If your landlord has filed for bankruptcy, contact the bankruptcy court and get in touch with the bankruptcy trustee in charge of the landlord's property to get information on how this effects your tenancy, where you should pay rent and what will happen to your security deposit.

3. Know Your Manager

Many medium to large apartment complexes have managers. The owner wants to make money, but he wants somebody else to do the work of actually managing the rental property. More and more owners are hiring management corporations who specialize in managing lots of rental units and who get paid a percentage (usually between 5% and 10%) of the rental income. Such companies tend to be sticklers for rules and procedures, but are usually less emotionally involved than owners, and are often more rational at arriving at business-like compromises.[3] Often, however, the owner will simply give a student or older person free or reduced rent to look after his property on a part-time basis. This can be either good or bad as far as you are concerned, depending on the personality of the manager and whether he has any real authority to take care of problems. Just as there are all sorts of landlords, there is an equal variety of managers.

In dealing with a manager on a day-to-day basis, it is important not only to notice who he is and how best to deal with him; it is also important to notice his relationship to the owner. Remember, the owner and the manager may have very different interests. Some owners, for example, may want the property to yield a maximum amount of profit with a minimal amount of trouble, while others may be investing for long-term real property appreciation and be willing to be reasonably generous to tenants in the meantime. Similarly, some managers might want to do as little work as possible for their free rent, while others, especially those who are in the business, may want to do a bang up job in hopes that word will spread and they will get other jobs.

A landlord is legally responsible for the acts of a manager or management company. Should you be in a situation in which the premises are not being kept clean or in good repair or if the manager is obnoxious or invading your privacy, you will probably want to deal directly with the owner if possible. In any case, where communications are sticky or broken down, you should send duplicate copies of letters and other communications to the owner as well as to the manager.

---

[2] In a rent control area, the 30-day notice may not be used for this purpose unless the rent control ordinance lists it as one of the "just causes" for eviction. *Gross v. Superior Court* (1985) 171 Cal.App.3d 265.

[3] Usually a rental management corporation manages a lot of units in a relatively small geographic area. This makes checking their reputation fairly easy. It is wise to do so. If the building or development has 16 or more apartments, there must be a resident manager living there. California Administrative Code, Title 25, § 42.

B. The Landlord Business

You may choose not to read this section and still learn all you need to know about what you face as a tenant. For those who are interested, however, we thought it would be helpful to understand how the landlord business works. We believe that a tenant or group of tenants will be in a better position to make wise decisions if they have an idea of what it's like to walk a mile in their landlord's boots.

Making money as a landlord depends a great deal on making wise initial investment decisions and on having an ability to manage property. This is true whether the landlord owns one unit or a thousand units. Given average ability in these directions, however, it is pretty difficult to lose money in the landlord business. Indeed, many landlords achieve spectacular returns. This is possible because the landlord is able to take advantage of a number of favorable tax laws and is able to use your money to do it.

The landlord business works something like this. To buy a building or building complex the landlord must usually put down between 15%-30% of the purchase price. A bank or insurance company puts up the rest. If he buys a decent building he may be able to set the rents at a level that will allow him to cover all of his mortgage, tax and upkeep payments and pocket a little money besides. If you ask a landlord about his yearly profit, he will doubtless tell you that it is small, or perhaps even nonexistent, but will not tell you that each year he owns more of the building and in addition is receiving tax deductions on his personal tax returns. He will also not point out that in most areas the market value of the building normally goes up over time.

You have probably heard about "tax shelters" and "tax loopholes." There are still many of these available to landlords although they were severely curtailed by the Tax Reform Act of 1986. Here is how tax laws work to benefit landlords:

• All the money a landlord pays for building maintenance, upkeep expense and interest on his mortgage payments is subtracted from the landlord's profit figure before taxes are paid.

• All the money a landlord pays in local property taxes constitutes a tax deduction.

• A percentage of the value of a landlord's building is deductible each year under the heading of "depreciation." The depreciation deduction allows the landlord credit for wear and tear to his building and the fact that the building is supposed to get less valuable as it gets older. If a landlord claims that a particular building has a useful life of 27.5 years, he is able to deduct 3.6% of the building's value each year. In some situations, a landlord is able to take advantage of laws that allow him to take extra depreciation in the early years of a mortgage. The depreciation deduction is often a major windfall for a landlord. This is because in most cases a building is more valuable after 20 years than it was when first purchased. Thus, the landlord gets his yearly tax deduction and a more valuable building too! As soon as the depreciation credits are used up, the wisdom of the landlord business dictates that the building be sold to a new landlord, who then declares a new life expectancy for the building and starts the depreciation process all over again!

Usually the landlord will buy the building with a little bit of his own money and a lot of borrowed money. He collects rent from you and other tenants, then uses your rent money to pay off his loan and to pay property taxes and upkeep.

Landlords also get certain built-in advantages in times of inflation. In non-rent control areas, a landlord is able to raise rents while his mortgage and interest payments remain pretty constant. In a similar way, the landlord often gets a break on his real property taxes. Normally, a building is assessed for local property tax purposes on the basis of the original purchase price. In periods of inflation, however, rents often go up faster than do tax assessments.

With so much in the landlord's favor, it is truly amazing that any landlords are in unfavorable financial situations. When such is the case, however, it always goes hard on the tenants. If the landlord is a bad businessperson, he may get over-extended on his loans (that is, he may try to buy too much property without enough money, or may have paid too much for the property in the first place). Then he will have to raise rents or cut back on repairs and services. This can lead to a high turnover of dissatisfied or resentful tenants. Such circumstances can make the landlord harder to deal with.

Note: You may want to ask your landlord about his finances and problems, especially if you are on good terms. He might appreciate your interest (which might improve your relationship), and you may learn some things that will increase your understanding of his problems.

Landlords' profits can be hurt quickly:

1. by periods of deflation and depression (the 1930's was a bad time for landlords), when they can't fill up their buildings with tenants at favorable rents;

2. by any action by tenants to jointly withhold rents; and

3. by extremely tough rent control ordinances.

None of these conditions has been widespread in California in recent years. As a result, most landlords have done very well and in many cases have made enormous profits. To see that these profits keep coming, landlords have organized at the local, state and federal levels. Through real estate associations, apartment house owners associations and similar groups, landlords keep a close watch on government—from your local city council and planning commission to the state and federal legislatures. Lobbyists maintain offices in Sacramento and Washington with the specific purpose of furthering the landlord business and seeing to it that no law harmful to landlords is passed by any legislature anywhere. Landlord lobbyists are often very successful at getting legislation introduced and enacted that is favorable to landlords.

C. Renters' Tax Credit—California Income Tax

Beginning with the 1991 tax year, the California renter's tax credit has changed from a flat credit to one based on income.[4]

The amount of the credit is shown below.

- Married couples filing joint returns, heads of households and surviving spouses:

Adjusted gross income	Tax credit
$40,000 or less	$120
$40,000-41,000	$60
$41,001 or more	$0

- Other households (most single people)

$20,000 or less	$60
$20,000-20,500	$30
$20,501 or more	$0

If you pay taxes, you subtract the credit from the amount owed. If you don't pay taxes, you can still get the credit. This means you file a return and the state pays you. Married couples can only get one credit, but people living together can each claim one. In addition, tenants 62 years of age or older and tenants who are blind or disabled and whose annual income is $12,000 or less are eligible for tax benefits due to the fact that part of their rent is used to pay property taxes.[5] For technical details on these benefits, see the Individual Income Tax guide put out by the California Franchise Tax Board.

D. Lawyers

This book is not designed to replace an attorney. It is meant to give you a clear understanding of your rights and obligations and help you decide whether or not you need one.

---

[4]Revenue and Taxation Code § 17053.5.
[5]Revenue and Taxation Code § 20544.

Lawyers, like most of the rest of us, are in business to make money. They have to pay a lot of office overhead as well as support themselves and their families in a style to which they are, or would like to be, accustomed. Thus, most charge fairly high fees, normally in a range of $100 to $200 an hour. Clearly, when you have a dispute with your landlord which involves a few hundred dollars, it does not make good sense to pay someone as much (or more) than that to try to vindicate your position. In addition, there is always the danger that you will lose and end up paying both your landlord and your attorney, too.

Legal Research Note: Many people wish to do some of their own legal research before visiting a lawyer. County law libraries (which are located in many county courthouses) are free and open to the public. We review the basics of legal research in Section F of this chapter.

1. When Do You Need a Lawyer?

There is no simple answer to the question of when you need a lawyer. This is because there are many possible areas of dispute between landlord and tenant, and many levels of tenant ability to deal with problems. Throughout this book, we suggest times when the advice or other services of an attorney would be useful, but here are a few general pointers:

a. If a lease or written rental agreement allows attorney fees for your landlord, then California law says that the tenant is also entitled to recover attorney fees if he wins a lawsuit based on the terms of that agreement.

b. If your landlord sues you for a lot of money, or if you suffer a physical or emotional injury because of action or inaction by the landlord or manager, see an attorney.

c. If you have any problem that you can't understand or solve by reading this book, you should do some legal research yourself or get some professional advice.

2. What Lawyers Can Do For You

There are three basic ways a lawyer can help with the kinds of problems that face a tenant:

a. Consultation and Advice

The lawyer can listen to the details of your situation, analyze it for you, and advise you on your position and best plan of action. Ideally he will give you more than just conclusions—he can educate you about your whole situation and tell you all the various alternatives available. Then you can make your own choices. Or, you may just want a lawyer to look over the papers you have prepared, to be sure they are correct. This kind of service is the least expensive, as it only involves an office call and a little time. Find out the fee before you go in.

b. Negotiation

The lawyer can use his special talents, knowledge and experience to help you negotiate with the landlord to your best advantage. In case of serious problems, he can probably do this more successfully than you, especially if you are at odds with the landlord, or if your landlord has an attorney. Without spending much of his own time, he can often accomplish a lot through a letter or phone call. Receiving a message on an attorney's letterhead is, in itself, often very sobering to a landlord. A lawyer can sometimes possess considerable skill as a negotiator. Also, if bad turns to worse, a lawyer can convincingly threaten legal action. You can then decide at a later time whether to actually pursue it.

c. Lawsuits

In some instances your case may merit going into court with a lawsuit. Having your lawyer go into court can be expensive, and only rarely warranted. If the landlord sues you first, it is more likely that you will end up in court, and very likely that you will need a lawyer's help.

Whenever you think of using a lawyer, keep in mind this view of clients that is held by a lawyer-friend of ours: he imagines a man who has built a shack on some old railroad tracks in a high mountain valley. One day, when he puts his ear to the track, the man hears a distant vibration. A few days later he can hear the sound of a train rumbling on the warm breeze that blows up to the canyon, and soon the sound is distinctly audible. At this point he can begin to see the smoke of the engine, and not much later the train is running down on him, spitting fire and belching smoke. When the thing is 50 yards away, he picks up his phone, calls his lawyer and asks him to get an injunction against the railroad company! What we mean to say is, if you decide to use a lawyer, don't wait until it's too late.

3. Finding a Lawyer

Finding a lawyer who charges reasonable prices and whom you feel can be trusted is not always an easy task. There is always the danger that by just picking a name out of the telephone book you may get someone unsympathetic (perhaps an attorney who specializes in representing landlords) or an attorney who will charge too much. Here are some suggestions:

a. Legal Aid

If you are very poor, you may qualify for free help from your Legal Aid (often called Legal Services) office. Check your phone directory for their location, or ask your County Clerk. Legal Aid personnel may not be able to represent tenants in court, but may offer self-help materials.

b. Tenants' Rights Organizations

In a number of California communities, tenants have gotten together and established tenants advocacy organizations. (See Chapter 12.B.) Many of these groups provide free or low cost tenant counselling. Often counselling is provided by paralegals, and sometimes by volunteer lawyers. It often involves helping tenants understand their rights and sometimes extends to helping them prepare paperwork necessary to file or defend a lawsuit. Local bar associations also sometimes provide clinics for low-income tenants.

c. Personal Referrals

If you're looking for a lawyer on your own, this is the best approach. If you know someone who has consulted a lawyer on a landlord-tenant matter and was pleased with the lawyer, call that lawyer first.

d. Pre-Paid Legal Plans

Many unions, employers and consumer groups now offer membership in pre-paid legal plans. You can also sign up as an individual with plans offered by private companies such as Montgomery Ward.

The services provided by the plans vary widely. Some give legal services at reduced fees; some offer free advice. If a plan offers extensive free advice, your initial membership fee may be worth the consultation you receive, even if you use it only once. Most plans have renewal fees; it's common to join a plan for a specific service and then not renew.

There's no guarantee that the lawyers available through these plans are any good. Check out the plan, and if possible its lawyers, in advance. And when using any of these pre-paid plans, remember this: the lawyer is typically paid very little by the pre-paid plan for dealing with you. Some lawyers sign up in the hope they can talk you into buying extra services not covered by your monthly premium.

e. Private Law 'Clinics'

To market their services, law firms such as Jacoby & Meyers advertise on TV and radio, offering low initial consultation fees. This generally means that a basic consultation is cheap (often about $35), but anything after that isn't. If you consult a law clinic, the trick is to quickly extract what information you need and to resist any attempt to make you think you need further services.

f. Lawyer Referral Panels

Most county bar associations maintain lawyer referral services. Usually, you can get a referral to an attorney who specializes in landlord-tenant law, and an initial consultation for free or for a low fee. But the panels don't really screen the listed attorneys, and the attorneys participating may not have much experience or ability. If you contact an attorney this way, be sure to ask about experience with tenant problems, and make sure she's sympathetic to tenants' rights.

g. Yellow Pages

If all else fails, every Yellow Pages has an extensive list of lawyers (under Attorneys) both by specialty and in alphabetical order. Many of the ads quote initial consultation rates.

Shop around by calling different law offices and stating your problem. Ask to talk to a lawyer personally; if you can't, this should give you an idea of how accessible the lawyer is. Ask some specific questions. Do you get clear, concise answers? If not, try someone else. If the lawyer says little except to suggest that he handle the problem (with a substantial fee, of course), watch out. You are talking with either someone who doesn't know the answer and won't admit it (common), or someone who pulls rank on the basis of professional standing. Don't be a passive client or deal with a lawyer who wants you to be one.

Keep in mind that lawyers learn mostly from experience and special training, not from law school. Because you're already well informed (you've read this book), you should be in a good position to evaluate a lawyer's credentials.

Remember, lawyers whose offices and life styles are reasonably simple are more likely to help you for less money than lawyers who feel naked unless wearing a $1,000 suit. You should be able to find an attorney willing to represent you for either a flat rate or an hourly rate of between $100-$200, depending on where the lawyer's office is located (big city lawyers tend to be pricier) and how complex your case is.

4. Legal Advice over the Phone

Legal information and advice are becoming available in more and more forms. One of the newest is by telephone, from a group of lawyers in the Los Angeles area, Tele-Lawyer, Inc., which employs lawyers in many specialities, including landlord-tenant law. The lawyers at Tele-Lawyer give advice by phone for $3 a minute ($180 an hour). It may sound expensive, but compared to the conventional way of getting help from a lawyer, it can be a bargain. You're charged only for the time the lawyer spends on the phone; the average tenant's call lasts about eight minutes.

If the lawyer can't answer your question during the call, he will research it and call you back. All conversations are confidential. In addition to advice, here's the kind of the help you can get from Tele-Lawyer:

• The lawyers will review documents—such as a lease or rental agreement—without charge, and then call back with comments.

• If you need a certain form, the lawyer can retrieve it from Tele-Lawyer's 4,000-document collection, and send it to you free of charge. Tele-Lawyer will send blank pre-printed California court forms as well as sample documents such as contracts.

Tele-Lawyer offers only advice—it does not give referrals to lawyers, and its lawyers do not accept cases.

If you want to call Tele-Lawyer to find more about the service without charge or have your call billed to your credit card, call (800) 835-3529. If you want the charge to appear on your phone bill, call (900) 370-7000.

E. Typing Services

What if you don't want to hire a lawyer but don't want to do all your legal paperwork yourself? Now, there's a middle ground. A number of businesses, known as "legal typing services" or "independent paralegals," assist people doing their own legal work in filling out the forms. Most typing services concentrate on family law or bankruptcy, but some handle landlord-tenant matters, too.

Typing services aren't lawyers. They can't give legal advice and can't represent you in court—only lawyers can. You must decide what steps to take in your case, and the information to put in any needed forms. Typing services can, however:

• provide written instructions and legal information needed to handle your own case;

• provide the appropriate forms; and

• type your papers so they'll be accepted by the court.

Typing services commonly charge far less than attorneys, because typing service customers do much of the work and make the basic decisions. Also, most typing services handle only routine cases.

If you're looking for a typing service, check classified sections of newspapers under Referral Services, usually immediately following attorneys. Also check the yellow pages under "divorce assistance" or "legal clinics." A local legal aid office may provide a reference, as will the occasional court clerk. Many offices have display ads in local throwaway papers like the *Classified Flea Market*. You can also get a list of California typing services from the National Association for Independent Paralegals, at (800) 542-0034.

Occasionally, a typing service has taken money from a customer and then failed to deliver the services as promised. As with any other business rip-off, you, as a consumer, can sue in small claims or regular court, and report the matter to your local district attorney's consumer fraud division. But legal remedies are often ineffective. The best precaution is to select a reliable typing service at the beginning. As with finding a lawyer, a recommendation from a satisfied customer is best. Also, as a general matter, the longer a typing service has been in business, the better. The National Association for Independent Paralegals will mediate complaints about any member typing service.

F. Legal Research Notes

We don't have space here to show you how to do your own legal research in anything approaching a comprehensive fashion. *Legal Research: How to Find and Understand the Law*, by Steve Elias and Susan Levinkind, and *Legal Research Made Easy: A Roadmap Through the Law Library Maze*, a videotape on the same subject, are excellent resources if you wish to learn basic legal research skills, something we highly recommend. Both are published by Nolo Press. (See order information at the back of this book.) Our goal here is only to tell you how to find the basic laws that control your residential tenancy. In addition, we show you how to locate the important judicial decisions (most of which are mentioned in this book) which interpret these laws.

Before you can find the laws, though, you've got to find the law library. Every California county maintains a law library which is open to the public. All have the California statutes, written court opinions, and expert commentary. You can find and read any statute or case we've referred to at the law library by looking it up according to its citation.

Or you may want to start your research with a good background resource. We mention several of these (*The California Eviction Defense Manual*, for example) throughout the book.

Landlord-tenant laws and legal procedure are principally contained in two parts of California law—the Civil Code (CC) and the Code of Civil Procedure (CCP), both of which are available at all law libraries and most public libraries. The Civil Code is divided into numerous sections, dealing generally with people's legal rights and responsibilities to each other. Most of California's substantive landlord-tenant law is contained in Sections 1940 through 1991 of this code, with laws governing minimum building standards, payment of rent, change and termination of tenancy, privacy and security deposits, to name a few. The Code of Civil Procedure is a set of laws which tells how people enforce legal rights in civil lawsuits. Eviction lawsuit procedures are contained in Sections 1161 through 1179 of the Code of Civil Procedure. Also of interest are the small claims court procedures mentioned in Sections 116.110 through 116.950.[6]

In this book, we make frequent references to statutes found in sources like the California Code of Civil Procedure and California Civil Code. We use standard abbreviations like CCP and CC to make future references to these sources easier. For your convenience, there is a list of standard abbreviations used in this book located on the last page of the introductory chapter.

Although these codes contain the text of applicable laws passed each year by the legislature, they don't contain the text of any of the appellate court decisions which determine what those laws mean. Sometimes these cases are extremely important. For example, the case of *Green v. Superior Court* adopted a "common law" rule allowing tenants in substandard housing to withhold rent—without paying to make repairs themselves. To gain access to the printed reports of important court decisions, you have to go to a law library.

The best way to learn of the existence of written court decisions which interpret a particular law is to first look in an "annotated code." An annotated code is a set of volumes of a particular code, such as the Civil Code or Code of Civil Procedure mentioned above, that contains not only all the laws (as do the regular codes), but also a brief summary of many of the court decisions interpreting each law. These annotated codes—published by West Publishing Company (*West's Annotated California Codes*—blue volumes) and by Bancroft-Whitney (*Deering's California Codes* —brown volumes)—can be found in some public libraries and any county law library or law school library in the state. They have comprehensive indexes by topic, and are kept up to date each year with paperback supplements ("pocket parts") located in a pocket in the back cover of each volume. Don't forget to look through these pocket parts for the latest law changes or case decisions since the hardcover volume was printed.

Each brief summary of a court decision is followed by the title of the case, the year of the decision, and the "citation." The citation is a sort of shorthand identification for the set of books, the volume, and page where the case can be found. The "official" volumes of cases are published by the California Supreme Court as the *Official Reports of the California Supreme Court* (abbreviated "Cal.," "Cal.2d," or "Cal.3d," respectively, representing the first, second and third "series" of volumes, the third containing all cases decided since 1969) and by the California Courts of Appeal[7] as *Official Reports of the California Courts of Appeal* (similarly abbreviated "Cal.App.," "Cal.App.2d" and "Cal.App.3d"). The same cases are also published in "unofficial volumes" by the West Publishing Company. These are *California Reporter* (abbreviated "Cal.Rptr.") and *Pacific Reporter* (abbreviated "P." or "P.2d," respectively, for the first and second series). The case is the same whether you read it in the official or unofficial reporter.

---

[6]You can buy the Civil Code and the Code of Civil Procedure in law book stores. In addition, Nolo Press sells the least expensive paperback versions. (To order these books from Nolo Press, call (800) 992-6656.) If you are involved with questions of landlord-tenant law on a daily basis, it is almost essential that you own both.

[7]The Courts of Appeal are California's "intermediate" level appeals courts, on a lower legal level than the California Supreme Court, but "higher" than the superior, municipal and justice courts of the counties. There are six appellate districts in the state, with courts in San Francisco, Los Angeles, Sacramento, San Diego, Fresno, and San Jose. (The California Supreme Court is headquartered in San Francisco.)

Here are some examples of case citations:

Green v. Superior Court (1974) 10 Cal.3d 616, 11 Cal.Rptr. 704, 517 P.2d 1168

- case name
- year of decision
- volume number
- 3rd series of *Official Reports of the California Supreme Court*
- page number
- volume number
- the case also appears in *Calif. Reporter*, the unofficial reports
- page number
- volume number
- the case is also listed in 2nd series of *Pacific Reporter*
- page number

Glaser v. Myers (1982) 137 Cal.App.3d 770, 187 Cal.Rptr. 242

- case name
- year of decision
- 3rd series of *Official Reports of the California Courts of Appeal*, Volume 137, page 770
- the case is also listed in *Calif. Reporter*, the unofficial reports, Volume 187, page 242

Lee v. Vignoli (1979) 98 Cal.App.3d Supp. 24, 160 Cal. Rptr. 79

- case name
- year of decision
- 3rd series of *Official Reports of the California Courts of Appeal*, Volume 98, page 24 of the supplement in the back of the volume
- the case also appears in volume 160, page 79 of the *Calif. Reporter*

Lindsey v. Normet (1972) 405 U.S. 56, 92 S.Ct. 862, 31 L.Ed.2d 36

- volume 405, page 56 of *Official Reports of the United States Supreme Court*
- also published in volume 92, page 862 of the *Supreme Court Reports*, an unofficial source
- also published in the 2nd series of "Lawyers Edition" of the *U.S. Supreme Court Reports*, volume 31, page 36

The above examples should take some of the mystery out of legal research. If, in the course of your research, you still have questions, again we recommend Elias, *Legal Research: How to Find and Understand the Law* (Nolo Press).

G. Mediation

Mediation involves bringing in a neutral third party to help disputants settle differences. The mediator normally has no power to impose a solution if the parties can't agree. Generally, mediation works well in situations where the parties want to settle their disputes in order to work together in the future. In a landlord-tenant context, mediation can be extremely helpful in a number of areas, such as disputes about noise, the necessity for repairs, a tenant's decision to withhold rent because defects have not been repaired, rent increases, privacy and many more. Many tenants and especially groups of tenants with a list of grievances find that mediating disputes with a landlord is a better approach to problem solving than is withholding rent, filing a lawsuit, etc.

A mediator does not impose a decision on the parties, but uses her skills to facilitate a compromise. Mediation is most effective when procedures are established in advance. Typically, the tenant or landlord with a problem contacts some respected neutral organization, such as a city or county landlord-tenant mediation project (not every area has one, but many do), the American Arbitration Association, or a neighborhood dispute resolution center, such as San Francisco's Community Board Program, and arranges for this group to mediate legitimate landlord-tenant disputes. There are a great number of mediation programs in California, and if you ask around in your area, you should find one.

At the mediation session, each side gets to state their position. Just doing this often cools people off considerably and frequently results in a compromise. If the dispute is not taken care of easily, however, the mediator may suggest several ways to resolve the problem, or may even keep everyone talking long enough to realize that the problem goes deeper than the one being mediated. For example, a landlord who thinks he runs a tight ship may learn that the real problem from the tenant's point of view is that her manager is lazy and slow to make repairs. This, of course, may lead to the further discovery that the manager is angry at several tenants for letting their kids pull up his tulips and call him a "big dummy."

Because mediation lets both sides air their grievances, it often works well to improve the climate of stormy landlord-tenant relationships. And if it doesn't, you haven't lost much, especially if you make sure mediation occurs promptly and you use it only in situations where your landlord has some arguably legitimate position. If mediation fails, you can still fight it out in court.

chapter 2

Looking for a Place and Renting It

A. Get Organized .... 2 / 2
B. Learn About Rental Agreements .... 2 / 2
    1. Oral Agreements .... 2 / 3
    2. Leases and Written Rental Agreements .... 2 / 3
    3. Printed Forms: What to Watch Out For .... 2 / 4
    4. Which Is Better, a Lease or a Month-to-Month Rental Agreement? .... 2 / 8
    5. Model Lease and Model Rental Agreement .... 2 / 9
C. Fees and Deposits .... 2 / 9
    1. Holding Deposit .... 2 / 9
    2. Finder's Fees .... 2 / 10
    3. Credit Check Fees .... 2 / 10
D. Credit Reports .... 2 / 11
E. How To Check a Place Over .... 2 / 12
    1. Landlord Disclosures .... 2 / 12
    2. Housing Codes and Enforcement .... 2 / 12
    3. A Checklist of Things to Inspect .... 2 / 13
    4. What If the Place Does Not Meet the Above Standards? .... 2 / 15
F. How to Bargain for the Best Deal .... 2 / 15
G. Get All Promises In Writing .... 2 / 16
H. The Landlord-Tenant Checklist .... 2 / 18
I. Your Responsibilities as a Tenant .... 2 / 18
    1. Comply With Your Lease or Rental Agreement .... 2 / 18
    2. Pay Your Rent on Time .... 2 / 18
    3. Keep the Place Clean .... 2 / 20
    4. Repair Anything You Break .... 2 / 20
J. Co-Signing Leases .... 2 / 20

Looking for a house or apartment to rent is often a frustrating and time-consuming task. Since it is human nature to become harried and frazzled under pressure, many mistakes are made at this stage which later turn out to be costly, both in time and money. Try to stay cool.

A. Get Organized

Before you start looking for a place, decide:

- how much you want to pay,
- how long you plan on staying, and
- what sort of area you want to live in.

Be realistic both as to your budget and as to what is available, and set definite guidelines in advance. If you can't find a place that meets your guidelines, don't change them without taking time to think the matter over carefully. Some of the worst and most costly mistakes are made by people who sign a lease or put down a deposit at the end of a long, frustrating day only to realize later that the place is completely unsuitable.

It is extremely important that you keep all records. As part of your getting organized, get a large manila envelope or file folder in which to keep all papers having to do with your rental transaction. Misplacing and losing papers (deposit agreements, leases, rent receipts, etc.) is a common mistake that should be avoided. Your landlord is in business and has probably learned how not to make such basic mistakes, so you should do the same. Set up a safe place in which to save your papers, receipts, cancelled checks, and anything else that you think might possibly be important at a later time.

If you have trouble finding a place, you may get help from a "homefinding service." Some do a good job of trying to help people find a place to rent, but some are sloppy, and a few are actually crooked. For example, several homefinding services have been caught running ads about imaginary apartments in good locations at low rents, only to tell people who show up, "We just rented that one, but here's another one"—at a higher rent—"you will really like." Another problem is that companies often sell rental lists which are so outdated that most or all of the apartments have been rented. In other words, do a little investigating (for example, talk to some other home-seekers or check with the Better Business Bureau) before you pay anyone to help you find a home. If you feel an apartment locator service has seriously misrepresented its service, ask for your money back and file a complaint with the Consumer Fraud Division of your local district attorney's office.

B. Learn About Rental Agreements

Before you start looking for a place, you should know a little about rental agreements. First—the most important rule—*don't sign any papers until you understand what's in them, or you may regret it later!*

Fortunately, there are only three different kinds of rental agreements, and all you really need to know is what they are like and the consequences to you of each. If you know these things, you may be able to bargain for better terms, and you'll certainly know when to turn down an agreement altogether. If you read this chapter and still don't understand what's in your agreement, you should probably get some advice (see Chapter 1.D) before you make the deal.

The three basic ways that residential rentals are commonly made are:

- the lease,
- the written rental agreement, and
- the oral rental agreement.

An oral agreement is made without anything being written down—you just talk over what the deal is and agree to it. The other two, the lease and the written rental agreement, have all the terms you agree to written down on a paper which you and the landlord sign. Let's look at each in some detail.

1. Oral Agreements

It is perfectly legal to make a deal orally—that is, without writing anything down, and no signatures—as long as it covers a year or less. The landlord agrees to let you move in and you agree to pay a certain amount of rent on some schedule, like weekly, every other week or every month. The period between rent payments is what determines how much notice you are entitled to for rent raises or orders to get out. If you pay (a) weekly or (b) monthly, then you are entitled to (a) a week's or (b) 30 days' notice.[1]

The oral agreement has some advantages: it is relatively informal, you can move out on short notice, and you aren't subjected to the long list of terms and rules contained in most leases and written rental contracts. However, if you want the clarity of having everything written down, you will probably want your deal in writing. If you want long-term security from rent raises and orders to move out (unless you live in one of the rent control cities that provide these advantages to everyone—see Chapter 4), you will want a lease.

Oral agreements are legal and enforceable. But as time goes by and circumstances change, people's memories can have a funny habit of changing, too. Then, if something goes wrong, both sides end up in front of a judge who has to decide whose recollection of the agreement to believe. For this reason, even if you make an oral agreement, it is wise to get some of the landlord's promises in writing. For example, if your landlord promises to make repairs, allow you to have a pet, or do anything else which you want to make sure he remembers, ask him to write it down, date and sign it, as illustrated in Section G, below.

2. Leases and Written Rental Agreements

The lease and the written rental agreement are basically the same except for one terribly important difference. The lease fixes all the terms of the agreement so that no changes can be made for a given period of time—most commonly, one year. If you rent under a lease, your rent cannot be raised until the lease runs out, nor can you be told to move unless you break the terms of the lease. On the other hand, you are expected to perform your obligations under the lease (including rent payments) until it runs out, or a qualified substitute tenant is found to replace you.

The written rental agreement—often called a "month-to-month" agreement—has everything written down, just like the lease, but the time period of your tenancy is indefinite. This means that you can move out or your landlord can raise your rent or order you to move out on only 30 days' notice (sometimes less)[2]—except in certain communities which have rent control laws including requirements that landlords show "just cause" to evict. (See Chapter 4 for a list of cities with just cause eviction provisions and Chapter 11 for details on three-day and 30-day notices.)

---

[1] CC §§ 827, 1944 and 1946.

[2] CC § 1946 allows the notice of tenancy termination period to be shortened to any amount of time not less than seven days before the end of the month, by an agreement made at the time the tenancy is created. This is very rarely done.

Except for these very important differences, leases and written rental agreements are so much alike that they are sometimes hard to tell apart. Both of them cover the basic terms of rental (names, addresses, amount of rent and date due, deposits, etc.) and both of them tend to have a lot of other fine print provisions to protect the landlord.

Be careful! Since they look so much alike, some forms can look like a lease, and sound like a lease, and even cover a year's period, but if they contain a provision that rent can be raised or that the agreement can be terminated on 30 days' notice, then they are really only written rental agreements.

Read it carefully! It is crucial that you read the entire lease or rental agreement and understand it before you sign it. If the main document refers to another document such as "house rules," make sure you read a copy of these too. If there is any part of the written document that you don't understand, get advice—but not from the people who want you to sign it. If you want your rights protected, you will have to see to it yourself.

Legally, a written agreement can be typed or written down in longhand on any kind of paper, in any words, so long as the terms are understandable. However, as a practical matter, nearly all landlords use standard printed forms which they buy in stationery stores or get from landlord associations. These forms have been prepared by lawyers or real estate associations, and they are usually as favorable as possible to the landlord. These forms need not look like death certificates, nor read like acts of Congress, but such is often the case. Some of the worst ones include clauses requiring you to waive your privacy, accept shorter than normal notice periods for rent increases and termination, accept responsibility for fixing things that should be handled by your landlord, and generally leave the tenant in a very vulnerable position. We discuss the common provisions and tell you some things to watch out for below. At the back of this book you will find a lease and rental agreement form which is fair to *both* landlord and tenant.

If the lease offered to you by the prospective landlord is not satisfactory, it is legal and simple to change it if both parties can agree on the changes. All you do is cross out unwanted portions, write in desired changes, and have all parties who are going to sign the document initial the changes. Make sure that you sign the lease at the same time as the landlord and that you get a copy then and there. This assures both sides that no changes can be made after only one party has signed.

Whenever there is a written agreement, the law presumes that the parties wrote down all of the parts to it before they signed it. If the landlord makes promises which aren't written, it is assumed they weren't made. So again, get everything you want included in writing before you sign.

SPANISH LANGUAGE NOTE: If a lease or month-to-month rental agreement is negotiated primarily in Spanish, then the landlord must give the tenant a Spanish translation of the lease or rental agreement before it is signed.[3]

3. Printed Forms: What to Watch Out For

This section is about the fine print on the form agreements. There are probably hundreds of different printed forms and the provisions in them are all worded a little differently. It is often not at all obvious what some provisions mean. (Contrary to what some form writers seem to think, it is not illegal to use plain English and be clear.) We try to simplify the whole problem for you by setting out, in the list below, the most common kinds of printed form provisions, together with what they usually mean, and what to watch out for.

As will be seen, some of the provisions are illegal and therefore unenforceable. When it comes to these provisions, you should probably *not* waste your bargaining power by trying to get the landlord to scratch them out. It may sometimes help, however, to mention to him that these provisions are illegal, in

---

[3] CC § 1632.

order to show him how one-sided the agreement is, and then ask him to eliminate or change other (enforceable) provisions.

Whether you want to use your bargaining power on lease changes, however, rather than on trying to get repairs or a lower rent or lower security deposit, is a judgment you will have to make.

a. Provision Against Assignment or Sub-Lease Without Landlord's Consent

This provision might restrict your ability to get out of your lease by finding another tenant to take your place. It might also restrict your ability to bring in a new roommate to help you pay the rent. It is probably better for you if this provision is not included. Without this provision, you have the right to assign or sublease without your landlord's consent. Keep in mind, however, that even if this provision is included, the landlord might not be able to arbitrarily withhold her consent to your transferring your lease to someone else.[4]

For example, she cannot withhold consent simply because she thinks the rent set by the lease is too low and will not consent unless the rent is increased. It is not arbitrary, however, to withhold consent because the new tenant has a poor credit rating or poor housekeeping habits.

b. Provision that the Landlord Is Not Responsible for Damage and Injuries

This provision says that if the landlord is negligent in maintaining the place and you, your family, or your property is injured (for example, by falling down broken stairs), the landlord is not responsible for paying for your losses. This is called an "exculpatory" provision. Under state law, such a provision is invalid.[5]

c. Provision Making Tenant Responsible for Repairs

This provision requires the tenant to give up (waive) his legal rights to make repairs himself and deduct the cost from his rent. This waiver is not valid, so don't use up your bargaining power by making an issue of it.[6]

The agreement might instead contain a provision requiring you to repair or maintain the premises in exchange for lower rent. This provision does not relieve the landlord of his legal obligation to see that the place complies with the housing codes. It might, however, stop you from exercising any rights you have to "repair and deduct," if he fails to make repairs. (See Chapter 7.B.4.)

d. Waiver of Right to Legal Notice

This provision says the landlord can sue to evict you or can raise the rent or change the terms of the lease without giving notice (such as a three-day notice to pay your rent or vacate) required by law. It is not valid.[7]

e. Provision Setting Notice Period

This provision sets the amount of time the landlord must give you before his notice of termination or rent raise or change in terms becomes operative. If there is no such provision, and you are a month-to-month tenant, the law requires that he give you at least 30 days' notice. State law, however, permits such a provision to cut the notice period down to as low as seven days before the end of the term (for example, the landlord may serve a rent increase notice on June 24, to raise the rent due on July 1).[8] This is very bad for you. If there is such a provision in the agreement, try to get it scratched out. Tell the landlord that you

---

[4] *Kendall v. Pestana* (1986) 40 Cal.3d 488.
[5] CC § 1953.
[6] CC § 1942.1.
[7] CC § 1953.
[8] CC § 1946.

will need at least 30 days to find another place if he decides to terminate your tenancy or raise your rent.

f. Right to Inspect

Many forms have a provision which gives the landlord the right to come into your place to inspect it, or for other purposes. Under state law, the landlord's right to enter the dwelling is limited to certain reasons, and any attempt to add to these reasons in the lease or rental agreement is void.[9] We discuss your rights to privacy in detail in Chapter 6.

g. Right of Re-entry Provision

This provision permits the landlord to come in and throw you out if you don't pay the rent, without giving you legal notice or going to court. It is not valid.[10]

h. Waiver of Jury Trial

This provision says that you waive your right to a trial by jury in any eviction lawsuit brought by the landlord. It is not valid.[11]

i. Waiver of Right to Appeal

This provision prevents you from appealing a court decision in any eviction lawsuit. It is not valid.[12]

j. Treble Damages

This provision says that if the landlord sues to evict you and wins, he may get not just the actual damages he has suffered (usually unpaid rent), but three times as much. The law provides for this possibility anyway, so you might as well leave this provision alone.

k. Landlord's Attorney Fees

This provision says that if the landlord has to sue to evict you or collect rent, you will pay his attorney fees. This can amount to $200 to $400 or more. This provision is valid, and the landlord cannot get attorney fees unless he has such a provision. Therefore, you may want to ask that it be scratched out. If it stays and you lose your job or your income is otherwise cut off and you can't pay the rent, you risk getting a judgment against you for attorney fees in addition to back rent.

However, you should understand that whenever there is an attorney's fee provision in a lease or written rental agreement, the law says that the attorney's fee provision entitles you to collect your attorney fees from the landlord if you win the eviction lawsuit, even if the provision does not say this.[13] For this reason some tenants actually prefer to have an attorney fees clause—even a seemingly one-sided one—in their written agreement, feeling that if their landlord seriously violates a provision of the agreement and they have to sue her, they want to be able to collect their attorney fees.

l. Late Charges

This provision requires the tenant to pay a "late charge" if the rent is paid late. The charge may be set as a percentage of the rent (such as 4%), a flat charge (such as $10), or a flat charge per day (such as $5 each day the rent is late). This provision is probably valid, if the late charge set is a reasonable estimate of the amount the lateness of your payment will cost the landlord—that is, her administrative cost of processing the late payment and her loss of interest on your rent. However, if the charge is set higher than this, in an effort to "terrorize" you into paying your

---

[9] CC § 1954.
[10] CC § 1953.
[11] CC § 1953.
[12] CC § 1953.

---

[13] CC § 1717.

rent on time, the charge is probably a "penalty" provision, which is invalid. If the late charge seems suspiciously high to you (for example, a $30 charge on a $300 rent payment late by a few days), ask the landlord to justify it or lower it.

m. Restrictions on Occupants and Guests

Restrictions on the number of occupants and the length of time guests may stay are common in leases and rental agreements. These are valid so long as they are not arbitrary. The landlord has legitimate interests in seeing that the number of occupants does not get so high that there would be excessive wear on the apartment, common area and facilities. The landlord also has a legitimate interest in ensuring that new occupants and guests will not be obnoxious people who might disturb other tenants or wreck the place.

These restrictions may not, however, be based on the age or sex of the occupant or guest. A provision forbidding any overnight guests of the opposite sex of the tenant, for example, would be illegal.[14] So would a provision saying, "No overnight guests under 12 years of age."[15]

Restrictions on "guests" are generally not intended to apply to daytime guests, but to overnight guests. While the restriction may not be clear on this distinction—simply limiting guests—this word should usually be interpreted to apply only to overnight guests.

Some agreements require the tenant to give the landlord prior notice of overnight guests, or to obtain the landlord's prior consent. These provisions are probably valid, though a provision regarding consent would probably be read to mean that the landlord could not arbitrarily withhold his consent. These provisions can be annoying, however, as they allow the landlord to nose into the tenant's private affairs. You might ask the landlord to write in something like, "This restriction shall apply only to overnight guests who stay more than five nights in any 30-day period."

n. Restrictions on Pets

A landlord may completely restrict a tenant's right to keep any pet or restrict the right to keep certain types of pets (for example, no dogs, or cats, but birds are okay). However, a landlord may not prohibit properly trained dogs needed by a blind, deaf or physically disabled tenant.[16]

o. Entire Agreement

Somewhere in the fine print, usually at the end, most leases have a provision which says that the agreement is the entire agreement of the parties. That means that if the landlord made any promises which weren't written down, then they don't count and can't be enforced. It pays, under all circumstances, to get all promises from the landlord in writing. Do this either on the lease or rental agreement itself, or do it on a separate piece of paper (but make sure it states that the additional material is made a part of the lease or rental agreement).

---

[14]CC § 51. See also *Atkisson v. Kern County Housing Authority* (1976) 59 Cal.App.3d 89.

[15]CC § 51. See also *Marina Point, Ltd. v. Wolfson* (1982) 30 Cal.3d 721 and Chapter 5, Section B(2).

[16]CC § 54.1(b)(5).

p. Provision Restricting Water-filled Furniture

If the building where you rent was built after 1973, it is no longer legal for a landlord to ban water-filled furniture. A landlord may, however, require you to have $100,000 of liability insurance to cover potential damage, and meet other requirements specified by law.[17] A policy should be available for $100 to $250 a year. (See Chapter 13.) For property built before 1973, a landlord may legally refuse to allow waterbeds.

q. Provision Against Violating Law, Causing Disturbances, Etc.

This type of provision—which allows a landlord to evict if you violate the law in the use of the premises or seriously damage the property—is legal and many landlords insist on it. However, a court is unlikely to enforce this provision for trivial violations.

r. Liquidated Damages Provision

Occasionally, a lease includes a "liquidated damages" clause. Such a clause says that if you move out before the lease expires, you are supposed to pay the landlord a certain amount of money (damages) for the losses caused by your early departure. Usually, landlords set the amount of liquidated damages at several hundred dollars.

If you think that sounds unfair, you're right. As is discussed in Chapter 9, if you move out before your lease expires, you are legally responsible to pay the landlord only for the actual losses you cause. Further, the landlord is legally obligated to minimize those losses by trying to find a new tenant to replace you as soon as possible. Why should the landlord, who didn't lose any money when you moved out, get a windfall?

Courts don't look kindly on liquidated damages, either. If the amount of liquidated damages far exceeds the landlord's actual damages, a judge will probably rule that you don't have to pay them. Of course, it takes time and trouble to go to court, so it's better to get a clause like this crossed out of the lease before you sign it.

4. Which Is Better, a Lease or a Month-to-Month Rental Agreement?

If you have a lease for a substantial term, like a year or more, you are assured that the landlord cannot evict you or raise the rent so long as you pay your rent on time and meet your other obligations under the lease. This kind of security is extremely valuable where housing is hard to find and rents are rising, which, as you know all too well, describes the rental market in most California communities.

If your unit is covered by a local rent control and eviction control ordinance, your need for the protection which a lease provides is lessened. Nevertheless, such ordinances do allow some rent increases, and they usually allow the landlord to evict in order to move himself or a relative into the place, or to make certain repairs. A lease will normally protect you against these dangers.

Of course, if you expect to be moving in a very short time, you may prefer a month-to-month rental agreement, so that you can leave simply by giving 30 days' notice. But don't be too sure that a month-to-month tenancy is what you want. In today's tight rental market, it is usually not difficult to "break" a lease if you have to. We discuss this possibility in Chapter 9. Basically, the rule is that if you have a lease and move out before the term is up, the landlord can sue you for the rent as it comes due until the lease runs out, only as long as she makes a reasonable effort to find another tenant. But, because finding another tenant at the same rent or more is usually very easy these days with even minimal effort, there is normally little risk of loss to the tenant who leaves before a lease runs out. (But see Chapter 9 for the details.)

---

[17]CC § 1940.5.

All things being equal, a lease is commonly preferable to a rental agreement because it gives you additional security from rent increases and eviction, especially in cities that do not have a provision in their rent control ordinances requiring just cause for eviction. But if it is likely that you will be a very short-term tenant, you will probably wish to rent under a written rental agreement, as getting out of a lease does involve some trouble.

If you prefer a lease, but are worried about some specific event which might force you to leave the area, consider simply providing for that event in the lease. If your boss might transfer you to Phoenix, put a provision in your lease saying, "Tenant may terminate this lease upon 30 days' written notice, provided that, with such notice, Tenant also gives Landlord a copy of a note from Tenant's employer saying that Tenant is being transferred to a location out of the city." Such a provision might be especially important for a tenant who is in the military service.

The written rental agreement is often preferred by landlords. It gives them the right to raise the rent as often as they wish (unless there is a local rent regulation ordinance) and to get rid of tenants that they don't like. In most cases, from a tenant's point of view, the written rental agreement does not have the advantages of either a lease or an oral agreement.

On the other hand, the truth is that you often have to take what you can get.

5. Model Lease and Model Rental Agreement

Landlords' forms are often very unfair. They impose many requirements on the tenant and very few on the landlord. We offer a positive alternative for you to use, if you get the chance. You will find tear-out copies of both a lease and rental agreement which are fair to both parties at the back of this book. They require the tenant to pay his rent and keep up his apartment, while requiring the landlord to make repairs and not hassle the tenant. They leave out the harsh provisions found in most landlord's leases. Try to get your landlord to agree to use one of these forms instead of his. Read the sections above to help you decide whether you want to use the lease or the rental agreement.

C. Fees and Deposits

Almost every landlord requires the tenant to give a substantial security deposit, sometimes including "last month's rent." The laws concerning how much can be charged and when deposits must be returned are discussed in Chapter 10. Here we will discuss some other fees and deposits that are occasionally required.

1. Holding Deposit

Sometimes, if you make a deal with a landlord, he will want some type of cash deposit, then and there, to make sure you don't change your mind and back out of the deal. If you give him the cash, sometimes as much as a month's rent, he will "hold" the place for you until you bring him your first month's rent and any deposits or fees you agreed on, or pending the result of a credit check. This is called a "holding" or "bond" deposit.

If you give a landlord a holding deposit and later decide not to take the place, you probably will be unable to get your whole deposit back. Therefore, be sure you really want the place before giving this kind of deposit. The law is very unclear as to what portion of a holding deposit a landlord can keep if a would-be tenant changes his mind about renting the property or doesn't come up with the remaining rent and deposit money. The basic rule is that a landlord can keep an amount that bears a "reasonable" relation to the landlord's costs—for example, for more advertising and for pro-rated rent during the time the property was held vacant. A landlord who keeps a larger amount is said to be imposing an unlawful "penalty." Whatever you and the landlord agree on, such as your right to get half of the holding deposit back if you decide not to take the place within a certain number of days, be sure you write it down.

Be sure you and the landlord understand what is to happen to the deposit when you take the place. Usually it will be applied to the first month's rent. To make this clear, have the landlord give you a receipt for the deposit and have her write on the receipt what is to happen to the deposit when you come back with the rent.

2. Finder's Fees

Some landlords—especially in cities with rent control—try to collect high "finder's fees" and the like just for renting the place to the tenant.

It works like this. When a prospective tenant applies to a landlord or management company, he is told that he must either (1) pay a finder's fee directly to the landlord or management company to qualify to get a particular unit, or (2) go to an apartment locator service and pay a finder's fee. In some situations, the locator service will have been set up primarily to collect the fee and isn't really in the business of locating apartments.

In a rent control city, this sort of fee is probably a sneaky way to get a higher rent—illegally. To get the place, you may want to pay the fee. After you move in, however, try to get it back! You have a right to, as your payment of the fee was not really voluntary, and a tenant generally cannot be required to waive his rights under a rent control law. Contact your local rent control board, city attorney, or district attorney's office (consumer fraud unit)—or sue the landlord in small claims court.

Even in a city without rent control, a finder's fee which goes to the landlord (or his agent) rather than to a true finder is probably still illegal.[18] This issue is covered by state law, which allows fees and deposits to be used only to remedy tenant defaults in payment of rent, cleaning the premises, and paying for damage to the premises.[19] The landlord who simply pockets the finder's fee is probably violating this statute, and you can sue him in small claims court to get it back.

3. Credit Check Fees

Landlords can, and often do, charge a fee to check the credit of prospective tenants. Credit checks normally cost no more than $25, and we believe that charging more is unreasonable. Some landlords have been known to take credit check fees from a number of prospective tenants and pocket some or all of the money. Problems can also develop if the landlord takes a long time to check a tenant's credit and the tenant, not knowing whether or not the rental will be approved, rents another place. To avoid these and other possible areas of dispute, it is wise to sign a brief agreement with a landlord such as the following:

---

[18]*People v. Sangiacomo* (1982) 129 Cal.App.3d 364.

[19]CC § 1950.5.

Landlord-Tenant Agreement Regarding Tenant's Credit Information

```
                        CREDIT INFORMATION

    Tenant authorizes Owner to verify all credit information for the purpose
of renting the premises at _____
_____.
Owner shall not release such information for any other purpose without the
express written approval of the Tenant.
    If Owner does not agree to sign lease within _____ days of receiving a
deposit from Tenant for the purpose of reserving the premises, the total deposit
shall be refunded to Tenant, less the amount actually spent to verify credit
information.
    Tenant may withdraw from the agreement and receive a refund of the total
deposit (less an amount used to verify credit information) up until such time as
Owner/Agent signs the lease.


_____   and   _____
Owner                                      Tenant
```

D. Credit Reports

Several companies, called tenant-screening or credit reporting agencies or credit bureaus, collect and sell credit and other information about tenants—for example, if they pay their rent on time or if they've ever been evicted. These agencies, however, are prohibited from reporting unlawful detainer lawsuits in which the landlord has not won in court.[20] If asked to, these companies also will gather and sell "investigative reports" about a person's character, general reputation, personal characteristics or mode of living.

Larger landlords routinely request credit reports on prospective tenants from these agencies. If a landlord does not rent, or charges higher rent, to someone because of negative information in a credit report, the landlord must so notify the tenant and give the person the name and address of the agency that reported the negative information. The landlord must also tell the person that he has a right to obtain a copy of his file from the agency that reported the negative information, as long as he requests the file within 60 days.[21]

A landlord may also request an investigative report. Before the agency compiles the report, and within three days of the landlord's request, the agency must notify the person who is the subject of the report that such a report will be made.

For more information on credit reports, see *Money Troubles: Legal Strategies to Cope with Your Debts*, by Robin Leonard (Nolo Press).

---

[20]CC §§ 1785.13(a)(3), 1786.18(a)(4). Under these laws, no record of an eviction lawsuit can be reported unless the landlord obtains a judgment aginst the tenant by default or after a court hearing, or if a written settlement agreement provides that the case may be reported.

[21]CC § 1785.20.

E. How To Check a Place Over

If you see a place that you think you will like, take a walk around the neighborhood. Check out stores, schools and bus stops. Walk around the building you are interested in renting and try to meet some of the neighbors. Ask them how they have gotten along with the landlord. Make sure that you can feel at home in all respects. Take an especially close look at the condition of the unit you may rent. Look for dirt and damage, and carefully check all doors, windows, screens, stoves, furnaces, hot water heaters and any other appliances. Make lists of any defects you find—later you can negotiate with the landlord for improvements and repairs. At the very least, be sure to get her to sign an acknowledgment of the existing conditions, so she can't blame you later for causing them. The best way to do this is by completing the Landlord-Tenant Checklist discussed in Section H.

In the section below we cover the landlord's responsibilities for disclosing certain information and for the condition of the premises he rents. In addition, we show you exactly how to carefully check a place out to see if it meets legal standards.

1. Landlord Disclosures

California landlords are legally obligated to make several disclosures to prospective tenants.

Shared Utility Arrangements. State law requires property owners to disclose to all prospective tenants, before they sign any rental agreement or lease, any arrangements under which a tenant might wind up paying for someone else's gas or electricity use.[22] This would occur, for example, where a single gas or electric meter serves more than one unit, or where a tenant's gas or electric meter also measures gas or electricity that serves a common area—such as a washing machine in a laundry room or even a hallway light not under the tenant's control. Besides disclosing any shared utility arrangements, state law requires landlords to address this issue in lease or rental agreements.

Location Near Former Military Base. In addition, if the rental property is within a mile of a "former ordnance location"—an abandoned or closed military base in which ammunition or military explosives were used—the landlord must notify all prospective tenants in writing of that fact.[23]

Asbestos. Owners of apartment buildings that have 10 or more units and were constructed before 1979 must notify tenants and employees who work in the building if the building contains "asbestos-containing construction materials." The written notice must be given to each employee and tenant individually. Violation of the law can result in a fine of up to $1,000, imprisonment up to one year, or both.[24]

2. Housing Codes and Enforcement

Housing codes are laws which require a landlord to put apartments and houses in good condition before renting them and to keep them that way while people are living there. The landlord cannot escape this duty by trying to impose it on the tenant in the lease or rental agreement.

California has a State Housing Law.[25] The main part of this law is contained in a little book called the Uniform Housing Code. You can get a copy for $10.50 (plus applicable local sales tax) from the International Conference of Building Officials, 5360 Workman Mill Road, Whittier, CA 90601-2298. It is a crime to repeatedly violate the State Housing Law—if the violations are severe, they can lead to a fine of up to $5,000, or imprisonment for up to one year, or both.[26] The Civil Code imposes

---

[22] CC § 1940.9.

[23] CC § 1940.7.

[24] Health & Safety Code §§ 25915 through 25924.

[25] For a list of those conditions which violate the law, see Health & Safety Code § 17920.3.

[26] Health & Safety Code § 17995.3. First-time offenders face a fine of $1000 and up to six months in jail or both, Health & Safety Code § 17995.

basically the same requirements (CC § 1941.1; see Chapter 7).

Many cities and counties have also enacted housing codes. Local rules are at least as strict as the State Housing Law and sometimes stricter. Check with your City Clerk and County Clerk to see if you have such laws in your community.

The State Housing Law and local housing codes are enforced by local agencies. These are usually city and county Building Inspection and Housing Departments. Other local agencies which might help you with certain health and housing conditions are the Health Department and Fire Department.

If you call a local agency such as a Building Inspection Department and tell them that your landlord won't make repairs, they will send out a building inspector. He will inspect the place and make a report. If he finds housing code violations, he should send a letter to the landlord ordering her to make repairs. If she does not make them within a reasonable time, the inspector may order the building vacated until repairs are made, order the building demolished, or have the work done and charge the cost to the landlord.

In addition, you may be able to "enforce" the codes by suing the landlord, using rent money to make repairs, or withholding rent. These remedies are discussed in Chapter 7.

3. A Checklist of Things to Inspect

Here is a checklist of things you should look for when inspecting a place. All requirements mentioned are contained in the State Housing Law. While checking some items on this list may seem obvious almost to the point of being simple-minded, the unhappy truth is that many people do not check a rental unit thoroughly before moving in and have all sorts of trouble getting repairs made later. So please slow down and look carefully (and then look again) before you sign on the dotted line.

a. Check the STRUCTURE (floors, walls, ceiling, foundation)

The structure of the place must be weatherproof, waterproof and rodent proof.

"Weatherproof" means there must be no holes, cracks, or broken plaster. Check to see if all the walls are flush (that they meet directly, with no space in between). See if any floorboards are warped. Does wall plaster fall off when you touch it?

"Waterproof" means no water should leak in. If you see dark round spots on the ceilings or dark streaks on the walls, rain water might have been leaking through.

"Rodent proof" deals with cracks and holes which rats and mice could use.

b. Check the PLUMBING

The landlord must provide a plumbing system connected to your community's water system and also to its sewage system (unless you have a cesspool).

All plumbing must be in good condition, free of rust and leaks. Sometimes the condition of the plumbing is hard to discover, but there are several tests you can run to see if there might be problems.

Flush the toilet. Does it take too long to flush? Does it leak on the floor? Is the water discolored? If so, the pipes may be rusty or unclean.

If the water is connected, fill a sink with hot and cold water. Turn the faucets on all the way, and listen for vibrating or knocking sounds in the pipes. See if the water in the sink is discolored. Drain the sink, and see if it takes too long for the water to run out.

c. Check the BATHROOM

The State Housing Law requires that every apartment and house have at least one working toilet, wash basin, and bathtub (or shower) in it. The toilet and bathtub (or shower) must be in a room which gives privacy to the occupant and which is ventilated. All of these facilities must be installed and maintained in a safe and sanitary condition.

d. Check the KITCHEN

The State Housing Law requires that every apartment and house have a kitchen. The kitchen must have a kitchen sink, which cannot be made of wood or other absorbent material.

e. Check the HOT WATER

The landlord must see that you have both hot and cold running water (although he can require you to pay the water and gas bills). "Hot" water means a temperature of not less than 120 degrees F.

f. Check the HEAT

The landlord must provide adequate heating facilities. Unvented fuel-burning heaters are not permitted.

g. Check the LIGHT AND VENTILATION

All rooms you live in must have natural light through windows or skylights, which must have an area not less than one-tenth of the floor area of the room, with a minimum of 12 square feet (3 square feet for bathroom windows). The windows must be openable at least half way for ventilation, unless mechanical ventilation is provided.

Hallways and stairs in the building must be lighted at all times.

h. Check for signs of INSECTS, VERMIN AND RODENTS

The landlord must provide facilities to prevent insect and rodent infestation and, if there is infestation, provide for extermination services.

These pests can be hard to notice. Remember, however, that they are very shy and stay out of sight. Therefore, if you see any fresh signs of them, they are probably very numerous and will bother you later on. Also, these pests travel from house to house. If your neighbors have them, they will probably get to you.

Check for rodent trails and excrement. Rats and mice travel the same path day after day and leave a gray coloring along the floor and baseboards. Look at the kitchen carefully, for rodents go there for food supplies. Check in closets, cupboards, and behind appliances for cockroaches.

Check for possible breeding grounds nearby. Stagnant water is often a source of pests. So are garages and basements that have piles of litter or old couches.

As mentioned before, cracks and holes in the walls and floors can be entry points for pests.

i. Check the WIRING AND ELECTRICITY

Loose or exposed wiring can be dangerous, leading to shock or fires. The landlord must provide safe and proper wiring.

If electrical power is available in the area, the place must be connected to it. Every room you live in must have at least two outlets (or one outlet and one light fixture). Every bathroom must have at least one light fixture.

j. Check for FIRE SAFETY

The landlord must provide safe exits leading to a street or hallway. Hallways, stairways and exits must be free from litter. Storage rooms, garages, and basements must not contain combustible materials. State law requires that all multiple-unit dwellings offered for rental after January 1987 be equipped with smoke detectors.[27]

k. Check for adequate TRASH AND GARBAGE RECEPTACLES

The landlord must provide adequate garbage and trash storage and removal facilities. Garbage cans must have tight-fitting covers.

l. Check the general CLEANLINESS OF THE AREA

The landlord must keep those parts of the building which he controls (hallways, stairs, yards, basement, driveway, etc.) in a clean, sanitary, and safe condition.

4. What If the Place Does Not Meet the Above Standards?

If the place has serious problems, you should probably not rent it if you can possibly avoid it. A landlord who would even show you such a place probably won't or can't make the needed repairs. If the landlord promises to fix it up, be careful. First, ask other tenants how good the landlord is at keeping promises. Second, make him put his promises in writing and sign it, as illustrated in Section G of this chapter. Be sure he also puts down dates on which certain repairs will be completed. Also, get him to write down that you will not have to pay your rent if he fails to meet the completion dates. If he doesn't want to agree to these things, he probably isn't taking his obligation to repair very seriously.

If you like the place but it has a few problems, simply ask the landlord to promise to make the necessary repairs. You might point out to him that he is required to make such repairs before renting, under the State Housing Law, but you will rent the place and let him repair it later, if he makes his promise (with dates) in writing and signs it.

If the landlord refuses to make the repairs, or if the place is so bad you don't trust his promises to make repairs, you should not rent the place, but you should report him to your city or county Building Inspection Department. He is violating the law (the State Housing Law), so this is your duty as a citizen. Also, you may be helping the tenant who ends up having to take the place.

F. How to Bargain for the Best Deal

Once you decide that you might like to rent a particular place, then negotiate the terms of the rental with the landlord or his agent. Often you will be presented with a "take it or leave it" proposition, where the landlord is not open to making changes. Many times, however, landlords will be open to reasonable changes. Whether it be the rent that you are trying to change, or particular terms in the contract, it never hurts to try.

In your first negotiation, it is good to remember that if the landlord is impressed with you, she will be more likely to want you as a tenant. Take a moment to consider what sort of folks you would like to rent to if you were a landlord. In fact, you might think over the information in Chapter 1 about your landlord and his situation. Certainly, a good first impression can be made on the application form. Most

---

[27] Health & Safety Code § 13113.7.

landlords ask you to fill out an application listing your jobs, bank, cars, income and references. It is a good idea to make up your own form in advance, much as you would write a job resume. It's a good idea to photocopy your application. If you don't get the first place, it will be available to submit when you apply for other units.

How good a deal you can get from a landlord depends on how badly he wants you. If there are very few places available at the rent he is asking and a lot of people are looking, which is usually the case these days, he may tell you to take his deal (rent, security deposit and form lease) or forget the whole thing. Even an attempt to bargain may make the landlord reluctant to rent to you.

If you are in an area where there are lots of places for rent and not too many people looking (say a university area in the spring), you will have more bargaining power. The landlord wants to rent the place soon (to get the rent) and may be afraid of losing you to another landlord.

If you can, try to talk to the last tenant who lived in the place. She might give you some very valuable information on how to deal with the landlord, what is wrong with the place, and generally what it is like to live there. Other tenants or neighbors in the area might also be helpful on this.

The more you look like a responsible tenant, the more bargaining power you will have. Every landlord wants "responsible" tenants who will pay rent regularly, not mess up his place, and not complain about anything. The more you appear to be this way, the better the deal you will get. The landlord won't rent to you at all unless he trusts you, and if he trusts you, he may be willing to give you things you ask for in order to keep you.

If you have any bargaining power, try to use it. You are investing a lot of your money and energy for a long time to come, and you are entitled to shop around and bargain to get the best deal you can. Some people don't like to bargain, because they think others will think they are cheap. But don't forget that the landlord is trying to get as much as he can out of his tenants, and he is not considered cheap, but a "good businessman." You should be a "good consumer" and get as much as you can for a reasonable price.

Even if the rent is fair and the landlord won't budge on that, there are other things he might give you if you ask. He may have a better refrigerator in storage or he may be willing to eliminate some lease provisions you don't like, or he may do some other things mentioned in this book.

G. Get All Promises In Writing

Your future relationship with your landlord may be very pleasant. Hope for the best and try to be open, honest and friendly. However, at the same time, sensible steps should be taken for your own self protection, just in case things take a nasty turn.

It often happens that a tenant moves into an apartment which has not been properly cleaned, or which needs painting or repairs. The landlord may say that the tenant can leave it in the same condition when he leaves, or perhaps that he can deduct money from the rent in exchange for cleaning, painting or repairs. Whatever promises the landlord makes, you should be aware that it is very common for this sort of vague, oral agreement to lead to misunderstanding, bitterness and financial loss. The time to protect yourself is at the beginning. This may be your only chance to do so.

If you plan to attach cupboards, shelves, bookcases, air conditioners, room dividers or anything at all to the premises, you should get something in writing from the landlord permitting you to install such things, and (if you plan it) to remove them later. By California law, anything which is nailed, screwed or bolted to the premises becomes the property of the landlord.[28] If you remove the object when you leave, your landlord will have the right to recover compensation for any damage to the premises

---

[28]CC § 1019.

and may also be able to recover the value of the object removed, unless there is a written agreement to the contrary. In addition, most landlords are sensitive to having the premises altered without their consent and may get quite irritated if they discover changes after they have already been made.

If a landlord promises to clean, paint, build a deck, install a fence or reimburse you for material and work, or if there are any other kinds of promises you want to depend upon, get them in writing and include a date for completing the work. Asking for a promise in writing need not cause you tension or embarrassment. Just tell the landlord, politely, that you have made a simple list of what has been agreed to, and you want to go over it with him for clarification. If he agrees that the list is accurate, include a line saying that this list is made a part of the written lease or rental agreement and have him date and sign it. There should be two copies, one for the landlord and one for your own file. (See Sample Addendum to Lease or Rental Agreement.)

The use of written contracts is standard among business people and among friends when they are in a business relationship. The purpose of such writings is to remind people of what they once agreed to do. If the landlord balks at putting things in writing, be very careful in all dealings with him.

If the landlord won't paint, clean or make repairs, be sure to list the faults as particularly and completely as you can and get him to sign and date the list. Otherwise, when you move out he may claim that you caused the damage and refuse to refund all, or a part, of your deposit.

If the landlord doesn't want to sign your list, get a few of the most responsible of your friends to take a look at it and write a simple little dated note of what they saw. And, if possible, have a friend take photographs of all defects. After the photographs are developed, the person taking them should identify each photo on the back by location, date and signature. All notes and pictures should go into your file with your other records.

Sample Addendum to Lease or Rental Agreement

January 1, 19__

Landlord Smith Realty and Tenant Patricia Parker make the following agreement, which is hereby added to the lease (or rental agreement) they entered into on _____, 19__:

1. Patricia Parker agrees to buy paint and painting supplies not to exceed a cost of $120 and to paint apartment #4 at 1500 Acorn Street, Cloverdale, California, on or before February 1, 19__ and to forward all receipts for painting supplies and paint to Smith Realty.

2. Smith Realty agrees to reduce the payment due February 1, 19__ by $150 in consideration for the painting to be done by Patricia Parker and in addition to allow Patricia Parker to deduct the actual cost of paint and painting supplies (not to exceed $120) from the rent payment due February 1, 19__.

3. The premises are being rented with the following defects:

  a. dent in oven door,
  b. gouge over fireplace in wall.

These defects will be fixed by Smith Realty by _____, 19__.

_____
Smith Realty Company
By: B. C. Smith

_____
Patricia Parker

H. The Landlord-Tenant Checklist

Another good self-protection device for both landlord and tenant involves taking an inventory of the condition of the premises at the time you move in, and then again when you move out. This means no more than making a brief written record of the condition of each room and having it signed by you and your landlord. Not only does the inventory give both of you an accurate record of the condition of the unit, but the act of making it provides a framework for communication and the resolution of potential disputes. We include a tear-out copy of a landlord-tenant checklist in the Appendix at the back of this book.

When filling out your checklist, mark "OK" in the space next to items that are in satisfactory condition. Make a note—as specific as possible—next to items that are not working or are in bad condition. Thus, you might state next to the "Stove and Refrigerator" listing: "generally good, but crack in freezer door." Be sure to note things like worn rugs, chipped enamel, holes in screens, dirty cabinets, etc. If you need more space than provided on your checklist form, make a separate list for those items, signed by both landlord and tenant, and have it stapled to the checklist.

I. Your Responsibilities as a Tenant

Read your lease or agreement carefully to see what it requires you to do and prevents you from doing.

1. Comply With Your Lease or Rental Agreement

Your most important responsibility as a tenant is to comply with the provisions of your lease or rental agreement. If you do not, you may have to pay money to the landlord or you may be evicted, and sometimes both.

2. Pay Your Rent on Time

You must pay your rent on the day it is due. Most leases and rental agreements say rent is due on the first of the month. However, if the first falls on a Saturday or Sunday or a legal holiday, then the law says that the rent can be paid on the next business day.[29] If you do not pay your rent on time, you may have to pay a reasonable late charge, if your lease or rental agreement provides for this. (See Section B.3.l, above.) Also, your landlord may serve upon you a three-day notice to pay your rent in three days or get out. If you do not comply with the three-day notice, he can then sue to evict you, as discussed in Chapter 11.

You are entitled to a written receipt whenever you pay your rent.[30] Be especially sure to get one if you don't pay by check, as the receipt is proof that you paid your rent. Keep your receipts in a safe place—preferably in the file that you set up for all documents relating to the rental transaction. It is common for landlords to make mistakes in their bookkeeping and conclude that you are delinquent in your rent obligation. Keeping your receipts or cancelled checks is the surest way to prevent misunderstandings of this type.

---

[29] CCP § 13; Government Code § 6700 et seq.

[30] CC § 1499: "A debtor has a right to require from his creditor a written receipt for any property delivered in performance of his obligation."

LANDLORD-TENANT CHECKLIST—General Condition of Rooms
(see reverse side for furnished property)

Street Address _____ Unit Number _____ City _____

	Condition on Arrival	Condition on Departure	Est. Cost of Repair/Replacement
Living Room			
Floors & Floor Coverings			
Drapes & Window Coverings			
Walls & Ceilings			
Light Fixtures			
Windows, Screens & Doors			
Front Door & Locks			
Smoke Detector			
Fireplace			
Other			
Other			
Kitchen			
Floors & Floor Coverings			
Walls & Ceilings			
Light Fixtures			
Cabinets			
Counters			
Stove/Oven			
Refrigerator			
Dishwasher			
Garbage Disposal			
Sink & Plumbing			
Smoke Detector			
Other			
Other			
Dining Room			
Floors & Floor Covering			
Walls & Ceiling			
Light Fixtures			
Windows, Screens & Doors			
Smoke Detector			
Other			
Other			

	Condition on Arrival			Condition on Departure			Est. Cost of Repair/Replacement
Bathroom(s)	Bath 1	Bath 2		Bath 1	Bath 2		
Floors & Floor Coverings							
Walls & Ceilings							
Windows, Screens & Doors							
Light Fixtures							
Bathtub/Shower							
Sink & Counters							
Toilet							
Other							
Other							
Bedroom(s)	Bedroom 1	Bedroom 2	Bedroom 3	Bedroom 1	Bedroom 2	Bedroom 3	
Floors & Floor Coverings							
Windows, Screens & Doors							
Walls & Ceilings							
Light Fixtures							
Smoke Detectors							
Other							
Other							

	Condition on Arrival	Condition on Departure	Est. Cost of Repair/Replacement
Other Areas			
Furnace/Heater			
Air Conditioning			
Lawn/Ground Covering			
Garden			
Patio, Terrace, Deck, etc.			
Other			
Other			

Use this space to provide any additional explanation: _____
_____
_____
_____

☐   Tenants acknowledge that all smoke detectors were tested in their presence and found to be in working order, and that the testing procedure was explained to them. Tenants agree to test all detectors at least once a month and to report any problems to Owner/Manager in writing. Tenants agree to replace all smoke detector batteries as necessary.

3. Keep the Place Clean

The housing codes and almost all agreements require that you keep your place clean, safe and sanitary. You must properly dispose of all garbage and trash in your premises, placing it in the containers provided by the landlord.

4. Repair Anything You Break

Anything damaged by you, other occupants or guests must be repaired at your expense, unless the damage resulted from "normal wear and tear" during ordinary use. In other words, you are responsible for the loss of broken windows, toothbrushes in the toilet and other damages you cause. If you rent a furnished unit and a chair you sit on breaks from old age, you do not have to repair or replace it. If, however, your child breaks the chair in a temper tantrum, you must pay for it.

J. Co-Signing Leases

Some landlords have begun requiring a co-signer on leases and rental agreements as a condition of renting. Normally, they ask the co-signer to sign a contract saying that he will pay for any rent or damage losses that the tenants fail to pay. Several landlords have told us that inclusion of this sort of provision is mostly psychological and that they don't often sue the co-signer, even if the original tenant defaults. Psychological or not, it is possible that a co-signer will be sued if the tenant defaults, so don't co-sign if you are not fully ready to pay.

Important: Many co-signer clauses are not enforceable in court because they are so vague that they don't qualify as contracts. Also, if a landlord and tenant change the terms of their rental agreement—or even renew it—without the approval of the co-signer, she is no longer responsible.[31] Of course, any defenses that a tenant may raise—for example, breach of the warranty of habitability because of seriously defective conditions—may also be raised by the co-signer (see Chapter 7). In addition, if a landlord sues a tenant for eviction, the co-signer can't be sued as part of the same suit. The co-signer must be sued separately in either a regular civil lawsuit or in small claims court.

---

[31]See also CC § 2819; *Wexler v. McLucas* (1975) 48 Cal.App.3d Supp. 9.

chapter 3

Sharing a Home

A.	Is It Legal to Live Together?	3/2
B.	The Legal Obligations of Roommates to the Landlord	3/2
C.	The Legal Obligations of Roommates to Each Other	3/3
D.	Having a Friend Move In	3/5
	1. The Legal Relationship Between the Person Moving In and the Landlord	3/6
	2. The Legal Relationship Between the Person Moving In and the Person Already There	3/8
E.	Guests	3/10

It's more and more common for two or more unmarried people to rent a place together. Commonly a sexual relationship forms the basis of a decision to share, but often it does not. But whether or not it involves sharing a bed, sharing a home can have all sorts of legal ramifications. Of course, there are the legalities when it comes to dealing with the landlord, but sometimes the legal rules governing the relationship between the roommates are of even more importance.

A. Is It Legal to Live Together?

The answer is yes when two adults live together. And it makes no difference whether they are gay or straight, if one or both is married to someone else, or if they have or don't have a sexual relationship. There used to be laws against gay sexual conduct and against people living together when married to someone else, but since 1976 these laws no longer exist in California. Does the repeal of these laws mean that landlords must rent to gay couples or unmarried couples? Not directly, but there are other state and local laws and court decisions banning unlawful discrimination (see Chapter 5).

Three or more people used to have trouble setting up housekeeping together, even if they were all as celibate as nuns. Why? Because some communities had local zoning ordinances banning more than two unrelated persons from living together (excepting household help, of course). Usually these ordinances were in effect in conservative communities which were uptight about what they saw to be "hippie communes." The California Supreme Court has ruled that this sort of ordinance is unconstitutional under the California Constitution.[1] This means that as far as local law is concerned, three or more unrelated people can live together any place in California.

Even more important is that a landlord can legally limit the number of adult occupants. A landlord can, for example, insist on renting a unit to only two people even though there is space enough for more. As long as a landlord doesn't establish the number of people who can live in a unit in order to discriminate against families with children (see Chapter 5), this decision is up to her.

B. The Legal Obligations of Roommates to the Landlord

If two people—let's call them James and Helen—enter into a lease or rental agreement (written or oral), they are each on the hook to the landlord for all rent and all damages to the apartment—except "normal wear and tear". It makes no difference who—or whose friends—caused the damage, or who left without paying the rent. Let's look at several common situations.

EXAMPLE 1

James and Helen both sign a written rental agreement providing for a total monthly rent of $800 for a flat. They agree between them to pay one-half each. After three months James refuses to pay his half of the rent (or moves out with no notice to Helen and the landlord). In either situation, Helen is legally obligated to pay all the rent, as far as the landlord is concerned. James, of course, is equally liable, but if he is unreachable or out of work, the landlord will almost surely come after Helen for the whole amount. Since James and Helen have rented under a month-to-month written rental agreement, Helen can cut her losses by giving the landlord a 30-day written notice of intention to move. She can do this even if James is lying around the place, refusing to pay or get out.

If Helen ends up paying the landlord more than her agreed share of the rent, she has a right to recover from James. If payment is not made voluntarily, Helen can sue James in small claims court.[2]

---

[1] *City of Santa Barbara v. Adamson* (1980) 27 Cal.3d 123.

[2] See *Everybody's Guide to Small Claims Court*, Warner (Nolo Press).

EXAMPLE 2
The same fact situation as Example 1, except that this time there is a lease for one year. Again, both partners are independently liable for the whole rent. If one refuses to pay, the other is still liable, unless a third person can be found to take over the lease, in which case both partners are off the hook from the day that a new tenant takes over. As we discuss in Chapter 9, because of the housing shortage in most parts of the state, it is often easy for a tenant to get out of a lease at little or no cost, simply by finding an acceptable new tenant and steering him or her to the landlord. A newspaper ad will usually do it. The landlord has an obligation to limit his damages (called "mitigation of damages" in legal lingo) by renting to a suitable new tenant as soon as possible. Should the landlord fail to do this, he loses the legal right to collect damages from the original tenants.

C. The Legal Obligations of Roommates to Each Other

People sharing a home usually have certain expectations of each other. Sometimes it helps to write these down. After all, you expect to write things down with the landlord almost as a matter of course, so why not do the same with each other? Nothing that Helen and James agree to between themselves has any effect as far as the landlord is concerned, but it still may be helpful to have something to refresh their memories, especially if the relationship gets a little rocky. Here we have a sample agreement between roommates. Of course, there are many other terms that could be included in this type of agreement and you will probably wish to make some modifications.[3]

There are also mutual obligations roommates have to one another. Roommates have a mutual obligation to pay rent, as discussed in Section B above. Roommates also have a mutual obligation to not violate the lease or rental agreement (for example, by being too noisy and disturbing other tenants.) This means that if one of the roommates violates the lease or rental agreement, the other roommate is also responsible for the consequences of such violation, whether or not that person participated in or knew of the violation.

Another situation where roommates may have obligations to one another is the situation discussed in Section D.1 below. This is a situation where a person moves into an apartment (or home) where there is already another living there who has a lease or rental agreement with the landlord. The new person who moves in does not enter into a contract with the landlord, and therefore has no legal obligation to the landlord. That person's only possible legal obligations will be to the already-existing tenant.

---

[3] If you are interested in a comprehensive living together agreement, see *The Living Together Kit*, Ihara & Warner (Nolo Press), or *A Legal Guide for Lesbian and Gay Couples*, Curry, Clifford & Leonard (Nolo Press).

Sample Agreement Between Roommates

AGREEMENT

Helen Mattson and James Kennedy, upon renting an apartment at 1500 Redwood Street, #4, Philo, California agree as follows:

1. Helen and James are each obligated to pay one-half of the rent and one-half of the utilities, including the basic monthly telephone charge. Each person will keep track of and pay for his or her long distance calls. Rent shall be paid on the first of each month, utilities within ten days of the day the bill is received.

2. If either Helen or James wants to move out, the one moving will give the other person 30 days' notice and will pay his/her share of the rent for the entire 30-day period even if he/she moves out sooner. If both Helen and James wish to move, they will be jointly responsible for giving the landlord 30 days' notice.

3. No third persons will be invited to stay in the apartment without the mutual agreement of both Helen and James.

4. If both Helen and James want to keep the apartment but one or the other or both no longer wishes to live together, they will have a third party flip a coin to see who gets to stay. The loser will move out within 30 days and will pay all of his/her obligations for rent, utilities and for any damage to the apartment.

Here is an alternative for number 4.

4. If both Helen and James want to keep the apartment but no longer wish to live together, the apartment shall be retained by the person who needs it most. Need shall be determined by taking into consideration the relative financial condition of each party, proximity to work, the needs of minor children, if any, and *(list any other factors important to you)*. If Helen and James can't decide this issue by themselves or with the help of a mutually agreed upon mediator, the determination shall be made by a third party (the arbitrator). If it is not possible for Helen and James to agree on an arbitrator, the arbitrator will be chosen by *(fill in name)*. The arbitrator shall be paid by the person who gets to keep the apartment. The determination shall be made within ten days after either party informs the other that he or she wishes to separate, and after the arbitrator has listened to each person present his or her case. The arbitration award shall be conclusive on the parties, and shall be prepared in such a way that a formal judgment can be entered thereon in any court having jurisdiction over the dispute if either party so desires. After the determination is made, the person who is to leave shall have an additional ten days to do so. The person who leaves is obligated for all rent, utilities and any damage costs for 30 days from the day that the original determination to separate is made.

_____   _____
Date   Helen Mattson
_____   _____
Date   James Kennedy

D. Having a Friend Move In

Perhaps just as common as two or more people renting a home together is for one person to move into a place already rented and occupied by another. This is often simple and smooth when the landlord is cooperative, but can raise some tricky legal questions if the landlord raises objections.

In some situations, where the landlord is not in the area or is not likely to make waves, it may be sensible to simply have the second person move in and worry about the consequences later. But is this legal? Is a tenant required to tell his landlord when a second person moves in? It depends on the lease or rental agreement. If no mention is made as to the number of persons allowed in the apartment, use your own discretion and knowledge of your landlord. Some don't care, but most probably do. We suspect that as a general rule, even in the absence of a lease or rental agreement provision dealing with the area, moving someone in without the consent of a landlord is not the most sensible thing to do. The landlord will probably figure out what is going on before long and may resent your sneakiness more than she resents your roommate. We advise you to:

• Read the lease or rental agreement to see how many people are allowed to live on the premises and if there are any restrictions on additional people. Sometimes additional people will be allowed for a slight increase in rent.[4] Many landlords will not care whether you are married, living together or joined by the toes with rubber bands, but will expect to collect more money if more people live in their rental unit.

• Contact the landlord to explain what is happening. If you can't do this in person, you might send the landlord a letter when a new roommate moves in.

Sample Letter When a New Roommate Moves In

```
1500 Redwood Street #4
Philo, California
June 27, 19__

Smith Realty
10 Ocean Street
Elk, California

I live at the above address, and
regularly pay rent to your office.
As of July 1, 19__, there will be a
second person living in my apartment.
As set forth in my lease, I enclose
the increased rent due which now comes
to a total of $800. I will continue to
make payments in this amount as long
as two people occupy the apartment.

Should you wish to sign a new lease
specifically to cover two people,
please let me know. My friend, Helen
Mattson, is regularly employed and has
an excellent credit rating.


Very truly yours,


_____
James Kennedy
```

Remember: Under state law, a written rental agreement may be terminated on thirty days' notice without the necessity of the landlord giving a reason.[5] Thus, a landlord who wants to get rid of you can normally do so without too much trouble if you

---

[4] If you live in a rent control area, your local ordinance may restrict how much rent can be increased in this situation.

[5] In several populous areas, including San Francisco, Los Angeles, Berkeley, and Santa Monica (see Chapter 4 for a complete list), this rule has been changed by local rent control ordinances which prevent evictions except for reasons specified in the various enactments. These "just cause" for eviction rules are discussed in Chapter 11. Also, the eviction can't be for an improper reason, such as the type of discrimination prohibited under California law (see Chapter 5) or as retaliation for the tenant's exercise of certain rights.

don't have a lease. So it pays to be reasonable when moving roommates in and out.

If you have a lease, you are probably in a little better position to bargain with the landlord if a friend moves in. This is because, to get you out before the lease expires, he would have to establish that you have violated one or more lease terms. If your lease has a provision allowing occupancy only by one person, your landlord probably has the right to terminate your tenancy if a second person moves in without his permission. However, if the landlord accepts rent with the knowledge that you are living with someone, many courts would hold that he can no longer enforce that right. Of course, if you cause the landlord too much grief, he can simply refuse to renew your lease when it runs out. Again, you will probably come out ahead by being reasonable and cooperative.

1. The Legal Relationship Between the Person Moving In and the Landlord

If Helen moves into James's apartment, what is the relationship between Helen and James's landlord? Is Helen obligated to pay rent if James fails to pay? What if James moves out, but Helen wants to remain? If James ruins the paint or breaks the furniture, does Helen have any obligation to pay for the damage?

Since she has not entered into a contract with the landlord, Helen has no legal obligations to him regarding the rent, nor does she have an agreement with him regarding her right to live in the apartment. Helen's only possible legal obligation is to James. Of course, if Helen damages the property, she is liable just as a visitor, a trespasser, or a thief who caused damage would be liable. James is completely liable for the rent and also for damage to the premises whether caused by Helen or himself, because he has entered into a contract which may be in the form of a lease, written rental agreement or oral rental agreement. If James leaves, Helen has no right to take over his lease without the landlord's consent.

Helen can, of course, enter into a lease or rental agreement contract with the landlord which would give her the rights and responsibilities of a tenant. This can be done by:

• signing a new lease or rental agreement which specifically includes both James and Helen as tenants.

• making an oral rental agreement with the landlord. Be careful of this one, as an oral agreement can consist of no more than a conversation between Helen and the landlord in which she says she will pay the rent and keep the place clean and he says okay. There may be some legal question as to whether an oral agreement between Helen and the landlord is enforceable if there is still a written lease or rental agreement between the landlord and James which doesn't include Helen, but it is our belief that most judges would bend over backwards to give Helen the rights and responsibilities of a tenant if she seemed to be exercising them.

• the actual payment of rent by Helen and its acceptance by the landlord, especially if it is done on a fairly regular basis. As in the preceding paragraph, this would set up a month-to-month tenancy between Helen and the landlord and would mean that either could end the tenancy by giving the other a 30-day written notice of intention to end it.

Should the situation ever arise that James wants to move out and Helen remain, it is important that the legal relationships be clarified. James should give the landlord a written notice of what he intends to do at least 30 days before he leaves. If he does this, he is off the hook completely in a written or oral rental agreement situation. If a lease is involved and James is leaving before it runs out, he might still be okay, because the landlord has a legal duty to take steps to limit her loss as much as possible (mitigate damages—see Chapter 9). This means finding a new tenant to pay the rent. In our example, as long as Helen is a reasonably solvent and non-destructive person, the landlord would suffer no loss by accepting her as a tenant to fill out the rest of James's lease. If the landlord refuses Helen without good reason, James will probably be legally absolved of future responsibility and any loss is legally the landlord's problem, not his. (Again, see Chapter 9 for details.)

Rent Control Note: If Helen has attained the status of a tenant, the landlord will probably not be able to raise the rent after James leaves, except as otherwise permitted by the local rent control ordinance. If, on the other hand, Helen has not become a tenant, the rent probably can be raised in most areas covered by rent control which contain a provision called "vacancy decontrol," which allows a landlord to raise rent as much as he wants when a tenant moves out. Berkeley, Santa Monica, and several smaller cities are exceptions to this rule, since in those areas rents are controlled regardless of who is living in the premises. When more than one tenant shares an apartment or house, the rule in some cities with vacancy-decontrol is that the rent can't be raised more than the annual increase allowed by the ordinance until all of the original tenants whose names were on the lease or rental agreement leave. At this point, the landlord can raise the rent as much as he wants under the vacancy-decontrol provision. But please be aware that since this rule is subject to a number of different interpretations, depending both on the city and the exact situation, it's up to you to check locally.

For use if you have a *rental agreement*:

Sample Letter When One Tenant Moves Out and the Other Remains (Rental Agreement)

```
1500 Redwood Street #4
Philo, California
June 27, 19__

Smith Realty
10 Ocean Street
Elk, California

I live at the above address and
regularly pay rent to your office. On
July 31, 19__, I will be moving out.
As you know, my friend, Helen Mattson,
also resides here. She wishes to
remain and will continue to pay rent
to your office on the first of each
month.

We will be contacting you soon to
arrange for the return of my security
deposits of $500, at which time Helen
will give you a similar deposit. If
you have any questions, or if there is
anything we can do to make the transi-
tion easier for you, please let us
know.

Very truly yours,


_____
James Kennedy
```

For use if you have a *lease*:

Sample Letter When One Tenant Moves Out and the Other Remains (Lease)

```
1500 Redwood Street #4
Philo, California
January 7, 19__

Smith Realty
10 Ocean Street
Elk, California

I live at the above address under a
lease which expires on October 30, 19__.
A change in my job makes it necessary
that I leave the last day of February.
As you know, for the last six months my
friend, Helen Mattson, has been sharing
this apartment. Helen wishes either to
take over my lease or enter into a new
one with you for the remainder of my
lease term. She is employed, has a
stable income, and will, of course, be a
responsible tenant.

We will soon be contacting your office
to work out the details of the transfer.
If you have any concerns about this
proposal, please give us a call.


Very truly yours,

_____
James Kennedy
```

2. The Legal Relationship Between the Person Moving In and the Person Already There

Alas, it seems all too common that big-brained monkeys go through violent changes in emotional feelings. A relationship that is all sunshine and roses one minute may be more like a skunk cabbage in a hurricane the next. Sometimes, when feelings change, memories blur as to promises made in happier times and the nicest people become paranoid and nasty. Suddenly, questions such as "Whose apartment is this, anyway?" may turn into serious disputes. We suggest that when feelings are relaxed (preferably at the time that the living arrangement is set up), both people make a little note as to their mutual understandings, either as part of a comprehensive living together arrangement or in a separate agreement. If this is done in good faith, as an aid to the all too fallible human memory, it need not be a negative experience. We include here an example that you might want to change to fit your circumstances.

Important: If you get into a serious dispute with your friend involving your shared home and have no agreements to fall back on, you will have to do the best you can to muddle through to a fair solution. Here are a few ideas to guide your thinking.

• If you live in San Francisco, your living relationship may be covered by the city's rent control ordinance, which recognizes the concept of the "master tenant." A master tenant is a tenant with a formal relationship with the landlord (lease or written rental agreement). Other tenants can be evicted without a need to demonstrate "just cause" by the master tenant, who can also charge the others a disproportionate amount of the rent-controlled rental amount.

• Outside of San Francisco, if only one of you has signed the agreement with the landlord and that person pays all the rent, then that person probably should have the first claim on the apartment, especially if that person occupied the apartment first. The other should be given a reasonable period of time to find another place, especially if she has been contributing to the rent and/or has been living in the home for any considerable period of time.

• If you both signed a lease or rental agreement and/or both regularly pay rent to the landlord, your rights to the apartment are probably legally equal, even if one of you got there first. Try to talk out your situation, letting the person stay who genuinely needs the place the most. Some people find it helpful

Sample Agreement Between New Tenant and Old Tenant

```
                           AGREEMENT

    Helen Mattson and James Kennedy make the following agreement:
    1. James will move into Helen's apartment and will give Helen one-half
of the monthly rent ($400) on the first of each month. Helen will continue
paying the landlord under her lease and James will have no obligation under
the lease.
    2. James will pay one-half of the electric, gas, water, garbage and
monthly telephone service charges to Helen on the first of each month; Helen
will pay the bills.
    3. Should James wish to move out, he will give Helen as much written
notice as possible and will be liable for one-half the rent for two weeks from
the time he gives Helen written notice. Should Helen wish James to move out,
she will give him as much written notice as possible, in no case less than two
weeks. In any case of serious dispute, it is understood that Helen has first
choice to remain in the apartment and James must leave on her request.


_____           _____
Date                               Helen Mattson


_____           _____
Date                               James Kennedy
```

to set up an informal mediation proceeding with a third person helping the parties arrive at their own solution. If this doesn't work, you may wish to locate a neutral third party arbitrator to hear the facts and make a decision.[6] If you do this, make sure that the arbitrator is not a close friend, as the person who loses is likely to have hard feelings. Lean over backwards to be fair about adjusting money details concerning such things as last month's rent and damage deposits. Allow the person moving out a reasonable period of time to find another place. *We have found that the best compromises are made when both people feel that they have gone more than half way.*

• Each person has the right to his or her belongings. This is true even if they are behind in their share of the rent. Never lock up the other person's property.

• It is a bad idea to deny a person access to his home except in extreme circumstances. If you are going to lock out a person, you should also be ready to sign a formal police complaint or go to court and get a restraining order under California's Domestic Violence Prevention Act.[7] You can get more information about this procedure from your county clerk's

---

[6] A number of California cities and counties have free or low cost landlord-tenant mediation and arbitration services. In addition, the nonprofit Community Board program offers excellent mediation services in many San Francisco neighborhoods.

[7] CCP § 541.

office. In many instances, locking out a person is not legal and you can be sued for damages.

E. Guests

What about overnight guests—particularly those who stay over often? What relationship, if any, do these people have with the landlord? More important, is the landlord entitled to any legal recourse if you have a "regular" guest? The answer to this question often depends on what it says in a lease or written rental agreement or written tenant rules authorized by one of these documents. (See Chapter 2.B.) Many restrict the right to have overnight guests to a certain number of days per year and require registration if a guest will stay more than a few days. While these sorts of lease provisions aren't often strictly enforced, they are legal and, in the case of persistent or serious violations, can be grounds for a landlord evicting a tenant who has a lease. Even in rent control areas which require just cause for eviction, a tenant who violates guest rules may be evicted, but under the terms of many ordinances, the tenant must first be given a written notice to correct the violation—that is, to follow the "guest" provision of the lease or written rental agreement.

Absent a specific lease or rental agreement provision dealing with the area, there is no precise line between guests and roommates. A person may be a frequent overnight visitor—four or five times a week—but still qualify as a guest, whereas a roommate may be in residence only a couple of days a week, as is common with flight attendants. A person's status as guest might be considerably enhanced by a showing that she maintains a separate residence complete with furniture and mailing address. However, to the landlord who sees the person on the premises more than the actual tenant, this might not prove persuasive.

Where the landlord is seeking to evict on the basis of a lease provision which prohibits occupancy of more than a certain number, he must (absent a provision limiting the number of days a guest can stay in the premises) prove that the extra occupant is in fact a resident. However, as we mentioned earlier in this chapter (Section D), in many parts of the state the landlord can evict for no reason at all if you have no lease. Accordingly, unless you live in an area covered by a just cause for eviction rent control ordinance (see Chapter 11), or have a lease, it might be a good idea to clarify your guest's status with your landlord at the outset instead of leaving things to his imagination.

chapter 4

All About Rent

A. When Is Rent Due?	4/2
B. Late Charges	4/2
C. Partial Rent Payments	4/3
D. Rent Increases: General Law	4/4
E. Rent Increase Notices	4/4
F. Rent Control	4/5
G. General Types of Rent Control Laws	4/9
1. Weak Rent Control	4/9
2. Strict Rent Control	4/9
3. Moderate Rent Control	4/10
4. Rent Mediation Laws	4/10
H. Rent Control Board Hearings	4/10
1. Initiating the Hearing	4/10
2. Preparing for the Hearing	4/11
3. The Actual Hearing	4/12
4. The Decision	4/13
I. What to Do If the Landlord Violates Rent Control Rules	4/14
J. Rent Control Chart: Specific Provisions of Rent Control	4/14

Today, most tenants pay 35% or more of their incomes on rent—sometimes over $1,000 a month. This money obviously means a lot to you, so you should understand your rights regarding when to pay, how much to pay, and whether the landlord can increase the rent. Rent is also very important to the landlord, who usually wants to get as much as she can get as soon as she can get it. And non-payment of rent is taken very seriously by the courts.

A. When Is Rent Due?

Under state law, rent is due at the end of the term of the tenancy—for example, at the end of the month, in a month-to-month tenancy—unless the lease or rental agreement provides otherwise.[1] Almost every lease and rental agreement (whether written or oral) does provide otherwise, however. Most require payment at the beginning of the term. Thus, rent for use of the place in March would be due on March 1 under the terms of the agreement.

If you fail to pay your rent on the date it is due, the landlord may not throw you out or sue to evict you the next day. He must first serve you with a written notice demanding that you pay the rent or get out in three days. If the third day falls on a Saturday, Sunday, or holiday, you get until the next business day to pay the rent.[2] Only after that day can he file a lawsuit to evict you. (See Chapter 11 for details on three-day notices.)

If you run into trouble paying your rent on time, three days isn't much time to come up with it. You might expect such trouble if your income is from alimony and child support, or a job which might involve lay-offs or strikes. If you know this might happen, you might wish to ask the landlord to put in the lease or rental agreement a provision that she will not serve a "three-day notice" on you until some time (like 10 days or 20 days) after the first of the month. If she objects, next suggest the provision be written so that it gives you the extra time only if your income is temporarily cut off or delayed.

Both the tear-out model lease and the model rental agreement in the Appendix at the back of this book contain a special provision (Section 14) which tries to deal with this problem in a fair way. It provides that the tenant may notify the landlord on or before the due date that he will be unable to pay the rent, and then the parties will try to work out a procedure for rent payment as soon as possible. If they can't do so within 10 days, then the landlord may serve a three-day notice to pay rent or quit on the tenant.

Ask the landlord to use the model lease or model rental agreement. If he won't, then he might at least allow you to include Section 14 in the forms he wants to use.

Note on Rent Withholding: If a landlord fails to fulfill his obligation to keep up the premises, the tenant's duty to pay rent is affected correspondingly. Under state law, a tenant may claim that the landlord's failure to repair and maintain the property justifies withholding rent. (See Chapter 7 for details on rent withholding.)

B. Late Charges

A fairly common landlord practice is to charge a fee to tenants who are late with their rent. Some cities with rent control ordinances regulate the amount of late fee charges. Check any rent control ordinance applicable to your properties. Most California cities and unincorporated areas, however, do not regulate what you can charge for late fees.

Unfortunately, some landlords try to charge excessive late fees. This is not legal. Late charges must be reasonably related to the amount of money it costs the landlord to deal with your lateness. Rental agreements and lease clauses that provide for unrea-

---

[1] CC § 1947.
[2] CC § 11, CCP § 12A.

sonably high late charges are probably not enforceable.[3]

While there are no statutory guidelines as to how much a landlord can reasonably charge as a late fee, here are some guidelines which will help you decide if the amount is excessive:

• A reasonable late charge might be a flat charge of no more than $20-$40, depending on the amount of rent. It is common for a landlord to give a tenant a grace period of from one to five days, but there is no law that requires this. A late charge that is out of proportion to the rent (say $75 for being one day late with rent on a $450 per month apartment) would probably not be upheld in court.

• If your landlord imposes a late charge which increases with each additional day of lateness, it should be moderate and have an upper limit. For example, $10 for the first day rent is late, plus $5 for each additional day, with a maximum late charge of $40-$50, would probably be acceptable to a judge, unless the property carries a high rent, in which case somewhat higher amounts might be allowed.

Some landlords try to disguise excessive late charges as a "discount" for early payment of rent. One landlord we know concluded he couldn't get away with charging a $50 late charge on a late $425 rent payment, so instead he designed a rental agreement calling for a rent of $475 with a $50 discount if the rent was not more than three days late. Ingenious as this sounds, it is unlikely to stand up in court, unless the discount for timely payments is very modest. This is because the effect of giving a relatively large discount is the same as charging an excessive late fee, and a judge is likely to see it as such and throw it out.

C. Partial Rent Payments

On occasion you may be short of the money to pay your full rent on time. One way to deal with this is to discuss the problem with your landlord and try to get her to accept a partial payment. Except in the unusual situation where your lease or rental agreement gives you the right to make partial payments, the landlord is under no obligation to accept part of the rent on the due date along with your promise to catch up later.

Unfortunately, there is normally nothing to stop the landlord from accepting a partial rent payment on one day and serving you with a three-day notice to pay the rest of the rent or quit the next. However, if you can get your landlord to specifically agree in writing that you can have a longer time to pay, the landlord is bound by this agreement. Here is a sample:

---

[3] See *Fox v. Federated Department Stores* (1979) 94 Cal.App.3d 867, 156 Cal. Rptr. 893, where the court held invalid a late charge clause in a promissory note because the charge exceeded reasonable administrative costs.

Sample Agreement for Partial Rent Payments

```
            SAMPLE AGREEMENT FOR PARTIAL RENT PAYMENTS

        John Lewis      , Landlord and      Betty Wong      , Tenant
agree as follows:
     1. That      Betty Wong      has paid   one-half of her $500 rent for
Apartment #2 at 111 Billy St., Fair Oaks, CA,    on  March 1, 19  , which is
the date the rent for the month of   March   is due.
     2. That    John Lewis    agrees to accept all the remainder of the rent
on or before    March 15, 19    and to hold off on any legal proceeding to evict
       Betty Wong          until after that date.


_____          _____
Date                              John Lewis, Landlord


_____          _____
Date                              Betty Wong, Tenant
```

D. Rent Increases: General Law

Rent may not be increased during a fixed-term lease unless the lease allows it.

If you live in public housing or "Section 8" housing, in most cases the rent may not be increased to an amount more than 30% of your income (after certain deductions are taken). A rent increase is invalid if you live in an area covered by rent control and it exceeds the amount allowed by the rent control ordinance. We discuss rent control below.

A rent increase is invalid if the landlord imposed it in order to retaliate against you because you exercised some legal right, such as complaining about the condition of the building or organizing a tenants' union. See Chapter 7.B.4, and Chapter 11.B, for more on retaliation.

A rent increase is invalid if the landlord imposed it in order to discriminate against you on the basis of race, sex, children, or any other prohibited reason mentioned in Chapter 5.

Other than these restrictions, there is nothing in state law to prevent the landlord from doubling the rent or even tripling the rent. Again, you are legally protected against such acts only if you are lucky enough to live in a city or county which has a local rent control ordinance.

E. Rent Increase Notices

Subject to the provisions of any local rent control law, a landlord may raise the rent on a month-to-month tenancy by "serving" a written notice on the tenant saying that the rent will be increased in 30 days (or more). (If the tenant has a *lease*, no rent increase is appropriate until the lease ends.)

Questions often arise over the manner in which the rent increase notice is delivered. It has been our experience that most landlords simply mail notice of rent increases to their tenants. Under California law,[4] this is not technically proper service of the notice. The notice must be served as follows:

1. By handing it to the tenant personally, or

2. *If the tenant is absent from home and work,* by leaving the notice with "a person of suitable age and discretion" at home or work, *and* mailing a copy to the tenant, or

3. *If the landlord cannot find the tenant or anyone else of suitable age and discretion at home or work, or the landlord doesn't know where the tenant is employed,* then the landlord may complete the service by doing all three of these things:

• posting the notice in a conspicuous place on the property, such as the front door,

• leaving a copy with someone residing in the rented premises (if such person can be found), and

• mailing a copy to the tenant.

In other words, if you received a rent increase by mail only, it is not legally effective (unless you voluntarily comply with it). In this situation you are within your rights to tell the landlord that because his notice is ineffective, you are not going to pay the increase. Obviously, however, if the amount of the increase seems fair and you have a good relationship with the landlord, you may want to simply pay the increase and not question the way in which you were served the notice.

F. Rent Control

Rent control is a local phenomenon, established either through the initiative process or by the act of a city council or a county board of supervisors.[5]

Some form of rent regulation now exists in 15 California communities, including Los Angeles, San Jose and San Francisco.

Cities With Rent Control Ordinances

Berkeley

Beverly Hills

Campbell (mediation only)

Cotati

East Palo Alto

Hayward

Los Angeles

Los Gatos

Oakland

Palm Springs

San Francisco

San Jose

Santa Monica

Thousand Oaks

West Hollywood

Rent control ordinances generally control more than how much rent a landlord may charge. Many cities' ordinances also govern how and under what circumstances a landlord may terminate a tenancy, even one from month to month, by requiring the landlord to have "just cause" to evict. Many cities,

---

[4] CCP § 1162, referred to by CC § 827.

[5] The California Supreme Court upheld the right of cities and counties to enact rent control ordinances in *Birkenfeld v. City of Berkeley* (1976) 17 Cal.3d 129. The U. S. Supreme Court agreed with that decision in *Fisher v. City of Berkeley* (1986) 475 U.S. 260, 106 S.Ct. 1045.

most notably Los Angeles, require landlords to register their properties with a local rent control agency.

Before we describe how rent control works, a few words of caution:

• Cities change their rent control laws frequently, and court decisions affect them. Landlords' groups have mounted campaigns to weaken the rent control provisions of strict laws, such as Berkeley's. In short, you should read the material here only to get a broad idea of rent control. It is absolutely necessary that you also contact your city or county to find out whether rent control presently exists, and if it does, to get a copy of current ordinances and any regulations interpreting it.

• State law requires local rent control agencies in cities that require registration of rents to provide, upon request of the landlord or tenant, a certificate setting out the permissible rent for a particular unit.[6] The landlord or tenant may appeal the rent determination to the rent control agency within 15 days. If no appeal is filed, the rent determination is binding on the agency. If an appeal is filed, the agency must provide a written decision in 60 days.

• No two rent control ordinances are exactly alike. Some cities have elected or appointed boards which have the power to adjust rents; others allow a certain percentage increase each year as part of their ordinances. Some cities have enlightened ordinances with just cause for eviction provisions which require landlords to give and prove valid reasons for terminating month-to-month tenancies. Some cities have "vacancy decontrol," which means that when a tenant moves out voluntarily (or is asked to leave for a just cause), the unit can be re-rented at the market rate. Some cities with vacancy decontrol in effect encourage landlords to evict by allowing unlimited rent increases on units when they are vacated (see the Rent Control Chart below and Chapter 11.D) and by not protecting existing tenants by requiring just cause for eviction.

In order to summarize how each ordinance works, we have prepared a "Rent Control Chart" which outlines the major points of each ordinance. Here are brief explanations of key terms we use in the Chart and the discussion below:

Exceptions: No city's rent control ordinance covers all rental housing within the city. New buildings as well as owner-occupied buildings with four units or less are often exempt from rent control ordinances.[7] Some cities also exempt single-family dwellings and luxury units that rent for more than a certain amount.

Administration: Most rent control ordinances are administered by rent control boards whose members are appointed by the mayor, city council, or board of supervisors (the boards are elected in Santa Monica and Berkeley). The formal name, address and phone number of the board is given.

Registration: The cities of Berkeley, Cotati, East Palo Alto, Los Angeles, Palm Springs, Santa Monica, Thousand Oaks and West Hollywood all require the owners of rent-controlled property to register the property with the agency that administers the rent control ordinance. This allows the "rent board" to keep track of the city's rental units, as well as to obtain operating funds from the registration fees.

These cities forbid landlords who fail to register their properties from raising rent. In fact, cities may require a landlord to refund past rent increases if the increases were made during a period in which the landlord failed to register property. The courts have ruled that it is unconstitutional for rent control ordinances requiring registration to allow tenants to withhold rents just because the property isn't registered.[8]

---

[6] CC § 1947.8.

[7] One hearing officer for the San Francisco rent board estimates that the majority of illegal evictions there involve landlords falsely claiming to occupy the building.

[8] *Floystrup v. Berkeley Rent Stabilization Board* (1990) 219 Cal.App.3d 1309.

STACEY'S

The Bay Area's Booksource since 1923:

STACEY'S BOOKSTORES

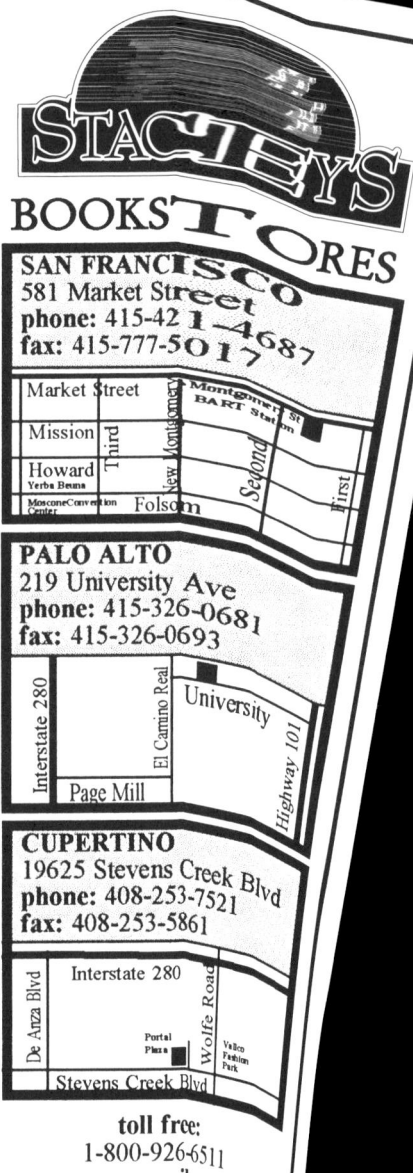

SAN FRANCISCO
581 Market Street
phone: 415-421-4687
fax: 415-777-5017

PALO ALTO
219 University Ave
phone: 415-326-0681
fax: 415-326-0693

CUPERTINO
19625 Stevens Creek Blvd
phone: 408-253-7521
fax: 408-253-5861

toll free:
1-800-926-6511
e-mail:
STACEYSBK@AOL.COM
1994 Prentice Hall
"Magnet Store of the Year."
**Members Northern California
Independent Booksellers Association**

Some cities, including Berkeley and Santa Monica, impose administrative penalties (fines) on landlords who fail to register property. However, both of these types of penalties are now limited by a state law[9] in cases where the landlord's failure to register was not in bad faith and was quickly corrected (that is, the landlord registered the property) in response to a notice from the city. To make things easier for landlords who make honest mistakes, state law now requires cities to allow landlords any rent increases, which would have been allowed had the property been registered, to be phased in over future years if the following conditions are met:

• The landlord's original failure to register the property was unintentional and not in bad faith;

• The landlord has since registered the property as required by the city and paid all back registration fees; and

• The landlord has paid back to the tenant any rents collected in excess of the lawful rate during the time the property wasn't properly registered.

Rent Formula and **Individual Adjustments**: Here you will find a brief summary of the mechanism each city follows to allow rent increases. Each city has a slightly different mechanism for allowing rent increases. All cities allow periodic (usually yearly) across-the-board increases. The amount of the increase may be set by the rent control board, or the ordinance may allow periodic increases of either a fixed percentage or a percentage tied to a local or national consumer price index. In most cities, landlords (and sometimes tenants) may petition the board for higher (or lower) rents based on certain criteria.

Vacancy Decontrol: Most cities allow landlords free rein to raise the rent when a unit is vacated. This feature, called vacancy decontrol, is built into their ordinances. In practice it means that rent control applies to a particular rental unit only as long as a particular tenant (or tenants) live there. If that tenant voluntarily leaves, or in some cities is evicted for just cause (defined below), this property, in most cities, is subject to rent control again after the new (and presumably higher) rent is established. If, however, a tenant acquires a roommate, and the landlord treats the new occupant as a tenant (by accepting rent from him or her, for example), the landlord may not be able to raise the rent when the original tenant leaves.[*] However, in the cities of Hayward and Thousand Oaks, the property is no longer subject to rent control following a voluntary vacancy.

Cities with Vacancy Decontrol

Beverly Hills
Hayward
Los Angeles
Los Gatos
Oakland
San Francisco
San Jose
Thousand Oaks
West Hollywood

When more than one tenant shares an apartment or house, the rule in some other cities with vacancy decontrol is that the rent can't be raised more than the annual increase allowed by the ordinance until all of the original tenants whose names were on the lease or rental agreement leave. At this point the landlord can raise the rent as much as he wants under the vacancy-decontrol provision. But this rule is subject to a number of different interpretations, depending both on the city and the precise situation, so check locally with the rent board.

---

[9]CC § 1947.7.

[*]See *Getz v. City of West Hollywood*, 233 Cal.App.3d 625, 284; Cal. Rptr. 631 (1991).

EXAMPLE

Tom rents an apartment in Oakland for $800 a month. While Tom is there, his landlord may raise the rent only as much as the city's rent control law currently allows—for example, 6% a year. When Tom moves out and Tina then becomes the tenant, the landlord may charge Tina an initial rent of $1,000, $5,000, or anything he likes! With this new starting point, further increases to Tina will be limited by the rent control law. But when Tina moves out, the landlord will once again be able to raise the rent as much as the market will tolerate. (If you think this gives the landlord a strong incentive to evict tenants, you are right.)

Vacancy decontrol really weakens the protections which rent control can give tenants. A study in Los Angeles showed that, overall, rents there went up just about as much as in surrounding cities—even though Los Angeles had rent control and the other cities did not! This was because Los Angeles has vacancy decontrol.

In cities without vacancy decontrol (Santa Monica, Berkeley, Cotati, East Palo Alto and Palm Springs), the limits on rent increases apply even when a tenant moves out and a new tenant moves in. The new tenant must be charged the same rent as the old one, unless it is time for a city-wide increase. The landlord gets a fair increase, a fair rent, and a fair profit, but she can't exploit a new tenant just because he is new. We think this is a better way to do it.

Eviction Protection (Just Cause for Eviction): If a city has a vacancy decontrol provision (in other words, the rent can be raised when a tenant moves), it is essential to the success of the ordinance that a tenant can be evicted only for just cause. This is because if the rents can be raised as much as the landlord wants when a tenant leaves, landlords will have a motive to avoid rent control by giving a 30-day notice to a month-to-month tenant whose rents are controlled. A just cause eviction provision requires landlords to give (and prove in court, if necessary) a valid reason for terminating a month-to-month tenancy. The most common reason for just cause eviction is tenant failure to pay rent on time. What constitutes just cause to evict is discussed in some detail in Chapter 11.D, and for reasons of space is not repeated here.

Cities that Require Just Cause for Eviction

Berkeley
Beverly Hills
Cotati
East Palo Alto
Hayward
Los Angeles
San Francisco
Santa Monica
Thousand Oaks
West Hollywood

Note: San Jose, Oakland and Los Gatos, three of the "weak" rent control cities, do not have just cause eviction. Their ordinances, however, penalize a landlord who tries to evict a tenant in retaliation. The tenant has the burden of proving that the landlord's motive was retaliatory. See Chapter 11 for details on retaliatory evictions.

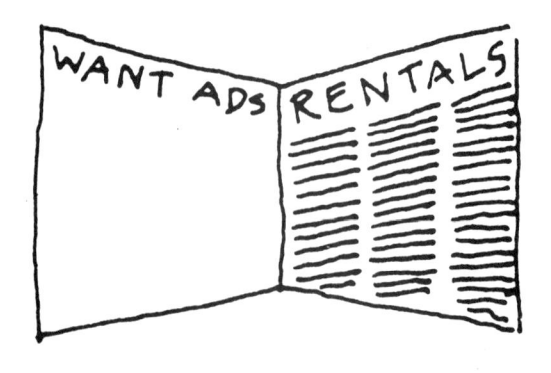

G. General Types of Rent Control Laws

As noted above, although no two cities' rent control laws are identical, they can be broadly categorized into three types. Obviously, this sort of gross classification isn't perfect, but it should help you place your city in the scheme of things.

1. Weak Rent Control

Let's start with the Bay Area cities of San Jose, Oakland, Hayward and Los Gatos, all of which have weak rent control ordinances. Although the rent control ordinances of these areas set forth a certain formula (usually fairly generous to landlords, in the 5-8% range) by which rents can be increased each year, it is possible for a landlord to raise the rent above this figure and still stay within the law. This is because each of these cities' ordinances require a tenant whose rent is increased above the formula level to petition the board within a certain period (usually 30 days) and protest the increase. If you do not protest the increase within the time allowed, the increase is effective, even though it is higher than the formula increase allowed. If the increase is protested, a hearing is held, at which the board decides if the entire increase should be allowed.

In addition, except in Hayward, the rent control ordinances in these cities do not require the landlord to show just cause for eviction. In other words, your landlord can evict you following normal procedures under state law. This means, of course, that this sort of rent control ordinance is so weak that it's almost gutless. It is, however, illegal for landlords in these cities to encourage this type of fear by threatening retaliation against tenants who protest rent increases. (See Chapter 11.B, for more on illegal retaliation.)

Finally, all these cities have vacancy decontrol, none of their ordinances require landlords to register their units with the board, and only Oakland's applies to single-family homes.

2. Strict Rent Control

California's best rent control laws (from a tenant's point of view) are found in the cities of Berkeley, Cotati, East Palo Alto, Santa Monica and West Hollywood. Often single-family rentals are covered by these cities' laws, unless a rental property has four or fewer units and the landlord lives on the property. Landlords must register their units with the board, which decides on the amount of the across-the-board rent increase allowed city-wide each year. Because inflation is presently low, this increase also tends to be low. A landlord who increases rent by a greater percentage faces civil penalties, unless the board has allowed an additional increase following the landlord's application. The burden of justifying a higher than routinely-allowable rent increase is entirely on the landlord.

Finally, as you might have guessed, there is no vacancy decontrol (except for West Hollywood). Again, this means that even if a tenant moves out, the maximum rent for a property remains fixed. A landlord must show just cause for eviction to evict a tenant in all "strict" rent control cities.

Of the strict rent control cities, Berkeley and Santa Monica also allow tenants to petition for lower rents based on landlord's failure to maintain or repair rental units.

Rent Agreed to by the Tenant: In cities with moderate and strict rent control, which require the landlord to petition the board before increasing the rent over a certain amount, a landlord can't circumvent the ordinance by having the tenant agree to an illegal rent. Even if a tenant agrees in writing to pay a higher rent, and pays it, he can sue to get the illegal rent back.[10] This cannot happen, however, in weak rent control cities that require the tenant to object to a rent increase if he wants to stop it from going into effect.

---

[10]*Nettles v. Van de Lande* (1988) 207 Cal.App.3d Supp. 6.

3. Moderate Rent Control

The rent control laws of Los Angeles, San Francisco, Beverly Hills, Palm Springs and Thousand Oaks are somewhere between strict and weak, and for lack of a better term we call them "moderate." Although these moderate laws differ somewhat from city to city, they all require landlords who wish to increase the rent by more than a fixed formula amount to petition the board for a higher increase. In addition, most of them provide for some form of vacancy decontrol and require just cause for eviction.

Otherwise, there is little similarity in the rent control laws of these cities. For more detailed information, consult the Rent Control Chart in Section J, below.

Decreases in Services as Illegal Rent Increases. If for some reason you're not getting all the use out of your apartment that you were promised when you moved in, the rent board may determine that you've been given an illegal rent increase. In one San Francisco case, elderly tenants successfully argued that their services had been decreased when the landlord moved their garbage cans up a flight of stairs.

4. Rent Mediation Laws

In a few cities where city councils have felt tenant pressure, but not enough pressure to enact rent control ordinances, so-called voluntary rent "guidelines," or landlord-tenant "mediation" services have been adopted. The chief beneficiaries of these dubious standards and procedures seem to be the landlords, since voluntary programs have no power to stop rent increases. On rare occasions, however, voluntary mediation or guidelines may work, particularly with smaller landlords who are trying to be fair. If your city or county isn't on the rent control list, check to see if it has a voluntary program.

H. Rent Control Board Hearings

Almost all cities with rent control provide for a hearing procedure to deal with certain types of complaints and requests for rent adjustments. In cities with weak rent control, a tenant's protest of a rent increase higher than that allowed by the applicable rent increase formula will result in a hearing at which the landlord must justify the increase. In other rent control cities, the landlord must request a hearing in order to increase rent above the formula amount. Finally, a few cities—such as Santa Monica and Berkeley—allow tenants to initiate hearings to decrease rents on the basis of the landlord's alleged neglect or lack of maintenance on the property.

In the first two types of hearings above, whether initiated by a tenant who protests a rent increase over the formula amount in a weak rent control city, or by a landlord in a city that requires him to first obtain permission before exceeding the formula increase, the landlord must demonstrate at the hearing that he needs a rent increase higher than that normally allowed in order to obtain a fair return on his investment. This most often means establishing that taxes, maintenance costs, utility charges, or other business expenses, as well as the amortized cost of any capital improvements, make it difficult to obtain a fair return on one's investment, given the existing level of rent.

1. Initiating the Hearing

A hearing is normally initiated by the filing of a "petition" or "application" with the rent board. In describing this process, let's assume that a landlord is filing a petition in a "strict" or "moderate" rent control city that requires her to obtain permission before raising rents above the formula increase allowed. You, the tenant, wish to protest the increase. Remember, this process is approximately reversed in weak rent control cities that require the tenant to protest such an increase.

In some cities, including Los Angeles and San Francisco, there are two types of petitions a landlord seeking an above-formula rent increase can file. If an increase is sought on account of recent capital improvements the landlord has made, a "petition for certification" of such improvements is filed. If a rent increase is sought on other grounds, a "petition for arbitration" is filed.

2. Preparing for the Hearing

As a general rule, you will greatly increase your chances of prevailing if you appear at the hearing fully prepared. The hearing officer will be much better disposed to listen to your concerns if you are thoroughly familiar with the issues and make your presentation in an organized way.

As part of planning your preparation, first obtain a copy of the ordinance and any applicable regulations for the area in which your property is located. Then determine which factors the hearing officer must weigh in considering whether to give the landlord an upward individual adjustment from the formula increase. Your job is to show that the increase being requested is either not justified at all, or too high. To do this you will need to carefully review the landlord's claimed expenses and compare them to what is allowed under the ordinance. For example, San Francisco's ordinance allows the consideration of the cost of capital improvements, energy conservation measures, utilities, taxes, janitorial, security, and maintenance services.

You should also be prepared to produce a witness who is familiar with any items that you think might be contested. If for some reason your witness cannot appear in person, you may present a sworn written statement or "declaration" from that person. The statement should be as specific as possible. At the end, the words, "I declare under penalty of perjury under the laws of California that the foregoing is true and correct" should appear, followed by the date and the person's signature.

Before the date set for your hearing, go and watch someone else's. (Most cities' hearings are open to the public, and even if they are sometimes closed, you can almost always arrange to attend as an observer if you call ahead.) Seeing another hearing may even make the difference between winning and losing at yours. This is because both your confidence and your capabilities will grow as you understand what the hearing officers are interested in and how they conduct the hearing. By watching a hearing, you will learn that while they are relatively informal, all follow some procedural rules. It is a great help to know what these are so you can swim with the current, not against it.

You are permitted to have an attorney or any other person, such as an employee or volunteer from a local tenants' rights group, represent you at a rent adjustment hearing. (Many landlords are represented at such hearings by their apartment managers or management companies.) Hiring someone to speak for you is probably not necessary. If you do a careful job in preparing your case, you will probably do as well alone as with a lawyer or other representative. One good alternative is for a group of tenants similarly situated to chip in and consult with an attorney or someone else thoroughly familiar with rent board hearings to discuss strategy. After the lawyer provides you with advice and information, you can handle the hearing yourself.

3. The Actual Hearing

Once you've prepared for the hearing, it's time to make your case. Here's how to be most effective.

a. Before the Hearing Begins

Arrive at the hearing room at least a few minutes before it is set to begin. Check in with the clerk or other official. Ask to see the file that contains the papers relevant to the application (either yours or the landlord's, depending on the type of ordinance). Review this material to see if there are any comments by office workers, rent board investigators, your landlord, or other tenants. Read the comments very closely and prepare to answer questions from the hearing officer on any of these points.

As you sit in the hearing room, you will probably see a long table, with the hearing officer seated at the head. In a few cities, the hearing is held before several members of the rent board, and they may sit more formally on a dais or raised platform. In any event, you, the landlord, your representatives (if any), and any witnesses will be asked to sit at a table or come to the front of the room. A clerk or other employee may make summary notes of testimony given at the hearing. Or, in some cities, hearings are tape recorded. If, under the procedure followed in your city, no record is kept, you have the right to have the proceedings transcribed or tape recorded, though at your own expense.

b. The Hearing Officer's Role

The hearing officer (who may be a city employee or volunteer mediator or arbitrator) or chairperson of the rent board will introduce herself and the other people in the room. If you have witnesses, tell the hearing officer. The hearing officer, or sometimes an employee of the rent board, will usually summarize the issues involved in the hearing. At some point, you will be sworn to tell the truth; it is perjury to lie at the hearing. When these preliminaries are complete, you and your landlord will have an opportunity to present your cases.

Many hearing officers, rent board employees and members of rent boards tend to be sympathetic to tenants. This is not the same thing as saying that they will bend over backwards to help you. Like most judges (who on balance are probably more sympathetic to landlords), most make an honest effort to follow the law. In other words, your job is to work to make your legal position as unassailable as possible.

A rent adjustment hearing is not like a court hearing. There are no formal rules of evidence. Hearing officers will usually allow you to bring in any information that may be important, though in a court of law it might not be admissible. Relax and just be yourself.

c. Making Your Case

Present your points clearly, but in a non-argumentative way. Sometimes an outline on a 3' x 5' card will help you to focus. Don't get carried away with unnecessary details. You probably won't be given much time, so be prepared and get to the point quickly. The hearing officer may ask you questions to help you explain your position. Make sure you present all documentary evidence and witnesses necessary to back up your case. Later, the hearing officer will give the landlord or his representative a chance to present his case and to ask you questions. Answer the questions quietly. It is almost always counterproductive to get into an argument. Even if you feel the landlord is lying or misleading, don't interrupt. You will be given time later to rebut the testimony. Direct all your argument to the hearing officer, not to the landlord or her representative.

When your witnesses are given the opportunity to testify, the normal procedure is simply to let them have their say. You may ask questions if the witness forgets something important, but remember, this is not a court and you don't want to come on like a lawyer. Very likely, the hearing officer will also ask your witnesses questions. The landlord has the right to ask the witnesses questions as well.

In rare instances, you may get a hearing officer or rent board chairperson who dominates the hearing or seems to be hostile to you, or perhaps to tenants in general. If so, you will want to stand up for your rights, without needlessly confronting the hearing officer. Obviously, this can be tricky, but if you know your legal rights and put them forth in a polite but direct way, you should do fine. If you feel that the hearing officer is simply not listening to you, politely insist on your right to complete your statement and question your witnesses.

Just before the hearing ends, the hearing officer should ask if you have any final comments to make. Don't repeat what you have already said, but make sure all your points have been covered and heard.

At the end of the hearing, the hearing officer will usually tell you when you can expect the decision. A written decision will usually be mailed to you within a few days or weeks of the hearing. Some cities, however, do not issue written decisions; the hearing officer just announces the decision at the end of the hearing.

4. The Decision

Depending on the city and the hearing procedure, you may or may not end up with a written decision and an explanation of why it was so decided.

In most cities, if a landlord's application for an increase was heard by a hearing officer, you have the right to appeal to the full rent board if the increase is allowed and you still feel it is improper. Your landlord has this same right if you prevail. If you make an appeal, you must file within a certain time and state your reason for the appeal. You may or may not have the opportunity to appear in person before the rent board.

The rent board will probably take the findings of the hearing officer at face value and limit its role to deciding whether the hearing officer applied the law to these facts correctly.[11] On the other hand, the rent boards of some cities (including Los Angeles) will allow the entire hearing to be held again. (This is sometimes called a "de novo" hearing.) In addition, the board will not usually consider any facts you raise in your statement which you could have brought up at the earlier hearing, but didn't. If you discover a new piece of information after the original hearing, however, the board might consider it.

If it's your landlord who is appealing and you are satisfied with the earlier decision, you will want to emphasize the thoroughness and integrity of the earlier procedure and be ready to present detailed information only if it seems to be needed.

The rent board will generally have more discretion to make a decision than does a single hearing officer. If your case is unique, the board may consider the implications of establishing a new legal rule or interpretation.

If you again lose your decision before the board, or if your city permits only one hearing in the first place, you may be able to take your case to court, if you are convinced that the rent board or hearing board failed to follow either the law or their own procedures. However, if the hearing officer or board has broad discretion to decide issues such as the one you presented, you are unlikely to get the decision overturned in court. Speak to an attorney about this as soon as possible, as there is a time limit (usually 30 days) for filing an appeal. To appeal a rent board decision, you must have a transcript of the hearing to give to the court.[12]

---

[11] There is an exception to this general rule in some cities. If you arranged to have a transcript of the hearing—or a taped recording of the hearing—prepared, then the rent board may review it.

[12] *Buckhart v. San Francisco Rent Stabilization and Arbitration Board* (1988), 197 Cal.App.3d 1032.

I. What To Do If the Landlord Violates Rent Control Rules

Take the following steps if you suspect your landlord has in any way violated your city's rent control rules:

• Get a copy of your local ordinance—and any regulation interpreting it—and make sure you are right. You may want to call the local rent board to confirm that what the landlord is doing violates the law. Contact any local tenants' rights organization and get the benefit of its advice.

• If you think your landlord may have made a good faith mistake, try to work the problems out informally.

• If that doesn't work, file a formal complaint with your city rent board.

• If the landlord's conduct is extreme, talk to a lawyer. You may have a valid suit based on the intentional infliction of emotional distress, for invasion of privacy, or on some other grounds, including those provided in the ordinance itself.

J. Rent Control Chart: Specific Provisions of Rent Control

The Rent Control Chart on the following pages summarizes the major features of California's local rent control laws. However, for more specifics and any recent changes not reflected in this book, it is absolutely essential that you obtain a copy of your local ordinance and any regulations interpreting it from the address listed after "Administration."

RENT CONTROL CHART

BERKELEY

Ordinance Adoption Date	6/3/80; latest amendment 11/90 (ballot measure).
Exceptions	Units constructed after 6/3/80, owner-occupied single-family residences and duplexes. [Sec. 5.]
Administration	Elected 9-member Rent Stabilization Board, 2100 Milvia Street, Berkeley, CA 94704, (510) 644-6128.
Registration	Required, or landlord can't raise rents.[13] Stiff penalties for noncooperation. [Secs. 8, 11.f.4, 11.g.]
Rent Formula	Annual general adjustments by Board after investigation and hearings. [Secs. 10, 11.] In 1991, Board allowed property owners to increase what was the base rent in 1980 by 45%. In 1992 and 1993 further increases of $26 and $20, respectively, were allowed per rental unit.
Individual Adjustments	Landlord may petition for further increase based on increased taxes or unavoidable increases in utility or maintenance costs, and on costs of capital improvements necessary to bring property up to minimum legal requirements. Increase not allowed based on increased debt service cost due to recent purchase. (If tenant agrees to join in landlord's request, a "fast track" petition method, under which a decision will be made within 30 days and without a formal hearing, may be used.) Tenant may apply for rent reduction based on poor maintenance. [Sec. 12.]
Notice Requirements	None in addition to state law.
Vacancy Decontrol	No increase allowed upon vacancy.
Eviction	Landlord must show just cause to evict.
Penalties	Violation of ordinance is misdemeanor punishable by maximums of $500 fine and 90 days imprisonment (first offense) and $3,000 fine and one year imprisonment (second offense). [Sec. 19.] Tenant may sue in court for excess rent collected plus up to $750. [Sec.15.a]
Other Features	Landlord must place security deposits in interest-bearing savings and loan account which is insured by the Federal Savings and Loan Insurance Corporation. Landlord must credit interest against rents each December, as well as when tenant vacates. [Sec. 7, Regulation Secs. 701, 702.]

---

[13] The provision that a tenant can withhold rents if the landlord fails to register was ruled unconstitutional in *Floystrup v. Berkeley Rent Stabilization Board* (1990) 219 Cal.App.3d 1309.

BEVERLY HILLS

Ordinance Adoption Date	(Beverly Hills Municipal Code, Chapter 5, Ord. No. 79-O-1731) 4/27/79; latest amendment 12/9/91.
Exceptions	Units constructed after 10/20/78, units that rented for more than $600 on 5/31/78, single-family residences, rented condominium units. [Sec. 4-5.102.]
Administration	Appointed 7-member Rent Adjustments Board 445 N. Rexford, Beverly Hills, CA 90210, (310) 285-1031.
Registration	Not required.
Rent Formula	Except for specific "surcharges" which must be justified and the rent-increase notice (see below), rents may not be increased in any 12-month period by more than 8% (10% where rents were over $600 in 1979) or a percentage based on the "Urban All Items Consumer Price Index for Los Angeles," whichever is less. (The CPI-based figure is calculated by adding the monthly CPI figures for the most recently-published 12-month period, subtracting from that a second CPI sum based on the 12-month period before that, and dividing the difference by the lesser of the two sums.) To this permitted increase, the landlord may add a "capital expenditure surcharge" so as to additionally increase the rent by up to 4% more (calculated by amortizing capital improvement costs), a "utility expense surcharge" based on owner-paid utility cost increases in excess of the allowed annual percentage increase, and a 10% surcharge for each adult tenant occupying the unit over and above any maximum number of adult occupants specified in the lease. The landlord may also pass through the amortized cost of any legally-required improvements. [Secs. 4-5.302-4-5.307.]
Individual Adjustments	Tenant who contests validity of any capital improvement surcharge or utility surcharge over and above the annual increase percentage may petition Board to request non-allowance of the surcharge. Landlord seeking increases above annual percentage increase and allowed surcharges may apply to Board for higher "hardship" increase. (Ordinance is silent on factors to be considered, but does not preclude hardship increase based on high debt service costs due to recent purchase.) [Sec. 4-5.402.]
Notice Requirements	Landlord must post in the lobby, hallway, or other "public" location on the property a notice stating the name, address, and telephone number of the owner or authorized agent, and must give each tenant a copy of the notice; failure to comply with this requirement precludes increase of rents. Rent-increase notice must state the basis justifying any rent increase above the basic rent formula and must advise the tenant that records and documentation verifying it will be made available for inspection by the tenant or the tenant's representative. [Sec. 4-5.309.] The justification should break down the increase into portions allowed under annual adjustment and individual surcharges.
Vacancy Decontrol	Landlord may charge any rent after a tenant vacates voluntarily, but not when landlord terminates tenancy. Once the property is re-rented, it is subject to rent control based on the higher rent. [Sec. 4-5.310.]
Eviction	Landlord must show just cause to evict.
Penalties	Violation of ordinance is a misdemeanor punishable by maximums of $500 fine and six months imprisonment. [Sec. 4-5.706.] Tenant may sue in court for three times any rent in excess of legal rent collected ($500 minimum), plus attorney fees. [Sec. 4-5.705.]

CAMPBELL

Ordinance Adoption Date	1983 (Campbell Municipal Code, Chapter 6.09)
Exceptions	Single-family residences, duplexes, and triplexes. [Sec. 6.09.030(l).]
Administration	Campbell Rent Mediation program, 1245 S. Winchester Blvd. Suite 200, San Jose, CA 95128, (408) 243-8565.
Registration	Not required.
Rent Formula	No fixed formula; rent increases must be "reasonable." [Sec. 6.09.150.]
Individual Adjustments	Tenants in 25% of the units (but at least three units) affected by an increase can contest it by filing a petition within 37 days, or lose the right to object to the increase. Disputes raised by tenant petition are first subject to "conciliation," then mediation. If those fail, either party may file written request for arbitration by city "Fact Finding Committee." Committee determines whether increase is "reasonable" by considering costs of capital improvements, repairs, maintenance, and debt service, and past history of rent increases. However, the Committee's determination is not binding. [Secs. 6.09.050-6.09.150.]
Notice Requirements	On written request by a tenant, an apartment landlord must disclose in writing to that person the apartment numbers of all tenants receiving rent increases that same month. [Sec. 6.09.040.]
Vacancy Decontrol	No restriction on raises after vacancy.
Eviction Features	Ordinance does not require showing of just cause to evict, so 3-day and 30-day notice requirements and unlawful detainer procedures are governed solely by state law.
Note	Because this ordinance does not provide for binding arbitration of any rent-increase dispute, it is not truly a rent control ordinance. Compliance with any decision appears to be voluntary only.

COTATI

Ordinance Adoption Date (Cotati Municipal Code, Chapter 19.19), 9/23/80 (ballot initiative); latest amendment 3/10/87.

Exceptions Units constructed after 9/23/80 (board has authority to remove exemption), owner-occupied single-family residences, duplexes, and triplexes. [Sec. 19.12.020.D.]

Administration Appointed 5-member Rent Appeals Board, 201 W. Sierra, Cotati, CA 94931, (707) 792-4600.

Registration Required, or landlord can't raise rents, and tenants can seek Board permission to withhold current rents (but may have to pay all or part of withheld rent to landlord after registration). [Sec. 19.12.030.O.][14]

Rent Formula 9/23/80 freeze at 6/1/79 levels, plus annual "general adjustments" by Board after investigation and hearings. [Sec. 19.12.050.] Annual general adjustment is to be adequate to cover operating cost increases and to permit net operating income to increase at 66% of the rate of increase in the CPI (Consumer Price Index [all items] for urban consumers, San Francisco-Oakland). [Regulation Secs. 3000-3002.]

Individual Adjustments Within 30 days after Board determines annual general adjustment, landlord may petition for further increase based on increased taxes or unavoidable increases in utility or maintenance costs, and on costs of capital improvements necessary to bring property up to minimum legal requirements. Increase not allowed based on increased debt service cost due to recent purchase. Tenant may apply for rent reduction based on poor maintenance. [Secs. 19.12.060, 19.12.070, Reg. Secs. 4001-4052.]

Notice Requirements None in addition to state law.

Vacancy Decontrol None. [Ordinance Sec. 19.12.030.P allows Board to decontrol only housing whose rental unit vacancy rate exceeds 5%; this is highly unlikely.]

Eviction Landlord must show just cause to evict.

Penalties Tenant may sue in court for three times any excess rent collected ($500 minimum) plus attorney fees, or tenant may simply credit any excess payments against future rent payments. [Sec. 19.12.110.]

Other Features Landlord must place security deposits in interest-bearing insured savings and loan account and credit interest to tenant when she vacates. [Sec. 19.12.150]

---

[14]Since the Board must first approve rent-withholding following a hearing, this provision may still be valid despite *Floystrup v. Berkeley Rent Stabilization Board* (1990) 219 Cal.App.3d 1309.

EAST PALO ALTO

Ordinance Adoption Date	11/23/83; latest amendment 4/88.
Exceptions	Units constructed after 11/23/83, units owned by landlords owning four or fewer units in city. [Sec. 5.]
Administration	Appointed 7-member Rent Stabilization Board, 2415 University Ave., East Palo Alto, CA 94303, (415) 853-3100.
Registration	Required, or landlord can't raise rents, and tenants can apply to Board for permission to withhold current rents (but may have to pay all or part of withheld rent to landlord after registration). [Secs. 8, 11.E.4, 15.A.1.][15]
Rent Formula	11/23/83 freeze at 4/1/83 levels, plus annual adjustments by Board after investigation and hearings. [Secs. 10, 11.]
Individual Adjustments	Landlord may apply for further increase based on increased taxes or unavoidable increases in utility or maintenance costs, and on costs of capital improvements necessary to bring property up to minimum legal requirements. Increase not allowed based on increased debt service due to recent purchase. Tenant may apply for rent reduction based on poor maintenance. [Sec. 12.]
Notice Requirements	Notices increasing rent by more than that allowed under annual across-the-board adjustment must state that it is subject to appeal by tenant petition to Board, and must list Board address and telephone number. [Sec. 12.E.]
Vacancy Decontrol	No increases allowed upon vacancy.
Eviction	Landlord must show just cause to evict.
Penalties	Violation of ordinance is misdemeanor punishable by maximums of $500 fine and 90 days imprisonment (first offense) and $3,000 fine and one year imprisonment (second offense). [Sec. 19.] Tenant may sue landlord in court for excess rent unlawfully collected plus up to $500. [Sec. 15.A.4.]
Other Features	Landlord must place security deposits in interest-bearing account at an insured bank or savings and loan and credit interest against rents each December, as well as when tenant vacates. [Sec. 7.]

---

[15]Since the Board must first approve rent-withholding following a hearing, this provision may still be valid despite *Floystrup v. Berkeley Rent Stabilization Board* (1990) 219 Cal.App.3d 1309.

HAYWARD

Ordinance Adoption Date	9/13/83; latest amendment 3/16/93.
Exceptions	Units first occupied after 7/1/79, units owned by landlord owning four or fewer rental units in the city. [Sec. 2(l).]
Administration	Administered by city-manager-appointed employees of Rent Review Office, 25151 Clawiter Rd., Hayward, CA 94545-2731, (510) 293-5540.
Registration	Not required.
Rent Formula	Annual rent increases limited in any 12-month period to 5%, plus increased utility costs if documented as specified. A landlord who has not increased the rent during a previous 12-month period may "bank" the increase by raising it 10% the next period. [Sec. 3(c),(d).]
Individual Adjustments	The tenant can contest an increase of over 5% by first contacting the person specified in the notice (see notice requirements, below) for an explanation of the increase. Tenant then must file petition with the Rent Review Office before the increase takes effect (30 days) or lose the right to object to it. Disputes raised in tenant petition are heard by a mediator; if mediation fails, arbitration is mandatory and binding on both parties. Landlord may be allowed to pass on increased utility and maintenance costs and "amortize" [spread out] capital expenditures. [Sec. 5.]
Notice Requirements	Landlord must give tenant a copy of ordinance at the beginning of the tenancy, and a document which gives the unit's rent history and lists improvements to the unit. [Sec. 4(a).] Failure to comply may be grounds for denial of an otherwise-proper rent increase. Rent-increase notices must be accompanied by a blank tenant petition form, and by a second notice which either states that the increase is allowed under the 5%-increase limitation or which gives specific reasons for an increase above 5%. The notice must also include the name, address, and telephone number of the landlord or other person able to explain the increase. [Sec. 4(b).]
Vacancy Decontrol	Rent controls are permanently removed from each unit after a voluntary vacancy (that is, without any legal action by or notices from the landlord, even for cause), followed by the expenditure of $200 or more on improvements by the landlord, and city certification of compliance with city Housing Code.[Sec. 8.]
Eviction	Landlord must show just cause to evict, even where rent control removed by vacancy decontrol, above.
Penalties	Failure to provide required information to tenant is an infraction (petty offense) punishable on first, second, or third offense within 12-month period by fines of up to $100, $200 and $500, respectively. Fourth offense within 12 months is misdemeanor punishable by maximums of $1,000 fine and six months imprisonment. [Sec. 20.b.] Tenant may sue in court for excess rent collected, treble that amount or $500 (whichever is greater), and attorney fees. [Sec. 20.a.]
Other Features	Ordinance requires landlords holding security deposits longer than a year to pay annual interest at a rate determined by Rent Review Officer by November 1st of each year, based on local passbook savings rates. Interest must be credited against the tenant's rent on his anniversary date and when deposit refunded at end of tenancy. There is, however, no requirement for separate account. Violation can subject landlord to liability for three times the amount of unpaid interest owed. [Sec. 13.]

LOS ANGELES

Ordinance Adoption Date — (Los Angeles Municipal Code, Chapter XV), 4/21/79; latest amendment 2/19/91.

Exceptions — Units constructed (or substantially renovated with at least $10,000 in improvements) after 10/1/78, "luxury" units (defined as 0,1,2,3, or 4+-bedroom units renting for at least $302, $420, $588, $756, or $823, respectively, as of 5/31/78), single-family residences, except where three or more houses are located on the same lot. [Sec. 151.02.G,M.]

Administration — Appointed 7-member Rent Adjustment Commission, 215 West 6th St., Suite 800, Los Angeles, CA 90014, (213) 485-4727. For questions regarding ordinance, call (213) 624-7368.

Registration — Required.[16] [Sec. 151.11.B] Tenant may defend any unlawful detainer action on the basis of the landlord's failure to register the property [Sec. 151.09.F].

Rent Formula — Except with permission of Commission or Community Development Department, rents may not be increased by more than a 3%-to-8% percentage based on the "All Urban Consumers Consumer Price Index" for the Los Angeles/Long Beach/Anaheim/Santa Monica/Santa Ana areas. The figure is published each year by the Community Development Department on or before May 30th, and applies to rent increases to be effective the following July 1st through June 30th of the next year. The actual percentage is calculated by averaging the CPI over the previous 12-month period beginning the September 30th before that, but in any event cannot fall below 3% or exceed 8%. In addition, if the landlord pays for gas or electricity for the unit, she may raise the rent an additional 1% for each such type of utility service. [Secs. 151.06.D, 151.07.A.6.]

Individual Adjustments — Landlord may apply to the Rent Adjustment Commission for higher increase to obtain "just and reasonable return." (This does not include "negative cash flow" based on recent purchase, but does include negative "operating expense," not counting landlord's mortgage payment.) [Sec. 151.07.B] Also, landlord may apply to Community Development Department for permission to pass on to the tenant 50% of the cost of capital improvements not directly benefitting the landlord—for example, new roof costs would be considered, but not costs of renovations to manager's units or advertising signs—spread out over five or more years [Sec. 151.07.A].

Notice Requirements — Landlord must post conspicuously or give tenant a copy of current registration statement showing that the property is registered with Board. [Sec. 151.05.A.] Landlord who applies to Board for a rent higher than maximum is required to provide written justification for the difference. [Sec. 151.05.C.]

Vacancy Decontrol — Landlord may charge any rent after a tenant either vacates voluntarily or is evicted for non-payment of rent, breach of a rental agreement provision, or to substantially remodel. Controls remain if landlord evicts for any other reason, fails to remodel after evicting for that purpose, or terminates or fails to renew a subsidized-housing lease with the city housing authority. Once a vacated unit is re-rented, it is subject to rent control based on the higher rent. [Sec. 151.06.C.]

Eviction — Landlord must show just cause to evict.

---

[16] The ordinance's provision that tenants may withhold rents for non-registration is unconstitutional, unless ordinance allows the landlord a hearing first. See *Floystrup v. Berkeley Rent Stabilization Board* (1990) 219 Cal.App.3d 1309.

Penalties

Violation of ordinance, including failing to include proper information in eviction notices, is a misdemeanor punishable by maximums of $500 fine and six months imprisonment. [Sec. 151.10.B.] Tenant may sue in court for three times any rent in excess of legal rent collected, plus attorney fees. [Sec. 151.10.A.]

Other Features

Landlord must pay 5% annual interest rate on deposits held over a year. Interest payments need only be made every five years, and when deposit refunded at end of tenancy.

Los Angeles also has a Rent Escrow Adjustment Program (REAP) ordinance that applies to all rent-controlled units. Under this ordinance, a tenant whose landlord has received a 30-day notice from local health or building inspectors to correct serious housing code violations may withhold rent and pay it to a city escrow fund, if the landlord has failed to correct the violation within the 30-day period. (See Chapter 7 for details on REAP.)

LOS GATOS

Ordinance Adoption Date (Los Gatos Town Code, Chapter 24), 10/27/80; latest amendment 12/5/83. (Later amendments apply to mobile home parks only.)

Exceptions Property on lots with two or fewer units, single-family residences, rented condominium units. [Sec. 24.20.015.]

Administration Los Gatos Rent Mediation program, 1245 S. Winchester Blvd., Suite 200, San Jose, CA 95128, (408) 243-8565.

Registration Not required. (However, a "regulatory fee" to pay for program is added to annual business license fee, when business license is required.)

Rent Formula Rents may not be increased more than once within 12-month period (except to pass through regulatory fee), and are limited to 5% or 70% of the All Urban Consumers Consumer Price Index for the San Francisco-Oakland area. [Secs. 24.30.010, 24.70.015(3).]

Individual Adjustments Tenants in 25% of the units affected by an increase greater than the formula above can contest it by filing a petition within 30 days, or will lose the right to object to the increase. Disputes initiated by tenant petition are first attempted to be resolved by "conciliation." If that fails, either party may file a written request for mediation, and, if that fails, binding arbitration. [Secs. 24.40.010-24.40.050.] Mediator/arbitrator may consider costs of capital improvements, repairs, maintenance, and debt service, and past history of rent increases. [Regulation Secs. 2.03-2.05.]

Notice Requirements Rent-increase notice for increases above 5% (or separate statement served with it) must state, "You have the right to use the Rental Dispute Mediation and Arbitration Hearing Process. For further information contact Los Gatos Rent Mediation Program," giving program's address and telephone number. On written request by a tenant, an apartment landlord must disclose in writing to that person the apartment numbers of all tenants receiving rent increases that same month. [Sec. 24.30.030.]

Vacancy Decontrol Landlord may charge any rent after a tenant vacates voluntarily or is evicted following 3-day notice for nonpayment of rent or other breach of the rental agreement. Once the property is re-rented, it is subject to rent control based on the higher rent. [Sec. 24.70.015(1).]

Eviction Ordinance does not require showing of just cause to evict, but tenant has other defenses.

Other Features Mediation/arbitration process applies not only to rent increases and evictions, but also to provision of "housing services". [Sec. 24.40.010.] Since ordinance requires that every lease and rental agreement include a provision to agree to binding arbitration [Sec. 24.40.040], a party invoking the process can in effect keep a "housing services" dispute out of the courts—this will make any binding arbitration award final.

OAKLAND

Ordinance Adoption Date	10/7/80; latest amendment 10/28/86.
Exceptions	Units constructed after 1/1/83, buildings "substantially rehabilitated" at cost of 50% of that of new construction (as determined by Chief Building Inspector) properties with HUD-insured mortgages. [Sec. 2.i].
Administration	Appointed 7-member Residential Rent Arbitration Board, 300 Lakeside Drive, Oakland, CA 94612, (510) 238-3721 (to leave message) or call Sentinel Fair Housing at (510) 836-2687.
Registration	Not required.
Rent Formula	Rents may not be increased more than 6% in any 12-month period for occupied units, and 12% in any 12-month period for units vacated after the landlord terminated the tenancy. [Sec. 5.]
Individual Adjustments	Tenant can contest an increase in excess of that allowed (but only if his rent is current) by filing a petition with the Board. The petition must be filed within 30 days. Hearing officer may consider costs of capital improvements, repairs, maintenance, and debt service, and past history of rent increases. [Sec. 5.c.,7.]
Notice Requirements	Landlords are required to notify tenants of the Residential Rent Arbitration Board at outset of the tenancy, in an addendum to the lease or rental agreement. [Sec. 5.d.]
Vacancy Decontrol	Landlord may charge any rent after a tenant vacates voluntarily. Controls remain if tenant vacates "involuntarily," though 12-month rent-increase ceiling increases to 12% from 8%. Once the property is re-rented, it is subject to rent control based on the higher rent. [Sec. 5.b.] Controls may be permanently removed if landlord spends at least 50% of new-construction cost to "substantially rehabilitate" property.
Eviction	Ordinance does not require just cause to evict, but there are other requirements.
Penalties	Violation of ordinance is infraction (petty offense) punishable on first, second, and third offenses within 12-month period by fines of up to $50, $100, and $250, respectively. A fourth offense within 12 months is a misdemeanor punishable by maximums of a $500 fine and six months imprisonment. [Sec. 9.1.]

PALM SPRINGS

Ordinance Adoption Date   (Palm Springs Municipal Code, Title 4), 9/1/79 (ballot initiative); latest amendment 4/10/90.

Exceptions   Units constructed after 4/1/79, owner-occupied single-family residences, duplexes, triplexes, and four-plexes, units where rent was $450 or more as of 9/1/79. [Secs. 4.02.010, 4.02.030.]

Administration   Appointed 5-member Rent Review Commission, 3200 E. Tahquitz Canyon, Palm Springs, CA 92262, (619) 778-8465.

Registration   Required, or landlord can't raise rents. [Sec. 4.02.080.]

Rent Formula   Rent as of 9/1/79, plus annual increases not exceeding 75% of the annual All Urban Consumers Consumer Price Index for the Los Angeles/Long Beach/Anaheim metropolitan area. (Step-by-step calculation procedure is set forth in ordinance.) [Secs. 4.02.040, 4.02.050.]

Individual Adjustments   Landlord may petition for further increases based on "hardship." Commission consent for increase is not necessary if tenant agrees in writing, but landlord may not coerce consent under threat of eviction or nonrenewal of lease, and may not include general waiver in lease or rental agreement. [Secs.4.02.060, 4.02.065.]

Notice Requirements   Before raising rent, landlord must notify tenant in writing of the base rent charged on 9/1/79, the present rent, and the date of the last previous rent increase. [Sec. 4.02.080(d)(2).] This information can be included on the rent-increase notice.

Vacancy Decontrol   No increases allowed when vacancy occurs.

Eviction   Just cause to evict is not required, but there may be other restrictions.

Penalties   Tenant may sue in court for any excess rent collected, attorney fees, and a penalty of up to $300. [Sec. 4.02.090.] Tenant may also seek the $300-plus-attorney-fees penalty against landlord who coerces consent to rent increase. [Sec. 4.02.060(c).]

SAN FRANCISCO

Ordinance Adoption Date	(San Francisco Administrative Code, Chapter 37), 6/79; latest amendment 12/8/92.
Exceptions	Units constructed after 6/79, buildings over 50 years old and "substantially rehabilitated" since 6/79, owner-occupied single-family residences, duplexes, triplexes, and four-plexes. [Sec. 37.2(p).]
Administration	Appointed 5-member Residential Rent Stabilization and Arbitration Board, [Sec. 37.4], 25 Van Ness Avenue, Suite 320, San Francisco, CA 94102, (415) 554-9550 and (415) 554-9551.
Registration	Not required.
Rent Formula	Rents may not be increased by more than 7% in any 12-month period. (Increase allowed each year is 60% of the All Urban Consumer Price Index for the San Francisco-Oakland Metropolitan Area, but not more than 7%.) The figure is published each year by the Board. [Sec. 37.3.] A landlord who has not increased the rent during a previous 12-month period may accumulate his/her rights to increases and impose them in later years. Landlord may apply to Board for certification of capital improvements the amortized cost of which may also be passed through to the tenant, but such increases are limited to 10% of the base rent each year. [Sec. 37.7.]
Individual Adjustments	Landlord may apply to Board for higher increase based on increased costs, including utility and capital-improvement costs. Hearing officer decides case based on various factors, including operating and maintenance expenses, but not "negative cash flow" based on recent purchase. Hearing officer may also consider rent-increase history and failure to make repairs. Tenant may contest any claimed passthrough of utility costs, or request rent reduction based on decrease of services or poor maintenance. Either party may request an "expedited hearing." [Secs. 37.8.]
Notice Requirements	Landlord must give tenant written itemized breakdown of rent increases—for example, what portion reflects costs of capital improvements—on or before the date of service of the rent-increase notice. [Sec. 37.6(b).]
Vacancy Decontrol	Landlord may charge any rent after a tenant vacates voluntarily or is evicted for good cause. Once the property is re-rented, it is subject to rent control based on the higher rent. [Sec. 37.3(a).]
Eviction	Landlord must show just cause to evict. [Sec. 37.9.]
Penalties	Violation of ordinance, including wrongful eviction or eviction attempts, is a misdemeanor punishable by maximums of a $2,000 fine and six months imprisonment. [Sec. 37.10.]
Other Features	Landlord must pay 5% annual interest on deposits held over a year, with payments made on tenant's move-in anniversary date each year, and when deposit refunded at end of tenancy. [Administrative Code, Chapter 49.]

SAN JOSE

Ordinance Adoption Date (San Jose Municipal Code, Title 17, Chapter 17.23) 7/7/79; latest amendment 7/19/91.

Exceptions Units constructed after 9/7/79, single-family residences, duplexes, and condominium units. [Sec. 17.23.150.]

Administration Appointed 7-member Advisory Commission on Rents, 4 N. Second St., Suite 600, San Jose, CA 95113-1305, (408) 277-5431.

Registration Not required.

Rent Formula Rents may not be increased more than 8% in any 12-month period, and may not be increased more than once within the 12 months. However, a landlord who has not raised the rent for 24 months is entitled to a 21% increase. [Secs. 17.23.180, 17.23.210.]

Individual Adjustments Tenant can contest an increase in excess of that allowed by filing a petition before rent increase takes effect (30 days), or lose the right to object. Disputes initiated by tenant petition are heard by a mediation hearing officer, who may consider costs of capital improvements, repairs, maintenance, and debt service, and past history of rent increases. Either party may appeal mediator's decision and invoke binding arbitration. Tenant can also petition to contest rent based on housing-code violations or decrease in services. [Secs. 17.23.220-17.23.440.]

Notice Requirements Where rent increase exceeds 8%, rent-increase notice must advise tenant of her right to utilize the Rental Dispute Mediation and Arbitration Hearing Process, giving the address and telephone number of the city's rent office. The notice must also indicate the time limit within which the tenant may do this. [Sec. 17.23.270.]

Vacancy Decontrol Landlord may charge any rent after a tenant vacates voluntarily or is evicted following 3-day notice for nonpayment of rent or other breach of the rental agreement. Once the property is re-rented, it is subject to rent control based on the higher rent. [Sec. 17.23.190.]

Eviction Ordinance does not require showing of just cause to evict.

Penalties Violation of ordinance by charging rent in excess of that allowed following mediation/arbitration, by retaliation against the tenant for asserting his rights, or by attempting to have tenant waive rights under ordinance is a misdemeanor punishable by maximums of a $500 fine and six months imprisonment. [Secs. 17.23.515-17.23.530.] Tenant may sue landlord in court for excess rents charged, plus treble damages or $500 (whichever is greater) [Sec. 17.23.540.]

SANTA MONICA

Ordinance Adoption Date	(City Charter Article XVIII), 4/10/79 (ballot initiative); latest amendment 9/13/91.
Exceptions	Units constructed after 4/10/79, owner-occupied single-family residences, duplexes, and triplexes, single-family houses not rented on 7/1/84. [Charter Amendment (C.A.) Secs. 1801(c), 1815, Regulation (Reg.) Secs. 2000+, 12000+.]
Administration	Elected 5-member Rent Control Board, 1685 Main St., Room 202, Santa Monica, CA 90401, (310) 458-8751.
Registration	Required, or landlord can't raise rents.[17] [C.A. Secs. 1803(q), 1805(h).]
Rent Formula	4/10/79 freeze at 4/10/78 levels, plus annual adjustments by Board. [C.A. Secs. 1804, 1805(a),(b), Reg. Secs. 3000+.]
Individual Adjustments	Landlord may apply for further increase based on increased taxes or unavoidable increases in utility or maintenance costs, capital improvements, but not "negative cash flow" due to recent purchase. Tenant may apply for rent reduction based on poor maintenance or decrease in services. [C.A. Sec. 1805(c)-(h), Reg. Secs. 4000+.]
Notice Requirements	Rent-increase notice must state, "The undersigned [landlord] certifies that this unit and common areas are not subject to any uncorrected citation or notices of violation of any state or local housing, health, or safety laws issued by any government official or agency, and that all registration fees have been paid to date." [Reg. Sec. 3007(f)(3)]. Otherwise, tenant may refuse to pay increase and successfully defend unlawful detainer action based on failure to pay increase.
Vacancy Decontrol	None. [C.A. Sec. 1803(r) allows Board to decontrol any category of property only if the rental unit vacancy rate exceeds 5%; this is a virtual impossibility.]
Eviction	Landlord must show just cause to evict.
Penalties	Violation of the charter amendment is a misdemeanor punishable by maximums of a $500 fine and six months imprisonment. Tenant may sue landlord in court for violating ordinance in any way, and may recover attorney fees; tenant may recover rents unlawfully charged, plus treble damages and attorney fees. [C.A. Sec. 1809(a)-(d).]
Other Features	Landlord must place security deposits in interest-bearing account at insured savings and loan or bank. Landlord need not pay tenant any of the interest, but failure to do so is a "factor" in the city denying an individual landlord's requested rent increase (or granting a tenant's requested rent decrease). Landlord cannot raise security deposit during tenancy, even if rent is raised, unless tenant agrees. [City Charter Article XV111, Chapter 14.]

---

[17]Since the Board must first approve rent-withholding following a hearing, this provision may still be valid despite *Floystrup v. Berkeley Rent Stabilization Board* (1990) 219 Cal.App.3d 1309.

THOUSAND OAKS

Ordinance Adoption Date	7/1/80; latest amendment 3/24/87.
Exceptions	Units constructed after 6/30/80, "luxury" units (defined as 0,1,2,3, or 4+-bedroom units renting for at least $400, $500, $600, $750, or $900, respectively, as of 6/30/80), single-family residences, duplexes, triplexes, and four-plexes, except where five or more units are located on the same lot. [Sec. III.L.]
Administration	Appointed 5-member Rent Adjustment Commission, 2150 W. Hillcrest Drive, Thousand Oaks, CA 91320, (805) 497-8611, ext. 657.
Registration	Required. [Sec. XIV.]
Rent Formula	Rents may not be increased by more than 7% in any 12-month period. Increase allowed each year is 75% of the All-Urban Consumer Price Index for the greater Los Angeles area, but not less than 3% nor more than 7%. [Secs. III.G,H, VI.]
Individual Adjustments	Landlord may apply to the Rent Adjustment Commission for higher increase based on capital improvement costs, or to obtain "just and reasonable return" (does not include "negative cash flow" based on recent purchase.) [Sec. VII.]
Notice Requirements	Landlord must prominently post in the apartment complex a listing or map of rental units, showing which are subject to the ordinance and which are not. [Sec. VI.C.]
Vacancy Decontrol	Property that becomes vacant after 5/1/81 due to tenant voluntarily leaving or being evicted for nonpayment of rent is no longer subject to any provision of the ordinance. [Sec. VI.]
Eviction Features	Landlord must show just cause to evict.
Penalties	Tenant may sue in court for three times any rent in excess of legal rent collected, plus a penalty of up to $500 and attorney's fees. [Sec. IX.]
Other Features	Landlord can exempt property from rent control by offering "freedom leases" with five-year term and yearly increase of no more than 3% where the tenant is over age 65, or three-year term with yearly increase of no more than 75% of the All-Urban Consumers CPI for the greater Los Angeles area, for non-elderly tenants.

WEST HOLLYWOOD

Ordinance Adoption Date (West Hollywood Municipal Code, Article IV, Chapter 4), 6/27/85 (ballot initiative); latest amendment 10/21/92.

Exceptions Units constructed after 7/1/79 ("just-cause" eviction requirements do apply, however). However, all exemptions (except a standard "boarding" exemption) must be applied for in registration document (see below). [Sec. 6406.]

Administration Appointed 5-member Rent Stabilization Commission, 8704 Santa Monica Blvd., (mailing address is 8611 Santa-Monica Blvd.) West Hollywood, CA 90069, (310) 854-7450.

Registration Required, or landlord can't raise rents. [Sec. 6407.]

Rent Formula 11/29/84 freeze at 4/30/84 levels, plus annual adjustments by Board of no more than 75% of the All-Urban Consumer Price Index for the greater Los Angeles area. Landlords who pay for tenants' gas and/or electricity may increase an additional 1/2 % for each such utility. [Secs. 6408, 6409.]

Individual Adjustments Landlord may apply for further increase based on unavoidable increases in utility or maintenance costs or taxes, and for capital improvements. Tenant may apply for rent reduction based on poor maintenance. [Sec. 6411.] Also, Board may initiate hearing on same basis. [Sec. 6414(k).]

Rent-Increase Notification Rent-increase notice must contain statement to the effect that landlord is in compliance with ordinance, including filing and payment of required registration documents and fees. [Sec. 6409.G, Regulation Sec. 40000(f).]

Vacancy Decontrol When tenant of property other than a single-family dwelling voluntarily vacates or is evicted for cause, landlord may increase rent by additional 10%; however, no more than one such increase is permitted within any 60-month period. When tenant of single-family dwelling (where there's one unit per parcel only) voluntarily vacates or is evicted for cause (other than for occupancy by owner or relative), landlord can raise rent to any level; once the single-family dwelling is re-rented, it is subject to rent control at the new higher rent. In either case, landlord must file "vacancy increase certificate" with city and show she has repainted and cleaned carpets and drapes within previous six months, that all appliances are in working order, and that the premises are free from health or safety violations. Certificate must be filed within 30 days after re-occupancy, or landlord cannot raise rent under this provision. [Sec. 6410.]

Eviction Landlord must show just cause to evict.

Penalties Violation of ordinance is misdemeanor punishable by maximums of $1,000 fine and six months imprisonment. [Sec.6414.E.] Tenant may sue landlord in court for three times any rents collected or demanded in excess of legal rents, plus attorney fees. [Sec. 6414.C.]

Other Features Landlord must credit 5-1/2% annual interest on security deposits against rents, with payments made on tenant's move-in "anniversary date" at least once every five years, as well as when tenant vacates. [Sec. 6408.B.]

WESTLAKE VILLAGE

This small city (population 10,000) has a rent control ordinance that applies to apartment complexes of five units or more (as well as to mobile-home parks, whose specialized laws are not covered in this book.) Because the city's only apartment complex of this size has undergone conversion to condominiums, there is therefore now no property (other than mobile-home parks) to which the ordinance applies, so we don't explain the ordinance here.

chapter 5

Discrimination

A.	Forbidden Types of Discrimination	5/2
B.	Legal Reasons to Discriminate	5/4
	1. Landlord-Occupied Premises	5/5
	2. Families with Children and Overcrowding	5/5
C.	How to Tell If a Landlord Is Discriminating	5/7
D.	What to Do About Discrimination	5/7
	1. Complain to the California Department of Fair Employment and Housing	5/7
	2. Complain to the U.S. Department of Housing and Urban Development	5/8
	3. Sue the Discriminating Landlord	5/8
E.	Sexual Harassment by Landlords or Managers	5/9

There was a time when a landlord could refuse to rent to just about anyone she didn't like. All sorts of groups—including blacks, Asians, Chicanos, women, unmarried couples, gays, families with children and many more—were routinely subjected to discrimination. Fortunately, our state and federal legislatures have taken steps to end these abuses.

Today it is illegal for a landlord to refuse to rent to you or engage in any other kind of discrimination on the basis of a group characteristic which is not closely related to the legitimate business needs of the landlord. To put this more specifically, a combination of statutes and cases forbid discrimination on the following grounds:

- Race
- Religion
- Ethnic background
- Sex
- Marital status
- Physical disability
- Families with children (unless the rental units are specifically designated for older citizens, as is the case with retirement communities).

In addition, the California Supreme Court has held that state law forbids landlords from *all* arbitrary discrimination. The Court indicated that discrimination against the following groups would be arbitrary: Republicans, students, welfare recipients, "entire occupations or avocations, for example, sailors or motorcyclists," and "all homosexuals."[1]

A. Forbidden Types of Discrimination

It is illegal for a landlord to refuse to rent to a tenant, or to engage in any other kind of discrimination (such as requiring more rent or larger deposits or targeting advertising) on the basis of a group characteristic, such as race or religion. It is legal to discriminate against people for reasons closely related to the landlord's legitimate business needs, as would be the case where a prospective tenant has a bad credit history or references. (See Section B, below.) State law, and in some cases federal law, absolutely forbids discrimination on the following grounds, regardless of a landlord's claim of a legitimate business need:

Race: This is forbidden by California's Unruh Civil Rights Act,[2] the Fair Employment and Housing Act,[3] the U.S. Civil Rights Act of 1866,[4] and the Federal Fair Housing Act of 1968.[5]

Religion: This is forbidden by all the laws listed above, except the Civil Rights Act of 1866.

Ethnic Background and National Origin: Same as Religion, above.

Sex (including sexual harassment—see Section E): Same as Religion, above.

Marital Status (including discrimination against couples because they are unmarried): This is forbidden under California law by both the Unruh and Fair Employment and Housing Acts.[6]

Age: This is forbidden by state law.[7]

---

[1] *Marina Point, Ltd. v. Wolfson* (1982) 30 Cal.3d 721.

[2] CC § 51-53.

[3] Government Code §§ 12955-12988.

[4] 42 USC § 1982—see *Jones v. Mayer Co.* (1968) 329 US 409.

[5] 42 USC §§ 3601-3619.

[6] See *Atkisson v. Kern County Housing Authority* (1976) 59 Cal.App.3d 89 and *Hess v. Fair Employment and Housing Comm.* (1982) 138 Cal.App.3d 232. See also *Donahue v. Fair Employment and Housing Commission*, 281 Cal. App.3d 446, 2 Cal.Rptr.2d 32 (1991). In this case, the court ruled that a landlord may legally discriminate agianst an unmarried couple based on the landlord's religious belief that it is a sin for unmarried couples to live together. This ruling appears to be in direct contradiction to the state Unruh Act and Fair Employment and Housing Act, which prohibit discrimination on the bases of both religion and marital status. It is currently being appealed to the California Supreme Court.

[7] CC § 51.2.

Families with Children: Discrimination against families with children is forbidden by the federal Fair Housing Amendments Act of 1988[8] and by the Unruh Civil Rights Act,[9] except in housing reserved exclusively for senior citizens.[10] In addition, San Francisco, Berkeley, Los Angeles, Santa Monica and Santa Clara County (unincorporated areas only) have local ordinances forbidding this sort of discrimination.

Physical Disability: It is illegal for a landlord to refuse to rent to a person with a physical handicap on the same terms as if he were not handicapped. The landlord must permit the tenant to make reasonable modifications to the premises if necessary for the tenant to fully use the premises. The landlord may, however, require the tenant to restore the interior of the premises at the end of the tenancy. In addition, a landlord must rent to an otherwise qualified blind, deaf or physically-handicapped person with a properly-trained dog, even if he otherwise bans pets. Discrimination on the basis of physical disability is forbidden by CC § 54.1, the federal Fair Housing Act and the federal Fair Housing Amendments Act of 1988.[11]

Sexual Orientation: This includes homosexuality. Discrimination on this basis is forbidden by the Unruh Civil Rights Act.[12] In addition, a number of California cities specifically ban discrimination for this reason.

Smoking: Discrimination against smokers has not been tested in California courts.

Animals: Although it is generally legal to refuse to rent to people with pets, it is illegal to do so in the case of properly-trained dogs for the blind, deaf or physically handicapped.[13]

Public Assistance: Discrimination against people on public assistance is forbidden by the Unruh Civil Rights Act.[14]

Other Unlawful Discrimination: After reading the above list outlining the types of discrimination forbidden by California and federal law, you may assume that it is legal for a landlord to discriminate for other reasons—say because a person owns a computer. Or, because none of the civil rights laws specifically prohibit discrimination against men with beards or long hair, you might conclude that such discrimination is permissible. This is not true. Although federal civil rights laws have generally been interpreted by the courts to prohibit only those types of discrimination specifically covered by their terms (that is, discrimination based on "race, color, religion, national origin, or sex"), California's Unruh Civil Rights Act has been construed by various California appellate courts to forbid all forms of "arbitrary" discrimination which bear no relationship to a landlord's legitimate business concerns. So, even though the Unruh Act contains only the words "sex, race, color, religion, ancestry, or national origin" to describe types of discrimination that are illegal, the courts have ruled that these categories are just examples of types of arbitrary and illegal discrimination. On this basis, the California Supreme Court has ruled that landlords can't discriminate against families with children, and has stated that discrimination against other groups, such as "Republicans, students, welfare recipients," or "entire occupations or avocations, for example, sailors or motorcyclists"[15] is also illegal.

---

[8] 42 USC § 3604.

[9] See CC § 51.2 and *Marina Point, Ltd. v. Wolfson* (1982) 30 Cal.3d 721.

[10] CC § 51.3 defines senior-citizen housing as that reserved for persons 62 years of age or older, or a complex of 150 or more units (35 in non-metropolitan areas) for persons older than 55 years. Under federal law, housing for older persons is housing solely occupied by persons 62 or older, or housing intended for people over 55 that has special facilities for older residents and is in fact 80% occupied by people 55 or older (42 USC § 3607).

[11] 42 USC § 3604.

[12] See *Hubert v. Williams* (1982) 133 Cal.App.3d Supp. 1.

[13] CC § 54.1(b)(5).

[14] See 59 Ops. Cal. Atty. Gen. 223 (1976).

[15] See *Marina Point, Ltd., v. Wolfson* (1982) 30 Cal.3d 721, 180 Cal.Rptr. 496.

Although the most common forms of illegal discrimination in rental housing consist of refusing to rent to prospective tenants for an arbitrary reason, or offering to rent to one person on tougher terms than are offered to others with no good reason for making the distinction, these aren't the only ways a landlord can be legally liable for unlawful discrimination. A landlord's termination, or attempt to terminate a tenancy, for a discriminatory reason, or discrimination in providing services, such as the use of pool or meeting-room facilities or other common areas, is illegal and can provide the discriminated-against tenant with a defense to an eviction lawsuit as well as a basis for suing the landlord for damages. (See Section D, below.)

EXAMPLE 1
Bill Lee rents apartments in his six-unit apartment building without regard to racial or other unlawful criteria. His tenants include a black family and a single Latin-American woman with children. When Constance Block buys the building from Bill, she immediately gives only these two tenants 30-day notices. Unless Constance can come up with a valid non-discriminatory reason for evicting these tenants, they can contest the eviction on the basis of unlawful discrimination. They can also sue Constance for damages in state or federal court.

EXAMPLE 2
Now, let's assume that Constance, having lost both the eviction lawsuits and the tenants' suits for damages against her, still tries to discriminate by adopting a less blatant strategy. One way she does this is by adopting an inconsistent policy of responding to late rent payments. When her Caucasian tenants without children are late with the rent, she doesn't give them a three-day notice to pay rent or quit until after a five-day "grace period," while non-white tenants receive their three-day notices the day after the rent is due. In addition, when non-white tenants request repairs or raise other issues about the condition of the premises, the speed of Constance's response mimics a turtle's walk after waking from a snooze in the sun. These more subtle (or not so subtle, depending on the situation) means of discrimination are also illegal, and Constance's tenants have grounds to sue her, as well as to defend any eviction lawsuit she brings against them.

B. Legal Reasons to Discriminate

The fact that all forms of arbitrary discrimination in rental housing are illegal does not mean that every time you are turned down for an apartment that you are being discriminated against for an illegal reason. The landlord may have had a lot of applicants and simply preferred someone else. Or the landlord may have discriminated against you for a legal reason. What are legal reasons that justify a landlord in discriminating against a prospective tenant? There is no list set out in a statute, but if a landlord discriminates against a prospective tenant because that person has objective characteristics that would tend to make him a poor tenant, the landlord is on solid legal ground. These characteristics include a bad credit history, credit references that don't check out, a past history of not paying rent or of using residential premises to run an illegal business (for example, drugs or prostitution), and anything else that honestly and directly relates to the quality of being a good tenant. A landlord can refuse to rent to a tenant, for example, on the basis of income, by requiring the tenant's income to be at least three times the amount of rent.[16]

Credit Disclosure Note: If a landlord relies on a credit report to take any action that negatively affects a tenant's (or prospective tenant's) interest, the tenant has a right to a copy of the report.[17]

1. Landlord-Occupied Premises

A few words should be said about situations where a tenant rents part of a house or apartment in which the owner resides, sharing common kitchen and bathroom facilities. You've undoubtedly seen roommate or house-sharing ads containing all sorts of restrictions like, "Young, female, non-smoking vegetarian who reads Asimov, wanted to share house," etc. Is this legal? Yes, because the California and federal civil rights laws apply only to housing rental operations that are considered to be "businesses." Although the renting of a single separate apartment or house (or even one half of an owner-occupied duplex)[18] constitutes the operation of a "business" to which these laws apply, renting out a portion of a dwelling in which the owner (or a tenant seeking a roommate) continues to reside normally does not. In other words, an owner (or tenant) occupant who will be sharing common kitchen or bathroom facilities with the tenant (sub-tenant) may, if she wishes, discriminate arbitrarily in renting a portion of the property, without violating any civil rights laws. One exception, however, is where the owner-occupant (or tenant) rents two rooms or portions of a dwelling (such as in a single-family house with three or more bedrooms). In this situation, California's civil rights laws do apply to make discrimination illegal,[19] although we haven't heard of any lawsuits challenging people's rights to choose only non-smoker, vegetarian, single mothers or some other narrowly-restricted group in this situation. Obviously, if a landlord in this situation discriminates on the basis of race or religion, there could well be cause for legal action.

2. Families with Children and Overcrowding

The fact that discrimination against families with children is illegal does not mean a landlord must rent you a one-bedroom apartment if you have a family of five. In other words, it is legal to establish reasonable space-to-people ratios. But it is not legal to use "overcrowding" as a euphemism justifying discrimination because a family has children, if a landlord would rent to the same number of adults.

A few landlords, realizing they are no longer able to enforce a blanket policy of excluding children, have now adopted criteria that for all practical purposes forbid children, under the guise of preventing overcrowding. These include allowing only one person per bedroom, with a married or living-together couple counting as one person. This would allow renting a two-bedroom unit to a husband and wife and their one child, but would allow a landlord to exclude a family with two children. Although the courts have not yet ruled on this practice, chances are they will soon find it illegal where the effect of its use is to keep all (or most) children out of a landlord's property. One court has already ruled against a landlord who did not permit more than four persons to occupy three-bedroom apartments.[20] Another court held that a rule precluding a two-child family

---

[16]*Harris v. Capitol Growth Investors XIV* (1991) 52 Cal.3d 1142.

[17]CC § 1787.2.

[18]An owner-occupant of a duplex or triplex, etc. is governed by civil rights laws in the renting of the other unit(s) in the building, even though he or she lives in one of the other units, because that person is renting out property for use as a separate household, where kitchen or bathroom facilities aren't shared with the tenant. See *Swann v. Burkett* (1962) 209 Cal.App.2d 685 and 58 Ops. Cal. Atty. Gen. 608 (1975).

[19]Government Code § 12927(c).

[20]*Zakaria v. Lincoln Property Co.* (1986) 185 Cal.App.3d 229, 500 Cal.Rptr. 699.

from occupying a two-bedroom apartment violated a local ordinance similar to state law.[21]

Until the courts spell out just what type of overcrowding standards a landlord can legitimately apply in a situation where he refuses to rent to children, we suggest that you refer to the Uniform Housing Code (which has been adopted by most California cities) to determine whether the landlord is requiring a lot more space per person than is reasonable.

The Uniform Housing Code[22] states that a unit is considered overcrowded if any bedroom has an area of less than 70 square feet for one or two occupants, plus 50 additional square feet for each additional occupant. When you think about it, this means that bedrooms can be fairly crowded. Many landlords may conclude that the code in fact allows too much crowding, and will want to adopt a somewhat stricter standard. Although it's impossible to be sure, we suspect that requiring somewhat more space per tenant will stand up should it be challenged in court. For example, if a landlord requires a sleeping area of 90 square feet for the first two occupants and 70 square feet for any additional occupant in the same bedroom, or restricts occupancy of studio apartments to one person, one-bedroom apartments to two people, and two-bedroom apartments to four people, no matter what the square-foot-to-people ratio, she will probably be on safe legal ground.

Also, look at the history of a landlord's rental policies. If he used to disallow children, before someone complained or sued about this, and then he adopted strict occupancy limits, it is likely that his intent is still to keep out children, and a court might well find his new policy illegal.

EXAMPLE
A couple and their three children seek to rent a small house. The landlord has a policy of requiring 90 square feet sleeping space for a couple and 70 square feet for any additional person in the same bedroom. The house has two bedrooms, one measuring 12' x 14' (168 square feet), and a smaller one measuring 10' x 10' (100 square feet). Under even the strict standards discussed above, three persons (the couple and one child) could share the larger bedroom, with 90 square feet required for the couple and 70 more, for a total of 160 square feet, for the child. The other two children could share the 10' x 10' bedroom, since its 100 square feet accommodate two people. Therefore, if a landlord claims overcrowding as an excuse not to rent to them, she is probably guilty of discriminating against children. However, if there were only two small bedrooms, overcrowding would be a legitimate criterion for refusing to rent. It is not legal for a landlord to inquire as to the age and sex difference of the two children who will be sharing the same bedroom. This is your business, not the landlord's.

Children Born to Tenants: Often a child will be born after you have already resided in a place for some time. Is your landlord entitled to evict you if the birth of the new child would result in a seriously overcrowded situation? Legally, yes, especially if your lease or rental agreement makes it clear that the property can only be occupied by a set number of people, and the baby is one too many. However, if you face this situation and feel the landlord is in fact using the crowding issue as an excuse to get you out, carefully research the landlord's rental policies on *other* apartments. For example, if you find situations in which the landlord is allowing four adults to occupy a unit the same size as yours, and she moves to evict you because the birth of your second child means your unit is now occupied by four people, you clearly have a good case.

Your landlord has the right, however, to insist on a reasonable increase in rent after a child is born if your lease or rental agreement specifically limits occupancy to a defined number of people—unless you're in a rent control city such as San Francisco

---

[21]*Smith v. Ring Brothers Management Corp.* (1986) 183 Cal.App.3d 649, 228 Cal.Rptr. 525.
[22]UHC § 503(b).

which prohibits landlords from charging extra rent for a newborn child.

C. How to Tell If a Landlord Is Discriminating

Occasionally an apartment house manager—and rarely a landlord himself—will tell you that he will not rent to blacks, Spanish-surnamed people, Asians, etc. This does not happen often any more, because these people are learning that they can be penalized if it is proved that they are discriminating.

Today, most landlords who wish to discriminate try to be subtle about it. When you phone to see if a place is still available, the landlord might say it has been filled, if he hears a southern or Spanish accent. If he says it is vacant, then when you come to look at it he sees that you are black, Chicano, etc., he might say it has just been rented. Or, he might say he requires a large security deposit which he "forgot to put in the ad." Or he might say that the ad misprinted the rent, which is $645, not $465. Many variations on these themes can be played.[23] If you suspect that the landlord is discriminating against you, it is important that you do some things to check it out. For example, if you think she is asking for a high rent or security deposit just to get rid of you, ask other tenants what they pay. The best way to check is to run a "test." Have someone who would not have trouble with discrimination (for example, a white male without kids) revisit the place soon after you do and ask if it is available and, if so, on what terms. If the response is better, the landlord was probably discriminating against you. Be sure that your friend's references, type of job and life style are similar to yours, so the landlord cannot later say he took your friend and turned you down because of these differences.

If you need help with testing, contact a civil rights organization or your local Human Relations Council.

D. What to Do About Discrimination

There are several different legal approaches to the problems raised by discrimination. Regardless of what you do, if you really want to live in the place, you must act fast, or the landlord will rent it to someone else before he can be stopped.

1. Complain to the California Department of Fair Employment and Housing

The State of California Department of Fair Employment and Housing takes complaints on discrimination in rental housing. This department enforces laws which prohibit housing discrimination. It has the power to order up to $1,000 damages for a tenant who has been discriminated against.

If you believe that you have been discriminated against, you can contact the office nearest you. You will be asked to fill out a complaint form and an investigator will be assigned to your case. You must file your complaint within 60 days of the date of the violation or the date when you first learned of the violation. The investigator will try to work the problem out through compromise and conciliation. If this fails, the Department may conduct hearings and maybe take the matter to court. However, because it has been our experience that in recent years the Department has been slack in enforcing anti-discrimination housing laws, we recommend that you consult a private attorney and consider suing the discriminating landlord.

---

[23]Larger landlords increasingly rely on rental agencies to take applications for them. These organizations utilize a variety of criteria to screen the prospective tenants, and are adept at choosing a legal reason (for example, credit history) if challenged as to why one person (say a white man) got an apartment instead of another (say a black man or woman). In addition, several computerized services are offered to landlords. For a fee, firms will sell landlords information about a prospective tenant's credit or, rental history, whether the tenant has ever been sued in an unlawful detainer proceeding, etc.

California Department of Fair Employment and Housing Offices

Bakersfield
1001 Tower Way, #250
(805) 395-2728

Fresno
1900 Mariposa Mall, Ste. 130
(209) 445-5373

Los Angeles
322 West First St., Rm. 2126
(213) 897-1997

Oakland
1330 Broadway, Ste. 1326
(510) 286-4095

Sacramento
2000 "O" St., #120
(916) 445-9918

San Bernardino
1845 S. Business Center Dr., #127
(714) 383-4711

San Diego
110 West C Street, Ste. 1702
(619) 237-7405

San Francisco
30 Van Ness Ave.
(415) 557-2005

San Jose
111 No. Market St., Ste. 810
(408) 277-1264

Santa Ana
28 Civic Ctr. Plaza, Rm. 538
(714) 558-4159

Ventura
5720 Ralston St., #302
(805) 654-4513

2. Complain to the U.S. Department of Housing and Urban Development

You can also lodge a complaint with the U.S. Department of Housing and Urban Development (HUD) if the discrimination is based on race, religion, national origin, sex, family status or physical disability. This federal agency has most of the same powers as does the state but must give the state agency the opportunity (30 days) to act on the case first. The HUD equal opportunity office for California is located at 450 Golden Gate Ave., San Francisco (Phone: (415) 556-0800).

You can also call HUD's housing discrimination hotline at (800) 669-9777. HUD's power of investigation and sanctions are similar to those of the state. The experience of the authors has been that HUD is far more militant in going after discriminating landlords than is the state. However, the fact that HUD can't act until 30 days after the state has received the complaint reduces its efficiency a great deal.

3. Sue the Discriminating Landlord

We think that normally the most effective thing you can do is to see a lawyer and sue the landlord. If you have been discriminated against because of sex, race, religion, physical disability or marital status, a lawsuit may be brought in state court. Suits in federal court work only for racial, religious and sex discrimination. If you can prove your case, you will almost certainly be eligible to recover money damages.

Many, if not most, attorneys have had little experience with discrimination lawsuits. This is particularly true of lawsuits brought in federal court. Rather than try to find an attorney at random, you would be wise to check with an organization in your area dedicated to civil rights and fighting discrimination. They will undoubtedly be able to direct you to a sympathetic attorney.

Attorneys have become more interested in taking these cases in the last few years, because the amount of money that can be recovered is now substantial. For racial, religious and sex discrimination, you may sue in federal court and collect damages to compensate you for your loss as well as substantial punitive damages and attorney's fees.[24] For discrimination based on these three areas and discrimination based on marital status, disability, having children, homosexuality, or any other arbitrary category, you may sue in state court and collect damages to compensate you for your loss as well as a penalty of $250 or more and attorney's fees.[25]

E. Sexual Harassment by Landlords or Managers

Sexual harassment in housing covers a wide range of behavior—from a landlord's or manager's offensive sexual comments to physical encounters, even outright rape. A tenant who has been led to believe she must sleep with her landlord to have repairs made or to avoid eviction has been sexually harassed, as has a tenant whose manager enters her apartment without her permission and pinches or fondles her against her will.

Sexual harassment by a landlord or manager is illegal under state and federal laws prohibiting discrimination on the basis of sex: California's Unruh Civil Rights Act,[26] the Fair Employment and Housing Act,[27] and the Federal Fair Housing Act of 1968.[28] Harassment which involves a violation of a tenant's privacy rights is illegal under state law.[29]

It's against the law for a landlord or manager to retaliate against a tenant for having exercised any right under the law, such as the right to be free from sex discrimination, including sexual harassment. Retaliation includes increasing rent, giving a termination notice or even threatening to do so.[30]

Here are some things you can do to stop sexual harassment and protect your rights as a tenant.[31] These are also crucial steps to take if you later decide to take formal action against the harassment.

1. Document the harassment

Write down what the landlord or manager said or did to you and the place and dates of the incidents. Keep copies of any sexually explicit material or threatening letters the landlord or manager sent you. Note names of any witnesses and talk with other tenants to find out whether they have been harassed.

2. Clearly tell the harasser what you don't want

As much as possible, deal directly with the harassment when it occurs—whether it's to reject repeated requests for a date or express your distaste for sexually explicit comments or physical contact.

---

[24] 42 USC § 3612; *Morales v. Haines*, 486 F.2d 880 (7th Cir. 1973); *Lee v. Southern Home Sites Corp.*, 42 F.2d 290 (5th Cir. 1970).

[25] Federal Fair Housing Act of 1968 (42 USC § 3612). For racial discrimination, you may also sue under the Civil Rights Act of 1866, which allows greater punitive damages. *Morales v. Haines*, 486 F.2d (7th Cir. 1973).

[26] CC§ 51-53.

[27] Government Code §§ 12955-12988.

[28] 42 USC §§ 3601-3619.

[29] CC § 1954. See Chapter 6 for a discussion of legal limits on a landlord's right to enter rented property.

[30] See Chapter 11 for advice on defending yourself against retaliatory eviction.

[31] See *Sexual Harassment on the Job* by Petrocelli and Repa (Nolo Press) for detailed strategies for stopping sexual harassment in the workplace. Many of these strategies can also be used for stopping harassment by a landlord or manager. The book also provides details on filing a sexual harassment lawsuit.

3. Report the incidents

If the apartment manager persists in sexually harassing you, or if you're uncomfortable speaking face-to-face, write him a letter spelling out what behavior you object to and why, and send a copy to the owner or property management firm. If the owner is the harasser, write him a letter demanding that he stop these actions. If you feel the situation is serious or bound to escalate, say that you will take action against the harassment if it doesn't stop at once. Include a copy of the state and federal laws prohibiting discrimination on the basis of sex. (Most public libraries have the statutues, or you can contact the state or federal housing agencies for copies.) If other tenants have been harassed, ask them to send a joint letter. Keep copies of all correspondence.

4. Complain to the California Department of Fair Employment and Housing or the U.S. Department of Housing and Urban Development

Section D provides more information on how these government agencies can help, although, as we note, there are limits to their assistance.

5. File a lawsuit

If the harassment continues or if you're threatened with retaliatory eviction but the state or federal housing agency fails to produce satisfactory results, considering filing a civil lawsuit. For example, if you have been physically harmed or threatened, consider filing an assault or battery action or a criminal complaint against the harasser.

While only a few tenants have filed suits for sexual harassment in housing, litigation is expected to increase as tenants become more aware of their rights in this area. In one of the largest settlements in California fair housing history, a group of women tenants settled a civil lawsuit in 1991 for more than $1 million against owners of a Fairfield, California apartment complex. In this case, the apartment manager tormented the tenants, mostly single mothers, by sexually harassing them both verbally and physically, spying on them, opening their mail and threatening eviction to those who complained. When tenants did complain to the building's owners, the owners refused to take any action—and the manager stepped up his harassment in retaliation. Finally, the tenants banded together and sued, and the details of the manager's outrageous and illegal conduct were exposed.

Several of the tenants involved in this case went on to form an advocacy group to help tenants fight sexual harassment in housing: Women Refusing to Accept Tenant Harassment (WRATH). For information and referrals on sexual harassment in housing, write to WRATH at 607 Elmira Road, Suite 299, Vacaville, CA 95687.

chapter 6

The Obnoxious Landlord and Your Right to Privacy

A. Your Landlord's Right of Entry 6/2
    1. Entry in Case of an Emergency 6/2
    2. Entry with the Permission of the Tenant 6/2
    3. Entry to Make Repairs 6/3
    4. Entry to Show Property 6/3

B. What to Do About a Landlord's Improper Entry 6/4

C. Other Types of Invasions of Privacy 6/6
    1. Putting For Sale or For Rent Signs on the Property 6/6
    2. Allowing Others to Enter the Premises 6/6
    3. Giving Information About You to Strangers 6/6
    4. Calling or Visiting You at Work 6/7
    5. Unduly Restrictive Rules on Guests 6/7

Some landlords can get pretty obnoxious. This is also true of plumbers, butchers, and English teachers, but since this book is for tenants, we will concentrate on the landlords.

Typically, problems arise with landlords who cannot stop fidgeting and fussing over their property. Normally, smaller landlords develop this problem to a greater extent than do the bigger, more commercial ones. Nosy landlords are always hanging around or coming by, trying to invite themselves in to look around and generally being pests. Sometimes you may run into a manager on a power trip.

If your landlord is difficult or unpleasant to deal with, she can make your life miserable and you may not be able to do anything about it. There is no law which protects you from a disagreeable personality, and, if you have no lease, you are especially unprotected from all but the most outrageous invasions of privacy or trespass. Things can get unpleasant, but if your right to privacy and peaceful occupancy are not disturbed, you may have to grin and bear it or look for another place.

A. Your Landlord's Right of Entry

Section 1954 of the Civil Code establishes the circumstances under which a landlord can enter his tenant's home, and Section 1953(a)(1) provides that these circumstances cannot be expanded, or the tenant's privacy rights waived or modified, by any lease or rental agreement provision. The first thing to realize is that there are only four situations in which your landlord may legally enter rented premises while you are still in residence. They are:

1. to deal with an emergency;

2. when you give permission for the landlord to enter;

3. to make needed repairs (or assess the need for them); and

4. to show the property to prospective new tenants or purchasers.

In most instances (emergencies and tenant permission excepted), a landlord can enter only during "normal business hours" and then only after "reasonable notice," presumed to be 24 hours. Because this is so important, let's examine Section 1954 of the Civil Code carefully to make sure you thoroughly understand the details of how your right to privacy works.

1. Entry in Case of an Emergency

Under CC § 1954, your landlord or manager can enter the property without giving advance notice, in order to respond to a true emergency which threatens injury or property damage if not corrected immediately. For example, a fire, or a gas or serious water leak is a true emergency which, if not corrected, will result in damage, injury, or even loss of life. On the other hand, a landlord's urge to repair an important but non-life- or property-threatening defect, say of a stopped-up drain, isn't a true emergency that allows entry without proper notice.

To facilitate a landlord's right of entry, he is entitled to have a key to the premises, including keys to any locks you may add.

2. Entry with the Permission of the Tenant

A landlord can always enter rental property, even without 24 hours' notice, if you so agree without pressure or coercion. For example, if your landlord (whom you like and feel is well motivated) has a maintenance problem that needs regular attending to—for example, a fussy heater or temperamental plumbing—you might want to work out a detailed agreement with him allowing entry in specified circumstances.

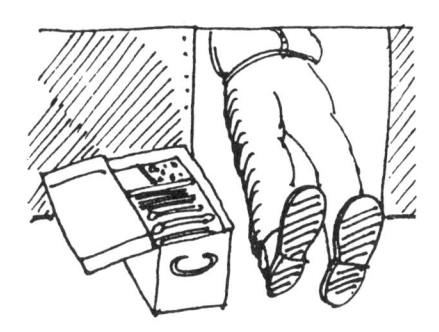

3. Entry to Make Repairs

Section 1954 allows a landlord or repairperson, contractor, etc. to enter to make and assess the need for and cost of routine repairs or alterations. In this situation, however, the landlord must enter only during normal business hours and must first give reasonable notice. Customarily, "normal business hours" means 9 a.m. to 5 p.m., Monday - Friday, but no exact hours are specified in the statute. As we noted above, CC § 1954 contains a presumption that an advance notice of at least 24 hours is reasonable. However, you should understand that if your landlord can establish a really good reason for it under the circumstances, giving a reasonable but shorter notice is legal. Under the statute, the 24-hour notice period is presumed to be reasonable, but it is not absolutely required.

EXAMPLE

If your landlord arranges to have a repairperson inspect a wall heater at 2 p.m. on Tuesday, she should notify you on or before 2 p.m. on Monday. But if she can't reach you until 6 p.m.—for example, you can't be reached at home or at work—less than 24 hours' notice is probably okay. Of course, if you consent to your landlord's plan, the notice period is not a problem.

In some situations, the 24-hour notice period will not be a problem, as you will be delighted that your landlord is finally making needed repairs and will cooperate with his entry requirements. However, there are definitely situations when a landlord will be totally unreasonable, as would be the case when a repairperson simply knocks at your door with no advance notice and asks to make a non-emergency repair when you are in the middle of cooking dinner for your mother-in-law. If this occurs, you have a legal right to deny entry.

Inspection Note: Your landlord can't legally use his right to access your unit in order to harass you. Repeated inspections, even when 24-hour notice is given, might fall into this category. To fight back in this situation, see Section C, below. If you have a waterbed, a landlord may "inspect the bedding installation upon completion (of installation) and periodically thereafter, to insure its conformity" with the standards a landlord may impose.[1]

4. Entry to Show Property

Section 1954 also allows your landlord to enter your property to show it to prospective tenants (toward the end of a tenancy) and to prospective purchasers if she wishes to sell it, as long as she complies with the "business hours" and "reasonable notice" provisions discussed above.

As noted, your landlord may show the property to prospective buyers or mortgage companies. This situation often arises when a property that is for sale is a rented single-family house or condominium unit, but can also occur where a multiple-unit building is placed on the market. Again, remember that under Section 1954, 24 hours is presumed to be reasonable notice to you.

Unfortunately, problems often occur when an overeager real estate salesperson shows up on your doorstep without warning or calls on very short notice and asks to be let in to show the place to a possible buyer. In this situation, you are within your rights to say politely but firmly, "I'm busy right now—try again in a few days after we've set a time convenient for all of us." Naturally, this type of misunderstanding is not conducive to your peace of mind, especially if you fear that the landlord or real estate person may use a pass key to enter when you are not home.

---

[1] CC § 1940.5(g).

There are several ways to deal with this situation:

• You can stand on your rights and notify your landlord to follow the law or you will sue for invasion of privacy (see Section B, below); or

• You can try to work out a compromise with your landlord by which you agree to allow the unit to be shown on shorter than 24-hour notice in exchange for a reduction in the rent or other benefit. For example, you might agree in advance that two-hour notice is reasonable for up to eight house showings a month, in exchange for having your rent reduced $200 per month. This kind of tradeoff is perfectly logical—your rent pays for your right to treat your home like your castle, and any diminution of this right should be accompanied by a decrease in your rent obligation.

Lock Box Note: Under no circumstances should you allow your landlord to place a key-holding "lock box" on the door. This is a metal box that attaches to the front door and contains the key to that door. It can be opened by a master key held by area real estate salespeople. Since a lock box allows a salesperson to enter in disregard of the 24-hour notice requirement, it should not be used—period.

B. What to Do About a Landlord's Improper Entry

Suppose now your landlord does violate your rights of privacy—what can you do about it?

As you have probably figured out by now, it is one thing to have a right, and quite another thing to get the benefits of it. This is especially true for tenants who do not have a lease and do not live in a city where a rent control ordinance requires just cause for eviction. In this situation, if you set about aggressively demanding your rights, you may end up with a notice to vacate. It is also generally true that you can rarely accomplish good results with hard words. This doesn't mean not to be firm or determined, but rather, not to be offensive.

Here is a step-by-step approach that usually works in dealing with a landlord who is violating your right to privacy:

Step 1: Talk to the landlord (or manager) about your concerns in a friendly but firm way. If you come to an understanding, follow up with a note to confirm it.

Step 2: If this doesn't work, or if your landlord doesn't follow the agreement that you have worked out, it's time for a tougher letter. Here is a sample:

Sample Letter When Landlord Violates Privacy

```
Roper Real Estate Management Co.
11 Peach Street
San Diego, CA

Dear Mr. Roper:

Several times in the last two months your
employees have entered my dwelling without
my being home and without notifying me in
advance. In no situation was there any
emergency involved. This has caused me
considerable anxiety and stress, to the
point that my peaceful enjoyment of my
tenancy has been seriously disrupted.

This letter is to formally notify you that
I value my privacy highly and insist that
my legal rights to that privacy, as
guaranteed to me under Section 1954 of the
Civil Code, be respected. Specifically, in
non-emergency situations, I would like to
have 24 hours' notice of your intent to
enter my house.

I assume this notice will be sufficient to
correct this matter. If you want to talk
about this, please call me at 121-2121
from 9:00 a.m. to 5:00 p.m.

Yours truly,


Sally South
```

Step 3: If, despite this letter, the invasions of your privacy continue, document them and either see a lawyer or take your landlord to small claims court.

One difficulty with a lawsuit against a landlord guilty of trespass is that it is hard to prove much in the way of money damages. Assuming you can prove the trespass occurred, the judge will probably readily agree that you have been wronged, but he may award you very little money. Most likely, he will figure that you have not been harmed much by the fact that your landlord walked on your rug and opened and closed your door. However, if you can show a repeated pattern of trespass (and the fact that you asked the landlord to stop it) or even one clear example of outrageous conduct, you may be able to get a substantial recovery. In this situation the landlord may be guilty of a number of "torts" (legal wrongdoings), including harassment,[2] breach of your implied covenant of quiet enjoyment (your right to enjoy your home free from interference by your landlord),[3] intentional infliction of emotional distress, and negligent infliction of emotional distress. In a suit by a tenant alleging that a landlord was guilty of the intentional infliction of emotional distress, the court ruled that it was necessary to prove four things: (1) outrageous conduct on the part of the landlord; (2) intention to cause or reckless disregard of the probability of causing emotional distress; (3) severe emotional suffering; and (4) actual suffering or emotional distress.[4]

If your landlord or manager comes onto your property or into your home and harms you in any way, sexually harasses you (see Chapter 5, Section E), threatens you or damages any of your property, see an attorney. You should also report the matter to the police. Some California police departments have taken the excellent step of setting up special landlord-tenant units. The officers and legal experts in these units have been given special training in landlord-tenant law and are often helpful in compromising disputes and setting straight a landlord who has taken illegal measures against a tenant. If your city hasn't done this, why not?

Probably the time that a landlord is most likely to trespass is when the tenant has failed to pay her rent. The landlord, faced with the necessity of paying a lot of money to legally get a tenant to move out, may resort to threats or even force. While it may be understandable that a landlord in this situation should be mad at the tenant, this is no justification for illegal acts. All threats, intimidation and any physical attacks on the tenant should be reported to the police. Of course it is illegal for the landlord to come on the property and do such things as take off windows and doors, turn off the utilities or change the locks. If this is done, the tenant should see an attorney at once. Do not over-react when a landlord gets hostile. While a tenant has the right to take reasonable steps to protect himself, his family and his possessions from harm, the steps must be reasonably related to the threat. The wisest thing to do, whenever you have good reason to fear that you or your property may be harmed, is to call the police.

You should know that a landlord's repeated abuse of a tenant's right to privacy gives a tenant under a lease a legal excuse to break it by moving out, without liability for further rent.

---

[2] CCP § 527.6.
[3] *Guntert v. Stockton* (1976) 55 Cal.App.3d 131.

[4] *Newby v. Alto Riviera Apartments* (1976) 60 Cal.App.3d 288.

der a lease a legal excuse to break it by moving out, without liability for further rent.

Note: Here's another idea for dealing with a nosy landlord who ignores repeated requests to respect your privacy: put a small chain lock (that opens with a key) on the door. This will keep him from nosing around, but not from breaking the chain if a real emergency arises.

C. Other Types of Invasions of Privacy

Entering a tenant's home without his knowledge or consent isn't the only way a landlord can interfere with the tenant's privacy. Here are a few other commonly-encountered situations, with advice on how to handle them.

1. Putting For Sale or For Rent Signs on the Property

Occasionally, friction is caused by landlords who put "For Sale" or "For Rent" signs on tenants' homes, such as a For Sale sign on the lawn of a rented single-family house. Although a landlord may otherwise be very conscientious about respecting your privacy when it comes to giving 24 hours' notice before showing property to prospective buyers or renters, the erection of a sale or rental sign on the property is a virtual invitation to prospective buyers or renters to disturb you with unwelcome inquiries. There is little law on the subject of your rights in this situation. However, it is our opinion that as you have rented the unit, including the yard, the landlord has no right to trespass and erect a sign, and if your privacy is completely ruined by repeated inquiries, you may sue for invasion of privacy, just as if the landlord personally had made repeated illegal entries.

Keep in mind that in this age of computerized multiple-listing services, many real estate offices can, and commonly do, sell houses and all sorts of other real estate without ever placing a For Sale sign on the property, except perhaps during the hours when an open house is in progress. If a real estate office puts a sign advertising sale or rental in front of the property you rent, you should at least insist that it clearly indicate a telephone number to call and warns against disturbing the occupant in words like, "Inquire at 555-1357—Do Not Disturb Occupant." If this doesn't do the trick and informal conversations with the landlord do not result in removal of the sign, your best bet is to simply remove it yourself and return it to the landlord or to write the landlord a firm letter explaining why your privacy is being invaded and asking that the sign be removed. If the violations of your privacy continue, document them and consider suing in small claims court. Of course, you will want to show the judge a copy of the letter.

2. Allowing Others to Enter the Premises

Except in the circumstances set out above (in Section A), your landlord has no right to enter your premises. It follows that the landlord also has no right to give others permission to enter. A landlord may not, for example, consent to a police search of premises occupied by a tenant.[5]

3. Giving Information About You to Strangers

Your landlord may be approached by strangers, including creditors, banks and perhaps even prospective landlords, to provide credit or other information about you. As with letting a stranger into your home, this may cause you considerable anxiety. Basically, your landlord has a legal right to give out normal business information about you as long as it's factual. However, if your landlord spreads false stories about you—for example, says you filed for bankruptcy if

---

[5]*People v. Escudero* (1979) 23 Cal.3d 800, 806; *People v. Roman* (1991) 227 Cal.App.3d 674, 278 Cal.Rptr. 44.

credit rating is adversely affected or you don't get a job), you have grounds to sue the landlord.

In addition, if a landlord or a manager spreads other types of gossip about you (whether or not true), such as who stayed overnight in your apartment or that you drink too much, you may be in good shape to sue and obtain a substantial recovery, especially if the gossip damages you. This is because spreading this type of information usually has no legitimate purpose and is just plain malicious. If flagrant and damaging, this sort of gossip can be an invasion of privacy for which you may have a valid reason to sue.

4. Calling or Visiting You at Work

Should a real need arise for your landlord to call you at work (say when your Uncle Harry shows up and asks to be let into your apartment), try to be understanding. However, situations justifying a landlord calling you at work are fairly rare. If a landlord calls you to complain about late rent payments or other problems, politely tell him to talk to you at home. If this doesn't work, follow up with a brief note. If the landlord persists, or tries to talk to your boss or other employees about the problem, your privacy is definitely being invaded. Consider going to small claims court, or see a lawyer.

5. Unduly Restrictive Rules on Guests

A few landlords, overly concerned about their tenants moving new occupants into the property, go overboard in keeping tabs on the tenants' legitimate guests who stay overnight or for a few days. Often their leases, rental agreements, or rules and regulations will require you to "register" any overnight guest. While your landlord has a legitimate concern about persons who begin as "guests" becoming permanent unauthorized residents of the property (see Chapter 2), it is overkill to require you to inform your landlord of a guest whose stay is only for a day or two. As with other subjects we mention in this chapter, extreme behavior in this area—whether by an owner or a management employee—can be considered an invasion of privacy for which you may have a valid cause of action.

chapter 7

Repairs and Maintenance

A. The Landlord's Duties 7/2
    1. The Law 7/2
    2. The Lease or Rental Agreement 7/3
B. Remedies 7/3
    1. Complain to the Landlord 7/3
    2. Move Out 7/4
    3. Call the Building Inspector 7/5
    4. Repair and Deduct 7/7
    5. The Implied Warranty of Habitability 7/9

From time to time, things need fixing and maintaining on any piece of property. Most landlords are willing to take care of the building because that is their job, because the law requires it, or because they don't want the place to become run down. Some landlords, however, are slow and reluctant to fulfill their responsibilities.

Section A of this chapter sets out the landlord's *duties*. The rest of the chapter deals with *remedies*—what you can do about a landlord who won't properly repair or maintain the place.

A. The Landlord's Duties

There are basically two sources of the landlord's duties to repair and maintain the premises: the law and the lease (or rental agreement).

1. The Law

The law is contained in the State Housing Law, the Uniform Housing Code, and local ordinances. These are described in Chapter 2, which also spells out in great detail exactly what the landlord must do. See Chapter 2.E, "How to Check a Place Over." These duties occur at the outset of the tenancy and also continue during the tenancy.

The law is also contained in CC § 1941.1. This is shorter than the laws described above, but it imposes basically the same requirements, in a more summary fashion. The reason it is important is that all judges have the Civil Code right on their desks, whereas very few have the Uniform Housing Code, etc., available.

Civil Code § 1941.1 is a bit long, but it is so important that we've decided to set it out here for you. It requires the landlord to provide:

"(a) Effective waterproofing and weather protection of roof and exterior walls, including unbroken windows and doors.

(b) Plumbing or gas facilities which conformed to applicable law in effect at the time of installation, maintained in good working order.

(c) A water supply approved under applicable law, which is under the control of the tenant, capable of producing hot and cold running water, or a system which is under the control of the landlord, which produces hot and cold running water, furnished to appropriate fixtures, and connected to a sewage disposal system approved under applicable law.

(d) Heating facilities which conformed with applicable law at the time of installation, maintained in good working order.

(e) Electrical lighting, with wiring and electrical equipment which conformed with applicable law at the time of installation, maintained in good working order.

(f) Building, grounds and appurtenances at the time of the commencement of the lease or rental agreement in every part clean, sanitary, and free from all accumulations of debris, filth, rubbish, garbage, rodents and vermin, and all areas under control of the landlord kept in every part clean, sanitary, and free from all accumulations of debris, filth, rubbish, garbage, rodents, and vermin.

(g) An adequate number of appropriate receptacles for garbage and rubbish, in clean condition and good repair at the time of the commencement of the lease or rental agreement, with the landlord providing appropriate serviceable receptacles thereafter, and being responsible for the clean condition and good repair of such receptacles under his control.

(h) Floors, stairways, and railings maintained in good repair."

It's important to understand that these are minimum requirements. Other conditions in the property may make it not "habitable," which means that you have several legal remedies available. (See Section B.)

Also, be aware that Civil Code Section 1941.4 and Public Utilities Code Section 788 makes residential landlords responsible for installing a telephone jack in their residential units and placing and maintaining inside phone wiring.

Finally, Health and Safety Code Section 13113.7 requires all units in multi-unit buildings to have smoke detectors.

2. The Lease or Rental Agreement

As you can see, the laws discussed above deal with basic living conditions only—heat, water, weatherproofing, etc. They do not deal with "amenities"—other facilities which are not essential, but which make living a little easier. Examples are drapes, washing machines, swimming pools, saunas, parking places, intercoms, dishwashers, and the like. The law does not require the landlord to furnish these things, but if she does so, she might be required to maintain or repair them—not by the above laws, but by her own promise to do so.

This promise might be express or implied.

It is express when the lease or rental agreement contains language which says that the landlord will repair certain things or maintain them a certain way.

Such a promise may be implied when the landlord (or his rental agent, manager, etc.) said or did something which indicated that the landlord would repair or maintain something.

EXAMPLE
Tina sees Larry's ad for an apartment. The ad says "heated swimming pool." After Tina moves in, Larry stops heating the pool regularly, because his utility costs have risen. Larry has violated his implied promise to keep the pool heated.

EXAMPLE
When Larry's rental agent shows Tom around the building, she goes out of her way to show off the laundry room, saying, "Here's the laundry room—it's for the use of all the tenants." Tom rents the apartment. Later the washing machine in the laundry room breaks down, but Larry won't fix it. Larry has violated his implied promise to maintain the laundry room appliances in working order.

EXAMPLE
Tina's apartment has a built-in dishwasher. When she rented the apartment, neither the lease nor the landlord said anything about who was to repair the dishwasher if it broke. The dishwasher has broken down a few times and whenever Tina asked Larry to fix it, he did (or tried to). By doing so, he has shown that there is a "usage" or "practice" that he—not the tenant—is responsible for repairing the dishwasher during the tenancy.

If the landlord does violate some promise relating to the condition of the premises, you may sue her for money damages. In most instances you would do this in small claims court. There is no law allowing you to use the repair-and-deduct remedy (discussed in Section B.4, below) to deal with such problems. Whether you can legally use rent withholding here is not yet clear (though there are some good arguments that you should be able to, if the breach of promise really cuts into what you had a right to expect and negatively affects the habitability of the unit). If the property is subject to rent control, a decrease in promised services may be considered an illegal rent increase. (See Chapter 4.G.)

B. Remedies

If the landlord fails to meet his legal responsibilities to repair and maintain the premises, you have several options.

1. Complain to the Landlord

If the landlord fails to meet one of his duties to repair or maintain something, talk to him. If you can, talk directly to the owner of the building, not just his manager or caretaker. Sometimes the owner wants to do the right thing, but he has a lazy or incompetent employee who doesn't. If so, the owner might appreciate your telling him, and he might get the needed work done promptly.

Your complaint should be in writing. The letter should be polite, but firm—you are not begging for charity, but insisting on your rights as a tenant.

Here is what your letter might look like:

Sample Letter of Complaint

```
1500 Acorn Street, #4
Cloverdale, CA
March 24, 19__

Mr. Simon Landlord
10 Jones Street
Cloverdale, CA

Dear Mr. Landlord:

I reside in apartment #4 in your building
at 1500 Acorn Street and regularly pay my
rent to you. On March 19, 19__ the water
heater in my unit failed to function. On
that date I notified your manager, Mr.
Robert Jackson, of the problem. He called
PG&E on that date and they sent a man out
who put a tag on the machine saying that
it was no longer serviceable or safe and
that it should be replaced. I gave Mr.
Jackson a copy of the PG&E slip on March
20, 19__ and he said that he would see
about having the heater replaced immediately. So far the heater has not been
replaced and no one has told me when it
will be. I am sure you know that it is a
real hardship to be without hot water.

I've read Tenants' Rights, so I know my
rights and remedies. I would appreciate
hearing from you as soon as possible. My
phone number at work is 555-4111.

Very truly yours,


Tina Tenant
```

This letter might get results all by itself. Most landlords don't want further trouble from a tenant who stands up for her rights. "The squeaky wheel gets the grease!"

It is illegal for the landlord to try to evict you for complaining about the condition of the premises.[1]

The complaint letter also serves another function: it satisfies a legal precondition to your right to use other remedies, which we will now discuss.

2. Move Out

One remedy is simply to move out, even if you are in the middle of your lease or rental agreement. The law allows you to do this if the dwelling "substantially lacks" any of the things mentioned in CC § 1941[1] (see Section A.1, above), and the landlord has been notified of the problem (orally or in writing), but failed to fix them in a "reasonable time."[2] If you have notified the landlord of the problems and given him a reasonable time to correct them, you don't have to give any notice that you are moving out.

---

[1] *Kemp v. Schultz* (1981) 121 Cal.App.3d Supp. 13.
[2] CC § 1942(a).

This is called the doctrine of "constructive eviction," because the landlord has made things so miserable that you pretty much have to leave. Leaving might be a good idea, because if the landlord won't fix this problem, she will probably be a lousy landlord throughout your tenancy. If you leave, you may also sue her for money damages for the trouble she has caused you.

When you move out, it is a good idea to tell the landlord why you are doing so—and the legal basis for moving. This should decrease the likelihood of her suing you for violating your lease. Here is an example of a notice you might send her:

Sample Letter When Moving Out Because of Defects in the Premises

```
1500 Acorn Street, #4
Cloverdale, CA
March 29, 19__

Mr. Simon Landlord
10 Jones Street
Cloverdale, CA

Dear Mr. Landlord:

I have resided in apartment #4 at 1500
Acorn Street and regularly paid my rent
to you.

As you know, on March 19, 19__ the water
heater in my unit broke down. Although I
have repeatedly requested repairs, no
action has yet been taken. Because of the
weather and because of the size of my
family, I cannot continue to live
comfortably without such an essential
service, so I am therefore compelled to
exercise my rights under California Civil
Code Section 1942 to vacate the premises.

Sincerely yours,



Tina Tenant
```

For many tenants, however, moving out is not really a good alternative. Because of low vacancy rates in most communities, it is just too hard to find another place at a reasonable rent. If you are in this situation, you should consider the remedies we discuss next.

3. Call the Building Inspector

The State Housing Law and local housing codes are supposed to be enforced by a city or county agency. Codes are usually enforced by an agency called the "Building Inspection" or "Housing" Department (or some similar name). Violations creating immediate health hazards (such as rats or broken toilets) are also enforced by the Health Department. Violations creating fire hazards (such as trash in the basement) are also enforced by the Fire Department. State law provides jail terms of up to one year for repeated severe violations of the state housing law and fines up to $5,000.[3]

These agencies have the power to close the building and even demolish it if the landlord will not comply with their orders to correct code violations. They very seldom go to this extreme, however. Usually they inspect the building, send a letter to the landlord ordering him to make repairs, and later reinspect the building and send more letters until the landlord complies.[4]

---

[3] Health & Safety Code § 17995.3.

[4] If the landlord has failed for six months or more to comply with agency orders to repair, the enforcement agency may notify the state's Franchise Tax Board. (Enforcement agencies have the discretion to do so in 90 days.) The Board then may deny the landlord any deduction on his state income tax form for interest, taxes, or depreciation on the building. California Revenue & Taxation Code §§ 17299 and 24436.5. Also, if the landlord has not made the repairs within 60 days of the letter ordering him to make repairs, the tenant may sue the landlord and recover any actual damages, plus "special damages" of between $100 and $1,000, plus attorney fees. CC § 1942.4. You may file such a lawsuit in small claims court, so long as you do not use a lawyer and do not ask for more than $5,000. If you do file suit, be sure to ask for the full $1,000 in "special damages."

This sort of pressure works on many landlords, so your reporting code violations to the agency and asking for an inspection can sometimes help you. If you decide to do this, it is best to go to the agency and make your complaint in writing.

a. Drawbacks of Reporting Code Violations

There are, however, some things to watch out for before deciding to report code violations.

First, if the landlord owns a lot of slum property or has been in this business for a while, he probably knows what to do to keep the agency off his back. He may be friendly with the building inspectors. He may know how to take appeals which can delay enforcement of the codes for years. He may make a few repairs and let the others go, knowing just how much it takes to temporarily satisfy the agency that he is "trying." The landlord is less likely to get away with these tricks if there is a real health or fire hazard, like rats or open gasoline on the premises. The Health or Fire Department will usually be tougher than the Building Inspection Department.

Second, there is a danger that the landlord will find out that you reported her to the agency and will try to evict you because of this. This is called a "retaliatory eviction." The landlord will usually do this simply by giving you a 30-day notice terminating your month-to-month tenancy, giving no reason for doing so. Or, she might give you a 30-day notice that your rent is being increased, as an indirect way of getting you out.

Retaliatory evictions for reporting code violations are illegal for 180 days after the date the report was made (if you are paid up in your rent).[5] Unfortunately, however, one California case indicates that it's up to the tenant to prove that any eviction was retaliatory.[6] So, if you refuse to get out and the landlord sues to evict you and you prove that he is doing it because you reported the code violation, you will win the lawsuit. The problem is that if the landlord can show that he is evicting you for some good reason (for example, you violated the rental agreement), you might lose. However, by attempting a retaliatory eviction, the landlord is taking a big chance. If you get out because of his 30-day notice but can prove it was retaliatory, you can sue for money damages later.[7] To prove that the landlord acted in retaliation, you will need written evidence that you complained to officials before the landlord began eviction proceedings. Keep careful records of all your contacts with government personnel, including dates and names.

If you have a lease, you are pretty well protected from retaliatory evictions, since the landlord must prove a breach in order to kick you out before your lease is up. If you have only a month-to-month rental agreement, you do face the danger of retaliatory evictions, unless you have a provision like Paragraph 16 of our model month-to-month rental agreement, in the Appendix. That paragraph requires the landlord to state her reasons when trying to terminate your tenancy or increase the rent, and to prove that these reasons are true if you question them. Also, tenants in certain rent control cities can be evicted only for "good cause" as specified in the law. (See Chapter 11.)

When deciding whether to withhold rent, sue the landlord, or take other action against him, you may wish to find out if he has had trouble with the housing code inspectors before. In the past, many code inspectors have refused to show tenants their records without the landlord's permission. A state statute, however, expressly declares that all records of notices and orders directed to the landlord concerning serious code violations[8] and the inspector's acts

---

[5]CC § 1942.5(a). Even if a retaliatory eviction occurs later than 180 days from the date of your complaint, it may be illegal under common law theories. *Glaser v. Meyers* (1982) 137 Cal.App.3d 770.

[6]*Western Land Office v. Cervantes* (1985) 175 Cal.App.3d 724.

[7]*Aweeka v. Bonds* (1971) 20 Cal.App.3d 278; CC §1942.5(f).

[8]Violations listed in CC § 1941.1.

regarding those violations are public records.[9] Every citizen has the right to inspect any public record.[10]

b. If You Must Move Because of Code Violations

If a court rules that a building's condition "substantially endangers the health and safety of residents," the local enforcement agency will send you a copy of the court order. Then, if the owner repairs the premises and you can't live there while the renovation proceeds, the owner must pay you certain relocation benefits. If you must move, the landlord is required to:

• provide you with comparable temporary housing nearby, or if that's not possible, pay you the difference between your old and new rent for 120 days;

• pay your moving expenses, including packing and unpacking costs;

• insure your belongings in transit, or pay you the replacement value of property lost, stolen or damaged in transit;

• pay utility connection charges; and

• give you the first chance to move back into the old place when repairs are completed.[11]

4. Repair and Deduct

When your landlord refuses to make repairs, California law gives you the right to make the repairs yourself (or hire someone to do them) and deduct the cost from your next month's rent. There are, however, some restrictions on this right, and there are certain procedures you must follow to exercise this right.[12]

a. Restrictions on the Right to Repair and Deduct

First, this remedy can be used only for certain defects. It can be used only if your place substantially lacks any of the things listed in CC § 1941.1. (See Section A.1, above.)

Second, you are not allowed to use this remedy if you interfered with the landlord's attempt to repair the defect, or if the defect was caused by your violation of any of the following duties (under CC § 1941.2):

• to keep your premises clean (unless the landlord has agreed to do this);

• to properly dispose of your garbage and trash (unless the landlord has agreed to do this);

• to properly use all electrical, gas and plumbing fixtures and keep them as clean as their condition permits;

• not to permit any person on the premises to damage the premises or the facilities willfully, or to do so yourself;

• to use each room only for the purpose for which it was intended (for example, you can't cook on the spare heater).

Finally, your repair of a defect may not require an expenditure of more than one month's rent and you cannot use your "repair-and-deduct" remedy more than twice in any 12-month period.[13]

b. How to Exercise Your Right to Repair and Deduct

You can use the repair and deduct remedy if none of the above restrictions apply to you.

To do so, you must first notify the landlord of the defects she should repair. You should put this in writing, date it and keep a copy so you can later prove you did it. Below is a form notice you might use. A tear-out form appears in the Appendix. (Be sure to keep a copy of this notice to use if you later go to court.)

---

[9] Government Code § 6254.7(c).
[10] Government Code § 6253.
[11] Health & Safety Code § 17980.7.
[12] The law on this subject is stated in CC §§ 1941-1942.5.

[13] CC § 1942.

Sample Notice to Repair

```
                          NOTICE TO REPAIR

     To _____, Landlord of the premises
located at _____.
          NOTICE IS HEREBY GIVEN that unless certain defects on the premises are
     repaired within a reasonable time, the undersigned tenant shall exercise any
     and all rights accruing to him pursuant to law, including those granted by
     California Civil Code Sections 1941-1942.
          The defects are the following:
          _____
          _____
          _____
          _____

     Date:_____                    _____
                                                    (signature of tenant)
```

Next you must wait a reasonable time to give the landlord a chance to make the repairs. After a reasonable time passes, you can do the repairs. What is a reasonable time? This will depend on the circumstances. If the heat doesn't work in January, a reasonable wait may mean only a few days, at most. If it breaks down in June, and it is expensive to repair quickly, you should wait a little longer. If you have complained to the landlord about the defect before, then you should not have to wait too long. The law says that 30 days is "presumed" to be a reasonable time. This means that if you do not wait 30 days, if the case goes to court, you must prove the wait was reasonable. If you wait 30 days, the landlord must prove the wait was unreasonable.

If the landlord has not made the repairs after a reasonable time, you may do the repairs or hire someone to do them. Keep a record of all the time you put in and all amounts you spend on labor and materials. When the next month's rent is due, give the landlord a written statement itemizing the expenses of the repairs, including compensation of your time. If this adds up to less than the rent, you must pay him the balance.

c. Retaliation for Using Repair and Deduct Remedy

If you have a month-to-month rental agreement instead of a lease, the landlord might try to retaliate against you by giving you a 30-day notice terminating your tenancy or raising your rent. Civil Code § 1942.5(a) prohibits such retaliation, with the following restrictions:

• The tenant is protected for only 180 days after he gives notice of the defects. After that, the landlord can terminate the tenancy or raise the rent, even if the tenant can prove that the landlord is doing it to retaliate.

• The tenant may raise the defense of retaliatory eviction in the eviction suit only if she is paid up in her rent when she raises the defense.

• The tenant may raise the defense only if he has not raised this defense in another eviction action brought by the same landlord in the past 12 months.

5. The Implied Warranty of Habitability

Under a famous 1974 decision of the California Supreme Court, *Green v. Superior Court*,[14] all leases and rental agreements are now deemed by law to include an "implied warranty of habitability." This means that whether it is written down or not, and whether the landlord likes it or not, he is required to keep the place in a habitable condition at all times.

What is habitable? According to the Supreme Court, this will usually mean substantial compliance with local building and health codes and with the standards set out in CC § 1941.1. (See Section A.1, above.) Put differently, a "material" violation of these codes and standards will usually constitute a breach of the implied warranty of habitability.

The law has not clearly defined material violations, but here are some guidelines the court has set out. Both the seriousness of the defect and the length of time it persists are relevant factors in deciding if it was material. Minor violations will not be considered material. Thus, failure to correct heavy rat infestation for a month would be clearly material, while a few ants which came in on one occasion when it rained would not. No heat for a week in January might be material, while a doorway an inch lower than allowed by the codes would not. Until the rules on this issue are more fully developed, you will just have to use common sense as to what is material.

In *Green*, the Supreme Court held that the implied warranty of habitability is so important that any provision in a lease or rental agreement that forces the tenant to waive her rights under the warranty is invalid. In a later case, the Supreme Court held that the tenant does not waive his rights under the warranty simply by moving in while knowing that the place is substandard.[15]

There is no breach of the implied warranty if the defect was caused by you or someone living with you or visiting you.

The courts have not clearly decided whether the landlord must be notified of the defects before she can be found to have breached the implied warranty. Nevertheless, it is obviously a good idea to notify her. You can use the Notice to Repair form (Section 4.b, above).

Suppose the landlord does breach the implied warranty of habitability. What can you do about it? The courts have established two very important remedies: rent withholding and suing the landlord for money damages.

a. Rent Withholding

The rent withholding remedy established by the courts is direct and powerful: you simply stop paying your rent until the landlord fixes the problems. The courts have reasoned that if the landlord doesn't fulfill his obligation to you, then your duty to him (to pay rent) "abates" until he shapes up. There is no requirement that you use any of your rent to make repairs. There is no requirement that you put your rent money into any bank or "escrow" account, but it is a good idea for you to set aside the rent money rather than spend it.[16] Unlike the repair-and-deduct remedy, you do not have to have all your rent paid up before you withhold rent because of the condition of the premises.

This can give the landlord a much stronger incentive to repair than your use of the repair-and-deduct remedy. There, he at least gets you to make some of the repairs, and you must pay him the bal-

---

[14] 10 Cal.3d 616.

[15] *Knight v. Hallsthammar* (1981) 29 Cal.3d 46.

[16] If the landlord sues to evict you for nonpayment of rent and you succeed in proving that he breached the implied warranty, the judge will determine a "reasonable" rent, which you must pay within five days to avoid eviction. (See Chapter 11, Section E.)

ance of the rent. With rent withholding, however, he gets nothing until he does his job. (Note, however, that the defects must be more material to justify rent withholding than to justify repair-and-deduct).

Here is how the rent withholding remedy works.

If the landlord fails to properly make the repairs, do not make your next rent payment. Although not required by law, it is an excellent idea to give the landlord a note at this time telling her what you are doing.

It might look like this (A tear-out form appears in the Appendix):

Sample Notice of Rent Withholding

```
                    NOTICE OF RENT WITHHOLDING

      To _____, Landlord of the premises located at
_____.

         NOTICE IS HEREBY GIVEN that because of your failure to comply with your
    implied warranty of habitability by refusing to repair defects on the premises, as
    previously demanded of you, the undersigned tenant has elected to withhold this
    month's rent in accordance with California law. Rent payments will be resumed in the
    future, as they become due, only after said defects have been properly repaired.

    Date:_____                    _____
                                                (signature of tenant)

    Authority: Green v. Superior Court, 10 Cal.3d 616 (1974).
```

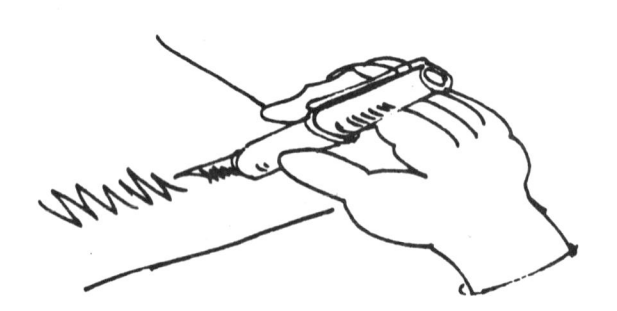

If the landlord then makes the repairs, you must resume your regular rent payments the next month, but you do not have to pay him the full amount of the rent you already withheld. You owe him only a "reasonable rent" out of that. What is a reasonable rent? That depends on the circumstances, and has not yet been clearly defined by the law. In one New Jersey case where the landlord had failed to provide heat, hot water, elevator service and incinerator use, the court required the tenant to pay only 25% of the agreed rent.[17] A West Virginia case allows the reasonable rent to be measured by determining the tenant's damages for "discomfort and annoyance," and then subtracting this amount from the agreed rent.[18] It is not clear whether California courts will allow this, however.[19] If you and your landlord can't agree on this, you could keep the money and let him take you to court if he wants to. If he does go to court, and if you prove that he materially breached his implied warranty of habitability, the court will decide what is a reasonable rent and make you pay only that amount.

Los Angeles and Sacramento Note: The City of Los Angeles has established a Rent Escrow Account Program, which lets tenants stop paying rent to landlords who don't correct health and safety violations for which they have been cited by the city. Tenants can pay rent into the city-run escrow account and will be protected from eviction for nonpayment of rent. When repairs are made, the city will return the money, minus administration fees, to the landlord. (Sacramento established a similar program in 1991.)

If you follow the procedures in this section, when you refuse to pay your rent it is possible that the landlord will give you a "three-day notice" to pay your rent in three days or get out. Then, when you fail to do either, she'll sue to have you evicted. (See Chapter 11 for a full discussion of the eviction procedure.) While normally she would easily win in such a suit, in this case you have a good defense, and she will not be allowed to evict you if you can prove that she breached her implied warranty of habitability.

When you raise this defense in your case, the judge might then order you to make future rent payments into court until the lawsuit is concluded. (He may not order you to pay into court the rent you already withheld.)

On occasion, a tenant has claimed in court that she had a valid reason for withholding rent because of substandard conditions, when in fact the unit was clearly habitable. These tenants were simply trying to get out of paying rent. This has resulted in some judges being cynical about all cases where tenants have withheld rent under the theory that the landlord has breached the duty to provide a habitable dwelling. When you add this fact to another one—some judges are more likely to be sympathetic to landlords than to tenants—you can see that a tenant is sometimes at a disadvantage in a rent withholding case. We don't mean to scare you so much that you will not use the rent withholding remedy, but we do want to prepare you for what you may face. How can you counter this possible disadvantage in a rent withholding case? Make sure to tell the judge clearly that you have the money to pay the rent, have always paid rent in the past, and will immediately start paying rent as soon as the proper repairs are made. Also, be sure that you have strong documentation that the uninhabitable condition really exists. This normally involves producing photographs and witnesses (the more technically knowledgeable the better).

At the end of the trial, if you have proved your case, the court will decide what was a reasonable rent while the defects on the premises were not corrected. When this is decided, that portion of any rent money which you paid into court which represents reasonable rent will be paid to the landlord, and the balance will be returned to you.

---

[17] *Academy Spires, Inc. v. Brown*, 111 N.J. Spr. 477, 268 A.2d 556, 562 (1970). In a California case, rent was reduced by 50%. *Strickland v. Becks* (1979) 95 Cal.App.3d Supp. 18.

[18] *Teller v. McCoy*, 253 S.E.2d 114, 128 (W. Va Supreme Court, 1978).

[19] *Quevado v. Braga* (1977) 72 Cal.App.3d Supp. 1. But see *Stoiber v. Honeychuck* (1980) 101 Cal.App.3d 903.

The judge will also order you to pay the reasonable rent portion of the rent which you withheld. He will give you only a few days to do this, so it's a good idea for you to keep this money put away rather than spending it. If you fail to pay this reasonable rent to the landlord in the time ordered by the judge, you will be deemed the loser of the lawsuit: you will be evicted, and a judgment for the landlord's costs, attorney fees (if the lease or rental agreement so provides), and reasonable rent will be entered against you. If you do pay the reasonable rent to the landlord on time, then you are the winner and you are entitled to a judgment for your court costs and (if the lease or rental agreement so provides) attorney fees.

Also, the court can order the landlord to make repairs and correct the conditions which consitute a breach of the landlord's obligations. The court must order the monthly rent to be limited to the reasonable rental value of the premises until repairs are completed. If the court orders repairs, corrections or both, the court may continue to oversee the matter to make sure the landlord complies with the order.[20]

If you do not have a lease, the landlord might try to retaliate against you simply by giving you a 30-day notice to vacate (rather than a three-day notice to pay the rent or get out). If you can prove in the eviction suit he brings that he gave you the notice in order to retaliate against you for rightfully withholding your rent, then this might well be held to be an attempted illegal retaliatory eviction and you will not be evicted.[21] A California statute seems to protect against retaliation in such a situation, since it forbids a landlord from retaliating against a tenant's lawful exercise of his rights.[22]

Rent withholding is a powerful strategy. If all goes according to the law stated above, you can stay in the premises, withhold rent and win eviction actions until the premises are brought up to code. Unfortunately, you might get into a lawsuit and require an attorney's services. Quite often, however, the written threat of rent withholding is sufficient to solve the problem.

Warning: Rent withholding can be risky! If you withhold rent, do not pay it in response to a three-day notice, and the landlord sues to evict, it is possible that you might then fail to convince the court that the landlord breached the implied warranty of habitability. If this happens, you will lose the action. Also, you will probably be evicted—even though your rent withholding was honest and in good faith, and even though you are now willing to pay the full rent rather than be evicted! You may ask the judge to "reinstate" your tenancy (see Chapter 11), but she is not required to do it.

So do not follow through with your threat to withhold rent unless you are pretty sure that you can prove that the defects which the landlord failed to fix were pretty serious, and that you did not cause them.

A safer strategy—though not usually as immediate and powerful as rent withholding—is to keep paying the rent, but sue the landlord for money damages for his breach of the implied warranty of habitability.

Note on Drug Dealing and Rent Withholding: Tenants who are threatened or victimized by the presence of drug-dealing in the same building may be able to start withholding their rent. (See Chapter 8.C.)

b. Sue the Landlord

The courts have held that one remedy you have against the landlord who fails to obey the implied warranty is to sue him for money damages. In one leading case, the court held that the tenant might recover damages for the discomfort and annoyance of

---

[20] CCP § 1174.2.

[21] See *Barela v. Superior Court* (1981) 30 Cal.3d 244, 178 Cal.Rptr. 618; *Robinson v. Diamond Housing Corp.*, 463 F.2d 853 (D.C. Cir. 1972).

[22] CC § 1942.5(c).

having to live in substandard conditions, and punitive damages if the landlord's failure is willful![23]

If repairs have not been made within 60 days of the building inspector or housing department ordering the landlord to make necessary repairs, the tenant may sue the landlord for actual damages, and receive "special damages" of between $100 and $1,000 (in the judge's discretion) plus attorney fees.[24]

If the landlord has not corrected health and safety violations ordered by the court, tenants can sue and ask the court to appoint a receiver. The receiver would be authorized to collect rents, manage the property and supervise the necessary repairs.[25]

Civil Code § 1942.4 now allows courts who award damages for untenantable buildings to also order the landlord to repair any substandard conditions at the residential dwelling which significantly or materially affect the health or safety of the people who live there. Section 1942.4 also provides that if the court orders repairs or corrections, the court may continue to oversee the matter to make sure the landlord complies with the order.

A model complaint to use when suing a landlord for damages for breach of the implied warranty appears in the Forms section in the back of the latest supplement to the *California Eviction Defense Manual* (Continuing Education of the Bar).

You may file a suit yourself for up to $5,000 in small claims court. For how to do this, see the description of small claims courts in Chapter 10 and see Warner, *Everybody's Guide to Small Claims Court* (Nolo Press).

If the landlord's breach of warranty caused any sickness or injury to you or anyone in your family, be sure to see a lawyer. Your claim might be worth much more than $5,000, and a lawyer can help you get what you should.

You may also sue the landlord for breach of any promise (express or implied) to provide or maintain appliances, swimming pools, or anything else relating to the premises.

It is illegal for the landlord to try to evict you or raise your rent in retaliation for your exercising your right to file a lawsuit against him.[26]

---

[23] *Stoiber v. Honeychuck* (1980) 101 Cal.App.3d 903.
[24] CC § 1942.4.
[25] Health & Safety Code § 17980.7.
[26] CC § 1942.5(c).

chapter 8

Injuries to a Tenant Due to Substandard Housing Conditions

A.	Standard of Care Imposed on Landlords	8/2
B.	Landlord Liability for Defects in the Premises	8/2
C.	Landlord's Duty To Protect Tenant from Injury Caused by Others	8/3
	1. Injuries to Others by Third Parties	8/3
	2. Locks and Security Systems	8/4
	3. Drug-Dealing Tenants	8/4
	4. Other Obnoxious Tenants	8/5
D.	Landlord Liability for Damage to Your Property	8/5

When we start talking about personal injuries, we get into an area that lawyers call "torts." Whole books have been written on this subject and many lawyers make a nice living filing lawsuits on behalf of people who have been injured as a result of the "negligent" or "intentional" acts of others. The last several years have seen a great increase in the ways a landlord might be held responsible for injuries caused to a tenant. Landlords are liable for physical injuries caused by faulty premises (a broken stair, for example) and for mental suffering or emotional distress caused by slum conditions, wrongful evictions, invasions of privacy and harassment. A tenant (or in some situations, a visitor) may even recover against the landlord for maintaining a nuisance, if the premises are substantially below code or abnormally messy or loud tenants are allowed to remain in other units in the building. If you are injured, either physically or mentally, as a result of some act or failure to act of your landlord, you should see a lawyer. (If your injury is worth $5,000 or less to you, you may want to go to small claims court.)

A. Standard of Care Imposed on Landlords

It used to be that a landlord could put a clause in a lease or rental agreement which freed him from most responsibilities for injuries suffered by a tenant, even if the injury was a direct result of the landlord's negligence. This is no longer the law, although you still find this sort of unenforceable clause in some leases and rental agreements.[1]

Today a landlord is held to a strict duty of care toward her tenants when defective conditions which existed at the time the tenant moved in caused an injury. Termed "strict liability," this duty of care extends to visitors. It is important to understand that this duty exists even though the landlord did not know about the existence of the injury-causing defect. When it comes to defects, the rule that resulted from a 1985 case (*Becker v. IRM Corp.*) is that a landlord must act toward his tenants and visitors to the building like a retailer in the business of providing housing.[2]

Because the doctrine of strict liability is so important, a few words about it are appropriate.

"Strict" liability means liability without fault. In other words, to prevail in a case based on strict liability, a plaintiff (person suing) does not have to prove that the defendant (person sued) was negligent. This doctrine is often applied in "products liability" cases, where a manufactured appliance, automobile or other device breaks for no apparent reason and causes injury or property damage. For example, if the steering mechanism on a new car fails, or an elevator falls causing an accident, the people injured are entitled to recover damages from the manufacturer without having to prove the manufacturer was negligent. Although there are a number of reasons for applying strict liability in this situation, it comes down to a conclusion that steering mechanisms on new cars are supposed to work and elevators are not supposed to fall, and if they fail the manufacturer is legally responsible without the injured people having to mount an elaborate case proving negligence.

B. Landlord Liability for Defects in the Premises

Here are some examples of situations in which a landlord has been held liable for injuries caused by defects in the premises.

- Mental distress from slum conditions.[3]
- Fall through a handrail on stairway.[4]

---

[1] CC § 1953.

[2] 38 Cal.3d 454.

[3] *Stoiber v. Honeychuck* (1980) 101 Cal.App.3d 903.

[4] *Brennan v. Cockrell* (1973) 35 Cal.App.3d 796.

• Fire caused by defective heater.[5] This case also states that a landlord can be strictly liable (the tenant doesn't have to prove that the landlord acted in an unreasonable way) if he installs an appliance without knowing whether or not it is defective.

• Fire as a result of defective wiring.[6] Here a defective wall plug (that the tenant had asked the landlord to fix) forced the tenant to plug a refrigerator into another socket with an extension cord, which resulted in a fire.

• Tenant trips over rock on common stairway.[7]

• Emotional distress from intimidation by landlord in course of eviction.[8]

• Injury from a fall into a shower door made of untempered glass. The landlord didn't know of the defect but was nevertheless held to be liable.[9]

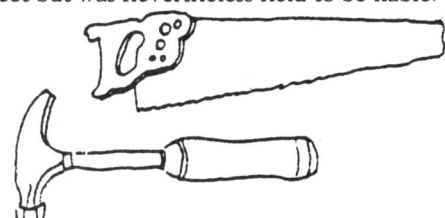

C. Landlord's Duty To Protect Tenant from Injury Caused by Others

Under certain circumstances, a landlord may be liable for property damage or injuries to a tenant that result from the acts of other tenants or third persons who were on the premises.

1. Injuries to Others by Third Parties

Depending on the situation, a landlord may be held liable for injuries resulting to tenants (or anyone else) by criminal actions committed by others, even if no prior similar acts have occurred.[10] If a tenant is assaulted, raped, bitten by a dog or robbed, a landlord may or may not be legally responsible. It depends on whether the landlord reasonably had a duty of care in the circumstances, and whether or not she fulfilled it. Generally, if you are injured by a violent act that the landlord could neither foresee nor prevent, the landlord will not be legally liable for your injury. Both of these questions are for a jury to decide. For example, landlords have been held liable for tenants' injuries caused by others in the following situations:

• A tenant is raped as a result of poor security or lighting in common areas, or after complaining of defective locks in apartment.[11]

• A tenant's vicious dog bites another tenant's visitor. Although the tenant owning the dog was held to be liable to the other tenant's visitor, the landlord was also found to be liable for doing nothing about the dog, even though he knew it was vicious.[12]

• Tenant's visitor killed in dim, empty parking area with broken security system and a history of violent crimes.[13]

• Tenant robbed and assaulted in dimly lit common area where landlord knew or should have known about earlier robberies and assaults.[14]

---

[5]*Golden v. Conway* (1976) 55 Cal.App.3d 948.

[6]*Evans v. Thompson* (1977) 72 Cal.App.3d 978.

[7]*Henrouille v. Marin Ventures, Inc.* (1978) 20 Cal.3d 512.

[8]*Newby v. Alto Riviera Apts.* (1976) 60 Cal.App.3d 288.

[9]*Becker v. IRM Corp.* (1985) 38 Cal.3d 454.

[10]*Isaacs v. Huntington Memorial Hospital* (1985) 38 Cal.3d 112.

[11]*Olar v. Schroit* (1984) 202 Cal.Rptr. 457, *Kwaitkowski v. Superior Trading Corp.* (1981) 123 Cal.App.3d 324, 176 Cal.Rptr. 494, *O'Hara v. Western Seven Trees Corp.* (1977) 75 Cal.App.3d 798, 142 Cal.Rptr. 487, and *Frances T. v. Village Green Properties* (1986) 42 Cal.3d 490 (Condominium Owners' Association held liable).

[12]*Ucello v. Landenslayer* (1975) 44 Cal.App.3d 504, 118 Cal.Rptr. 741. For more on landlord liability for tenants' dogs, see *Dog Law*, by Mary Randolph (Nolo Press).

[13]*Gomez v. Ticor* (1983) 145 Cal. App. 3d 622, 193 Cal. Rptr. 622.

[14]*Penner v. Falk* (1984) 153 Cal. App. 3d 858, 200 Cal. Rptr. 661, and *Isaacs v. Huntington Memorial Hospital* (1985) 38 Cal. 3d 112, 211 Cal. Rptr. 356.

2. Locks and Security Systems

The ordinances of many cities and counties require all rental units to be equipped with deadbolt locks. If your unit is not so equipped and you are burglarized or injured by an intruder, your chances of recovering from your landlord are excellent. If the landlord won't make good your loss, see a lawyer.

Security systems—such as garage doors that open on electronic signal, and television monitors in lobbies and hallways—are often advertised as desirable features which justify a higher-than-normal rent. While there is generally no legal requirement mandating the installation of these systems, a tenant is justified in relying on them if they exist. Generally, a landlord's legal liability increases should a tenant (or his property) be injured when a security system is broken. It's obviously up to your landlord to fix any defective security system immediately. If she fails to do so and you or your property are injured, your chances of recovering your losses are excellent.

3. Drug-Dealing Tenants

Trafficking in illegal drugs, most notably cocaine, has turned some formerly placid neighborhoods into battle zones. To combat this seeming intractable problem, the law is targeting landlords who rent to dealers.

The legal theory boils down to this: Landlords have a responsibility to keep their properties safe. That means it's up to the landlord to keep dealers out or, failing that, to kick them out pronto when they are discovered. When they allow drug-dealing tenants to annoy, frighten or even prey upon other tenants and neighbors, law-abiding tenants may start withholding rent, and neighbors or the government may bring costly lawsuits against the landlord.

a. Rent Withholding

Although no statute specifically allows it, some courts have said that tenants may withhold rent if the landlord fails to protect their security.[15] (See Chapter 7 for details on rent withholding.) A landlord who does nothing about a tenant's drug-dealing is certainly open to this accusation.

If the landlord tries to evict the complaining tenants for nonpayment of rent, a court might rule that the tenants were within their rights to withhold rent until the property again became reasonably safe and peaceful.

b. Lawsuits Against Landlords

Tenants and others who become victims of the crime that surrounds a drug dealer's home may also sue a landlord who does nothing to stop drug-dealing on his property.

In 1989, 19 neighbors plagued by the crime, noise and fear generated by a "crack house" in Berkeley won $2,000 each in small claims court against an absentee owner who had ignored their complaints for years (the California small claims court maximum has since risen to $5,000). In San Francisco, a similar rash of small claims suits cost a landlord $35,000. Soon after the verdicts, both landlords evicted the troublesome tenants. In another example, a group of San Francisco neighbors successfully sued the city Housing Authority for allowing drug-dealing and related crime to flourish on its property. They won a total of $25,500.[16] Also, tenants may sue the landlord in federal court, under the federal Racketeering Influenced Corrupt Organizations (RICO) Act, if they can prove the landlord is tolerating drug dealing.[17]

---

[15] *Secretary of HUD v. Layfield* (1979) 88 Cal.App.3d Supp. 28.

[16] *San Francisco Chronicle*, Nov. 2, 1990.

[17] *Spinosa v. University Students Cooperative Assn.*, __F.2d__ (9th Cir., 1991).

Many cities are passing new laws aimed at getting drug-dealing tenants evicted. The laws make it easier for landlords to evict and punish landlords who sit by while drug-dealing takes place on their property. In Los Angeles, for example, the police department can notify landlords when tenants are arrested or convicted of drug-related offenses. In Pasadena, a landlord who refuses to evict the tenants after a request from the city can be fined up to $5,000.

Under state law, cities and counties can bring suit to have a drug-dealer-infested building declared a public nuisance. Any city or county resident can do the same by filing a lawsuit in superior court.[18]

Landlords who fail to respond can even lose their property. Federal or local law enforcement authorities can take legal action to have housing used by drug dealers seized and turned over to the government, even if the owners' part in the crime is just that he ignored it. In 1988, the San Mateo County, district attorney brought just such a suit against the owner of a 60-unit drug haven in the city of East Palo Alto. The owner was fined $35,000 in civil penalties and had to shut the building down and pay tenants' relocation expenses.

4. Other Obnoxious Tenants

If other tenants are driving you crazy by creating excessive noise, damaging the property, running an illegal business or throwing trash in common areas, your first course should be to complain to the manager and landlord. The more tenants who complain, the more likely you will get fast action.

If the landlord doesn't take action, you can file a lawsuit against him for allowing the tenant to stay on the property. If all the tenants (or neighbors in other buildings) threaten to sue the landlord at one time, the landlord will probably respond quickly.

If you still don't get results, each tenant should file a separate small claims court case, on the ground that the landlord is allowing a nuisance on his property. When every tenant asks for a few hundred dollars or more, the amount quickly adds up and is sure to get the landlord's attention.

Note on Hiring an Attorney: We discuss how to deal with lawyers in Chapter 1. You will want to re-read that chapter, but you should also realize that personal injury cases are special; a lawyer normally does not charge the client any money up front, but takes a portion of any recovery. This is called a "contingency fee" and means that the lawyer gets nothing if you lose. Depending on how much work is involved, the fee can typically be from 25% to 40% of the recovery. It is wise to shop around to see what various lawyers offer. If you have a strong case, you should get someone to help you for 25% of the eventual recovery.

Here is another idea that might prove helpful. Contact the landlord or his insurance company yourself and see what they will offer you without an attorney. Then, if you think you should get more, hire an attorney on a contingency fee arrangement so that he gets a cut only of the amount he can recover for you over and above what you were offered without his help.

D. Landlord Liability for Damage to Your Property

If you start a fire or let the water overflow your bathtub and your property is damaged, you, not the landlord, are responsible. For this reason, many renters buy renter's insurance, which also provides valuable personal liability protection. (Renter's insurance is discussed in Chapter 13.)

But what happens if your property is damaged by someone else's negligence? For example, suppose a fire starts in a common area of a multi-unit dwelling and burns down the whole building? While it has not

---

[18]Health & Safety Code § 11570, 11571 and 11581.

been finally ruled on by the courts, it is logical to assume that the landlord is legally liable under the strict liability theory outlined in Section A above. Even if the courts do not rule that the *Becker* case applies to property damage as well as to personal injury, the landlord will be judged liable if your loss resulted from her negligence (say flammable material was improperly stored in a common area). However, if your loss can in no way be traceable to the landlord (for example, another tenant starts a fire in a perfectly safe fireplace and forgets to use a screen, allowing the fire to spread), the landlord is not liable. If you can demonstrate that the other tenant was negligent, you can win a lawsuit against him. If your loss or damage is due to an earthquake or other unusual hazard, you're out of luck unless you have renter's insurance and extra earthquake coverage. (See Chapter 13.)

chapter 9

Breaking a Lease, Subleasing, and Other Leasing Problems

A. What Happens When the Lease Runs Out	9/2
B. Subleases and Assignments	9/2
C. Subleasing With the Idea of Returning Later	9/3
D. How to Break a Lease	9/3
1. General Rules	9/5
2. Self-Protection When Breaking a Lease	9/6
3. Possible Legal Action	9/7
E. Belongings You Leave Behind	9/8

A. What Happens When the Lease Runs Out

Often a tenant wishes to stay in a dwelling after a lease term expires. If you are in this situation, read your lease carefully, as it may have a provision covering what happens at the end of the lease term. The terms of the lease apply, unless they call for an illegal automatic renewal. In the absence of a lease provision, state law provides that if a lease runs out and the landlord thereafter accepts rent, the tenant becomes a month-to-month tenant under the same terms outlined in the old lease.[1] All the terms of the original lease, with the exception of the period-of-occupancy clause, are still binding and become, in effect, a written agreement. (See Chapter 2.B.) This means that either the landlord or the tenant can terminate the tenancy with a 30-day written notice; likewise, the rent can be increased after a 30-day notice.[2]

Sometimes a lease will contain a provision calling for automatic renewal if the tenant stays beyond the end of the lease term. This would mean that if a tenant held over one day after a one-year lease expired, he would have renewed the lease for another year. This provision is legal only if the renewal or extension provision is printed in at least eight point boldface type, immediately above the place where the tenant signs the lease. If a renewal provision is not set forth in this way, it may be legally disregarded (voided) by the tenant.[3]

B. Subleases and Assignments

A sub-tenant is a person to whom a tenant subleases all or part of the property. This can occur where the tenant moves out temporarily—for example, for a couple of months in the summer—and rents the entire dwelling to someone else, or where he rents one or more rooms while continuing to live there. (See Chapter 3.D, for a discussion of adding a roommate.)

Typically, a sub-tenant does not have a separate agreement with the landlord. Their right of occupancy depends on:

• the continuing existence of the tenancy between the landlord and the tenant; and

• whatever implied, oral or written rental agreement the sub-tenant has with the tenant, who functions as the sub-tenant's landlord.

But what about the tenant who has no intention of returning, such as a tenant with a year lease who stays six months and sublets to someone else for the remaining six months of the lease term? According to technical lease jargon, this is not a sublet, but an "assignment," under which the tenant has legally "assigned" all her rights to the property to someone else. We distinguish the term assignment from "sublet" in part because lawyers often do, and to explain why many lease and rental agreement forms forbid both assignments and sublets without the owner's consent.

There is one important technical difference between an assignment and sublease. Where an assignment is involved, the new tenant (the "assignee") is responsible to the landlord for everything the original tenant was liable for—even without an agreement between that person and the landlord.[4] (The previous occupant (assignor) remains liable to the landlord also, unless the landlord agrees otherwise in writing.) This should be distinguished from the situation in which a tenant sublets to a second tenant who is responsible to the first tenant, not the landlord.

---

[1] CC § 1945.

[2] Some rent control cities have special guidelines requiring just cause for the termination of a tenancy. See Chapter 4.

[3] CC § 1945.5

[4] CC § 822.

As a tenant, you normally face the need to sublease or assign your tenancy in the following situations:

• You have a lease or a rental agreement and want to leave for some set period of time and then return and get your home back (see Section C, below);

• You have a lease and want to leave permanently before it ends (see Section D, below);

• You want to bring in a roommate (see Chapter 3).

C. Subleasing With the Idea of Returning Later

Technically speaking, you are entitled to sublease only when you have a lease yourself in the first place. In addition, most leases and rental agreements require the landlord's consent in advance for subletting. If you sublet without it, the sublease is probably invalid.[5] If a tenant sublets on the sly when a lease or rental agreement prohibits it, the landlord can evict both the original tenant and the sub-tenant. In addition, you can't sublease what you don't have a right to. So if you have a month-to-month tenancy, you can sublet on that basis, but you can't give someone a one-year sublease. If you have a one-year lease, you can't sublease beyond that period—though in practice many landlords continue to accept monthly rent after a fixed-term lease expires. Legally, that converts the fixed-term tenancy to a month-to-month one.[6]

Whenever you let anyone move into your place for a while, it is important to have a written agreement, incorporating your lease or rental agreement, which sets out all the terms of the arrangement. We include here an example of a possible sublease arrangement with the warning that it will have to be modified to suit your individual circumstances. Also, your landlord may require your sub-tenant to sign a separate rental agreement, giving the new person all the rights and responsibilities of a tenant.

D. How to Break a Lease

If you want to move out before your lease expires, you probably won't have too much of a problem. In most areas of California, the same shortage of housing that gives the landlord an advantage at the time of the original rental also makes it possible for a tenant to get out of a lease fairly easily.

---

[5]One case, although it doesn't specifically apply to residential tenancies, indicates that a landlord cannot unreasonably withhold consent. *Kendall v. Pestana* (1986) 40 Cal.3d 488.

[6]In some communities covered by rent control ordinances which require "just cause" to evict, a determined sub-tenant may be able to prevent you from reclaiming your rental unit unless you can establish "just cause" under the rent control ordinance.

Sample Sublease Agreement

SUBLEASE AGREEMENT

This is an agreement between Leon Hernandez of 1500 Acorn Street #4, Cloverdale, California and Joan Ehrman, now residing at 77 Wheat Avenue, Berkeley, California.

1. In consideration of $300 per month payable on the first day of each month, Leon Hernandez agrees to sublease apartment #4 at 1500 Acorn Street, Cloverdale, California to Joan Ehrman from August 1, 19__ to December 30, 19__.

2. Leon Hernandez hereby acknowledges receipt of $1,200 which represents payment of the first and last months' rent and a $600 security deposit.[7] The security deposit will be returned to Joan Ehrman on December 30, 19__ if the premises are completely clean and have suffered no damage.

3. A copy of the agreement between Smith Realty and Leon Hernandez is stapled to this agreement and is incorporated as if set out in full. Joan Ehrman specifically covenants and agrees to adhere to all the rules and regulations set out in Sections 1-10 of this lease.

_____   _____
Date   Leon Hernandez

_____   _____
Date   Joan Ehrman

---

[7] The rules which limit the amount of money that a landlord can charge a tenant for deposits discussed in Chapter 10 also apply to sublease agreements.

1. General Rules

When you sign a lease, you promise to pay rent on certain premises for a certain time. Simply moving out does not get you off the hook as far as paying is concerned. You have made a contract and are legally bound to fulfill it. This means that you are legally bound to pay rent for the full lease term, whether or not you continue to occupy the dwelling.[8] If you do not pay, your landlord can sue you, get a judgment and try to collect the money by doing such things as attaching your wages.

But the law requires a landlord to take all reasonable steps to keep his losses to a minimum—a concept known as mitigation of damages.[9] This means that when a tenant leaves in the middle of the lease term, the landlord must make all reasonable efforts to rent the premises to another tenant at the best price possible.

If the landlord re-rents the property quickly, and doesn't lose any rent, the former tenant doesn't owe the landlord anything. But if the landlord loses money because the old tenant moved out early, the landlord is entitled to payment from the former tenant. Because of a general shortage of rental units in most areas of California, the landlord should be able to get a new tenant fairly quickly, for about the same rent as paid by the original tenant. The result is that the tenant who breaks the lease is obligated for little or no damages.

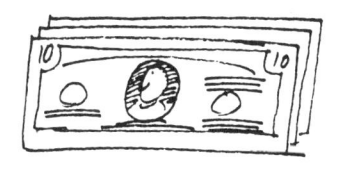

EXAMPLE
Susan Wong rented an apartment from Stephan Leness in January for a term of one year, at the monthly rent of $1,000. Everything went well until September, when Susan had to move to be closer to her invalid mother. Under the general rule, Susan is theoretically liable to Stephan for $3,000—the rent for October, November, and December. However, if Stephan mitigated these damages by taking out an ad and re-renting on October 15, Susan would owe much less. If the new tenant paid $500 for the last half of October and $1,000 in November and December, Stephan must credit the total $2,500 he got from the new tenant against Susan's $3,000 liability. This leaves Susan liable for only $500, plus Stephan's advertising costs of $20, for a total of $520.

To summarize, a fixed-term tenant who leaves before the end of the lease is responsible for:

• the remaining rent due under the lease, plus any reasonable advertising expenses incurred in finding a new tenant minus

• any rent the landlord can collect from a new tenant between the time the original tenant leaves and the end of the lease term.

Liquidated Damages Note: If your lease contains a liquidated damages clause—requiring you to pay the landlord a certain amount of money as damages for breaking the lease—you should know that a court probably won't make you pay it. If the amount of liquidated damages far exceeds the amount the landlord actually lost, the court will consider it an invalid "penalty." You will have to compensate the landlord only for his actual losses.

The landlord cannot legally take the amount of liquidated damages out of your security deposit. If the landlord keeps your deposit in payment of these damages, remind him, promptly and in writing, that state law strictly limits the ways that a landlord can use the security deposit. (See Chapter 10.C.)

---

[8] CC § 1951.2.
[9] CC § 1951.2.

2. Self-Protection When Breaking a Lease

Notify your landlord in writing as soon as you know that you are going to move out before the end of a lease term. The more notice you give the landlord, the better your chances are that he will find another tenant.

After sending the landlord your written notice it is wise to stop by and talk to him. He may have another tenant ready to move in and not be concerned by your moving out. In some cases the landlord may demand an amount of money to compensate him for his trouble in re-renting the place. If the amount is small, it may be easier to agree to pay rather than to become involved in a dispute. If your landlord has a deposit, you might even offer to let him keep a part of it in full settlement of all possible damage claims arising from your leaving in the middle of the lease term. As noted above, since the landlord has a duty to try and re-rent the place (mitigate damages) and since this is reasonably easy to do, you should not agree to pay much in the way of damages. Get any agreement you make in writing. A sample agreement is shown below.

If it is not possible to deal rationally with your landlord, or if she won't make a written release, you should take steps to protect yourself. Don't let your landlord scare you into paying her a lot of money. Simply put an advertisement in your local paper to lease your dwelling at the same rent that you are paying. When people call, show them the place, but tell them that any lease arrangement must be worked out with your landlord. Also request that the potential tenants contact the landlord directly. To protect yourself, keep a list of all tenants who appear suitable and who express an interest in moving in. Include information on your list that shows that the potential tenants are responsible—for example, include

Sample Agreement

```
                          AGREEMENT

     This agreement is between Leon Hernandez of 1500 Acorn Street #4,
Cloverdale, California, and Smith Realty Co., of 10 Jones Street, Cloverdale,
California, and by its owner, B. R. Smith.
     In consideration of the amount of $75, Smith Realty Co. hereby agrees to
cancel the lease of Leon Hernandez on Apt. #4 at 1500 Acorn Street,
Cloverdale, California as of October 31, 19__. The $75 payment is hereby
acknowledged to be made this date by subtracting it from Leon Hernandez's $600
security deposit.


_____          _____
Date                                 B. R. Smith


_____          _____
Date                                 Leon Hernandez
```

something about their job or family. Write a letter to your landlord with a list of the names and keep a copy for your file. She has a right to approve or disapprove of whomever you suggest as a tenant, but she may not be unreasonable about it; she must keep her losses to a minimum (mitigate damages) as discussed above. Also, when you move out be sure the unit is clean and ready to rent to the next tenant, so that your landlord has no basis to claim that it was not in rentable condition and that you are responsible for rent during the time it took her to get it cleaned.

Sample Letter to Landlord Suggesting Potential Tenants

```
1500 Acorn Street #4
Cloverdale, California
October 1, 19__

Smith Realty Co.
10 Jones Street
Cloverdale, California

As I told you on September 15, 19__, I
plan to move out of this apartment on
October 31, 19__. Because I wish to keep
damages to a minimum, I am giving you the
names, addresses, and phone numbers of
four people who have expressed an
interest in renting this apartment on or
about November 1, 19__ at the same rent
that I pay. I assume that you will find
one of these potential tenants to be
suitable, unless of course you have
already arranged to rent the apartment.

(include list of names, addresses and phone numbers)

Very truly yours,


_____
Leon Hernandez
```

3. Possible Legal Action

If you move out and break a lease, the landlord may sue you for the rent he lost and the expense of getting a new tenant. This is not likely if the landlord has gotten a new tenant to move in almost immediately after you've moved out, because in such a situation there would be little or no damages. However, occasionally it takes the landlord a little time or expense (for advertising) to get a new tenant. This is especially likely in a resort area (off season) or near a university in the summer. In this case, a landlord may sue either in small claims court or in municipal court.

If you are sued, you will receive legal documents setting out the landlord's claim. Read them carefully to see if the amount the landlord asks for is fair. As explained above, if you take the proper steps to protect yourself, she should be entitled to little or nothing. In unusual situations, however, the landlord may be entitled to some recovery. For example, if a tenant with a year's lease at a $600 per month rental moved out in mid-year and no new tenant could be found who would pay more than $575 per month, then the landlord would likely recover damages. In this case, the old tenant would be liable for the $25 a month difference between what he paid and what the new tenant paid, multiplied by the number of months left in the lease at the time he moved out. A tenant might also be liable for damages if it took the landlord some period of time, such as a month, to find a new tenant. In this case the first tenant would be liable for the month's rent (*if* the landlord had made diligent efforts to find a new tenant).

If you are sued in small claims court for an amount that seems excessive, simply tell the judge your side of the case and bring with you any witnesses and written documentation that would help tell your story. If you are sued in municipal court, you may want to see a lawyer, especially if there is a lot of money involved. (See Chapter 1.)

E. Belongings You Leave Behind

If you leave belongings on the premises when you move out, you must ask the landlord for them, in writing, within 18 days. Your request must describe the property and must give the landlord your mailing address. Within five days of receiving your request, the landlord may demand, in writing, that you pay reasonable costs for storage. You must pay the charges and pick up the property within 72 hours of receiving the landlord's demand.

If the landlord doesn't comply with your request, you can sue for your actual damages and, if the landlord acted in bad faith, for another $250 in damages.[10]

Alternately, the landlord may notify you, in writing, that the property is still there. The notice should describe the property and tell you where the property can be claimed, how long you have to claim it, and that you may have to pay reasonable costs for storage. The landlord must give you at least 15 days (18 days, if the notice is mailed) to claim the property.

If the property is worth less than $300, the landlord is free to dispose of it. If it is worth more than that, the landlord must sell it at a public sale, subtract costs of sale and storage, and turn the rest over to the county. You have a year to claim the net profit from the sale.[11]

---

[10] CC § 1965.

[11] CC §§ 1983. 1988.

chapter 10

Security Deposits and Last Month's Rent

A.	Amount of Deposit	10/2
B.	Non-Refundable Deposits	10/3
C.	What the Deposits May Be Used For	10/3
D.	Landlord's Duty to Return Deposit	10/4
E.	Effect of Sale of Premises on Security Deposits	10/4
F.	May the Landlord Increase the Security Deposit?	10/5
G.	Avoiding Deposit Problems	10/5
H.	If the Landlord Won't Return Your Deposit	10/6
	Step 1. Make a Formal Demand	10/6
	Step 2. Consider Compromise	10/6
	Step 3. Sue In Small Claims Court	10/6
	Step 4. Call the District Attorney	10/9
I.	Rent Withholding as a Way to Get Deposits Back In Advance	10/9
J.	Interest on Security Deposits	10/10
K.	Last Month's Rent	10/10

Almost all landlords require their tenants to put up some money before moving in. This payment might be called a "security deposit," "cleaning fee," "last month's rent," or something else by the landlord.

Security deposits can add up to a lot of money—often over $1,000. The landlord usually wants to get as much as she can so she won't have to go chasing after you for unpaid rent or any costs of repairing the premises after you leave. The tenant, who usually wants to fork over as little as possible, often finds that it's very difficult to talk a landlord into reducing a deposit. Unfortunately, there is little we can say that will help you to get a potential landlord to be reasonable in this regard, assuming the deposit he charges is within the statutory maximum discussed below. However, because security deposits constitute a big investment on your part, and because deposits have historically been a major source of friction between landlord and tenant, it is essential that you understand the legal rules in this area.

A. Amount of Deposit

State law provides that the total of all deposits and fees required by the landlord—for security, cleaning, last month's rent, etc.—may not exceed an amount equal to two months' rent, if the premises are unfurnished. If the premises are furnished, the limit is an amount equal to three months' rent.[1] If you have a waterbed, the maximum allowed deposit increases by half a month's rent—to 2.5 times the monthly rent for unfurnished property and 3.5 times the monthly rent for furnished property.[2]

Suppose the landlord supplies the stove and refrigerator, but no other "furniture." Does this make the place "furnished"? We don't think so—though the statute is not clear on this. If the landlord provides basic furniture (beds, tables, etc.), obviously it is furnished and she is legitimately entitled to a higher deposit because the potential for damage is high. But, in our opinion, she is not exposed to that much risk of loss if she provides only the stove and refrigerator, and therefore should only be allowed to require a deposit of up to two months' rent. Also, in the rental business, "furnished" is usually taken to mean the inclusion of all basic furniture.

State law also says: "This subdivision does not preclude a landlord and a tenant from entering into a mutual agreement for the landlord, at the request of the tenant and for a specified fee or charge, to make structural, decorative, furnishing, or other similar alterations, if the alterations are other than cleaning or repairing for which the landlord may charge the previous tenant as provided by subdivision (e)."[3] The intent of this provision is clearly to allow the landlord to require compensation for strange or unusual alterations requested by the tenant. This, of course, is reasonable. However, there is a danger that some landlords may improperly try to reintroduce all sorts of extra or nonrefundable fees under this exception to the basic deposit rules. Be awake to this possibility!

If the landlord is forced to use some of the security deposit during your tenancy (for example, because you broke something and didn't fix it or pay for it), he may require you to replenish the security deposit.

EXAMPLE
Millie pays her landlord Maury a $700 security deposit. Millie goes on vacation, leaving the water running. By the time Maury is notified, the overflow has damaged the paint on the ceiling below. Maury repaints the ceiling at a cost of $350, taking the money out of the security deposit. Maury is entitled to ask Millie to replace that money.

---

[1] CC § 1950.5(c).
[2] CC § 1940.5(h).

[3] CC § 1950.5(c).

Note on Paying Installments: The landlord may let you pay a hefty deposit in installments over three months or so. If you miss a scheduled payment, the landlord can evict you for breaching the lease or rental agreement.

B. Non-Refundable Deposits

No lease or rental agreement may call any deposit "non-refundable."[4] Nor may a landlord escape this rule by demanding a "cleaning" or "security" or "pet fee" instead of a deposit. Under the law, the security deposit rules we discuss here apply to any "payment, fee, deposit or charge."[5]

For example, a San Francisco apartment complex charged tenants a $65 move-in fee and a $50 transfer fee if they moved from one apartment to another within the complex. A court ruled that the fees were "deposits" under the law, and because they weren't used for the purposes allowed by law, they had to be refunded to the tenants.[6]

C. What the Deposits May Be Used For

State law says that the deposit may be used by the landlord "in only those amounts as may be reasonably necessary" to do the following four things *only:*[7]

1. to remedy defaults in payment of rent;

2. to repair damage to the premises caused by the tenant (except for "ordinary wear and tear");

3. to clean the premises, if necessary, when the tenant leaves.

4. if the rental agreement allows it, to pay for the tenant's failure to restore or replace personal property.

One of the biggest sources of tenant-landlord dispute centers around the often vague language in leases and rental agreements regarding cleaning. For example, some provisions merely say "Cleaning deposit: $200," and nothing else in the agreement says anything about cleaning. How clean must the tenant leave the premises when he vacates? As clean as they were when the tenant moved in? "Perfectly" clean? "Reasonably" clean? May the tenant merely sweep the floor, or must the floor also be washed and waxed? Must the freezer be defrosted and the oven be cleaned? The words "cleaning deposit" do not answer any of these questions; nor does the vague statutory language that allows the deposit to be used for such cleaning as is "reasonably necessary."[8]

The unhappy result of all this vagueness is that there is often an argument about cleaning when a tenant moves out. The best way to avoid such a fight is to spell out clearly what you both mean by cleaning right in the lease or rental agreement. You and your landlord don't have to use any fancy legal language—just state exactly what you both expect to be done.

If you are stuck with an agreement which has unclear language and you want to be sure to get your deposit back, we advise that you do two things:

• Clean the place thoroughly. This doesn't normally mean you have to shampoo rugs, dry clean the drapes, or wash the ceiling. A good thorough cleaning, including the refrigerator, stove, bathroom fixtures, etc. should be adequate.

• Carefully document your cleaning work through pictures, witnesses, etc. (See Section H, below.)

And according to state law, if an agreement is unclear and leads to a conflict, a court will likely hold responsible the party that wrote or supplied the

---

[4] CC § 1950.5(l).

[5] CC § 1950.5(b).

[6] *People v. Parkmerced Co.* (1988) 244 Cal.Rptr. 22, 198 Cal.App.3d 683.

[7] CC § 1950.5(e).

[8] CC § 1950.5(e).

agreement.[9] Therefore, if the landlord wrote the language or provided the lease form, the language will be construed against her. "Cleaning deposit," therefore, should be interpreted to mean that the tenant would not have to do any extraordinary cleaning.

Another area of tenant-landlord disputes over the return of deposits has to do with damages to the premises. Some landlords try to charge tenants for everything from a worn spot on a hall rug to faded paint to missing light bulbs. The tenant is not responsible for any damage or wear and tear done to the premises by an earlier tenant.[10]

D. Landlord's Duty to Return Deposit

Within two weeks after you move out—whether voluntarily, by abandonment or by eviction—the landlord must do one of two things:

1. return all of your deposit, or

2. give you personally or by first-class mail an "itemized statement" in writing saying why he is retaining part or all of the deposit, and return any remaining part to you.[11]

The bad faith retention of a security deposit, or any portion of it, may subject the landlord to $200 punitive damages in addition to any actual damages. In addition, for rental agreements entered into or renewed on or after January 1, 1987, the tenant is entitled to 2% monthly interest on the unreturned balance of the deposit.

At least one court has ruled that a landlord who doesn't give a tenant an itemized statement of charges also loses the right to withhold anything from the deposit.[12] So if the landlord has the right to keep part of the deposit (for example, because you broke something), but fails to furnish the itemized statement in two weeks, he loses the right to keep that part.

When One Tenant Moves Out Early: When two or more co-tenants rent under the same rental agreement or lease, the landlord does not have to return or account for any of the deposit until all of the tenants leave. If you move out early, however, your landlord might voluntarily work out an appropriate agreement and return your share of the security deposit. If not, you should try to work things out with the remaining tenants (or a new roommate, if there is one).

E. Effect of Sale of Premises on Security Deposits

A landlord who sells the building is supposed to do one of two things: return the deposit to the tenant, or transfer it to the new owner.[13]

It's been known to happen, however, that the landlord does neither and simply walks off with the money. The tenant often never knows of this. In fact, the tenant usually doesn't even know the building was sold until sometime later. But the new owner cannot require the tenant to replace any security deposit kept by the old landlord.[14]

The law requires the new owner to get all security deposits from the old landlord. Whether he does so or not, he becomes responsible for returning the

---

[9] CC § 1654. Also see CC § 1442, which says that any provision creating a forfeiture is interpreted most strongly against the person who would benefit from it.

[10] CC § 1950.5(e).

[11] CC § 1950.5(f).

[12] This ruling was made in an unpublished opinion by the Second Appellate District Court in 1990. The underlying case is *Granberry v. Islay Investments* in Santa Barbara County Superior Court. Although you may not rely on an unpublished opinion in court, this case illustrates some weight courts place on these itemized statements.

[13] CC § 1950.5(g).

[14] CC § 1950.5(h).

security deposit to the tenant at the end of the tenancy, just as if he were the old landlord.[15]

F. May the Landlord Increase the Security Deposit?

Tenants often ask if it's legal for a landlord to raise their security deposits after they move in. The answer is that it depends on the situation.

• If you have a fixed-term lease (for example, a lease for a year), the landlord may not raise the security deposit during that year unless the lease allows this.

• If you live in a city which has rent control, your ordinance probably restricts increases in security deposits while you remain a tenant of a particular landlord.

• If the security deposit and other fees already add up to twice the monthly rent (if the place is unfurnished) or three times the monthly rent (if the place is furnished), the security deposit may not be increased.

• If none of these three things applies, then the landlord may force you to pay more into the security deposit—if she does it right. To legally raise a deposit, she must give you at least 30 days' written notice of the increase and she must have it properly "served" on you. This means that she must try to have it handed to you at your residence or place of work; a notice served by mail alone is not legal unless you voluntarily go along with it.[16] See Chapter 4.E, regarding the law on how the landlord may change terms of a tenancy.

G. Avoiding Deposit Problems

Problems involving security deposits often arise like this:

• the tenant moves out,

• the landlord keeps all or part of the deposit on the ground of damage or lack of cleaning,

• the tenant says that the place was left in good condition.

If tenant and landlord can't reach a compromise, the tenant will probably sue the landlord for the money withheld, leaving it up to the judge to decide who is telling the truth. For both sides, this is a pretty risky, messy, and time-consuming way of handling things.

The best way to try to prevent this from happening is to arrange to meet with the landlord or manager after you've moved your belongings out and cleaned up, and just before you return the key. Tour the apartment together and check for any damage, dirt, etc. Assuming you made out a list of damage already there when you moved in (see Chapter 2.H), pull it out now and check it against the present condition of the place. Try to work out any disputes on the spot, and ask the landlord to give you the security deposit before you leave. Be reasonable, and be willing to compromise. It is better to give up a few dollars for some questionable damage than to have to sue for the whole deposit later.

If you cannot get the landlord to meet with you when you leave, then make your own tour. Bring at least one witness (a person who helped clean often makes a very convincing one) take some photos, and keep all your receipts for cleaning and repair materials, so you will be ready to prove your case if you later have to sue in small claims court in order to get your deposit back. (Remember, after you're out, it is usually too late to come back to take pictures.)

---

[15] CC § 1950.5(h).
[16] CC § 827; CCP § 1162.

H. If the Landlord Won't Return Your Deposit

Let's assume that two weeks have passed since the day you moved out and you have received neither your deposit nor an itemization of what it was used for. It's time to take action. We suggest the following step-by-step approach:

Step 1. Make a Formal Demand

If you feel that your landlord has improperly kept your deposit, the first thing you should do is ask for it, in writing. Here is a sample demand letter:

Sample Letter Demanding Security Deposit

```
1504 Oak Street #2
Cloverdale, CA
November 15, 19__

Smith Realty Co.
10 Jones Street
Cloverdale, CA

As you know, until October 31, 19__, I
resided in Apartment #4 at 1500 Acorn
Street and regularly paid my rent to
your office. When I moved out, I left
the unit cleaner than it was when I
moved in.

As of today, I have received neither my
$600 security deposit nor any accounting
from you for that money. Please be aware
that I know about my rights under
California Civil Code Sec. 1950.5, and
that if I do not receive my money within
the next week, I will regard the reten-
tion of these deposits as showing bad
faith on your part and shall sue you not
only for the $600 in deposits, but also
for the $200 punitive damages allowed by
Sec. 1950.5 of the Civil Code.

May I hear from you promptly.

Very truly yours,


Leon Hernandez
```

Step 2. Consider Compromise

If the landlord offers to meet you or offers a compromise settlement, try to meet him half way, but don't go overboard. After all, a law—requiring that your deposits be returned if you leave a rental property clean and undamaged—is there to protect you. You might suggest that the dispute be mediated.

Many cities, counties and nonprofit organizations such as San Francisco's Community Boards offer tenant-landlord mediation services designed to help you and the landlord arrive at a mutually satisfactory settlement.

Step 3. Sue In Small Claims Court

If the formal demand doesn't work and there is no reasonable prospect of compromise, you should consider suing the landlord. If you rent under a lease or rental agreement which provides for the landlord's attorney fees, then you, too, are entitled to attorney fees if you win your lawsuit.[17] In such situations, you might ask an attorney to handle the matter for you. Be sure you thoroughly discuss her fee arrangements ahead of time, however.

---

[17]CC § 1717.

In most cases, however, deposit disputes should probably be brought in small claims court, where lawyers aren't allowed. The rules governing small claims proceedings are contained in the Code of Civil Procedure, beginning with Section 116. The cost for filing papers and serving the landlord will be modest. The best source of information on how to prepare and present a small claims court case and collect money if you win is *Everybody's Guide to Small Claims Court*, Warner (Nolo Press), which devotes a chapter to tenant-landlord cases, including how to prepare and present a deposit case.

To sue your landlord in small claims court, go to your local courthouse (there may be more than one, so call first to make sure you go to the right place) and find the clerk of the small claims court. The clerk is required by law to help you fill out the papers necessary to sue your landlord. On the court form, you must state how much you are claiming the landlord owes you. This amount cannot exceed $5,000. You figure the amount you want to claim by asking for the total deposit, less anything that should reasonably be withheld for unpaid rent, damage, or dirty conditions. Add $200 in "punitive damages" (and interest at 2% per month on the uncollected balance starting from 14 days after you moved out) if you believe the landlord's failure to return your deposit (or reasonably itemize expenses) constitutes bad faith. If this adds up to more than $5,000, then you either have to waive the excess over $5,000 or else not use the small claims court. If you have to decide between suing in small claims court or in regular municipal court (for an amount more than $5,000), consider that you may not easily win the full $200 in punitive damages.

If your rental agreement is oral, you must file your lawsuit against the landlord within two years after the two weeks (for the landlord to return your deposit) run out.[18] However, whether the agreement is written or oral, we advise you not to wait, but to file promptly. Judges are just not very sympathetic to old disputes.

After you file the form with the small claims clerk, he will normally send a copy of it to the landlord by certified mail, with an order for her to appear in court for a trial on the suit at a certain date and time. To find out that date and time, ask the clerk. That date must be not less than 15 nor more than 40 days after the date of the order to appear, if the landlord lives within the county. If she doesn't live in the county, the date must be not less than 30 nor more than 70 days after the date of the order to appear.[19] If the landlord does not sign for the certified mail notice, you will have to arrange for a new court date and arrange to have the papers served by personal service.

Small claims court trials are very informal. No lawyers are present and there are no formal rules of evidence. There is no jury. When you come to court for your hearing, bring the file or envelope with your records. All papers or pictures that you believe help your case should be included, such as a copy of your lease or rental agreement (if any). Also bring with you all witnesses who have first-hand information about the facts in dispute, especially any people who helped in the cleanup. If you do not have any experience with a court, you can go down a day or two before and watch a few cases. You will see that it is a very simple procedure.

NOTE: If you cannot speak English and cannot find a volunteer interpreter or afford to hire an interpreter, the court will probably be able to arrange for a volunteer for you. Have a friend call the clerk about this in advance.

On the day your case is to be heard, get to the court a little early and check for your courtroom (referred to as a "department"). Tell the clerk or bailiff that you are present and sit down and wait until your case is called. When your turn comes, stand at the large table at the front of the room and

---

[18] CCP § 339.5.

[19] CCP § 116.330(c).

tell the judge clearly what is in dispute. Remember, the judge hears many cases every day, and she will not be particularly excited by yours. If you are long-winded, she may stop listening and start thinking about what she is going to eat for lunch.

Start your presentation with the problem (for example, "Lester Landlord has failed to return to me $500 in security deposits in the six weeks since I moved out of his house at 222 Spring Street") and then present the directly relevant facts which explain why you should win (for example, "The house was clean, undamaged, and my rent was paid in full"). Again, be brief and to the point—don't ramble. You may show pictures and documents to the judge. When you are done with your oral presentation, tell the judge you have witnesses who want to testify.

The landlord will also have a chance to tell his side. You can expect it to be very different from yours, but stay cool! When he is done, you may ask him questions if you feel that he has not told the truth or if he has left some things out. But often asking the landlord a lot of vague questions just gives him more opportunity to tell his side of the case. It is especially important not to argue with the landlord or any of his witnesses—just get your facts out, and back them up with convincing evidence.

In a case where a landlord has not returned your cleaning deposit after you have moved out and asked for it, you might present your case something like this:

"Good morning, Your Honor. My name is Susan Smit and I now live at 2330 Jones Street. From January 1, 19__ until July 1, 19__, I lived at 1500 Williams Street in a building owned by the Jefferson Realty Company. When I moved out, the Realty Company refused to refund my $700 cleaning deposit even though I left the place spotless. I carefully cleaned the rugs, washed and waxed the kitchen and bathroom floors, washed the inside of the cupboards and washed the windows. Your Honor, I want to show you some pictures that were taken of my apartment the day I moved out. (*If you completed a checklist of the condition of the premises, you will want to show it to the judge at this time.*) These were taken by Mrs. Edna Jackson, who is here today and will testify. Your Honor, I don't have much else to say, except that in addition to the amount of my deposit, I am asking for the full $200 in punitive damages allowed by law. I am entitled to these damages because I don't believe the landlord had any reason at all to withhold my deposits."

If you have any evidence that the landlord commonly withholds deposits with no good reason, be sure to introduce it. You would then ask your witness to testify.

In most courts, your witnesses do not take the witness stand, but remain at the table in front of the judge and simply explain what they know about the dispute. Typical testimony might go like this:

"Good morning, Your Honor. My name is Mrs. Edna Jackson and I live at 1498 Williams Street. On July 1, 19__ when the plaintiff moved out, I helped her move and clean up. The place was very clean when we finished. And just to show how clean it was, I took the pictures that you were just shown. I'm sure those are the pictures I took because I signed and dated them on the back after they were developed."

Punitive Damages Note: If the landlord acts in "bad faith" and does not return the money or properly account for any part that he keeps, he may be liable for up to $200 in punitive damages over and beyond the amount of the deposits unjustly retained. As noted, small claims courts may award these punitive damages.[20] However, many tenants who have been through small claims court have told us that an award of all, or part, of the punitive damage amount is extremely rare because judges tend to be biased in favor of landlords. How can you counter this bias where it exists? The best way to do it is to thoroughly prepare your case and document that the landlord's failure to return your deposits within 14 days was not only a mistake, but was without any reasonable basis in fact. In addition, bad faith might also

---

[20]CC § 1950.5(m).

be shown by proof that the landlord has a practice of failing to return security deposits. This can often be done with the assistance of your local tenants' organization.

If you win in small claims court and need help collecting the money from the landlord, see *Collect Your Court Judgment*, Scott, Elias and Goldoftas (Nolo Press).

Step 4. Call the District Attorney

If your landlord has a habit of refusing to return security deposits to tenants, your local district attorney might bring a criminal action against him for fines and an injunction requiring the landlord to return the deposit.[21]

I. Rent Withholding as a Way to Get Deposits Back In Advance

Suppose, after you move in, you learn from other tenants that your landlord has a tendency to cheat tenants out of their security deposits—perhaps by inventing or exaggerating a need for repairs or cleaning after they move out. When you decide to leave, you fear the same sort of trouble, and you'd rather not deal with the risk and hassle of suing the landlord in small claims court.

There is a way to handle this problem that many tenants use: a month or two before you leave, tell the landlord that you are not making your usual rent payment, and she should keep your deposit and apply it to the rent.

Your letter might look like this:

Sample Letter Requesting Landlord to Apply Deposit to Last Month's Rent

```
1500 Acorn Street #4
Cloverdale, CA
September 15, 19__

Smith Realty Co.
10 Jones Street
Cloverdale, CA

Dear Sirs:

As you know, I occupy Apartment #4 at
1500 Acorn Street and regularly pay
rent to your office once a month.

Please take note that this is a formal
written notice of my intention to
vacate Apartment #4 on October 31,
19__.

In speaking to other tenants in this
area, I have learned that from time to
time the return of cleaning deposits
has been the subject of dispute
between you and your tenants.
Accordingly, I have decided on the
following course of action: Instead of
sending you the normal $600 rent pay-
ment today, I am sending you instead
$200 and ask that you apply the $400
cleaning deposit to my last month's
rent.

I will leave the apartment spotless
and undamaged so that you will suffer
no damage whatsoever. If you should
doubt this or want to discuss the
matter further, please give me a call
and come over. I think that you will
be satisfied that I am dealing with
you honestly and in good faith and
that the apartment, which is clean and
in perfect repair now, will be in the
same condition when I leave.

Very truly yours,


_____
Leon Hernandez
```

---

[21] *People v. Sangiacomo* (1982) 129 Cal.App.3d 364.

Technically, this type of "rent withholding" is not legal. You have no legal right to compel the landlord to apply your deposit to unpaid rent, and if you do not pay your rent on time, he can serve you with a "three-day notice" (ordering you to pay the rent or get out, in three days). If you do not comply with such a notice, however, it is very unlikely that the landlord will follow it up with a suit to evict you for non-payment of rent. (He cannot simply lock you out.) It would probably take him at least a few weeks to bring his case to trial, and he knows you plan to leave soon anyway.

Nevertheless, we do not recommend that you use this rent withholding device against a landlord unless you are pretty sure that she is the type that cheats on security deposits. The fair landlord has a legitimate right and need to get the rent on time and to keep the security deposit until she is sure that the tenant has left the place in good shape.

J. Interest on Security Deposits

As a matter of fairness, the landlord should pay you interest on your security deposit. It is your money—not his—and he is merely holding it for you. He should put it into some type of interest-bearing account and pay the interest to you.

None of the form leases and rental agreements customarily used by landlords require them to pay interest on your security deposit. In fact, the only forms we know of which require this are the model lease and model rental agreement in the Appendix at the back of this book.

A few local rent ordinances, including those of Berkeley, Cotati, East Palo Alto, Hayward, Los Angeles, San Francisco, Santa Monica and Santa Cruz, require payment of interest on security deposits. Most of these are rent control cities. (See Chapter 4 for details on these local ordinances.)

No state law clearly says that landlords must pay interest on security deposits. But the Legislature has enacted statutes imposing such obligations on trustees—people who hold money for someone else. And the courts have held that a landlord acts as a trustee when she holds a tenant's security deposit, and the landlord cannot put it to her own use.[22] A trustee must invest trust funds and pay any interest or profits over to the owner of the money.[23] Therefore, it appears to us that the law presently requires landlords to pay interest on security deposits. Unfortunately, the only court to rule on this question disagreed, concluding that landlords do not have to pay interest on deposits unless the rental agreement or local law says they do. The court based its decision on the fact that the legislature has repeatedly refused to pass a law requiring landlords to pay interest on deposits.[24]

Note: As discussed in Section H, Step 3, a landlord who illegally withholds all or part of your deposit after you leave is liable for interest on the withheld portion at the rate of 2% per month.[25]

K. Last Month's Rent

Many landlords require some payment for "last month's rent." The legal effect of such a requirement should depend largely upon the exact language used in the lease or rental agreement.

If the lease or rental agreement says "security for last month's rent," or has a heading called "Security" and then lists "last month's rent" as one of the items on the list, then you have not actually paid the last month's rent, but just provided security for it. So, if the landlord legally raises the rent before you move out, you must pay the difference between the final rent and your security for last month's rent. For

---

[22] *Ingram v. Pantages* (1927) 86 Cal.App. 41; *City Investment Co. v. Pringle* (1925) 73 Cal.App. 782, 788-789. See also Legislative Counsel Opinion #4187 (3/3/75, to Senator Petris).
[23] Prodate Code §§ 16040, 16042, 16200, 16220, 16223.
[24] *Korens v. R.W. Zukin Corp.* (1989) 261 Cal.Rptr. 137.
[25] CC § 1950.5(k).

example, suppose when you moved in the monthly rent was $400, and the rental agreement said, "Security: ...last month's rent: $400." After two years, the rent has been raised to $500, and the tenant leaves. The tenant owes the landlord the $100 difference for the last month's rent.

If, however, the lease or rental agreement does not say that the payment is for security, but simply says "last month's rent: $400," then in our opinion, the tenant has paid the last month's rent—well in advance of the last month. This money is not a security payment, and the landlord can do what he likes with it. He does not hold it as a trustee for the tenant. However, a rent increase later on will not affect the amount of the last month's rent, which the tenant has already paid. So, in the above example, the tenant would not owe an additional $100 to the landlord.

Despite this common sense approach, some judges are inclined to rule that the tenant must pay the extra $100. If the rental agreement is unclear as to whether this payment is intended as security, point out to the judge that since the landlord provided the form agreement, it should be interpreted against him.[26]

---

[26] CC § 1654.

chapter 11

Evictions

A.	Illegal Self-Help Evictions	11 / 3
	1. Utility Cut-Offs	11 / 3
	2. Lock-Outs	11 / 4
B.	Illegal Retaliatory Evictions	11 / 4
C.	Overview of Eviction Procedure	11 / 5
	1. The Notice to Quit	11 / 5
	2. The Summons and Complaint	11 / 5
	3. Your Response	11 / 6
	4. Trial	11 / 6
	5. Actual Eviction	11 / 6
	6. Timeline for Eviction	11 / 6
D.	Termination of Tenancy Notices	11 / 8
	1. Notice to End a Fixed-Term Lease	11 / 8
	2. The Three-Day Notice Because of a Tenant's Violation	11 / 8
	3. The 30-Day Notice to Terminate a Month-to-Month Tenancy	11 / 10
E.	Your Options After a Three-Day or 30-Day Notice Is Served	11 / 12
F.	The Eviction Lawsuit	11 / 13
	1. The Complaint and Summons	11 / 13
	2. Responding to the Summons	11 / 13
	3. The Motion to Quash	11 / 14
	4. The Demurrer	11 / 22
	5. The Answer	11 / 28
	6. Setting Aside a Default Judgment	11 / 35
	7. Discovery: Learning About the Landlord's Case	11 / 36
	8. Negotiating a Settlement	11 / 39
	9. Summary Judgment	11 / 43
	10. The Trial	11 / 43
	11. The Judgment	11 / 45

G. Stopping an Eviction	11 / 46
H. Postponing an Eviction	11 / 48
I. Appeal From an Eviction	11 / 50
J. After the Lawsuit—Eviction by the Sheriff	11 / 50

Many tenants become terrified when they receive a Three-Day Notice to Pay Rent or Quit from the landlord. They believe that if they do not pay or get out in three days, they will be thrown out onto the street on the fourth day. The law simply does not allow this. The landlord must first file a lawsuit in court and notify you of it so that you have an opportunity to defend yourself. If you are going to fight the eviction, you must respond quickly—within five to 15 days from the time you are notified of the lawsuit, depending on the circumstances (see Section F)—or risk losing the suit.

Even if you lose the lawsuit, the court must still issue an order authorizing a law enforcement officer to remove you from the premises. All of this takes time, often more than a month or two, depending on whether you contest the eviction or let the law take its course. The chart in Section C.6 (Eviction Timeline With 30-Day Notice) will give you an idea of how long different types of eviction cases normally take.

This chapter will help you go to court and defend yourself if you choose to do so. It will also help you understand what your lawyer is doing, if you choose to hire one.

The material set out here is by no means a complete summary of every defense or litigation device available to a tenant. To give you that would make this volume look like a metropolitan phone book. Instead, we concentrate on the basic and most commonly-used tools suitable for use in defending against most straightforward eviction proceedings.

You can supplement this information by consulting the *California Eviction Defense Manual*, and the *California Residential Landlord-Tenant Practice Book*, both of which are published by Continuing Education of the Bar (CEB) in Berkeley, California. The *California Eviction Defense Manual* is the source most often used by lawyers when defending unlawful detainer cases. Unlike many law books, it is not difficult to use. You should be able to find them in your county law library. Be sure you consult the latest *Supplements* to these books, which contain the most recent cases and statutes.

A. Illegal Self-Help Evictions

The most basic thing a tenant should know is that California law clearly states that if a landlord wishes to evict a tenant, she must first go to court, giving the tenant prior notice of the court proceedings. She cannot legally take the law into her own hands by locking the tenant out, taking the tenant's belongings, removing doors and windows, cutting off the utilities or harassing the tenant in any other way.

1. Utility Cut-Offs

Any landlord who causes any utility service (including water, heat, light, electricity, gas, telephone, elevator or refrigeration) to be cut off with intent to terminate a tenant's occupancy is liable to the tenant for certain damages.[1] This law applies whether the utilities are paid for by the landlord or the tenant, and whether the landlord cuts off the utilities directly or indirectly—for example, by not paying the utility bill.

The tenant may sue the landlord and recover the following amounts:

• actual (out-of-pocket) losses including such things as meat spoiling in the refrigerator after the electricity is turned off or motel bills if the tenant has to find a temporary place to live because the utilities were turned off;

• punitive damages of up to $100 for each day or part thereof that a utility was turned off (but not less than $250 in punitive damages for each separate violation);

• a reasonable attorney fee;

---

[1] CC § 789.3.

- a court order compelling the landlord to turn on the utilities.

You can bring your suit in small claims court (for up to $5,000), or retain a lawyer to sue for you in municipal court (for up to $25,000) or superior court (over $25,000).

Tenants can also sue for mental anguish if the landlord's acts were especially outrageous. In 1988, a jury awarded 23 tenants of a San Francisco residential hotel $1.48 million from their landlord. The landlord had cut off water, entered tenants' rooms without notice, and threatened the tenants, most of whom were elderly or disabled.[2]

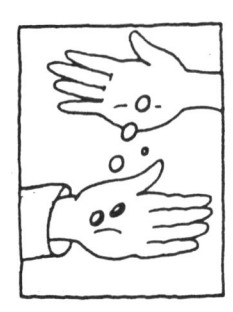

2. Lock-Outs

If the landlord locks you out, removes outside doors or windows, or removes your personal property from your home with the intention of terminating your tenancy, he is in violation of state law.[3] The damages are the same as set out above for utility cut-offs. You can collect damages in small claims court, but if you want quick action to get back into your home, see a lawyer, because the statute allows you to collect attorney fees. The lawyer might also sue the landlord for "forcible entry and detainer."[4]

You might also call the police or district attorney, because these acts are crimes (forcible entry, malicious mischief and unauthorized entry). Even if the police won't arrest the landlord, they might persuade him to let you in. Ask the police to write a report on the incident; it might help you in a later lawsuit against the landlord.

Tenants who live in residential hotels (apartment buildings that are called hotels) are also protected against lock-outs.[5]

B. Illegal Retaliatory Evictions

It is illegal for a landlord to retaliate against a tenant "for having exercised any right under the law." Retaliation includes reducing services, giving a 30-day rent increase or termination notice, or even threatening to do so. In recent years, the courts have prevented evictions brought to punish tenants who:

- complain to health authorities or exercise statutory rights, such as the right to repair and deduct (see Chapter 7);

- exercise rights under rent control ordinances (see Chapter 4);

- organize rent strikes or other tenant protests (see Chapter 12); or

- exercise any other statutory or constitutional right, such as the right to be free of discriminatory treatment based on factors such as race or religion (see Chapter 5) and the right to privacy (see Chapter 6).

Retaliation for Complaints to Government Agencies: If a tenant whose rent is paid up complains to a government agency about defects in the premises, and if the landlord subsequently raises rent, decreases services or evicts the tenant within 180 days, retaliation is presumed. If the tenant goes to court, the landlord must prove that the action was not retaliatory [CC § 1942.5(a)]. After 180 days, the tenant can still sue, but retaliation is no longer presumed.

---

[2] The trial judge had tripled the amount based on the San Francisco rent control law. The landlord appealed the verdict, however, and the appellate court ruled that the San Francisco rent control ordinance does not allow tripling awards for mental anguish. *Balmoral Hotel Tenants Association v. Lee* (1990) 226 Cal.App.3d 686, 276 Cal.Rptr. 640.

[3] CC § 789.3.

[4] CCP § 1159; *Jordan v. Talbot* (1961) 55 Cal.2d 597.

[5] CCP § 1159; CC § 1940.

Aside from limitations in any applicable rent-control ordinance, a landlord can legally raise the rent or terminate the tenancy at any time, if there is a legitimate non-retaliatory reason. But if challenged, the landlord will have to prove that his actions were not retaliatory.

Retaliation for Other Acts: If the tenant asserts any other legal right—that is, other than complaining to a government agency about defects in the premises—the tenant must prove retaliation is the motive for any rent increase, decrease in services or eviction which follows. Under both statutory and common law, the tenant may raise the defense of retaliation or sue the landlord for retaliatory eviction at any time, and it doesn't matter whether or not the tenant is paid up in rent.[6] (Even so, as time goes on, it becomes harder for the tenant to establish that the landlord still has a retaliatory motive.)

A landlord's conduct can be proof of his motive. In deciding whether a landlord acted with a retaliatory motive, judges look at such things as:

• how soon the landlord raised the rent or terminated the tenancy after the tenant exercised a legal right;

• how the landlord treated the complaining tenant as compared to other tenants;

• whether the landlord appears to have had a legitimate reason for the actions.

C. Overview of Eviction Procedure

The rest of this chapter, which deals with how you can defend against a formal unlawful detainer (eviction) procedure, is pretty technical and complicated. For this reason, we believe it will help you to carefully read this overview of the eviction process first. In addition, if you live in a rent control city listed in Chapter 4 that requires "just cause" for eviction, it is essential that you get a copy of your local ordinance and regulations from your rent control board and study it. Although we will remind you of the many special rights residents in cities covered by rent control enjoy when it comes to defending against eviction, it is impossible for us to deal with each city's ordinance in detail.

1. The Notice to Quit

A landlord who wants to get you out must properly deliver a termination notice to you. (The method of delivery is required by law and called "service.") The landlord must then wait until the notice period expires before filing an eviction lawsuit (unless you have a fixed-term lease that has expired, in which case no notice is required unless the lease itself provides for it).

For an eviction based on an alleged breach of your lease or rental agreement, the notice may give you three days to perform—for example, to pay the rent or get rid of the dog. To terminate a month-to-month tenancy, the notice need not state a reason but must give you 30 days to vacate, unless you live in an area that requires a just cause for eviction, in which case the just cause must also be stated. Some local rent control ordinances also require landlords to include other things—for example, the phone number of the Rent Board—in the notice. Section D describes the specific notice requirements.

2. The Summons and Complaint

If you have not met the landlord's demand when the notice period runs out, he may file a "Complaint" against you in court. Filing a Complaint begins a lawsuit. The landlord will then have a copy of the Complaint served on you, together with another document called a Summons. The Summons will tell you to respond to the court in writing, usually within five days. Section F provides details.

---

[6] CC § 1942.5(c). Also, see *Glaser v. Meyers* (1982) 137 Cal.App.3d 770.

3. Your Response

If you don't respond in writing to the landlord's lawsuit within the time allowed, the landlord may ask the court for a default judgment against you. That means you lose without a trial. (See Section J for details on eviction by the sheriff.)

If you choose to respond, you have several options:

• If the Summons was not properly served on you, or the wrong court is named, or for certain other technical reasons, file a Motion to Quash Service of Summons (see Section F.3);

• If the Complaint is not in proper technical form or does not properly allege the landlord's right to evict you, file a Demurrer (see Section F.4); or

• If you want to deny statements in the Complaint or allege new facts showing why you should win, file an Answer (see Section F.5).

These responses (called "responsive pleadings") are not mutually exclusive. So your response may be a Motion to Quash Service of Summons, then a Demurrer, and then an Answer, depending on the court's rulings. Or, you may simply file an Answer as your response. Section F will help you choose the appropriate response.

4. Trial

After your Answer is filed, the case will either be decided summarily by a judge or will go to trial. The trial will be heard by a judge (assuming the case isn't settled first), unless either side demands a jury. (See Section F.10.)

5. Actual Eviction

If you lose the trial, the judge may, in rare circumstances, allow you to stay on if you pay everything you owe the landlord (see Section G). Otherwise, the landlord will get a "Writ of Possession," which the sheriff (or marshal or constable) will serve on you. This will give you five days to leave. If you are not out on the fifth day, the sheriff will physically throw you out, unless a court grants a temporary stay of the eviction to give you a few extra days to move. (See Sections H and J.)

You may also appeal the trial court's ruling, on the theory that the court made some error of law. (Section I shows you how to do this.) Your eviction will be delayed (stayed) during the appeal if you can show the judge that a delay will cause hardship to yourself but won't irreparably harm the landlord. During any delay, you will have to pay reasonable rent.

Stopping an Eviction by Filing for Bankruptcy: If a tenant files for bankruptcy, the landlord must stop all attempts to evict. The landlord, however, can almost always go to the bankruptcy court and get permission to proceed again within a week or two.

Some non-lawyer eviction defense organizations (primarily in the Los Angeles area) routinely help tenants file for bankruptcy as a means of buying a little more time to find new premises. While the extra time may seem like a minor miracle at the time, we recommend against filing for bankruptcy solely to stave off an eviction. It can hurt your credit rating and may cause you to lose property you wanted to hang on to. However, if other reasons justify filing for bankruptcy, stopping an eviction temporarily may be a beneficial side effect. For more information, see *How to File for Bankruptcy,* by Elias, Renauer and Leonard (Nolo Press).

6. Timeline for Eviction

How long does the entire eviction process take? Of course, it varies from case to case. Every lawyer who has defended a lot of eviction cases has a story about how he or she brilliantly created a paper blizzard and staved off an eviction for many months. On the other hand, an eviction can occur in a blindingly short period of time if the landlord does everything right and you do nothing.

Nevertheless, the time estimates we set out here (two to three months) should prove broadly accurate, assuming the following facts:

- You have received a 30-day notice;
- The Summons and Complaint are personally served on you;
- You contest the action by filing written responses with the court;
- All papers (after the Summons and Complaint) are served by mail where this is permitted (the usual practice); and
- The landlord (or her attorney) stays on top of her case and files all papers as fast as possible.

Eviction may occur earlier if the landlord:

- Personally serves all papers on you instead of mailing them; or
- Wins a "summary judgment" (see Section F, Step 9) and doesn't have to go to trial.

The timeline will be longer if the landlord lets time slip by between any of the procedural steps necessary to move an eviction case along.

It is rare that a landlord's case marches along without one snag or another, many of them caused either by the landlord's attorney's schedule, by courthouse delays or by the sheriff's backload of papers to serve. Practically speaking, if you added two (and sometimes as many as four) weeks to the timeline, you would have a better picture of how long the typical contested eviction takes. On the other hand, if you fail to take one of the steps indicated in the timeline, or you lose on your Motion to Quash or Demurrer, you should deduct the appropriate number of days.

Because the primary elements of a basic eviction suit are discussed in detail later on in this chapter, we suggest you look at the timeline for a general idea now, and then review it after you have had more time to study the actual process.

Eviction Timeline with 30-Day Notice

MINIMUM RESPONSE TIME		ACTION			MAXIMUM RESPONSE TIME
30 days		30-Day Notice			30 days
5 days		Date Complaint Is Served			5 days
		Tenant's First Response			
0 days	no?	Motion to Quash	yes?		7 days
0 days	no?	Demurrer	yes?	win?	10 days
				lose?	5 days
20 days		Answer			20 days
5 days		Trial			10 days
60 days TOTAL		ACTUAL EVICTION			102-107 days TOTAL

Note: If you receive a Three-Day Notice, this timeline will range from 33 days to 75-80 days.

D. Termination of Tenancy Notices

Now that you have an overview of the eviction process, it's time to deal with the specifics. We start with the paper the landlord uses to notify you that your tenancy is being terminated. This will be either a three-day or 30-day notice and is commonly referred to as a "Notice to Quit."

One very important principle applies to all notice requirements in eviction cases: Because the landlord is trying to evict you from your home, and because the law gives the landlord special privileges in eviction cases (a quicker lawsuit), the landlord must *strictly comply* with all of the law's notice requirements.[7] If the landlord makes even a small mistake in a required notice, and/or you don't receive the notice, the eviction itself might be invalid and the landlord may have to start the process over.

1. Notice to End a Fixed-Term Lease

When a fixed-term lease expires, you are supposed to move out right away, unless your city has a rent control ordinance that requires the landlord to have just cause to evict you. If you don't move, the landlord may file an eviction lawsuit immediately, without first serving any notice on you. (See Section D.3, below regarding expiration of a fixed-term lease, and Chapter 4 for details on rent control.)

If you live in a city with a rent control ordinance requiring just cause for eviction, expiration of the lease does not by itself justify an eviction. You are entitled to remain unless you are evicted for one of the reasons listed in the rent control ordinance.

If the landlord wants to evict you during the term of your lease for your breach of the lease (such as nonpayment of rent), then she will have to serve a notice on you before suing to evict. The notice is normally a three-day notice.

2. The Three-Day Notice Because of a Tenant's Violation

The landlord can serve you with a three-day notice if you or another tenant have violated the terms of your lease or rental agreement.

a. Kinds of Three-Day Notices

There are basically three types of three-day notices.

Three-Day Notice to Pay Rent or Quit: If you fail to pay your rent on time, the landlord must serve a three-day notice on you before he may sue to evict you on that ground. The notice must tell you to pay the rent or move in three days. The notice must state the amount of rent you must pay to avoid eviction, and this amount may not be more than what you actually owe in rent. (The three-day notice can ask for less than what you owe, but not more.) It must not, for example, include late charges, check-bounce or other fees of any kind, or interest or utility charges. The landlord can deduct these amounts from the security deposit or sue for them in small claims court.

Some judges also require landlords to include the dates for which the rent is due. Because rent is almost always due at the beginning of a month (or other rent period), the landlord is entitled to request the total rent for the period for which rent is late, less any partial payments you have made. Thus, if your $350 rent is due on the first of the month, the landlord has the right to ask you in a three-day notice for the entire $350 on the second day of the month.[8]

If you pay before the end of the three days, the notice is cancelled, and you don't have to leave.[9] After three days, the landlord may refuse your money and proceed with the eviction. If he accepts the rent after the three-day period, however, he waives his right to evict for the late payment.[10]

---

[7] *Kwok v. Bergren* (1982) 130 Cal.App.3d 596, 599.

[8] CCP § 1161(2); *Werner v. Sargeant* (1953) 121 Cal.App.2d 833.
[9] CCP § 1161(3).
[10] *EDC Associates Ltd. v. Gutierrez* (1984) 153 Cal. App.3d 169.

Three-Day Notice to Perform Covenant (Correct Violation) or Quit: If you are accused of violating some other provision of your lease or rental agreement, the three-day notice must tell you to stop the conduct if it's curable. For example, suppose the landlord believes that you have a dog, in violation of a lease provision which prohibits pets. The notice must say in effect, "Either get rid of the dog in three days *or* move out in three days." In all cases, the violation of the lease or rental agreement must be substantial, not minor, in order to justify evicting you from your home.[11]

Unconditional Three-Day Notice to Quit: A landlord can serve you with a three-day notice to vacate if she believes that you are committing "waste" (that is, wrecking the place) creating a "nuisance" on the premises (for example, dumping garbage in the backyard or seriously and repeatedly disturbing other tenants or neighbors) or using it for an illegal purpose (such as to sell illegal drugs). In this situation, however, the notice need not give you the alternative of stopping your misbehavior.[12] The landlord can also give you this kind of three-day notice if you sublet the premises, contrary to a lease or rental agreement provision prohibiting sublets.

b. How a Three-Day Notice Must Be Served on You

To be effective, the three-day notice must be properly served on you.[13] First, the landlord (or his agent) must try to find you and hand it to you. If he tries to find you at home and at work but can't, he may then hand it to "a person of suitable age and discretion" at your home or work and also mail a copy to you. If he can't find someone at your home or work to leave it with, then—and only then—may he serve it on you by the "nail and mail" method. This involves posting a copy in a conspicuous place on your premises, such as the front door, and mailing another to you.[14]

Landlords are often sloppy about following these procedures. It is common, for example, for a landlord to make one attempt to find the tenant at home, no attempt to find the tenant at work, and then simply nail the notice to the tenant's door and mail a copy. This is not proper service.

Sloppy landlords often fall back on a legal doctrine that states that if the tenant actually receives the notice, it doesn't matter that it wasn't served properly. The theory is that actual receipt of the notice "cures" any defect in service. If the case later goes to court, the landlord can prove you received the notice by calling you to the witness stand and asking you. For this reason, it is usually unwise for a tenant who actually received the notice to rely on a landlord's faulty service of notice as a defense.

c. Counting the Three Days After Service

You have three full days to comply with the demands in a three-day notice. If you do comply, then the landlord may not sue to evict you—unless it's an Unconditional Three-Day Notice to Quit, where your compliance or change in behavior won't make a difference.

---

[11]*McNeece v. Wood* (1928) 204 Cal. 280, 285. CCP § 1161(3).
[12]CCP § 1161(4).
[13]If there is more than one tenant, it is legally sufficient for a landlord to serve just one. *University of Southern California v. Weiss* (1962) 208 Cal.App.2d 759, 769, 25 Cal.Rptr. 475.
[14]CCP § 1162.

If you receive an unconditional notice or don't comply with a three-day notice to pay rent or correct some other violation, the landlord may file his lawsuit on the fourth day (or later).

The date of service is the date you were handed the notice, if you were personally served. If the landlord left the notice with someone else at your home (or office) or posted a copy on the premises and mailed another copy, the date of service is the date the landlord took that action. It doesn't matter that you didn't actually receive the notice until later.[15]

To count the three days, do the following:

• Ignore the date of service and start counting on the next day;

• Count three days;

• If the third day falls on a Saturday, Sunday or holiday, ignore that day and move on to the next business day.

EXAMPLE 1
You are served with a three-day notice on Wednesday. To count the three days, do not count Wednesday; begin with Thursday. This makes Saturday the third day. But Saturday is a holiday, and so is Sunday. So the third day is Monday. Therefore, you have until the end of Monday to comply. If the landlord files his eviction lawsuit before Tuesday, it should be thrown out of court if you raise the issue. (You would do this by filing a Demurrer—see Section F.4.)

EXAMPLE 2
You're served on Friday. Saturday is the first day, Sunday is the second day, and Monday is the third day. Neither of the weekend days extends the three-day period.

d. After the Three Days

If the three-day notice does not say that your tenancy will be "forfeited" if you don't pay the rent or correct a violation in three days, then you may avoid eviction by offering to pay the rent or comply with your rental agreement after the three days runs out—so long as you do so before the landlord files an eviction lawsuit.[16] (Obviously, you won't have this choice with unconditional notices.)

EXAMPLE
On May 5, the landlord serves you with a three-day notice to pay $300 rent or vacate. It does not say anything about your tenancy being "forfeited" if you fail to comply with the notice. The three days run out on May 8. On May 10, you try to give the $300 to the landlord, but she returns it. On May 15, she files a lawsuit to evict you. If you can convince the judge (in your "Answer"—see Section F.5) that you tried to pay the rent on the 10th, you should win the case.

3. The 30-Day Notice to Terminate a Month-to-Month Tenancy

To terminate a month-to-month tenancy (for reasons other than non-payment of rent or breach of a rental agreement term), the landlord must normally serve you with a notice that simply says that you are to get out in 30 days (or more). The notice need not state why the landlord wants you out, unless a rent control ordinance requires that the notice state just cause to evict (discussed below), or you live in "Section 8" housing and your rent is partially paid by the federal government.

A 30-day notice is not required if the landlord does not want to renew a tenant's lease; the tenant is entitled to stay until the end of the lease term, but no longer. However, many landlords use a 30-day notice near the end of a lease term as a practical way to inform the tenant that the lease will not be renewed.

You may also get a 30-day notice from a bank if your landlord's mortgage has been foreclosed upon and the lender who has obtained title to the property

---

[15]*Walters v. Meyers* (1990) 226 Cal. App. 3d.Supp 15, 277 Cal. Rptr. 316.

[16]*Briggs v. Electronic Memories & Magnetics Corp.* (1975) 53 Cal.App.3d 900, 905.

wants you out in order to sell it.[17] The bank (or other buyer) may do this even in the middle of a fixed-term lease.

a. How a 30-Day Notice Must Be Served on You

Here are some key points about 30-day notices:

• A 30-day notice may be served on any day of the month. It need not be served on the first day, the "rent day," or any other day—unless the rental agreement requires it to be served on a certain day.

• It may be served in the same manner as the three-day notice (see above), *or* by certified or registered mail.[18]

• When you count the 30 days, if the 30th day falls on a Saturday, Sunday or holiday, you have all day Monday to move if you want it.

EXAMPLE

You have a month-to-month tenancy and pay rent on the first. If your landlord serves you with a 30-day notice on July 15, you are supposed to vacate on August 15. But if it falls on a weekend or holiday, the next business day is "moving day."

b. Withdrawal of a 30-Day Notice

If the landlord accepts rent covering a period beyond the 30 days, he has probably legally withdrawn the notice by implication.[19]

EXAMPLE

The landlord serves you with a 30-day notice on June 10, requiring you to move on July 10. Your rent is $500 a month, due on the first. On July 1, you pay the usual $500 rent. If the landlord accepts it, he has accepted rent for the whole month of July, including the part beyond July 10. By doing so, he has probably impliedly withdrawn the notice.

c. The 30-Day Notice in Rent Control Cities With Just Cause Requirements

Many local rent control ordinances (including those of Los Angeles, San Francisco, Berkeley and Santa Monica) limit the landlord's right to evict. (See Chapter 4 for more on rent control.) These ordinances require the landlord to have a good faith "just cause" or "good cause" reason to evict, and they specify a list of acceptable reasons. It does not matter whether the tenant has a month-to-month tenancy or had a fixed-term lease that has expired.

Typically, the causes that these ordinances consider "just" fall into three classes:

• Wrongdoing by the tenant—such as nonpayment of rent or making a nuisance of yourself. As discussed in Section D.2, above, a three-day notice is typically used in this situation. Under the ordinances of some cities, including Berkeley, Santa Monica, Los Angeles and San Francisco, the landlord must first notify the tenant of certain types of lease or rental agreement violations—for example, moving in too many people, damaging the premises, or making too much noise—and give her a chance to correct it before serving the 30-day notice. In other types of situations—such as using the premises to sell illegal drugs—the notice need not give the tenant the alternative of stopping her misbehavior.

• Landlord needs to make major repairs or do large-scale remodeling on the premises. Under the terms of many ordinances, however, a tenant must be allowed the right to move back in, after the remodeling is completed, at the original rent plus an extra "passthrough" increase that allows the landlord to recover part of the cost of the improvements.

• Convenience of the landlord, such as to move in a parent or other family member. Most just cause ordinances allow a landlord to evict so she can move in herself or have certain close relatives move in, if the landlord has no other comparable vacant units.[20] Some landlords have abused this provision

---

[17] In a rent control area, the 30-day notice may not be used for this purpose unless the rent control ordinance lists it as one of the "just causes" for eviction. *Gross v. Superior Court* (1985) 171 Cal.App.3d 265.

[18] CC § 1946.

[19] *Highland Plastics, Inc. v. Enders* (1980) 109 Cal.App.3d Supp. 1.

[20] Cities define differently which relatives are eligible to evict a tenant. All include parents and children of the landlord, and some

by falsely telling the tenant that the landlord or a relative is going to move in, and later—after the tenant moves out—simply renting the place out at a higher rent.[21]

If this is your situation, or your landlord has similarly acted in bad faith—for example, he evicted you because he needed to make major repairs, but never made the repairs—you might have a good reason to contest the eviction. See discussion of affirmative defenses in Section F.5, Item 4.

E. Your Options After a Three-Day or 30-Day Notice Is Served

If you get a three-day or 30-day notice, sit down and think things over. Don't worry—you won't be thrown out on the fourth or 31st day. As we mentioned, the landlord must first sue to evict you, and you must be notified of the lawsuit. Only if you lose the lawsuit can you be evicted, and then only by the sheriff. At a minimum, it will take the landlord over a month to finish his lawsuit (much longer if you contest it) and if he wins, get the sheriff to give you an eviction order.

You have several choices:

• Comply with the notice—for example, pay the rent, get rid of the dog or simply move out. If the landlord is in the right and you are able to comply, this may be the best course. In the majority of eviction cases (except possibly in some rent control areas), the tenant ultimately ends up moving.

• Negotiate a solution with the landlord, either by yourself, through a neighborhood or city-sponsored mediation program, or through a lawyer. (See Chapter 1.G for a discussion of mediation services.) It will cost the landlord time and money if she has to file an eviction lawsuit, so she has some incentive to work out a fair deal with you.

• Let her file her eviction lawsuit—and then fight like hell to win. The discussion in this chapter should help you decide your chance of winning. You may also want to get some advice from a tenants' organization or an experienced tenants' lawyer. (See Chapters 1.D and 12.B for information on tenants' rights groups and how to find and use a lawyer.)

If you decide to fight the eviction, you can represent yourself or hire a lawyer. If your lease or rental agreement requires the loser to pay the winner's attorney fees—and your chances of winning look pretty good—you may well want to do the latter.

If you decide to represent yourself, prepare carefully. The key is to do your homework—both on the law and on the facts. Get your witnesses, receipts, photos and other evidence lined up, and learn the procedural rules set out in this chapter.

---

also include the landlord's brothers, sisters, and grandparents. In many cities, a landlord must own at least half of the property to qualify to move relatives in. In Los Angeles, a particular relative of a landlord may justify evicting a tenant only once, and the landlord must pay the evicted tenant's costs of finding another place to live and moving. Check your local ordinance on all of these details.

[21] In cities with ordinances allowing "vacancy decontrol," such as Los Angeles, the landlord can raise the rent as much as she likes whenever the place becomes vacant. See Chapter 4 for a discussion of vacancy decontrol and a list of rent control cities with this provision.

F. The Eviction Lawsuit

Until February 1992, landlords could, in some circumstances, use small claims court to evict a tenant. This is now illegal and eviction lawsuits may only be brougt in municipal court.[22]

An eviction lawsuit is technically called an "unlawful detainer" lawsuit. We use both terms interchangeably, but courts and lawyers almost always use the term unlawful detainer.

One very important rule cuts across all other rules in an eviction case: The landlord must strictly comply with all legal requirements.[23] This is the price the landlord pays for a special, quick procedure and reflects the seriousness of the matter, which seeks to deprive you of your home.

1. The Complaint and Summons

The Complaint is the paper the landlord files in court to get the case going. It states the basic facts that justify eviction and asks the court to order you out and to enter a judgment against you for unpaid rent, court costs, and sometimes attorney fees and other damages.

Before you can be evicted, you must receive proper notice of an unlawful detainer suit against you by being named in the Complaint and served with a Summons. The Summons is a notice from the court telling you that you must file a written response (Answer, Demurrer or Motion to Quash) with the court within five days or lose the lawsuit. The Summons also tells you whether you should give your response to the landlord's attorney or to the landlord. If the Summons and Complaint aren't served on you according to law, you can ask the court to throw out the lawsuit. (See Section 3, below.)

If you are living in the property but are not named as a defendant in the Complaint, you may protect yourself against eviction for a while by filing a form with the court, called "Claim of Right to Possession and Notice of Hearing."[24] (See Section J, below.) However, the sheriff, marshal or registered process server, when serving the Summons and Complaint on the named defendants, may ask whether any other occupants of the property aren't named in the Summons and Complaint. If there are occupants who aren't named, the sheriff, marshal or registered process server can then serve each of them, too, with a blank Prejudgment Claim of Right to Possession form and an extra copy of the Summons and Complaint. The unnamed occupants have 10 days from the date of service to file a Claim of Right to Possession; they can't file it later, when the sheriff is about to evict.[25] A blank Prejudgment Claim of Right to Possession is in the Appendix.

2. Responding to the Summons

Your first response to the Summons can be one of three documents, each of which is discussed below:

• Motion to Quash—if the Summons was not properly served on you;

• Demurrer—if the Complaint is not in proper technical form or does not properly allege the landlord's right to evict you;

• Answer—if you want to deny statements in the Complaint or allege new facts.

Note: Even if you've already moved out, you might want to file an Answer—for example, if the landlord is still suing you for money damages.

You have five days to file your written response. You must count Saturdays and Sundays, but not other judicial holidays, in the five days. However, if the fifth day is a Saturday or Sunday, you can file your response the next day court is open.[26]

---

[22] CCP §§ 86, 116.220.
[23] Vasey v. California Dance Co. (1977) 70 Cal.App.3d 742.
[24] CCP § 1174.3.
[25] CCP §§ 415.46, 1174.25.
[26] CCP § 1167.

EXAMPLE 1

Teresa is served with a Summons on Tuesday. She counts Wednesday as day 1, Thursday as 2, Friday as 3, Saturday as 4, and Sunday as 5. Because court isn't open on Sunday, she can file her response on Monday.

EXAMPLE 2

Joe is served with a Summons on Wednesday. His five days are over on Monday, too.

EXAMPLE 3

Laura is served with a Summons on Thursday. The next Monday is a court holiday. She counts Friday as day 1, Saturday as 2, Sunday as 3, Tuesday as 4, and Wednesday as 5. Wednesday is her last day to file a response.

If this is your first responsive pleading, you will have to pay a filing fee. The amount depends on how many defendants there are. It will probably be between $35 and $70. Call the municipal court clerk (civil division) for information on filing fees in your county. If you win, you will get your filing fee from the landlord as "costs."

3. The Motion to Quash

Once you become aware that the landlord has filed an unlawful detainer action against you, your first step is to decide whether or not the landlord has complied with the strict requirements for how the Summons must be served on you. If the landlord didn't follow the rules exactly, you are entitled to file a paper called a "Motion to Quash Service of Summons," asking the court to rule that service of the Summons was improper.[27] You can also file a Motion to Quash based on a defect in the Summons itself—for example, that the wrong court or judicial district is listed. If this ruling is in your favor, the landlord has to start all over again.

a. How the Summons Must Be Served

The landlord cannot get sloppy about service of the Summons and Complaint. Whether or not you actually receive these documents, the landlord's failure to strictly abide by the rules governing their service means that the court has no authority (jurisdiction) to hear the case.

There are two allowable ways to serve a Summons and Complaint: personal service and substituted service.

Personal Service: The landlord must first attempt personal service of the Summons and Complaint. Someone over the age of 18 who is not a named party to the lawsuit—someone other than the landlord—must personally hand you the papers.[28] Even if you don't accept the papers, service has properly been made as long as you are personally presented with them. It is a common practice, when people realize they are about to be served, to slam the door in the server's face. Forget it. The server can deposit the papers outside the door (after you slam it) and you will be considered served.

Substituted Service: If several unsuccessful attempts are made to personally serve you (three is the general rule) the server may make substituted service by:

• leaving a copy of the Summons and Complaint with a competent person in your house (this can be someone less than 18 years of age), or with a person over 18 at your business; and

---

[27] CCP § 418.10.

[28] CCP § 414.10.

- explaining the nature of the papers to the person with whom they are left; and

- mailing a copy of the papers to the address where the papers were left.[29]

If this method of service is used, your time to respond is extended from five to 15 days.

b. When to File a Motion to Quash Service of Summons

If you file a Motion to Quash, make sure you have a valid reason. Courts do not allow the filing of motions solely for the purpose of delay. However, if there are adequate legal grounds for a motion, the request will be granted and no inquiry into your motives will be made.

Typical grounds for a tenant's Motion to Quash based on defective service are:

- the Summons was served on one defendant but not the other;

- the wrong person was served;

- no one was served;

- the process server used substituted service without first trying personal service;

- the landlord himself served the Summons.

c. Overview of Motion to Quash

There are three parts to a Motion to Quash:

The Notice of Motion and Motion: This notifies the other side (the landlord or his attorney) that you are making the motion and have scheduled a court hearing on a certain day.

Your Declaration: This is a written statement made under penalty of perjury stating the facts supporting your conclusion that service of the Summons was improper.

Memorandum of Points and Authorities: This is a short statement of the legal authority for your position.

If you want to file a Motion to Quash, you must do so within your five-day period to respond.

d. Preparing the Motion to Quash

Step 1: Make several copies of the blank numbered legal paper in the Appendix, or buy some at a stationery store.

Step 2: Take a piece of numbered paper and put your name, address, telephone number and "Defendant in pro per" in the same location (and on approximately the same lines) as is shown in the sample. Don't go crazy about trying to line up your text exactly with the numbers. Just do the best you can.

Step 3: Put the county where you are being sued, the municipal court district, and the case number in the spaces as indicated on the sample. Get this information from the Summons and Complaint that were served on you.

Step 4: Call the municipal court clerk and ask when and in what department or division motions are heard. In large cities, this tends to be every morning. In less populous areas, motions may be heard only once or twice a week.

Step 5: Once you find out which dates and times are available, and which department hears motions, immediately fill in the blanks as follows:

❶ Pick a date that is no less than eight days and no more than twelve days from the date you plan to file the motion.

❷ Fill in the time the court hears motions.

❸ Fill in the department where motions are heard.

❹ Fill in the address of the court.

---

[29] CCP § 415.20(b).

Step 6: Prepare your Points and Authorities.

Skip a couple of lines after the last line of your Notice of Motion and Motion, type the words POINTS AND AUTHORITIES in capitals, and then begin typing your points and authorities. You can copy the first sentence directly from the sample. You also need to explain:

- what the landlord did wrong; and
- the specific statute the landlord violated.

If the Summons and Complaint weren't served by someone over 18 or if they were served by someone who was a party to the action, the landlord violated CCP § 414.10. If the server used substituted service without first unsuccessfully attempting personal service, the landlord violated CCP § 415.20(b). If some other requirement for substituted service was missed, Section 415.20(b) was violated.

If the landlord erred for some other reason, you will need to find a legal basis for your conclusion and put it in the Points and Authorities. Talk to a tenants' group or lawyer or research the law yourself.[30]

Step 7: Prepare a Declaration.

On a new sheet of paper, type the word DECLARATION in capitals, and type your statement, as shown in the sample. Number each paragraph. The judge will use your declaration in place of oral testimony as a basis for deciding whether to grant your motion. So use simple sentences and don't argue. ("Just the facts, ma'am.") Review your information to make sure it accurately and clearly tells the court what the landlord did wrong.

The following sample Notice of Motion to Quash, Declaration, and Memorandum of Points and Authorities is based on the scenario that your landlord handed the Summons and Complaint to you himself (a no-no) rather than having another person serve it. The papers will, of course, have to be modified appropriately if you bring your motion on another ground.

For more information on Motions to Quash, consult the *California Eviction Defense Manual* (CEB), available in most law libraries.

---

[30] See *Legal Research: How To Find and Understand the Law*, Elias (Nolo Press).

Sample Notice of Motion

```
TOM TENANT
2233 Apartment Lane
Anytown, CA 99000
(916) 555-6543

Defendant in Pro Per
```

IN THE MUNICIPAL COURT OF THE STATE OF CALIFORNIA

COUNTY OF _____, _____ DISTRICT

LENNY LANDLORD,
 	
       Plaintiff
 	
  v.
 	
TOM TENANT,
 	
       Defendant.
	No. _____
	
	NOTICE OF MOTION AND MOTION
	TO QUASH SERVICE OF SUMMONS

To: LENNY LANDLORD, plaintiff, and to LAURA LAWYER, his attorney:

PLEASE TAKE NOTICE THAT on _____, 19__, ❶ at _____ ❷ in Department No. _____ ❸ of the above-entitled court, located at _____, ❹ defendant, Tom Tenant, will appear specially pursuant to Code of Civil Procedure Section 418.10 and will move the court for an order quashing the service of Summons herein on the ground(s) that the Summons and Complaint in this case was personally served on him by Lenny Landlord, plaintiff in this case, in violation of Code of Civil Procedure Section 414.10, which requires service of the Summons and Complaint to be served by one not a party to the action.

The motion shall be based upon this notice, the memorandum of points and authorities in support thereof, the files and records of this case, and the declaration of Tom Tenant, attached hereto.

Dated: November 29, 19____

TOM TENANT
Defendant in Pro Per

POINTS AND AUTHORITIES

A defendant in an unlawful detainer action is entitled to file a Motion to Quash Service of Summons when service has not been validly completed. Code of Civil Procedure Sec. 418.10.

In this action, service of the Summons and Complaint was made personally by the plaintiff, Lenny Landlord.

Service by a party to the action violates Code of Civil Procedure Sec. 414.10, which requires that service of a Summons and Complaint must be made by a person over 18 who is not a party to the action.

Respectfully submitted,

TOM TENANT
Defendant in Pro Per

DECLARATION

TOM TENANT declares and says:

1. I am a tenant at 2233 Apartment Lane, Anytown, CA 99900.

2. On November 26, 19__ I was served with the Summons and Complaint in this case by my landlord, Lenny Landlord. I have not been served with those papers in any other manner or by any other person.

3. I declare under penalty of perjury under the laws of the State of California that the foregoing is true and correct.

Date: November 29, 19__

At: Anytown, California

_____
TOM TENANT
Defendant in Pro Per

e. How to Serve the Motion to Quash

After you have prepared your Motion to Quash, you must have it served on the landlord promptly, to give her enough time to respond before the hearing date. As a defendant, you cannot serve your own legal papers, but you can have a friend or relative do it. The server must be a person over 18 and not a party to the action—that is, not named in the Complaint as a plaintiff or defendant.

Step 1: Complete the document called Proof of Service by Mail, following the instructions in the box below. You will find a blank tear-out form in the Appendix; make several copies before using it, as you may need more later.

Step 2: Make two copies of your Notice of Motion and Motion, Declaration, Points and Authorities, and the filled in but unsigned Proof of Service by Mail. Print the server's name on the last line of both copies of the Proof of Service.

Step 3: Attach a copy of the unsigned Proof of Service to each set of your motion papers.

Step 4: Have your server mail one set of copies (the motion papers and the Proof of Service) to the landlord's attorney (listed on the Summons) or the landlord if there is no attorney. The papers must be mailed on the day indicated on the Proof of Service.

Step 5: Now have your server fill in the blanks in the last paragraph of the Proof of Service and sign the document. Attach it to the original motion.

Step 6: Take the original motion papers and one set of copies to the municipal court clerk.[31] Give the original set of papers to the clerk, who will stamp (or have you stamp) your copies with a "filed" message. This is your proof that you filed the originals with the clerk.

Step 7: The clerk will note the date you indicated for the hearing on the Notice of Motion and enter it on the court calendar after you leave.

Step 8: Courts sometimes make a tentative decision solely on the basis of the papers filed. This decision is usually posted outside the courtroom the day before your hearing. If the decision is for the landlord, some courts require you to call the landlord before the hearing if you want to argue your side.

Step 9: The day of the hearing, go a little early and check with the clerk's office to make sure your case is on the calendar. If it isn't, find out why. If it is, go to the courtroom indicated.

f. The Court Hearing on a Motion to Quash

The evening before the hearing, you should sit down, relax, and go over the points stated in your motion papers just to familiarize yourself with them. On the day of the hearing, you should dress conservatively, though you don't have to wear a business suit. Try to get to the courtroom a little early.

When your case is called, step forward. Some judges prefer to ask questions, but others prefer that the person bringing the motion (you) talks first. In any case, don't start talking until the judge asks you to begin. Your argument should be straightforward, and based on the facts and issues set forth in your declaration and motion papers, and the landlord's responses to your papers.

Don't refer to any facts not contained in the declarations, or state your opinion of the landlord, or argue the merits of your situation beyond what you have raised in your motion papers.

After the landlord or his lawyer has had a chance to argue his side, you can respond. The judge will then either rule on the motion or take the matter "under submission" and decide later.

If the judge denies the motion, you will have some time to file your next response (or whatever other action is required at that time). If you win, the landlord may have another Summons ready to serve on you right there, and you start all over again.

---

[31] It is possible to file papers by mail, but this is not advised, especially in unlawful detainer cases being handled by a tenant without a lawyer. The time limits are so tight in these kinds of cases that a postal foul-up or a mishandling in the clerk's office can cause you no end of grief.

> **Instructions for Completing the Proof of Service By Mail**
>
> Fill in the blanks in the Proof of Service by Mail with the following information:
>
> ❶ County where the server lives;
>
> ❷ Server's street address and city;
>
> ❸ Date you plan to have your motion filed and served;
>
> ❹ Name of document you're serving;
>
> ❺ City where Proof of Service will be mailed;
>
> ❻ Name, street address, city, state and zip code of landlord.
>
> You will complete the rest of the form when you follow the instructions to serve specific documents.

```
                        PROOF OF SERVICE BY MAIL

   I am a citizen of the United States and a resident of the county of

_____.❶ I am over the age of 18 years and not a party

to the above action; my residence address is: _____

_____,❷ California.

   On _____, 19___,❸ I served the within

_____❹ document on the Plaintiffs

in said action by placing a true copy thereof enclosed in a sealed envelope

with postage fully prepaid, in the United States Post Office mail box at

_____,❺ California, addressed as follows:

_____.❻

   I, _____(name of server)_____, certify under penalty of perjury

that the foregoing is true and correct. Executed on ____(date served)____,

19___, at _____(city)_____, California.

                                    _____
                                          (signature of server)
                                    _____
                                          (print name of server)
```

4. The Demurrer

Once the landlord has properly served you with a Summons and Complaint, you are entitled to file an Answer to the Complaint or a Demurrer.[32] You must either answer or demur within five days from the date the Summons and Complaint were properly served. If the fifth day falls on a holiday, the last day for your response is extended to the next business day. (See Section 2, above.)

When you file a Demurrer, what you are really saying is, "Assuming, only for the purpose of argument, that everything the landlord says in her Complaint is true, it still doesn't provide legal justification for the court to order me evicted."

Note that when you file a Demurrer, you assume the facts as stated by the landlord in his Complaint to be true only for the purpose of the particular pleading. You are not conceding the truth of anything in the Complaint. Once the court rules on your Demurrer, you will still have a chance to file a written Answer, in which you may deny any factual allegations in the Complaint you believe are false or don't actually know to be true.

a. When to File a Demurrer

Here are some of the principal legal grounds on which you may properly demur to a Complaint:

Ground 1. The three-day notice wasn't in the alternative. All three-day notices—including those based on nonpayment of rent—must be in the alternative, unless the landlord is alleging violation of a lease provision that is not curable within that time (Unconditional Three-Day Notice to Quit). For example, if you receive a Three-Day Notice to Quit because you have a dog (or failed to pay the rent) and the notice fails to say that you have the *alternative* of getting rid of the dog (or paying the rent) in three days, it is defective. See Section D.2 for details on three-day notices.

Ground 2. The Complaint was filed too soon. The date the Complaint was filed will be stamped on the first page of the Complaint. Look at this date. If it is before the three days or the 30 days given by the notice, you can demur.

b. Overview of the Demurrer

You need to prepare three documents to file a Demurrer:

- The Demurrer
- Notice of Hearing
- Memorandum of Points and Authorities

c. Filling Out the Demurrer

A blank Demurrer form is in the Appendix. For instructions on how to complete the Demurrer, refer to Steps 1-3 for preparing the Motion to Quash set out in Section F.3.d, above.

The list of legal grounds for a demurrer are discussed just above.

If Ground #1 applies to your situation, type in: "The three-day notice attached to the Complaint simply ordered me to vacate, without giving me the alternative of stopping any alleged breach of the rental agreement."

If Ground #2 fits your situation, type in: "The Complaint was filed prematurely, before the time set in the notice expired."

Sign and date the Demurrer.

---

[32] CCP § 430.10.

Sample Demurrer

```
_____
_____
_____
Defendant in Pro Per
```

IN THE MUNICIPAL COURT OF THE STATE OF CALIFORNIA

COUNTY OF _____, _____ DISTRICT

_____,	) No. _____
Plaintiff(s),	) DEMURRER OF
v.	) _____
	) (name of defendant)
_____,	) TO THE COMPLAINT OF
Defendant(s).	) _____
	) (name of plaintiff)

Defendant(s) demur to the Complaint on the following ground(s):

1. <u>The three-day notice attached to the Complaint simply ordered me to vacate, without giving me the alternative of stopping any alleged breach of the rental agreement.</u>

2. _____
_____
_____
_____

3. _____
_____
_____
_____

Dated: _____   _____
                                (signature of defendant)

d. Filling Out the Memorandum of Points and Authorities

On a blank piece of numbered legal paper (make some copies of the blank sheet in the Appendix), type "Points and Authorities in Support of Demurrer." Then skip a line and type "CCP § 430.10." Then, in numbered paragraphs, repeat each ground for your demurrer. (See the sample.) This time, however, you should follow each ground by an appropriate legal reference. For Ground #1, this is: CCP § 1161(3); *Feder v. Wreden Packing and Provision Co.* (1928) 89 Cal.App. 671. For Ground #2, put: CCP § 1161(2).

Attach your Points and Authorities to your demurrer.

Sample Points and Authorities

POINTS AND AUTHORITIES IN SUPPORT OF DEMURRER

CCP § 430.10

1. The three-day notice attached to the Complaint simply ordered me to vacate, without giving me the alternative of stopping any alleged breach of the rental agreement. Code of Civil Procedure Section 1161(3); Feder v. Wreden Packing and Provision Co. (1928) 89 Cal.App. 671.

2. _____

3. _____

Dated: _____   _____ (signature of defendant)

e. Filling Out the Notice of Hearing On Demurrer

A blank tear-out form for the Notice of Hearing is located in the Appendix and a sample is shown here. Turn back to Section F.3.c of this chapter and locate the instructions accompanying the Notice of Motion to Quash. Follow them for the Notice of Hearing on Demurrer with the following exceptions:

• Call the municipal court clerk and ask when Demurrers (rather than motions) are heard by the court.

• Select a hearing date at least 20 days after the day you plan to file your Demurrer. Put the day, the time the court hears Demurrers, the department that hears them, and the address of the court in the indicated spaces. Then, attach the Notice of Hearing to the front of the Demurrer and Points and Authorities.

f. Filing and Serving the Demurrer

After you have prepared your Demurrer, here's how to file and serve it.

Step 1: Complete the document called Proof of Service by Mail, following the instructions found in the box in the discussion of Motion to Quash (Section F.3, above). You will find a blank tear-out form in the Appendix; make several copies before using it, as you may need more later. The server must be a person over 18 and not a party to the action—that is, not named in the Complaint as a plaintiff or defendant. As a defendant, you cannot serve your own legal papers.

Step 2: Make two copies of your Demurrer papers (Notice of Hearing, Demurrer, and Points and Authorities) and the Proof of Service. Print the server's name on the last line of both copies of the Proof of Service.

Step 3: Attach one copy of the Proof of Service to each set of copies of your Demurrer papers.

Step 4: Have your server mail one set of copies (your Demurrer papers and an unsigned Proof of Service) to the landlord's attorney (listed on the Summons) or the landlord if there is no attorney.

Step 5: Now have your server fill in the blanks in the last paragraph of the Proof of Service and sign it, stating that the mailing has occurred. Attach this original to your original Demurrer papers.

Step 6: Take the original Demurrer papers and one set of copies to the municipal court clerk.[33] Give the original set of papers to the clerk, who will stamp (or have you stamp) your copy with a "filed" message. This is your proof that you filed the originals with the clerk.

Step 7: The clerk will note the date you indicated for the hearing on the Demurrer and enter it on the court calendar.

If the landlord desires to respond to your Demurrer, he must file a response at least five days before the hearing. If you wish to make a written response to those papers, you must do so at least two days before the hearing.

Step 8: Courts sometimes make a tentative decision solely on the basis of the papers filed. This tentative decision is posted outside the courtroom the day before your hearing. If you want to argue your side even if the tentative decision is against you, some courts require you to call the landlord and say you're still going to argue.

Step 9: On the day of the hearing, check to see that your case is on the calendar. If it isn't, ask the clerk why and get it rescheduled.

---

[33] It is possible to file papers by mail, but this is not advised. A postal service or clerk's office foul-up could cause grave problems given the short time limits in these kinds of cases.

Sample Notice of Hearing on Demurrer

```
1   _____
2   _____
3   Defendant in Pro Per
4
5
6
7
8           IN THE MUNICIPAL COURT OF THE STATE OF CALIFORNIA
9           COUNTY OF _____, _____ DISTRICT
10   _____,  )  No. _____
                                )
11           Plaintiff(s),      )  NOTICE OF HEARING ON DEMURRER OF
                                )
12      v.                      )  _____
                                )        (name of defendant)
13   _____,   )
                                )  TO THE COMPLAINT OF
14           Defendant(s).      )
                                )  _____
15   _____    )        (name of plaintiff)

16      To: _____(defendant)_____
17      PLEASE TAKE NOTICE THAT on _____, 19___, at
18   _____ in Department No._____ of the above entitled
19   court, located at _____
20   a hearing will be held on defendant's demurrer to the Complaint, a copy of
21   which is served with this notice.
22
23
24   Dated:_____          _____(signature of defendant)_____
25
26
27
28
```

g. At the Hearing

See the discussion on hearings on a Motion to Quash (Section F.3.f, above).

Other procedures: Other motions may be appropriate at this stage of the proceedings. For instance, a "motion to strike" might be appropriate if the landlord's Complaint requests relief that is not justified by the allegations. For more on this, consult the *California Eviction Defense Manual*, by Moskovitz, published by Continuing Education of the Bar (CEB).

5. The Answer

The Answer is where you tell your version of what happened. You must file it with the court within five days of receiving the Summons and Complaint (15 days if substituted service was used), unless you file a Motion to Quash or Demurrer instead. If you miss the deadline, the landlord can take a default judgment against you. Defaults are discussed in Subsection 6, just below.

Even if you first file a Demurrer or Motion to Quash, you will have to file an Answer sooner or later, unless the landlord drops the case.

If your Demurrer is upheld by the court, the landlord will have to amend the Complaint. Then you can demur again, if you have grounds, or file an Answer. If, on the other hand, your Demurrer is overruled, you will have to file an Answer within five days after the date of the notice of the court order overruling the demurrer.

a. Filling Out the Form Answer

Fortunately, a form Answer has been developed (by the California Judicial Council) specifically for unlawful detainer cases. A blank tear-out copy is located in the Appendix, and you may obtain additional copies from the court. A sample is included here.

Top of the Form: This is self-explanatory. Put your name in both the top box—"Attorney or Party Without Attorney"—and the one marked "Defendant." You will find the name and address of the court and the case number on the Complaint.

Item 1: Fill in "2" for the number of pages, unless you add attachments. If you do, use 8-1/2" x 11" typing paper (numbered legal paper is not required), and clearly label each attachment with the number of the paragraph on the printed form answer to which it refers. (See Sample Attachment to Item 4.K, below.) Each attachment should be on one side of a separate sheet and should be stapled to the Answer.

Item 2: Fill in your name.

Item 3: If the Complaint expressly asks for more than $1,000 in damages, check Box b. If it does not, check Box a.

If you checked Box b (as our sample Answer does), you have a little more work to do before going to Item 4. Follow these directions and you should have no trouble:

Carefully read the Complaint, paragraph by paragraph. As you do, take the following actions for each paragraph.

(a) If you agree with *everything* in the paragraph, go on to the next one.

(b) If you disagree with *any* statement in a paragraph, enter the paragraph number in the space on the Answer form after 3.b.1. You may very well disagree with more than one paragraph. If so, enter the numbers of all such paragraphs. If you don't have enough space to list all the paragraphs, check the box labeled "Continued on attachment 3.b.1." and type up an attachment on a separate piece of paper.

(c) If you don't have enough information to agree or disagree with a statement in a paragraph, enter the paragraph number in the space on the Answer form labeled 3.b.2.

Do a careful job of reading each paragraph on the Complaint. Any paragraph that isn't listed after

Box 3.b.1. or 3.b.2. will be accepted as true by the court.

Item 4: Affirmative Defenses: An affirmative defense is any defense that involves a set of facts different from those raised in the Complaint. The Answer lists common affirmative defenses; check any that you plan to raise if your eviction goes to trial.

For example, suppose the landlord seeks to evict you because you didn't pay your rent. If your defense is that you didn't pay the rent because the rental unit was uninhabitable, as discussed in Chapter 7, it is based on different facts than are found in the Complaint and is therefore an affirmative defense—in this case, Item 4.a.

Another example is an eviction that was supposedly based on just cause—such as a landlord in a rent control city evicting a tenant on the grounds that he needed to make major repairs. (Section D.3.c above, discusses just cause requirements.) If this eviction was made in bad faith—for example, the tenant checked with the city and found out that the landlord had not taken out the necessary building permits—the tenant would have an affirmative defense to the eviction. In this case, Item 4.f.

In Item 4.k., state the facts on which you base your affirmative defense. See the examples below. Generally, the fewer words you use to describe your defense, the better. However, even if you try to be brief, the room provided will probably not be enough. If you need more space, take a sheet of 8-1/2" x 11" paper, label it "Item 4.k." at the top, and then explain the facts regarding each affirmative defense. For example, if you need more room to explain Affirmative Defense 4.d.—"Plaintiff has failed to perform his obligations under the rental agreement"—state your additional facts under "4.d." on the attachment, which would look like this:

Sample Attachment to Item 4.k of Answer

```
      ATTACHMENT TO ITEM 4.k
STATEMENT OF DETAILS OF AFFIRMATIVE DEFENSES

   4.d.: The reason I didn't water the lawn
as required in rental agreement was that
landlord never provided the hose (which she
had agreed to do).
```

Affirmative Defenses in Rent Control Cities: If you live in a rent control area, it is possible that you have been charged more rent than the ordinance allows. (See Chapter 4.) If this is the case, the landlord's claim that you failed to pay rent can be defeated on the ground that the rent demanded in the three-day notice was higher than it should have been. Although this defense is technically raised by a simple denial in Item 3 of the Answer, it is also a good idea to describe your position in an affirmative defense—in this case, Item 4.f.

State law says that landlords in rent control cities that require registration of rents (Berkeley, Santa Monica, Cotati, East Palo Alto, Los Angeles, Palm Springs, Thousand Oaks, and West Hollywood) can't be penalized for good-faith mistakes in the amount of rent they charge.[34] Landlords may argue that the statute also protects them from having a three-day notice thrown out because it demanded the wrong rent. Your response should be that dismissal of a Complaint because of a deficient three-day notice is not one of the penalties covered by the statute.

If you receive a 30-day notice of eviction because the landlord or his relative plans to move in (a just cause for eviction in many rent control cities), do a little checking before you decide to leave. If the landlord says he is moving in himself, find out where he lives now. If he lives in a fancy neighborhood and you live in a not-so-fancy one, maybe he does not really plan to move in. If your rent is among the lowest rents in the building, the landlord may want

---

[34] CC § 1947.7.

Sample Answer

ATTORNEY OR PARTY WITHOUT ATTORNEY (NAME AND ADDRESS):	TELEPHONE:	FOR COURT USE ONLY
TOM TENANT 2233 Apartment Lane Anytown, CA 99000	(916) 555-6543	

ATTORNEY FOR (NAME): In pro per

Insert name of court, judicial district or branch court, if any, and post office and street address:

Santa Barbara County Municipal Court
118 E. Figueroa St.
Santa Barbara, CA 93101

PLAINTIFF:

Lenny Landlord

DEFENDANT:

TOM TENANT

ANSWER—Unlawful Detainer

CASE NUMBER:

---

1. This pleading including attachments and exhibits consists of the following number of pages: __2__
2. Defendants (name): TOM TENANT

   answer the complaint as follows:
3. **Check ONLY ONE of the next two boxes:**
   a. ☐ Defendant generally denies each statement of the complaint. (Do not check this box if the complaint demands more than $1,000.)
   b. ☒ Defendant admits that all of the statements of the complaint are true EXCEPT:
      (1) Defendant claims the following statements of the complaint are false (use paragraph numbers from the complaint or explain):

      Paragraphs 6 and 7

      ☐ Continued on Attachment 3.b.(1).
      (2) Defendant has no information or belief that the following statements of the complaint are true, so defendant denies them (use paragraph numbers from the complaint or explain):

      ☐ Continued on Attachment 3.b.(2).
4. **AFFIRMATIVE DEFENSES**
   a. ☐ (nonpayment of rent only) Plaintiff has breached the warranty to provide habitable premises. (Briefly state the facts below in item 4.k.)
   b. ☐ Plaintiff waived, changed, or canceled the notice to quit. (Briefly state the facts below in item 4.k.)
   c. ☐ Plaintiff served defendant with the notice to quit or filed the complaint to retaliate against defendant. (Briefly state the facts below in item 4.k.)
   d. ☒ Plaintiff has failed to perform his obligations under the rental agreement. (Briefly state the facts below in item 4.k.)
   e. ☐ By serving defendant with the notice to quit or filing the complaint, plaintiff is arbitrarily discriminating against the defendant in violation of the constitution or laws of the United States or California. (Briefly state the facts below in item 4.k.)
   f. ☐ Plaintiff's demand for possession violates the local rent control or eviction control ordinance of (city or county, title of ordinance, and date of passage):

   (Briefly state the facts showing violation of the ordinance in item 4.k.)

   (Continued)

Form Approved by the
Judicial Council of California
Effective January 1, 1982
Rule 982.1(95)

ANSWER—Unlawful Detainer

CCP 425.12
Post Record Catalog # 982.1(95)

SHORT TITLE: LANDLORD V. TENANT	CASE NUMBER:

ANSWER—Unlawful Detainer Page two

g. ☐ Plaintiff accepted rent from defendant to cover a period of time after the date stated in paragraph 8.b. of the complaint.
h. ☐ *(nonpayment of rent only)* On *(date):* defendant offered the rent due but plaintiff would not accept it.
i. ☐ Defendant made needed repairs and properly deducted the cost from the rent, and plaintiff did not give proper credit.
j. ☐ Other affirmative defenses. *(Briefly state below in item 4.k.)*
k. FACTS SUPPORTING AFFIRMATIVE DEFENSES CHECKED ABOVE *(Identify each item separately.)*

4.d. The reason I didn't water the lawn as required in rental agreement was that landlord never provided the hose (which she had agreed to do).

☐ Continued on Attachment 4.k.

5. OTHER STATEMENTS
   a. ☐ Defendant vacated the premises on *(date):*
   b. ☐ Defendant claims a credit for deposits of $
   c. ☐ The fair rental value of the premises in item 12 of the complaint is excessive *(explain):*

   d. ☐ Other *(specify):*

6. DEFENDANT REQUESTS
   a. that plaintiff take nothing requested in the complaint.
   b. costs incurred in this proceeding.
   c. ☒ reasonable attorney fees.
   d. ☐ other *(specify):*

TOM TENANT
(Type or print name)   *(Signature of defendant or attorney)*

(Type or print name)   *(Signature of defendant or attorney)*

(Each defendant for whom this answer is filed must be named in item 2 **and** must sign this answer unless represented by an attorney.)

VERIFICATION
(Use a different verification form if the verification is by an attorney or for a corporation or partnership.)
I am the defendant in this proceeding and have read this answer. I declare under penalty of perjury under the laws of the State of California that this answer is true and correct.

Date:
TOM TENANT
(Type or print name)   *(Signature of defendant)*

you out pretty badly, because he can make the greatest profit by evicting you and charging a higher rent to a new tenant. In either case, see if he owns other vacant apartments he could move into instead. If he does, most ordinances require that he occupy one of these.

If a landlord claims that a relative is moving in, try to find out if the relative really exists, and if it would make sense for the relative to want to live there. For example, if the landlord's daughter is going to college in another city, it is not likely that she would want to move into your place in the middle of the semester.

If you do move out because the landlord says that she or a relative is moving in, go back and check up on whether they moved in, and if they did, how long they stayed. If it turns out that this was merely a scheme to take advantage of vacancy decontrol, you might be able to file a profitable lawsuit. In San Francisco, tenants' lawyers have obtained "wrongful eviction" judgments against landlords in such cases for as much as $30,000. In 1987, a San Francisco landlord settled a wrongful eviction suit for $85,000.

State law requires that in rent-controlled cities that require landlords to register their properties with the rent board, landlords who evict tenants to move a relative (or the landlord) into the property must have the relative actually live there for six continuous months. If this doesn't happen, the tenant can sue the landlord.[35]

If a court determines that the landlord or relative never intended to stay in the unit, the tenant can move back in. The court can also award the tenant three times the increase in rent she paid while living somewhere else and three times the cost of moving back in. If the tenant decides not to move back into the old unit, the court can award her three times the amount of one month's rent of the old unit and three times the costs she incurred moving out of it. The tenant can also recover attorney fees and costs.[36] In a recent case, the court awarded a tenant $200,000 for a wrongful eviction based on a phony-relative ploy.[37]

Here are some brief examples of affirmative defenses, with references to sections in this book where these issues are discussed in greater detail.

Box 4.a.: Breach of Warranty of Habitability (see Chapter 7.B.5). If you are being evicted for nonpayment of rent and the landlord had reason to know that there are deficiencies in your apartment affecting its habitability, you should check box 4.a. and put the details in 4.k. or the attachment.

Sample Statement of Details

"On December 25, 19__, I notified my landlord (the plaintiff in this action), that the heating unit in my apartment was broken and asked that it be fixed. This was not done." Or, "On March 19, 19__, I notified my landlord that the roof was seriously leaking in three places. The roof has never been fixed."

---

[35] CC § 1947.10.

[36] See also *Brossard v. Stotter* (1984) 160 Cal.App.3d 1067, 207 Cal.Rptr. 108. In this case the landlord had earlier won an eviction lawsuit, on the basis that she didn't use the phony-relative ploy. Despite the landlord's win, the tenant was allowed to bring suit for damages, claiming that the landlord did use the phony-relative ploy, although it didn't become obvious until after the tenant was evicted and the property re-rented. The tenant won the case.

[37] *Beeman v. Burling* (1990) 216 Cal.App.3d 1586, 265 Cal. Rptr. 719.

Box 4.b.: Cancellation of Notice. Sometimes, after a three-day or 30-day notice is served, the landlord (or his agent) says something to indicate that he didn't mean it, that you can have more time, or something else inconsistent with the notice. If this happens, he may have impliedly waived or cancelled the notice, so check Box 4.b.

Sample Statement of Details
"After I received the notice, Plaintiff's resident manager told me that they had served the notice on me only to scare me, and as long as I paid by the end of the month, no eviction lawsuit would be filed."

Box 4.c.: Retaliatory Eviction. Retaliatory eviction is a very common defense. If you believe that your landlord is illegally retaliating against you (see Section B, above), check Box 4.c. and put the details in 4.k.

Sample Statement of Details
"After Plaintiff twice refused to respond to our request that he fix the toilet, we complained to the city health department. Forty-five days later, we received a 30-Day Notice to Quit. We believe that we are being evicted in retaliation for our complaint to the health department."

Box 4.d.: Landlord's Breach of Agreement (see Chapter 7.A.2.) If the landlord failed to perform some promise she made regarding the premises, then your failure to pay rent may have been justified.

Sample Statement of Details
"Plaintiff had promised to provide a laundry room (with washer and dryer) for all tenants, including us, but she closed up the laundry room in July and August. Therefore, our failure to pay all of the agreed rent for July and August was justified."

Box 4.e.: Discrimination (see Chapter 5). The landlord may not evict you because of your race, religion, sex, sexual preference, job, because you have children, or for any other arbitrary reason.

Sample Statement of Details
"Plaintiff served me with the 30-day notice because he doesn't want black people living in his rental units."

Box 4.f.: Just Cause for Eviction Ordinances (see Chapter 4 and Section D of this chapter). If you live in a community with a rent control ordinance that requires just cause for eviction, and you dispute the just cause alleged in the Complaint, simply deny that allegation of the Complaint (by putting the paragraph number in Item 3.b.1). If, however, the landlord committed some violation of the just cause ordinance that you cannot raise by a denial, then check Box 4.f.

Sample Statements of Details
"The rent control ordinance of the City of Santa Monica says that a three-day notice must tell me of my right to call the rent board for advice. The notice served on me by Plaintiff did not say this, so it is invalid." Or,
"The rent control ordinance of the City of San Francisco requires that the 30-day notice state a just cause to evict. The 30-day notice served on me by the landlord did not do this." Or,
"Landlord has sued to evict me because she wants her mother to live in the unit. This is not a just cause to evict because under the rent control ordinance of the City of San Francisco landlord must first establish that there are no other vacant units that her mother can live in. In fact, at the time she served me with the 30-day notice, she had two equivalent vacancies."

Box 4.g.: Acceptance of Rent Beyond Notice Period (see Section D.3.b, above). If the landlord served a 30-day notice and then accepted rent covering a period beyond the 30 days, he has impliedly withdrawn the notice, so check this box.

Box 4.h.: Landlord's Refusal to Accept Rent (see the discussion of three-day notices in Section D.2, above). If you tried to pay the rent during the time allowed you by a three-day notice but the landlord refused to accept it, check this box. If you tried to pay the rent after the three days (but before the lawsuit was filed) and the notice did not mention "forfeiture" of your tenancy, check this box.

Box 4.i.: Use of Repair and Deduct Remedy (see Chapter 7.B.4). If you used the repair-and-deduct remedy, and the landlord failed to give you credit in the three-day notice for the amount you deducted from your rent, check this box.

Box 4.j.: Other Affirmative Defenses. Sometimes landlords orally allow tenants to get behind on their rent or to make certain repairs to their premises in exchange for free rent, or they make other agreements on which the tenant relies because of a good relationship with the landlord. Then, when a falling-out occurs, the landlord will attempt an eviction on the basis of a particular tenant default and deny that any oral agreement was made. In such a case, you have an affirmative defense based on the agreement and should check this box and place the details on 4.k.

Item 5: Other Statements.

Box 5.a.: If you have moved out by the time you get around to filing this Answer, check this box. Remember, even though you've moved, the landlord may still be suing you for money damages. It is important to file this Answer to have your day in court on the money damages claim.

Box 5.b.: Add up all your security deposits and list them here. Generally speaking, all your deposits must be returned if you have left the premises clean and undamaged. (See Chapter 10.)

Box 5.c.: Although the landlord may not accept rent after the expiration of the notice to quit, the court will award the landlord the fair market rental value of the premises for the time between the expiration of the notice and the day the judgment is entered. This is normally computed by dividing the total rent amount by 30 to arrive at a daily rental, and then multiplying this amount by the number of days. If you believe that the "fair rental value" stated in the Complaint is too high, check this box. Then explain any habitability problems on the premises, any change in the neighborhood that might have affected rental value, or any other reason you think the landlord's estimate is excessive.

Box 5.d.: This box gives you a chance to say anything relevant and not covered by the other boxes.

Item 6: Defendant Requests.

Here you need check only Box 6.c.—"reasonable attorney fees"—unless you feel you are entitled to some other remedy. You are entitled to reasonable attorney fees if you win and your rental agreement or lease provides for landlord's attorney fees. (See Chapter 2.B.3.k for a discussion of attorney fees)

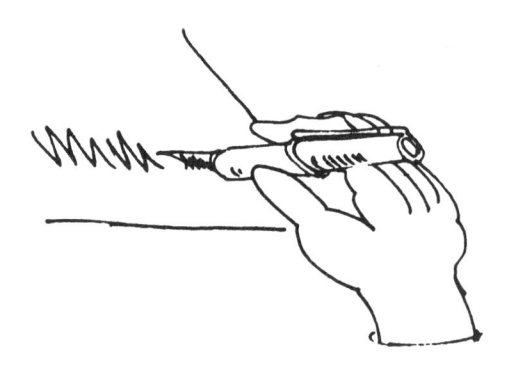

b. Signing and Verifying Your Answer

Here are the rules:

• The Answer must be signed by all of the named defendants.

• The Verification at the bottom of the Answer (the statement under penalty of perjury that the statements in the Answer are true) need be signed only by any one defendant.

c. Filing and Serving Your Answer

After you've prepared your Answer, here's how to file and serve it.

Step 1: Complete the document called Proof of Service by Mail, following the instructions found in the box in Section F.3, above. You will find a blank tear-out form in the Appendix; make several copies before using it, as you may need more later. The server must be a person over 18 and not a party to the action—that is, not named in the Complaint as a plaintiff or defendant. As a defendant, you cannot serve your own legal papers.

Step 2: Make two copies of your Answer and the unsigned but filled in Proof of Service by Mail. Print the server's name on the last line of both copies of the Proof of Service.

Step 3: Attach one copy of the Proof of Service to each copy of your Answer.

Step 4: Have your server mail one copy of the Answer and attached unsigned Proof of Service to the landlord's attorney (listed on the Summons), or the landlord if there is no attorney. The papers must be mailed on the day indicated on the Proof of Service.

Step 5: Now have your server fill in the blanks in the last paragraph of the Proof of Service and sign it, stating that the mailing has occurred. Attach this original to your original Answer.

Step 6: Take the original Answer and Proof of Service and a copy to the municipal court clerk.[38] Give the original set of papers to the clerk, who will stamp (or have you stamp) your copy package with a "filed" message. This is your proof that you filed the originals with the clerk.

Warning: Make sure your Answer is filed within five days of the day the Complaint was served (or your Motion to Quash or Demurrer was overruled). If you miss this deadline, you may find yourself having to dig yourself out from under a default judgment obtained by the landlord. See Section F.2, above, for how to compute the five-day period.

6. Setting Aside a Default Judgment

If you miss the deadline for responding to the landlord's Complaint, the landlord may ask the court for a default judgment against you. That means you lose without a trial and the landlord has the legal right to evict you. If this happens, you may file a motion asking the court to set aside the default judgment. If the motion is granted, you may then file your Answer and have your trial.

To persuade the judge to grant your motion to set aside a default, you must show all of the following:

• That you have a pretty good excuse (such as illness) for your failure to respond to the Summons in five days—for example, "I didn't know how to respond, and it took me a few days to get hold of a copy of *Tenants' Rights*" might work, but don't count on it.

• That you did not unnecessarily delay too long in filing your motion to set aside the default. There is no set period of time for which a delay is or is not excusable. It depends on the facts of each case.

• That you have a defense to the lawsuit.

In addition, be sure to ask for a stay (postponement) of the eviction (Section H, below) until the court rules on your motion to set aside the default.

Moving to set aside a default can be tricky. We recommend that you try to get a lawyer or tenants' rights advocate to help you with it. If you still want to do it yourself, the necessary forms and procedures are contained in the *California Eviction Defense Manual*, by Moskovitz, published by Continuing Education of the Bar (CEB), available in most county law libraries.

---

[38] It is possible to file papers by mail, but this is not advised. A postal service or clerk's office foul-up could cause grave problems given the short time limits in these kinds of cases.

7. Discovery: Learning About the Landlord's Case

"Discovery" is the process of finding out what evidence the other side has before the trial begins, so you can prepare your own case to meet it. Discovery is conducted in two basic ways.

One is to question the other party face to face in a proceeding called a deposition (discussed below.)

The second is to send the other party a written document that specifies what is being sought. This document typically consists of:

- questions (interrogatories),
- a request that certain documents be produced for inspection,
- a request that a physical inspection of the premises be allowed,
- a request that certain facts be admitted as true, or
- all of the above.

You can make any of these requests following the instructions below. The law provides a set period of time within which a party must respond to discovery requests. Usually, the response must be given within 20 days or within five days before trial, whichever is sooner.

a. Request for Inspection

A Request for Inspection is used to make the other side let you see and copy any documents or other things before trial. You may want to see copies of leases, building inspector's reports or checks. It can also be used to get into the apartment to take photos.[39]

The landlord must respond to your request within five days and must produce the documents for actual inspection within ten days. If the landlord refuses to respond adequately to your discovery request within that time, you may ask the court to impose sanctions on him—require him to pay your costs or prevent him from using certain evidence.[40]

Here is a sample Request for Inspection. You will find a blank tear-out copy in the Appendix. You'll need to fill in your name, address and telephone number; the county where you are being sued, the municipal court district, and the case number; the name of the plaintiff and plaintiff's attorney (if any); the documents you are requesting and where and when you want to see and copy these documents. If you want to inspect or photograph the rental premises, you'll also need to specify the location, date and time you wish to do this.

---

[39] CCP § 2031.
[40] CCP § 2023.

Sample Request for Inspection

```
1  _____
2  _____
3  Defendant in Pro Per
4
5
6
7
8          IN THE MUNICIPAL COURT OF THE STATE OF CALIFORNIA
9      COUNTY OF _____, _____ DISTRICT
10  _____,  )  No. _____
                              )
11       Plaintiff(s),        )  REQUEST TO INSPECT AND FOR
                              )  PRODUCTION OF DOCUMENTS
12    v.                      )
                              )
13  _____,  )  Code of Civil Procedure Sec. 2031
                              )
14       Defendant(s).        )
15   To _____, Plaintiff, and _____,
16  Plaintiff's attorney:
17     Defendant requests that you produce and permit the copying of the following
18  documents: _____(describe documents)_____.
19     Defendant requests that you produce these documents at the following
20  address: _____(your address or any other location)_____
21  at the following date and time: (within 20 days or five days before trial, whichever comes first).
22     Defendant further requests permission to enter, inspect, and photograph the
23  premises located at _____
24  at the following date and time: (within 20 days or five days before trial, whichever comes first).
25
    Dated:_____        _____(signature of defendant)_____
26
27
28
```

After you've prepared your Request for Inspection, you must file and serve it.

Step 1: Make one copy of your Request for Inspection.

Step 2: Complete the document called Proof of Service by Mail, following the instructions found in the box in Section F.3, above. You will find a blank tear-out form in the Appendix; make several copies before using it, as you may need more later. The server must be a person over 18 and not a party to the action—that is, not named in the Complaint as a plaintiff or defendant. As a defendant, you cannot serve your own legal papers.

Step 3: Make a copy of the Proof of Service by Mail, print our server's name on the last line of the copy and attach it to the copy of your Request for Inspection.

Step 4: Have your server place these papers in the mail with first class postage attached.

Step 5: Now have your server fill in the blanks in the last paragraph of the Proof of Service and sign it.

Step 6: Keep the originals of your Proof of Service by Mail and Request for Inspection in your records. You need not file these papers with the court clerk unless a dispute arises over your request.

b. Interrogatories

The discovery devices most often used in unlawful detainer cases are written interrogatories. These are questions you pose that the other side must answer. You can use a set of Form Interrogatories designed for eviction cases. These are set out in the Appendix. Here is how to use them:

• Read the interrogatories. If any is relevant to the issues in your case, check off the number of that interrogatory in the proper box of the blank tear-out "Form Interrogatories."

• Do not simply check off every box in the Form Interrogatories. If you do, the landlord may take you to court and get sanctions against you (usually a fine) based on the claim that you are using the interrogatories for purposes of harassment and delay. Make sure that the interrogatory pertains to some denial or affirmative defense you raised—for example, in your Answer—and that the landlord's answer might help you know what to expect at trial.

• Tear out the Interrogatories and follow these instructions:

Step 1: Complete the document called Proof of Service by Mail, following the instructions found in the box in Section F.3, above. You will find a blank tear-out form in the Appendix; make several copies before using it, as you may need more later. The server must be a person over 18 and not a party to the action—that is, not named in the Complaint as a plaintiff or defendant. As a defendant, you cannot serve your own legal papers.

Step 2: Make one copy of your Interrogatories and the Proof of Service by Mail. Fill in the server's name on the last line of the copy of the Proof of Service.

Step 3: Attach the copy of the Proof of Service to the copy of your Interrogatories.

Step 4: Have your server mail the copy package (the Interrogatories and the Proof of Service) to the landlord's attorney (listed on the Summons) or the landlord, if there is no attorney. The package must be mailed on the day indicated on the Proof of Service. You may also include a full set of the Interrogatories themselves if you wish.

Step 5: Now have your server fill in the blanks in the last paragraph of the Proof of Service and sign it. Attach this original to your original Interrogatories. Place these documents in your file. You don't have to file them with the court unless a dispute arises.

c. The Deposition

Depositions are oral statements made under oath. The other party must sit down with you in your lawyer's office or another site and answer questions. You must arrange to have (and pay for) a court reporter to take down the questions and answers. The transcript can be used against the person if he tries to change his story at trial.

Explaining how to set up and conduct a deposition is beyond the scope of this book. More to the point is what happens if the landlord's attorney serves a notice of deposition on you telling you to appear somewhere at a certain time for a deposition. All you have to do is appear and answer the questions. However, you may be tricked into giving an answer that later comes back to haunt you. For this reason, if possible, it is often a good idea to have a lawyer there to help you avoid the traps set by the landlord's attorney. (See Chapter 1.D.)

d. The Request to Admit

It is possible to find out just what you and the landlord agree and disagree about by requesting her to admit certain statements that you believe to be true. If they are admitted, it saves you the trouble of having to prove them in court. If, on the other hand, the landlord denies a statement, and you later prove it to be true, the landlord can be required to reimburse you for the cost of the proof. We don't provide you the forms for this discovery device, but if you are interested in using it, consult *Modern California Discovery*, published by Continuing Education of the Bar (CEB), available in most law libraries.

8. Negotiating a Settlement

At any point in a dispute, you may negotiate a settlement with the landlord. The keys to any settlement are (1) that each side has something the other wants, and (2) that each side is willing to talk to the other in a reasonable manner.

The landlord usually wants you to get out, pay back rent or both. She wants minimum expense and trouble. You have the power to cause her expense and trouble by your use of the defenses and procedural tools described in this chapter. Therefore, the landlord may be willing (reluctantly) to give you more time to get out, reduce the amount of her claim for back rent, or even pay your moving expenses if you are willing to give up your defenses and procedural tools and agree to get out on a specific, mutually agreeable day. If you are planning to move anyway, this sort of compromise may make excellent sense.

Of course, depending on the facts of your situation, you might instead hang tough, go to trial and win everything. But you always run some risk of losing. The landlord is often in the same boat. What this amounts to is that, commonly, it may be in both of your interests to lessen your risks by negotiating a settlement both of you can live with.

EXAMPLE

When Tom fails to pay his rent of $500 on May 1, Monica serves a three-day notice on him, and when that runs out without Tom paying the rent, Monica sues Tom for an eviction order and a judgment for the $500. Tom's Answer says that Monica breached the implied warranty of habitability by not getting rid of cockroaches. Monica tells Tom that at trial Monica will try to prove that the cockroaches were caused by Tom's poor housekeeping. Monica thinks she will win the trial, and Tom thinks that he will win. Each of them is sensible enough to know, however, that they might lose—and that it is certain that a trial will take up a lot of time and energy (and maybe some costs and attorney fees). So they get together and hammer out a settlement agreement: Tom agrees to get out by July 1, and Monica agrees to drop her lawsuit and any claim for back rent.

Here are a few pointers about negotiation:

• It is common for the tenant to receive forgiveness of past rent (or some of it) plus in some instances moving expenses, and sometimes even some financial help with a new security deposit, as a condition of moving out without a court fight.

• Be courteous, but don't be weak. If you have a good defense, let the landlord know that you have the resources and evidence to fight and win if she won't agree to a reasonable settlement.

• If you are in a rent control area and your defense is that the landlord breached rent control rules, consult the staff at your local rent board. They may be able to help.

• Put the settlement agreement in writing. If you can (and you may not be able to), try to avoid agreeing to a "stipulated judgment," which enables the landlord to get you out very quickly if he thinks you are not abiding by the settlement agreement. Also, credit reporting agencies get records of judgments, so a stipulated judgment may hurt your credit rating.

The following is a sample form settlement agreement that may be used with appropriate modification. A blank tear-out copy is in the Appendix.

Sample Settlement of Unlawful Detainer Action

SETTLEMENT AGREEMENT

1. _____ ("tenant") resides at the following premises: _____ ("premises").

2. _____ ("landlord") is the owner of the premises.

3. On _____ , 19___ landlord caused a Summons and Complaint in unlawful detainer to be served on tenant. The Complaint was filed in the Municipal Court for the County of _____ , _____ District, and carries the following civil number: _____ .

4. Landlord and tenant agree that tenant shall vacate the premises on or before _____ , 19___ . In exchange for this agreement, and upon full performance by tenant, landlord agrees to file a voluntary dismissal with prejudice of the Complaint specified in clause #3.

5. Also in exchange for tenant's agreement to vacate the premises on or before the date specified in clause #4, landlord agrees to:

(choose one or more of the following)

[ ] Forgive all past due rent

[ ] Forgive past due rent in the following amount: $_____

[ ] Pay the tenant $_____ to cover tenant's moving expenses, new deposit requirements, and other incidentals related to the tenant moving out.

6. Any sum specified in clause #5 to be paid by the landlord shall be paid as follows:

(choose one of the following)

[ ] Upon tenant surrendering the keys to the premises

[ ] Upon the signing of this agreement

[ ] $_____ upon the signing of this agreement and $_____ upon tenant surrendering the keys.

[ ] in the following manner:

7. The tenant's security deposit being held by landlord shall be handled as follows:

[ ] restored in full to the tenant upon surrender of the keys

[ ] treated according to law

[ ] other:

8. Tenant and landlord also agree:

a) to waive all claims and demands that each may have against the other for any transaction directly or indirectly arising from their landlord/tenant relationship;

b) that this settlement agreement not be construed as reflecting on the merits of the dispute; and

c) that landlord shall not make any negative representations to any credit reporting agency or to any other person or entity seeking information about whether tenant was a good or bad tenant.

9. Time is of the essence in this agreement. If tenant fails to timely comply with this agreement, landlord may immediately rescind this agreement in writing and proceed with his or her legal and equitable remedies.

10. This agreement was executed on _____, 19___ at _____.

Signed:_____

Signed:_____

9. Summary Judgment

Although the landlord is entitled to a trial date within three weeks after you file your Answer, she doesn't have to wait that long to obtain a judgment if she can convince the court that there is no substantial disagreement over the facts. For instance, if you both agree that you have been conducting a mail order business from your apartment, but disagree as to whether this is an illegal use of the premises, the court can decide the case without holding a full trial. This speedy procedure is termed a "summary judgment."

If the landlord files a Motion for Summary Judgment, you will be served with the Notice of Motion and an accompanying Declaration setting out the landlord's version of the facts. If you wish to contest the motion, you should file and serve a statement of your own, called a "Statement of Disputed and Undisputed Material Facts," setting forth your version of the facts. Your statement must respond specifically to the facts the landlord, in his declaration, said were undisputed. You can support your statement with declarations (from you or others) or references to other documents such as the Complaint. If your statement contradicts the landlord's facts in important particulars, and the difference in facts is important to the case, the judge should deny the motion and require the landlord to proceed to trial. Refer to the instructions for completing the Declaration accompanying the Motion to Quash, in Section F.3.e, for the required format. Your statement should be filed at least five days before the date scheduled for the summary judgment hearing (that you can find on the Notice of Motion served on you by the landlord) and should be served according to the method described for serving the Answer. (See Section 5, above.) For additional information, consult the *California Eviction Defense Manual*, published by Continuing Education of the Bar (CEB), available in most law libraries.

10. The Trial

After you file your Answer, the landlord may request the court clerk to set the case for trial. This is done by filing a "Memorandum to Set for Trial" with the municipal court clerk. Once the clerk receives this memo from the landlord, she is supposed to set the case for trial within 20 days.[41] You may file a motion to have this date extended, and it might be granted if you can show the judge that, for example, a key witness (such as you) must be out-of-town that day. Consult the *California Eviction Defense Manual* (CEB), which is available at law libraries, for how to file and serve this motion.

When you receive a copy of the landlord's Memorandum to Set for Trial, check to see whether he has requested a jury trial. If so, you needn't make a request of your own. However, the landlord usually doesn't want a jury trial, and, if you do, you will need to tell the court. Your right to demand a jury trial is secured by state law.[42] You probably should demand a jury if you will have a lawyer representing you at trial.[43] Requesting a trial often prompts the judge to try to get you and the landlord to settle the case before trial, which can be helpful to you. In the experience of most landlord-tenant lawyers, 12 ordinary people tend to be more sympathetic to tenants than one crusty old (or even young) judge. If, however, you will be representing yourself at trial, you might be better off having a judge decide the case. Judge trials are much more simple and informal than jury trials, which are usually too complicated for non-lawyers to comfortably handle by themselves.

---

[41] CCP § 1170.5(a).

[42] CCP § 1171.

[43] If you request a jury trial, you will have to post about $125-$135 with the court to pay for the jurors for one day of trial. If you win, you can recover these fees from the landlord. If the landlord posted the jury fee and wins, she can recover these from you.

Sample Demand for Jury Trial

```
_____
_____
Defendant in Pro Per




        IN THE MUNICIPAL COURT OF THE STATE OF CALIFORNIA
    COUNTY OF _____, _____ DISTRICT
_____,    )   No. _____
                               )
        Plaintiff(s),          }   DEMAND FOR JURY TRIAL
                               )
    v.                         )
                               )
_____,    )
                               )
_____Defendant(s)._____  )

    To the clerk of the above-entitled court:
    Defendant(s) hereby demand a jury trial in this action.



Date:_____        _____(signature of defendant)_____
```

You will find a blank tear-out Demand for Jury Trial form in the Appendix. Here are instructions for completing, filing and serving the Demand.

Step 1: Complete the document called Proof of Service by Mail, following the instructions found in the box in Section F.3, above. You will find a blank tear-out form in the Appendix; make several copies before using it, as you may need more later. The server must be a person over 18 and not a party to the action—that is, not named in the Complaint as a plaintiff or defendant. As a defendant, you cannot serve your own legal papers.

Step 2: Make copies of Demand For Jury Trial and Proof of Service forms.

Step 3: Attach a copy of the unsigned Proof of Service to a copy of the Demand For Jury Trial.

Step 4: Have your server mail one copy package to the landlord or his attorney, then fill in the last paragraph of the original Proof of Service and sign it.

Step 5: File the original Demand and original signed Proof of Service with the court. Have the court file stamp the second copy package for your files.

If you know ahead of trial which judge will hear the case, and you have reason to believe that this judge may not be fair to you, you may file a motion to disqualify the judge.[44] This is called a "peremptory challenge" and is described in the *California Eviction Defense Manual* (CEB). The motion must be filed at least five days before trial, together with a statement that you believe the judge will be prejudiced against you. You need not prove that the judge is prejudiced or even state detailed reasons for your belief—the disqualification is automatic. You may do this only once in any case. If you do it, you cannot be sure which judge will replace the one you disqualified—he might even be worse! So don't use your challenge lightly.

Before the trial, carefully organize your witnesses, documents, photographs and any other evidence you think is important. Ask yourself what it would take to convince a neutral person that you are right, and then organize that evidence for the judge.

At trial, be courteous and respectful to everyone. The purpose of a trial is to resolve disputes in a civilized manner; it's not a forum for yelling, sarcasm and the like. Address yourself to the judge and the witnesses only, not the other party or his attorney. It is an advantage to be forceful and to stand up for your rights, and a serious mistake to be rude or unnecessarily hostile. The most important thing is to present your side of the case clearly and with as few complications as possible. Try not to be repetitive. If you confuse, bore or annoy the judge, you lessen your chance of winning.

We do not have the space to discuss trial tactics here. If you are worried about representing yourself, watch several contested unlawful detainer trials before your court date.

11. The Judgment

If you win, the landlord cannot evict you, and you can get a judgment for your court costs—mainly your filing fee and jury fees if you paid them. If your lease or rental agreement provides for attorney fees for the prevailing party—or just for the landlord—you can recover them too.[45]

If the landlord wins, the judgment will award her possession of the premises. It may also award her money for unpaid rent (if the action was based on nonpayment of rent), damages, costs, and attorney fees (if provided by the lease or rental agreement).

If you asserted a habitability defense in your Answer, and the judge finds the landlord substantially breached his habitability obligations, you will be required to pay into the court, within five days,

---

[44] CCP § 170.6.

[45] CC § 1717.

the amount the judge determines is the reasonable rental value of the premises (in their "untenantable state") up to the time of the trial. If you don't make the payment on time, you will not be the "prevailing party" for purposes of awarding attorney fees and costs, and the court must award possession of the property to the landlord.[46] The landlord may try to collect the money part of the judgment by garnishing your wages or by going after your bank account or other property.

If you do make your payment on time and you are the "prevailing party," the court can order the landlord to make repairs, to charge only the reasonable rental value of the premises until the repairs are made, and the court can maintain continuing supervision over the landlord until the repairs are made.[47]

G. Stopping an Eviction

In rare cases, even if you lose an eviction lawsuit, the judge may give you "relief from forfeiture" of your tenancy—that is, save you from eviction. For example, suppose you didn't pay your rent because you felt the rental unit was uninhabitable, and the judge, while agreeing that there were problems, was not convinced that the rental unit was not habitable and therefore ruled against you. The judge may nonetheless stop the eviction.[48]

To persuade the judge to do this, you will probably have to show two things:

• That the eviction would cause a severe hardship on you or your family—for example, because your kids are in school, or you cannot find other housing, or you would have to move away from your job, or you are elderly or handicapped.

• That you are willing and able to pay both the money you owe the landlord (for costs and back rent) and the rent in the future.

You will find a blank tear-out Application and Declaration for Relief from Eviction form in the Appendix. Here are the instructions for completing it.

Step 1: Complete the document called Proof of Service by Mail, following the instructions found in the box in Section F.3, above. You will find a blank tear-out form in the Appendix; make several copies before using it, as you may need more later. The server must be a person over 18 and not a party to the action—that is, not named in the Complaint as a plaintiff or defendant. As a defendant, you cannot serve your own legal papers.

Step 2: Make copies of Application and Declaration for Relief from Eviction and Proof of Service forms.

Step 3: Attach a copy of the unsigned Proof of Service to a copy of the Application and Declaration for Relief from Eviction.

Step 4: Have your server mail one copy package to the landlord or his attorney, then fill in the last paragraph of the original Proof of Service and sign it.

Step 5: File the original Application and Declaration for Relief from Eviction and original signed Proof of Service with the court. Have the court file stamp the second copy package for your files.

---

[46] CC § 1174.2.
[47] CCP § 1174.2.
[48] CCP §§ 1179 and 1174(c).

Sample Application for Relief from Eviction

_____
_____
_____
Defendant in Pro Per

IN THE MUNICIPAL COURT OF THE STATE OF CALIFORNIA

COUNTY OF _____, _____ DISTRICT

_____,) No. _____
)
           Plaintiff(s),   } APPLICATION AND DECLARATION
) FOR RELIEF FROM EVICTION
    v.   )
) Code of Civil Procedure
_____,) Secs. 1174(c), 1179
)
_____Defendant(s)._____)

Defendant(s) _____,
hereby apply for relief from eviction, after judgment for plaintiff in this action.

If defendants are evicted, they will suffer hardship in the following way(s): _____(describe negative impact of eviction on you or your family)_____

_____.

Defendants are willing and able to pay all money they presently owe to Plaintiff, as a condition to this application being granted. Defendants are also willing and able to pay the rent as it comes due in the future.

I declare under penalty of perjury that the above statements are true and correct to the best of my knowledge.

Date:_____   _____(signature of defendant)_____

H. Postponing an Eviction

Even if the judge will not stop the eviction, she may postpone (stay) it for some limited time, for a good reason—for example, to give you more time to find another place—or to let you stay where you are while you appeal. If you need time to find another place, explain how difficult it is to locate available housing in your city and ask for a stay of about 30 days. File an application for a stay as soon as possible after you receive notice of the judgment.

If you seek a stay during an appeal, you must show the court that (1) you will suffer "extreme hardship" if you are evicted, and (2) that the landlord will not be hurt by the stay. Specifically, the stay must be conditioned on your paying rent into court as it comes due. The court may also impose other conditions on the stay. If the trial court denies a stay during appeal, you may ask the appellate court to grant a stay.[48] You will probably need a lawyer's help to accomplish this.

You will find a blank tear-out Application and Declation for Stay of Eviction form in the Appendix. Here are the instructions for completing it.

Step 1: Complete the document called Proof of Service by Mail, following the instructions found in the box in Section F.3, above. You will find a blank tear-out form in the Appendix; make several copies before using it, as you may need more later. The server must be a person over 18 and not a party to the action—that is, not named in the Complaint as a plaintiff or defendant. As a defendant, you cannot serve your own legal papers.

Step 2: Make copies of Application and Declation for Stay of Eviction and Proof of Service forms.

Step 3: Attach a copy of the unsigned Proof of Service to a copy of the Application for Relief from Eviction.

Step 4: Have your server mail one copy package to the landlord or his attorney, then fill in the last paragraph of the original Proof of Service and sign it.

Step 5: File the original Application and Declation for Stay of Eviction and original signed Proof of Service with the court. Have the court file stamp the second copy package for your files.

---

[48] CCP § 1176.

Sample Application for Stay of Eviction

```
_____
_____
_____
Defendant in Pro Per




        IN THE MUNICIPAL COURT OF THE STATE OF CALIFORNIA
   COUNTY OF _____, _____ DISTRICT

_____,     )  No. _____
                             )
        Plaintiff(s),        )  APPLICATION AND DECLARATION
                             )  FOR STAY OF EVICTION
   v.                        )
                             )
_____,     )
                             )
        Defendant(s).        )
```

Defendant(s) _____,
hereby apply for stay of execution from any writ of restitution or possession in this case, for the following period of time:
_____.

Such a stay is appropriate in this case for the following reason(s):
_____
_____.

I declare under penalty of perjury that the above statements are true and correct to the best of my knowledge.

Date:_____   _____
                                      (signature of defendant)

I. Appeal From an Eviction

To appeal a court's eviction order, you must file a paper called "Notice of Appeal" with the clerk of the municipal court. You must file it within 30 days of receiving notice that judgment was entered against you. The appeal is to the Appellate Department of the Superior Court.

On appeal, you may argue only issues of law, not fact. This means that you may argue that the trial court erred by ruling that, for example, there can be no breach of the implied warranty of habitability if the lease says that the tenant waives his rights under this doctrine—an issue of law. But you may not argue that the judge was wrong in believing the landlord's testimony rather than yours, because that is an issue of fact. After you file your Notice of Appeal, the appellate department will notify you about when your brief (the document in which you argue points of law) must be filed in that court.

Appeals are pretty technical, and we recommend that you get a lawyer if possible.

Warning: Filing a Notice of Appeal does not automatically stop the sheriff from carrying out an eviction. To do that, you must seek a stay of the eviction from the trial court judge, as discussed in the preceding section. If you plan to appeal and feel you have a good argument that the trial court misinterpreted the law, include these facts in your application for the stay.

You will find a blank tear-out Notice of Appeal form in the Appendix. Here are the instructions for completing it.

Step 1: Complete the document called Proof of Service by Mail, following the instructions found in the box in Section F.3, above. You will find a blank tear-out form in the Appendix; make several copies before using it, as you may need more later. The server must be a person over 18 and not a party to the action—that is, not named in the Complaint as a plaintiff or defendant. As a defendant, you cannot serve your own legal papers.

Step 2: Make copies of Notice of Appeal and Proof of Service forms.

Step 3: Attach a copy of the unsigned Proof of Service to a copy of the Notice of Appeal.

Step 4: Have your server mail one copy package to the landlord or his attorney, then fill in the last paragraph of the original Proof of Service and sign it.

Step 5: File the original Notice of Appeal and original signed Proof of Service with the court. Have the court file stamp the second copy package for your files.

J. After the Lawsuit—Eviction by the Sheriff

If the landlord wins the eviction case in court (or because you never responded in writing to the landlord's lawsuit within the time allowed—see Section F.2), the judge will sign a "writ of possession." The landlord will give this writ to the sheriff's department and pay a fee, which will be added to the judgment against you. A deputy sheriff will then serve the writ on you, along with an order that you vacate within five days. It might take the sheriff a few days to serve you with the writ. Some sheriffs serve such writs only on certain days of the week.

Sample Notice of Appeal

Defendant in Pro Per

IN THE MUNICIPAL COURT OF THE STATE OF CALIFORNIA

COUNTY OF _____, _____ DISTRICT

_____,) No. _____
)
    Plaintiff(s), } NOTICE OF APPEAL AND NOTICE
)   TO PREPARE CLERK'S TRANSCRIPT
  v.   )
)
_____,)
)
    Defendant(s).)

Defendant(s) _____,
hereby appeal to the Appellate Department of the Superior Court.

Defendant(s) hereby request that a Clerk's Transcript be prepared, and that this transcript include all documents filed in this action and all minute orders and other rulings and judgments issued by the court in this action.

Date:_____   _____
                                      (signature of defendant)

If you are served with the writ and are not out in five days, the sheriff will return and physically evict you and your family. He might also throw your belongings out with you, or have them stored by the landlord. (You may have to pay storage fees to get them back. See Chapter 9.E.)

If you are served with a five-day notice to vacate by the sheriff, it's time to move. It is much better to manage your own moving than be thrown out by the sheriff.

What if you occupied the premises on or before the date the eviction action was filed, but you are not named in the writ of possession or were not served with a Prejudgment Claim of Right to Possession? (See Section F.1, above.) If you're in this situation, you can delay your eviction by filing a form called a "Claim of Right to Possession and Notice of Hearing" after the sheriff serves the writ of possession on you or other tenants.[49] The sheriff or marshal who serves the writ of possession is required by statute to serve a copy of the form at the same time. We have included a copy here.

The sheriff should have filled in the case number on the front of the form.

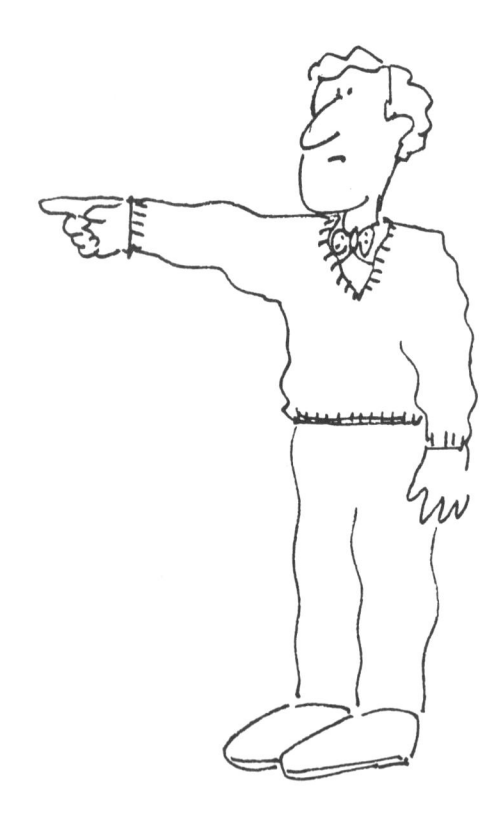

---

[49] CCP § 1174.3.

Here's how to make a claim:

1. Fill out the Claim of Right to Possession and Notice of Hearing form.

2. Give the form to the sheriff or marshal. Submitting the Claim form will stop the eviction. You can give the sheriff the form any time until and including when the sheriff comes back to evict you. You do not have to take it to the sheriff's office, although you may; you can just hand it to him.

3. Send the court the filing fee (or a form requesting waiver of the fee) within two court days, as explained on the Claim of Right to Possession and Notice of Hearing form. If you submit 15 days' rent with your filing fee, the hearing will be held within five to fifteen days. If you don't submit 15 days' rent with your filing fee, the hearing will be held in five days. (See sample letter to court.)

When the court holds its hearing, it will determine the validity of your claim. If the court rules in your favor, the Complaint will be deemed to have been served on you at the hearing, and you will be able to respond to it in any of the ways discussed above. (See Section F.) If the court rules against you, it will order the sheriff to proceed with the eviction.

Sample Letter to Court Regarding Claim of Right to Possession

```
(Date)

Municipal Court of California
_____ Judicial District
_____
_____, CA _____

Re: Unlawful Detainer Action, Case
No._____
Enclosed is a check for $_____ as
payment of the fee for filing a Claim of
Right to Possession. I filed a Claim of
Right to Possession to the premises
at_____ on
_____, 19__, by giving the Claim
to the sheriff/marshal of _____
County.
I have also enclosed a check for
$_____ , an amount equal to 15
days' rent of the premises.

Sincerely,

_____

Tom Tenant
```

Claim of Right to Possession and Notice of Hearing Form

CLAIMANT OR CLAIMANT'S ATTORNEY *(Name and Address)*:   TELEPHONE NO.:   FOR COURT USE ONLY

ATTORNEY FOR *(Name)*:
NAME OF COURT:
STREET ADDRESS:
MAILING ADDRESS:
CITY AND ZIP CODE:
BRANCH NAME:
PLAINTIFF:
DEFENDANT:

CLAIM OF RIGHT TO POSSESSION AND NOTICE OF HEARING

CASE NUMBER:

NOTICE TO LEVYING OFFICER:
☐ Claim granted ☐ Claim denied

Clerk, by _____

(For levying officer use only)
Completed form was received on

Date: _____ Time: _____

By: _____

Complete this form only if ALL of these statements are true:
1. You are NOT named in the accompanying form called Writ of Possession.
2. You occupied the premises on or before the date the unlawful detainer (eviction) action was filed. *(The date is in the accompanying Writ of Possession.)*
3. You still occupy the premises.
4. A Prejudgment Claim of Right to Possession form was NOT served with the Summons and Complaint.

I DECLARE THE FOLLOWING UNDER PENALTY OF PERJURY:

1. My name is *(specify)*:

2. I reside at *(street address, unit No., city and ZIP code)*:

3. The address of "the premises" subject to this claim is *(address)*:

4. On *(insert date)*: _____, the landlord or the landlord's authorized agent filed a complaint to recover possession of the premises. *(This date is in the accompanying Writ of Possession.)*

5. I occupied the premises on the date the complaint was filed *(the date in item 4)*. I have continued to occupy the premises ever since.

6. I was at least 18 years of age on the date the complaint was filed *(the date in item 4)*.

7. I claim a right to possession of the premises because I occupied the premises on the date the complaint was filed *(the date in item 4)*.

8. I was not named in the Writ of Possession.

9. I understand that if I make this claim of possession, a COURT HEARING will be held to decide whether my claim will be granted.

10. *(Filing fee)* To obtain a court hearing on my claim, I understand that after I present this form to the levying officer I must go to the court and pay a filing fee of $ _____ or file with the court the form "Application for Waiver of Court Fees and Costs." I understand that if I don't pay the filing fee or file the form for waiver of court fees *within two court days*, the court will immediately deny my claim.

11. *(Immediate court hearing unless you deposit 15 days' rent)* To obtain a court hearing on my claim, I understand I must also deliver to the court a copy of this completed claim form or a receipt from the levying officer. I also understand the date of my hearing will be set immediately if I don't deliver to the court an amount equal to 15 days' rent.

(Continued on reverse)

CP10 (Rev. January 1, 1991)   **CLAIM OF RIGHT TO POSSESSION AND NOTICE OF HEARING**   Code of Civil Procedure, §§ 715.010, 715.020, 1174.3

PLAINTIFF (Name):	CASE NUMBER:
DEFENDANT (Name):	

12. I am filing my claim in the following manner (check the box that shows how you are filing your claim. Note that you must deliver to the court a copy of the claim form or a levying officer's receipt):
    a. ☐ (With 15 days' rent payment) I presented this claim form to the sheriff, marshal, or other levying officer, AND within two court days I shall deliver to the court the following: (1) a copy of this completed claim form or a receipt, (2) the court filing fee or form for proceeding in forma pauperis, and (3) an amount equal to 15 days' rent. — OR —
    b. ☐ (Without 15 days' rent payment) I presented this claim form to the sheriff, marshal, or other levying officer, AND within two court days I shall deliver to the court the following: (1) a copy of this completed claim form or a receipt, and (2) the court filing fee or form for proceeding in forma pauperis.

IMPORTANT: Do not take a copy of this claim form to the court unless you have first given the form to the sheriff, marshal, or other levying officer.

(To be completed by the court)
Date of hearing: Time: Dept. or Div.:   Room:
Address of court:

NOTICE: If you fail to appear at this hearing you will be evicted without further hearing.

13. **Rental agreement.** I have (check all that apply to you):
    a. ☐ an oral rental agreement with the landlord.
    b. ☐ a written rental agreement with the landlord.
    c. ☐ an oral rental agreement with a person other than the landlord.
    d. ☐ a written rental agreement with a person other than the landlord.
    e. ☐ other (explain):

I declare under penalty of perjury under the laws of the State of California that the foregoing is true and correct.

WARNING: Perjury is a felony punishable by imprisonment in the state prison.

Date:

▶

(TYPE OR PRINT NAME)   (SIGNATURE OF CLAIMANT)

NOTICE: If your claim to possession is found to be valid, the unlawful detainer (eviction) action against you will be determined at trial. At trial, you may be found liable for rent, costs, and, in some cases, treble damages.

— NOTICE TO OCCUPANTS —

YOU MUST ACT AT ONCE if all the following are true:
1. You are NOT named in the accompanying form called Writ of Possession.
2. You occupied the premises on or before the date the unlawful detainer (eviction) action was filed. (The date is in the accompanying Writ of Possession.)
3. You still occupy the premises.
4. A Prejudgment Claim of Right to Possession form was NOT served with the Summons and Complaint.

You can complete and SUBMIT THIS CLAIM FORM (in person with identification)
(1) before the date of eviction at the sheriff's or marshal's office located at (address):

(2) OR at the premises at the time of the eviction. (Give this form to the officer who comes to evict you.)

If you do not complete and submit this form (and pay a filing fee or file the form for proceeding in forma pauperis if you cannot pay the fee), YOU WILL BE EVICTED along with the parties named in the writ.

After this form is properly filed, A HEARING WILL BE HELD to decide your claim. If you do not appear at the hearing, you will be evicted without a further hearing.

CP10 (Rev. January 1, 1991)   **CLAIM OF RIGHT TO POSSESSION AND NOTICE OF HEARING**   Page two

chapter 12

Tenants Acting Together

A. Tenant Organizing .... 12 / 2
B. Setting Up a Tenants' Organization .... 12 / 3
    1. Getting the Tenants Together at a Meeting .... 12 / 3
    2. The First Meeting .... 12 / 4
    3. Setting Up the Organization .... 12 / 4
    4. The Second Meeting .... 12 / 5
    5. Contact Other Groups .... 12 / 5
    6. How Many Tenants Do You Need Before Acting? .... 12 / 6
C. Getting Information on the Landlord .... 12 / 6
    1. Tax Assessor's Office .... 12 / 6
    2. Local Real Estate Offices .... 12 / 7
    3. Housing Code Inspection Departments .... 12 / 7
    4. Other Sources of Information .... 12 / 7
D. Tactics .... 12 / 8
    1. Petition the Landlord .... 12 / 8
    2. Call the Building Code Inspector .... 12 / 8
    3. Picketing and Publicity .... 12 / 9
    4. Rent Strikes .... 12 / 10
    5. Repair and Deduct Remedy .... 12 / 11
    6. Lawsuits Against the Landlord .... 12 / 11
    7. Landlord's Countertactics .... 12 / 11
E. Negotiations .... 12 / 12
    1. Preparations .... 12 / 12
    2. The Negotiating Meeting .... 12 / 12
F. The Agreement .... 12 / 13

So far in this book we have only discussed strategies and procedures for the tenant who is acting alone. While an individual can certainly solve her own tenant-landlord problems, a group of tenants working together is even more likely to achieve results.

This chapter will give you some ideas on how to set up a tenant organization, tactics to use in dealing with the landlord, and how to negotiate a good agreement with him.

Keep in mind, however, that a tenant organization is only as effective as the will of its members and leaders to make it effective. This takes time, energy, patience and the willingness to take risks. Most of all, it takes mutual understanding and a shared sense of community amongst the tenants. Of course it is important that you and others have a good feel for organization and that you understand your legal rights, yet in the end it is equally important that your group shares a common identity that will ensure each member's commitment to the cause. If you feel that this is lacking, and that it cannot be inspired, then you probably should give up the idea of forming a tenant organization. Find some way of dealing with the landlord by yourself.

A. Tenant Organizing

As we have seen, the odds are often against an individual tenant who is trying to get an unreasonable landlord to be more reasonable. The landlord has most of the power. Not only is state law somewhat weighted in her favor, but she normally has far more in the way of financial resources than does the tenant. Most landlords can afford attorneys—most tenants cannot. As long as tenants are divided, she can deal with each one separately and will usually come out on top.

In many ways the landlord/tenant situation today (especially in areas without strong rent control ordinances) is similar to the labor/management situation of 1900. One worker without a union had little chance of getting better working conditions or wages from a giant corporation. Indeed, a worker who showed the bad sense to make such a request would probably be walking the bricks in a big hurry. While one tenant dealing with a small landlord might be able to work out a sensible relationship, the individual tenant dealing with the large landlord has little chance of influencing his situation very much. In fact, he is in much the same situation as was the worker before unions came on the scene. The bigger the business, the more it is run like a machine, and the more humanity is forced out. The tenant, unless she is lucky enough to live in a city with an effective rent control ordinance, either conforms to the many rules in the lease and lets her rent be raised whenever it suits the landlord, or she is out on the street trying to find another place that will probably be just as bad.

There are two ways to restore the balance of power in landlord/tenant relationships, at least to some degree. One involves organizing to pass an effective rent control ordinance which both limits rent increases and requires just cause for eviction. We discuss rent control in some detail in Chapter 4. Suffice it to say that in many California cities rent control ordinances (which not only protect a tenant from outlandish rent increases, but also provide some security against arbitrary eviction) have been very successful. The second involves getting tenants together and bargaining with the landlord as a group.

A tenant organization begins as a group of tenants who want to change their relationship with their landlord. This can involve forcing him to make repairs, stopping a rent increase in a non-rent control area, or stopping arbitrary mistreatment of tenants. The tenant organization may fight the landlord and force him to sign an agreement—sometimes called a collective bargaining agreement—giving the tenants all or some of what they request. If the tenant organization is together enough, it will also force the landlord to deal with it on a continuing basis.

To understand why a tenants' organization can work, consider the landlord business, especially as it relates to large rental projects. Normally, the landlord has very little of her own cash tied up in the property. Most of the time she is simply taking money from tenants in the form of rent, giving it to the bank in the form of mortgage payments and to the city in the form of taxes, and pocketing the difference. In the long run the landlord hopes that the value of the property will increase, allowing her to sell out at a substantial profit.

To pay her bills in the meantime, the landlord is dependent upon the majority of her tenants paying the rent. While she can easily deal with a few tenants who hassle her, the landlord is usually not equipped to handle any sort of concerted tenant action. If all of a sudden no one pays the rent, she is in real trouble. She can, of course, bring an eviction suit against every tenant, but this is expensive. In the meantime, she is getting no rent for a considerable period of time and her bills are piling up.

Just as the labor union's ultimate weapon is its ability to withhold labor, so, too, the strike is the ultimate sanction of a tenants' organization. This does not mean, however, that a rent strike should be used often. Many labor unions rarely strike. They don't need to. They are well organized and able to negotiate from strength. Tenants should work to create a sound, well supported organization that can negotiate from strength and that seeks to arrive at understanding rather than conflict.

For example, suppose a tenants' organization tells the landlord that it is dissatisfied with her maintenance of the property: the common areas are dirty, the yard is filled with weeds, the asphalt in the parking area has a lot of holes, the washing machine is broken, etc. Chances are the amount of money necessary to deal with these problems is small compared to the combined rent of all the tenants. A sensible landlord, then, is almost sure to clean up the problems long before the tenants ever need to carry out the threat of a strike.

Tenant organizations are usually set up in a crisis situation, when some dispute arises. This is not always the case, however. Even when no dispute is going on, a tenant organization can be a good way for neighbors to get to know each other, as well as to establish a group to deal with the landlord when problems arise.

A tenant organization can also be an effective vehicle to work out problems among tenants. As any tenant in a multi-unit building knows, a neighbor with a loud stereo (or kid, dog or spouse) can cause more day-to-day misery than the most obnoxious landlord. In this context, an effective tenants' union can set up a voluntary mediation procedure to help members settle problems before they fester. Local mediation services, such as the Community Boards program in San Francisco, can help you do this. Never overlook the importance of solving disputes between tenants before turning to the landlord. For example, one of the authors formerly lived in a 14-unit project with an active tenants' organization. At one point there was even the hope that the tenants could buy the project and turn it into a co-op. Unfortunately, the whole organization fell apart when most meetings turned into disputes between those tenants who had dogs and those who didn't, leaving not enough time or energy to deal with the landlord.

B. Setting Up a Tenants' Organization

A number of organized tenants' groups describe themselves as "tenants' organizations" while others use the term "tenants' union." It makes no legal difference and we use the terms interchangeably.

1. Getting the Tenants Together at a Meeting

Two or three concerned tenants can start a tenants' organization, if they are willing to do the work.

First, set a meeting time and place. Both should be convenient for most of the tenants. If everyone lives in one large building or group of buildings, this is easy. If the landlord owns several smaller scattered buildings, you will need to allow some time both to contact people and to make sure that there are enough grievances in common to make organizing possible.

Next, contact the tenants and ask them to come to the meeting. If you can possibly afford the time, do this in person, door-to-door. Recruit other tenants to help you. Use posting or distribution of notices only as a last resort or as a supplement to personal contact. If there are different races or ethnic groups in the building, you may want to get someone from each group. If more than one building is involved, make sure you have the active involvement of someone from each.

2. The First Meeting

The first meeting should be conducted informally. People should get to know each other. They should be encouraged to speak about problems they have had with the building or the landlord. This way they will see what problems they have in common.

After this, explain to people the possibilities of collective action described here and the benefits of acting together.

Next, try to deal with tenants' fears. People will be afraid of being evicted if they fight the landlord. Even if not expressed, these fears are there, so you had better try to bring them out and deal with them, or else you will find the tenants committing now but dropping out later when the action starts.

Explain to the tenants that while some tactics involve a high risk of eviction (such as the rent strike), others do not (such as forming a tenants' organization, writing to the landlord or picketing), if the group has a competent lawyer to protect it from retaliatory evictions (which are prohibited by law). Also make sure that everyone realizes that it will be up to the group to democratically decide which tactics to use. Emphasize that absolutely no action will be taken until the group is ready, having first figured out a strategy, elected leaders, made work assignments, and lined up legal representation and community support. Tell them, however, that there is always some risk of eviction or rent raise (unless you are in a city with a tight rent control ordinance), and if anyone is not willing to take it, he had better drop out now so the others don't depend on him.

From the very beginning, try to deal with the problem of internal dissension. Among the group, there are very likely to be feuds, jealousies, and maybe even racial or ethnic prejudices. Try to bring these out in the open and resolve them as soon as possible, or else they will keep the group from working together if the going gets tough.

3. Setting Up the Organization

At the first meeting, if you feel that the tenants have the qualities needed to take on the landlord, and they more or less agree on the problems to be addressed, set up the organization of your tenant union. You might elect officers, including a president, vice president, secretary and treasurer. Or, you might elect a "steering committee" or four or five members (with a chairperson) to be responsible for running day-to-day operations, including establishing the time and place of meetings, etc.

In setting up an organization, the most important thing is to see that there is a person responsible for each job which is important to the group. Here are some of the jobs that will need to be done:

1. Line up a lawyer.

2. Find out the legal reality of your situation. This means learning your rights under state law. If you are in a city covered by rent control, it also means studying the ordinance and regulations.

3. Coordinate publicity.

4. Get support from other groups.

5. Handle the finances.

6. Coordinate communication among the tenants (set up further meetings, contact people, etc.).

7. Draw up a list of tenants' demands and plan negotiations with the landlord.

8. Gather information on the landlord. (See Section C, below.)

Each of these jobs can be assigned to a committee chairperson, or they can be handled by certain officers. The actual work on these jobs should be done by as many people as possible, so everyone feels involved and no one feels overburdened. But make sure that there is one person responsible for seeing that each job gets done, and that the chairperson or president is responsible for seeing that they get the job done.

Before adjourning the first meeting, the group should:

1. Select a name (for example, "540 Alcatraz Ave. Tenants' Union");

2. Decide the time and place of the second meeting; and

3. Assign to specific people the jobs needed to be done before the second meeting, such as lining up a lawyer and contacting other tenants.

4. The Second Meeting

If you face serious immediate problems with the landlord, the second meeting of the tenant union should be devoted to planning a strategy, and your lawyer should be present. Get some agreement on what are the most serious problems the tenants want resolved. Then have your "information" chairperson report on what she found out about the landlord and to which tactics the landlord might be most vulnerable. Then the lawyer should explain the possible consequences of using certain tactics and what he can do to protect the tenants.

Make sure that both the lawyer and the tenants understand that the lawyer is there only to give advice and to help protect the tenants. She is not there to make decisions for the group—only to supply necessary information to allow the group to choose a sensible course of action. If you get a lawyer who wants to run everything, get another. Also, see that tenants do not ask the lawyer to help solve their individual problems. She is there for the group, not for individuals, and if people fall back into an "individual" rather than "group" way of trying to solve problems, the tenant organization will fail.

Then the group should formulate a strategy. Make sure that there is general agreement on whatever strategy you decide on. A simple majority vote will not do if there is strong minority feeling opposed to it.

After the strategy is formulated, make specific work assignments to specific people, with deadlines for reporting to the chairperson or the group that the job is done.

5. Contact Other Groups

Assuming your strategy involves a fairly direct confrontation with the landlord, you should try as soon as possible to get support from other groups in the community which can help with publicity, political influence and moral support. Ask each tenant what groups he has contacts with which might help.

Be sure to contact groups which are concerned with tenants' rights. Some cities now have city-wide tenant associations. They can furnish technical advice as well as publicity and moral support. In the San Francisco Bay area, The Public Interest Clearinghouse publishes a directory of public interest organizations, including tenants' groups. It's available from PIC at 200 McAllister St., San Francisco, CA 94102, (415) 565-4695. In Los Angeles, contact the Coalition for Economic Survival, 1296 North Fairfax, Los Angeles, CA 90046, (213) 656-4410.

6. How Many Tenants Do You Need Before Acting?

There is no set number. Sometimes only a few tenants join initially, but many others may come in when the word spreads that the group is doing something and not just talking. If you cannot get a lot of people at first, try to get some key people who will influence others and bring them in later.

Obviously, the more tenants you have with you the more pressure the landlord will feel, so try to get as many tenants to join as you can.

C. Getting Information on the Landlord

In order to find out how to deal with the landlord, you will need information on her. Sometimes you need to find out who the owner is. You should try to find out what her financial situation is like to see where she is most vulnerable. You need to know something about her personality before you negotiate with her.

Here are some sources of information you might check out.

1. Tax Assessor's Office

The City or County Tax Assessor estimates the value of each piece of property and keeps a record of to whom the tax bill is sent and who pays the taxes. This information is kept according to address, so you can obtain it without first knowing the name of the owner.

This can help you identify the real owner. Usually he is the one who pays the taxes. If not, then investigating the person who does pay the taxes can lead you to the real owner. If taxes have not been paid, this indicates either the landlord's poor financial condition or possibly her intent to abandon the building to the city or county.

The amount of the tax is a significant part of the landlord's expense in running the building. You may want to know this for negotiations.

Some assessors keep an alphabetical list of people who pay property taxes, specifying each piece of property on which they pay taxes. This can tell you how much property the landlord owns in the city or county and where it is. If he has other rental buildings, talk to the tenants there and see if they are interested in joining your effort. This can really help you increase the pressure on the landlord.

2. Local Real Estate Offices

For income tax reasons, many buildings are put up for sale rather frequently, usually six to ten years after purchase. There is a fair chance that, at any given time, your building will be on the market.

You might send some substantial-looking person into a local real estate office to ask if the building is for sale and to express interest in buying it. The real estate agent might furnish him with some very helpful information concerning the building, especially information relating to income and expenses. While this information may be slanted to make the building seem more profitable than it is, this bias should make the figures useful to rebut the landlord's inevitable complaints that she is suffering financially from owning the building.

3. Housing Code Inspection Departments

The city or county housing or building inspection department can provide you with information about the condition of the building and the landlord's efforts (or lack of them) to repair.

First, since he must obtain a permit to make alterations in the building, you can find out when he last made substantial repairs and what he planned to do.

Second, find out when the agency last inspected the building and whether any violations were corrected. This documentation can be useful later for publicity or in court.

Also, find out if they have recorded any complaints by tenants. This can build your case that tenants have long been concerned about the landlord's failure to repair.

Records of the building inspector's dealings with the landlord are open to the public and may be copied.[1]

4. Other Sources of Information

If you want to do a thorough job, here are some other sources of information you might check out.

a. County Recorder's Office

If you know the name of the present owner, you can find out names of prior owners and who has mortgages, deeds of trust, or liens on the property.

b. Rent Control Board

In several California cities (including Berkeley, Santa Monica and West Hollywood), a landlord must register all rental property with the city rent control board. Comprehensive information telling you how much rent can be charged is available.

c. Title Insurance Companies

They can tell you everything about the ownership of the property, including mortgages, etc. They usually charge for their services, but some people (such as attorneys who do real estate work) can often get information from title companies for nothing.

d. Secretary of State

If the building is owned by a corporation, the Secretary of State can tell you who runs the corporation. Contact the California Secretary of State's Office, 1230 J Street, Sacramento CA 95814.

e. Newspapers

A look through the local newspaper's library of past issues ("morgue") can sometimes produce good information on a landlord. A reporter who has covered the neighborhood for some time might also be helpful.

---

[1] Government Code §§ 6253 and 7254.7(c).

f. Ex-Managers and Former Tenants

These people might tell you how the landlord has treated people in the past. Since they are out, they have nothing to lose, and if they were mistreated by the landlord, they might be willing to help.

D. Tactics

If you have problems with your landlord, a tenant organization can pursue several strategies.

1. Petition the Landlord

One good first step is to draw up a list of your complaints and demands and give it to the landlord.

This document should be worded politely but firmly. Remember that it might later get into the hands of other people, such as the newspapers or the courts, so you want to sound reasonable, even if the landlord deserves something stronger.

The demands should be clearly set out, and there should be a final request for a response or a meeting by a specific time (such as a week later). Although it is probably not wise to set out at this point exactly what you intend to do if the landlord is not cooperative (since you want to leave your options open until you are ready to act), the petition should carry the clear implication that the group means business.

It is usually better if all the tenants in the group sign the petition. This lets the landlord know that the people are united and serious enough about this to sign their names and risk possible reprisals. It also tends to make the people feel more committed.

The petition is a useful starting tactic, no matter what else you later decide to do. It forces the group to stop talking about general problems and decide what issues it will focus on. Often it will impress the landlord into agreeing to solve some, or all, of the problems. Even if it doesn't, the landlord's response will give you an idea of how to deal with her in the future. Also, if you start with a reasonable petition, you are in a positive position to demonstrate later to newspapers, courts, and other groups that you made every effort to be reasonable before you had to resort to pressure tactics.

A number of California cities and counties offer non-binding mediation programs. In some situations sitting down with your landlord to discuss the issues in this sort of forum can be a good idea. If no agreement is forthcoming in a reasonable time, you can always resort to tougher tactics later. Also, if the landlord refuses to be reasonable, it is likely to convince those tenants who are reluctant to organize and take a strong stand that doing so is the only way to accomplish your goals.

2. Call the Building Code Inspector

If your grievances have to do with the substandard condition of the premises, call the local code inspector and ask for an inspection of the building. (See Chapter 7.B.3, for a discussion of local agencies, such as the Building Inspection and Health Departments.) This can be useful for several purposes.

First, an inspection which results in a report that there are violations shows that the tenants have legitimate grievances and are not just making things up to cause trouble or withhold rent.

Second, if you end up in court, you have the inspector available as a neutral, expert witness who can testify as to conditions in the building.

Third, an inspection which results in an order from the agency that the landlord make repairs may get him to fix the place, because otherwise the agency might have it condemned. Many sophisticated landlords, however, know how to handle the agency so as to avoid making repairs until the last possible moment. They are friendly with the inspectors, know how to take appeals and get extensions, and might get the agency to hold off by doing a few things and saying he is "working on" the others. He is less likely to get away with this where there are serious health hazards, such as rats or no heat. In this case, call the Health Department rather than the Building Inspection Department.

There are some dangers in reporting code violations. First, if the building is really in bad shape, you may get too much action. The agency may condemn the building, or the landlord might decide it is cheaper to tear it down than fix it up. In either case, the tenants might be evicted.

Second, before calling the inspector, make sure that bad conditions were not caused by tenants, even in part. If they were, the inspector will probably find out about it and her report will probably do you more harm than good.

Finally, there is a danger of eviction if the landlord finds out who reported the violations. However, because retaliatory evictions are prohibited by law, you should prevail if you bring the facts to light in court.[2] Indeed, in some instances, reporting code violations provides protection for subsequent organizing activities, since a later eviction may be inferred to be retaliatory.

Before you call out a code inspector, try to find out if there is some inspector in the agency who will be sympathetic to what you are trying to accomplish. If there is, talk to him about these problems and see what he advises. He may be able to set things up so you get the most out of the inspection with the least risk.

Rent Control Note: In a few California cities, including Berkeley and Santa Monica, the existence of substandard housing conditions is a valid reason to petition the local rent control board for a rent reduction.

---

[2]CC § 1942.5.

3. Picketing and Publicity

Landlords don't like negative publicity, particularly if it affects their business or social lives. So it can be a very useful tactic to let the world know that your landlord owns units with serious health or safety problems.

Whenever you seek publicity by any means, make sure that you make specific charges and that what you are saying is true. This will keep you out of legal trouble and keep support on your side.

There are many ways to get publicity.

Picketing at the building itself involves no travel time or expense, so it is easier to get tenants out to picket. This lets tenants, prospective tenants, and the neighborhood in general know what is going on, and it can help muster support. Picketing at the landlord's office can put economic pressure on her by persuading her customers to stay away. This can be particularly effective when she is a rental agent or management company. A third possible location is the landlord's residence. This can be particularly effective if the grievances are truly serious.

Whenever you picket, be sure to notify local media and have lists of your grievances available for reporters. Their coverage will multiply the effect of your picketing.

Banners in the windows of tenants' apartments are another good way of letting tenants, prospective tenants and the neighborhood know what is happening. Leaflets can also serve this purpose, and they are good to use when picketing, so people passing by (including reporters) can get the details of the dispute.

A press conference can be a good way of getting to all of the media at once. To get reporters and TV people to come, however, you will have to call them personally, well ahead of time, and set up a time when they can come (that is, when nothing else of importance is happening). Also, try to make the dispute sound dramatic. If conditions in the building are bad, have the press conference at the building and show the reporters the worst conditions.

If picketing or other publicity is hurting the landlord, he might file a lawsuit to try to stop it. He may ask the court to limit the number of pickets, stop distribution of material he claims is untrue, or stop the campaign entirely. The law on these issues is not clear, and what happens depends a lot on how the judge feels about it. Therefore, it is very helpful to have a lawyer to advise you and ready to represent you when you start a publicity campaign.

4. Rent Strikes

The rent strike can be the tenants' most powerful tactic. It brings direct and immediate economic pressure to bear on the landlord. Without the income from rent, few landlords are able to keep up with their mortgage payments, property taxes, and other expenses for very long. If the landlord cannot break the strike quickly, she must come to the bargaining table.

A rent strike is now legal in California, if the landlord has materially breached his "implied warranty of habitability" by failing to correct serious housing code violations. How this doctrine works is discussed more fully in the section on rent withholding in Chapter 7.

If no material problems of habitability are involved in your dispute, a rent strike is not legal, but might work anyway, because the landlord might prefer to negotiate rather than try to evict.

If you decide that your landlord is being so unreasonable that no other course of action is open to you but a rent strike, there are some things you might do to minimize the danger of eviction.

First, line up a good lawyer. If she fights the eviction action very hard and takes advantage of the rights you have, it might take the landlord a long time to evict anyone, if he ever can. He might not be able to wait that long, so he might be willing to negotiate.

Second, inform the landlord that you are not simply pocketing the rent money, but are putting it in an "escrow account" which will be disposed of after the dispute is settled (by using it to make repairs, turning it over to the landlord or something else). This escrow account is *not* required by law. But it is sure to impress the judge that you are not just trying to get something for nothing, so she may rule in your favor, or she may at least give you a chance to pay the rent to avoid eviction if she finds that the landlord did not materially breach his implied warranty of habitability. Also, if you dangle a large escrow account in front of a landlord, he will be more willing to deal with you than if the money is simply lost.

An escrow account can be set up as a bank savings account. Everyone deposits his rent into the account. For withdrawals, the signatures of both a tenant organization officer and the tenant should be required. This assures each tenant that her money will not be spent without her consent. An easier way to set up an escrow is to rent a safe deposit box in a bank and have each tenant put a money order (or certified check) for the amount of the rent in the box as it comes due. Alternatively, you might put the money in your lawyer's account.

Whichever method you choose, make sure that every tenant follows it. If some tenants get a free ride, morale will suffer badly and the group might easily fall apart.

Third, be sure to put together good evidence on the housing code violations. Take pictures (in color), get a housing code inspector or other expert to look at the place, and have tenants ready to testify as to the conditions.

Finally, keep up your campaign for publicity and community support. This can help impress the judge that this is a very important issue.

5. Repair and Deduct Remedy

Another more modest form of rent strike is permitted in California. The "repair and deduct" remedy, described in detail in Chapter 7, might be used by a group of tenants to make repairs costing no more than the total of the monthly rents of the tenants participating. For example, if the plumbing doesn't work and it will cost $1,400 to fix, four tenants might notify the landlord that they will pool their next month's rent of $350 each and have it fixed, if he does not make the repairs within a reasonable time. If he fails to do so, the tenants can have the work done, pay the bill and deduct the amount from the next month's rent. There is presently no reported case in California where tenants have pooled their rents like this, but there seems to be nothing in the repair and deduct statute to prevent it.

Many times, of course, the threat of using this sort of remedy will produce action.

6. Lawsuits Against the Landlord

A lawsuit can be another means of pressuring the landlord to negotiate with you. You might want to sue if the landlord has locked someone out,[3] committed a retaliatory eviction or rent raise,[4] or refused to repair substantial housing code violations.[5] You may file a suit yourself for up to $5,000 in small claims court. See *Everybody's Guide to Small Claims Court*,

---

[3] *Jordan v. Talbot* (1961) 55 Cal.2d 597; 12 Cal.Rptr. 488; CC § 789.3.

[4] *Aweeka v. Bonds* (1971) 20 Cal.App.3d 278; CC § 1942.5(f).

[5] *Stoiber v. Honeychuck* [1980] 101 Cal.App.3d 903.

Warner (Nolo Press), or hire a lawyer and sue in regular court.

A lawsuit puts the landlord on the defensive psychologically. He is in danger of having to pay substantial money damages. He will have to pay attorney fees, which may be expensive.

If your lawsuit asks for punitive damages (an extra amount, intended to punish the landlord for outrageous conduct), your attorney is entitled to find out the landlord's entire financial position—naturally, your landlord may not be anxious to have this made public. Your attorney may also take the landlord's "deposition," requiring him to appear and answer questions which might make him uncomfortable.

You should be very careful about the effect that filing a suit might have on your tenant union, however. Often when such a suit is filed, the tenants begin to rely too much on the lawsuit and the lawyer to solve their problems for them. They tend to stop their other efforts, and the group gradually disintegrates. If this happens, even a victory in the lawsuit usually won't help the tenants much, since most of the tenants will probably move out before the suit is settled. Be sure to tell the people (and the attorney) that the lawsuit is only one part of the campaign against the landlord to force her to negotiate with the tenant union. If they cannot accept this, then you probably should not file the suit.

7. Landlord's Countertactics

There are several things the landlord is likely to try to defeat your movement. He might file lawsuits against the tenants or try to get the police to stop the picketing. He might try to evict the leaders of the tenant union, or, thinking that if just one person is evicted the tenant union will collapse, he might try to evict one person that he has good legal grounds to evict. He might try to pit certain tenants against others, making promises to some and blaming problems on others. A common tactic is to surprise the tenants by giving in to most of their demands right away with promises, then waiting for the group to disintegrate and doing little or nothing.

The tenants should be aware of these possibilities and be ready to deal with them. They should remember (1) always to stick together and (2) to work until they have the final action they seek.

E. Negotiations

Skill in negotiating is very important to maximize the results of your campaign against the landlord. Never forget, however, that the outcome will depend much more on who has the power outside the negotiating room—that is, what you can do to the landlord if she won't give you what you want, and what you can give her if she will. The most skilled negotiator can't do much for powerless people, but inarticulate amateurs can often succeed when their opponent understands that they can and will use some real power if she does not give in.

1. Preparations

The tenant organization should select a small negotiating team to speak for them.

These people should know as much as possible about the building, the tenants and the landlord. Psychologically, the landlord can gain control of the negotiating meeting if he overwhelms the tenants with his knowledge, so the tenants had better be prepared to keep up with him.

The negotiators should have a clear understanding of what their authority is—that is, what kind of deal the tenants will accept. The tenants should discuss their demands and tell the negotiators which demands are non-negotiable and which are expendable and can be traded off. In deciding this, the tenants must understand how strong they are and what they can realistically expect to get.

A role-playing session, with some tenants playing the landlord's role, can be very helpful to give the negotiators some experience.

The negotiators should have a proposed collective bargaining agreement ready at the meeting, so that they can get the landlord to commit herself in writing then and there. If there is nothing for her to sign, she might promise to sign something but change her mind later.

Finally, the negotiators should put together an overall strategy, knowing what they are after and how they are going to get there, so they can work together and not interfere with each other.

2. The Negotiating Meeting

The meeting should not take place at the landlord's office, where he will feel comfortable and the tenants intimidated. Have the meeting at the building or somewhere else in your neighborhood. In San Francisco, check with the Community Boards program for help arranging a site. In other California cities and counties, mediation programs will often help set up tenant-landlord negotiating sessions.

Have as many tenants as possible attend the meeting. This show of unity will impress the landlord and help the negotiators. It will also stimulate tenant interest and help strengthen the tenant union.

Make sure that the person you negotiate with is the owner or has the authority to make decisions binding on the owner. If this isn't made clear at the outset, you are wasting your time.

The negotiators should get across to the landlord—directly or subtly—what the union will do if negotiations break down and what they will give her if she comes to terms. On this latter point, you might tell the landlord that the tenant union and a collective bargaining agreement giving rights to tenants can increase tenant morale. This can cut down vandalism and vacancies and make rent payments more prompt.

One of the most important elements in negotiations is the psychological atmosphere. The landlord will try to be in control and keep the negotiators on the defensive. The negotiators should realize this and try to keep the landlord on the defensive. If you work with a third party mediator, this person should help establish a neutral atmosphere.

F. The Agreement

A written agreement (sometimes called a collective bargaining agreement) with the landlord is a key goal of the tenant organization or union. Labor unions seek such agreements in order to firmly establish a continuing bargaining relationship with an employer, as well as to settle specific points of dispute. Tenant organization agreements can do the same, so that the landlord has to deal with the union rather than the isolated tenant, and so the tenant can have the power of the union behind him whenever he has a grievance. The Appendix contains a sample Collective Bargaining Agreement.

Remember, however, that the agreement will only be as effective as the continued willingness of the tenant union to make it effective. Even though the agreement is legally binding on the landlord, experience has shown that it will simply fade away unless the tenant union (or some larger neighborhood organization) is continually around to see that the landlord complies with it.

When you and your landlord sign an agreement, have the signatures notarized. Take a copy of the signed and notarized agreement to the County Recorder's Office to have it recorded. This may prevent someone who buys the building from trying to avoid the agreement.

chapter 13

Renter's Insurance

Attitudes towards insurance vary—some people wouldn't be without it while others consider it a giant rip-off. Our job is not to argue this question one way or the other, but to tell you how renter's insurance works.

Renter's insurance is a package of several types of insurance designed to cover tenants for more than one risk. Each insurance company's package will be slightly different—types of coverage offered, the dollar amounts specified for coverage and the deductible will vary. There is nothing we can tell you here that will substitute for your shopping around and comparing policies and prices. It's a good idea to talk to friends and see if they are happy with their insurance—but realize that prices for renter's insurance can be very different depending upon where you live. In certain high theft areas it is almost unobtainable.

The average renter's policy covers you against losses to your belongings occurring as a result of fire and theft, up to the amount stated on the face of the policy, which is often $15,000 or $25,000. As thefts have become more common, most policies have included "deductible" amounts of $250, or even $500. This means that if your apartment is burglarized, you collect from the insurance company only for the amount of your loss over and above the "deductible" amount.

Many renters' policies completely exclude certain property from theft coverage, including cash, credit cards, pets, etc., while others limit the amount of cash covered to $200, the value of home computers and equipment to $3,000, and jewelry and furs to $500. If you live in a flood- or earthquake-prone area, you'll have to pay extra for coverage. Earthquake policies, for example, typically run from $2 to $4 for each $1,000 of coverage, with a deductible of 10%-15% of total coverage. Make sure your policy covers what you think it does. If it doesn't, check out the policies of other companies. As a general rule, you can get whatever coverage you want if you are willing to pay for it.

If you do take out insurance on valuable items, you should inventory them: note down their values and take photos or make videotapes. Include the estimated value of each item, backed up with information on the model number and date of purchase. Keep the inventory and photos at work or some other place other than your apartment, so that if there is a problem it won't suffer the same fate as your belongings.

Some tenants who don't have much property to lose don't see a reason to have fire insurance, especially if the unit is furnished. This is sensible enough, but does overlook the fact that if the rental unit suffers fire (or water) damage as a result of tenant negligence (for example, a grease fire in a frying pan spreads and damages the kitchen), the tenant is liable, and will need insurance coverage if he is to avoid having to make good the loss out of his own pocket.

In addition to fire and theft coverage, most renter's policies give you (and your family living with you), personal liability coverage to a certain amount stated in the policy ($100,000 is typical). This means that if you directly injure someone (for example, you hit them on the head with a golf ball), he is injured on the rental property that you occupy through your negligence (for example, he slips on a broken front step), or you damage his belongings (for example, your garden hose floods the neighbor's cactus garden), you are covered. There are a lot of exclusions to personal liability coverage, important among them being any damage you do with a motor vehicle, with a boat or through your business.

Important: Your landlord's "homeowner's" insurance won't cover you. Even if you live in a duplex with your landlord and the landlord has a homeowner's policy, this policy won't protect your belongings if there is a fire or theft. Of course, if you suffer a loss as a result of your landlord's negligence, you may have a valid claim against her. Most landlords have insurance specifically to protect against this sort of risk. If you have a loss, be sure your insurance company treats you fairly. You are entitled to the present fair market value (what the property would sell for, not the replacement cost), of anything stolen or destroyed by fire or any other hazard covered by the policy after the deductible amount of the policy is subtracted, unless your policy specifies "replacement value." If the company won't pay you a fair amount, consider taking the dispute to small claims court if it is for $5,000 or less. If the loss is a major one, you might consider seeing a lawyer, but agree to pay the lawyer only a percentage of what he can recover over and above what the insurance company offers you without the lawyer's help.

Recently many landlords have begun inserting a clause into their leases or rental agreements requiring that the tenant purchase renter's insurance. This is legal under California law. The landlord's motive for doing so is threefold:

1. If the tenant's property is damaged in any way that is not the landlord's legal responsibility and the damage is covered by the renter's policy, the landlord won't have to rely on his own insurance policy.

2. Anyone who suffers a personal injury on the property in a situation where the tenant is at fault is less likely to also sue the landlord.

3. A number of landlords believe that tenants who are willing to buy insurance are more responsible than other tenants.

chapter 14

Condominium Conversion

A. Legal Protection for Tenants .... 14 / 2
B. Changing the Law .... 14 / 2

Converting buildings from rental properties into condominiums was unusual several years ago. Now, however, the general shortage of new homes, coupled with favorable tax laws, has created a condominium boom.

Condominium ownership as an abstract idea can make great sense. People have a basic need to own their own spaces, and with the high cost of land and construction, condominiums are often the only way this need can find expression. But many tenants of existing rental properties are unable or unwilling to pay large sums of money to purchase their units.

Here is a little story about what this could mean to you.

One day the mail carrier delivers an identical letter to all the tenants in a multi-unit building. The owner, it seems, has decided to convert the building from rental units to owner-occupied condominiums. Everyone will either have to buy her apartment and a share of the common space (such as halls and grounds) or move out. Those with leases must leave when they run out, and those with month-to-month tenancies under a written rental agreement must leave in 30 days. The letter concludes politely that the owners hope that they have caused no inconvenience and are sure that many tenants will welcome this opportunity to buy their units at the rock bottom price of $200,000 each.

Is there anything a tenant can do if he wants neither to move nor buy his unit? Yes.

A. Legal Protection for Tenants

Your city or county may already have passed an ordinance restricting condominium conversions, and your first step is to get a copy if one exists. But beware: many ordinances purporting to strictly limit condominium conversions were, in fact, written by developers and have no real teeth.

State law also provides that:

1. Each tenant is given 180 days' written notice of the intent to convert before termination of tenancy due to the conversion, and

2. Each tenant is given the first right to buy her apartment on at least the same terms that the apartment will be offered to the general public. The tenant has 90 days to decide.[1]

The conversion of rental units to a condominium constitutes a "subdivision" under California law. This means that several local government agencies have the right to approve or disapprove the project. A public hearing must be held before the planning commission, with the right to appeal to the city council or county board of supervisors. Tenants acting together have stopped many conversions by exerting sufficient political pressure so that proposed conversions were denied the necessary approvals.

B. Changing the Law

Tenants can also band together to get the local government to pass an ordinance allowing condominium conversions only if a number of conditions have been met. A good condominium conversion ordinance should require most, if not all, of the following conditions, before a conversion can take place:

• That existing tenants be given first right to buy their units;

• That 50% of the current tenants approve of the conversion;

• That all tenants over 65 or disabled are allowed to continue as tenants for life if they wish;

• That no conversions be allowed where the landlord has evicted large groups of tenants or greatly raised rents to get rid of tenants just before the conversion;

• That no conversions of any kind be allowed when the rental vacancy rate in a city is below 5%

---

[1] Government Code § 66427.1.

unless new rental units are being built at least fast enough to replace those converted;

• That special scrutiny be given to conversion of units rented to people with low and moderate incomes, to see that the units are priced at a level that the existing tenants can afford;

• That the landlord provide adequate relocation assistance.

To stop a proposed condominium conversion, it is essential that tenants act together and that they create political alliances with sympathetic groups in the city. If you have not already done so, read Chapter 12, Tenants Acting Together. You will want to start by checking out your landlord carefully. Look for facts about the landlord that would tend to make local government agencies unsympathetic to the conversion. Among the best are the following:

• The landlord is from out of town and has recently bought your building (and perhaps others) as a speculation;

• The landlord has a long history of violating housing codes and generally is known as a bad landlord;

• The landlord raised rents excessively, terminated tenancies for no reason, and did other things to clear out the building before the conversion was announced;

• The building is occupied by many older people (or others on fixed incomes) who have no place to go, and the landlord has made little or no effort to either allow them to stay on at terms they can afford or find them a decent place to live;

• The landlord is making an excellent return on his money as rental units, and conversion to condominiums would result in huge profits.

Appendix

Checklist

Lease

Rental Agreement

Notice to Repair

Notice of Rent Withholding

Prejudgment Claim of Right to Possession

Blank Legal Lined and Ruled Paper

Proof of Service By Mail

Demurrer

Notice of Hearing on Demurrer

Answer

Request to Inspect and for Production of Documents

Form Interrogatories

Settlement Agreement

Demand for Jury Trial

Application and Declaration for Relief from Eviction

Application and Declaration for Stay of Eviction

Notice of Appeal and Notice to Prepare Clerk's Transcript

Collective Bargaining Agreement

LANDLORD-TENANT CHECKLIST—General Condition of Rooms
(see reverse side for furnished property)

Street Address _____ Unit Number _____ City _____

	Condition on Arrival	Condition on Departure	Est. Cost of Repair/Replacement
Living Room			
Floors & Floor Coverings			
Drapes & Window Coverings			
Walls & Ceilings			
Light Fixtures			
Windows, Screens & Doors			
Front Door & Locks			
Smoke Detector			
Fireplace			
Other			
Other			
Kitchen			
Floors & Floor Coverings			
Walls & Ceilings			
Light Fixtures			
Cabinets			
Counters			
Stove/Oven			
Refrigerator			
Dishwasher			
Garbage Disposal			
Sink & Plumbing			
Smoke Detector			
Other			
Other			
Dining Room			
Floors & Floor Covering			
Walls & Ceiling			
Light Fixtures			
Windows, Screens & Doors			
Smoke Detector			
Other			
Other			

	Bath 1	Bath 2	Bath 1	Bath 2	
Bathroom(s)					
Floors & Floor Coverings					
Walls & Ceilings					
Windows, Screens & Doors					
Light Fixtures					
Bathtub/Shower					
Sink & Counters					
Toilet					
Other					
Other					

	Bedroom 1	Bedroom 2	Bedroom 3	Bedroom 1	Bedroom 2	Bedroom 3	
Bedroom(s)							
Floors & Floor Coverings							
Windows, Screens & Doors							
Walls & Ceilings							
Light Fixtures							
Smoke Detectors							
Other							
Other							

	Condition on Arrival	Condition on Departure	Est. Cost of Repair/Replacement
Other Areas			
Furnace/Heater			
Air Conditioning			
Lawn/Ground Covering			
Garden			
Patio, Terrace, Deck, etc.			
Other			
Other			

Use this space to provide any additional explanation: _____

_____

_____

☐   Tenants acknowledge that all smoke detectors were tested in their presence and found to be in working order, and that the testing procedure was explained to them. Tenants agree to test all checctors at least once a month and to report any problems to Owner/Manager in writing. Tenants agree to replace all smoke detector batteries as necessary.

LANDLORD-TENANT CHECKLIST—Furnishings

	Condition on Arrival	Condition on Departure	Est. Cost of Repair/Replacement
Living Room			
Coffee Table			
End Tables			
Lamps			
Chairs			
Sofa			
Other			
Other			
Kitchen			
Broiler pan			
Ice Trays			
Other			
Other			
Dining Area			
Chairs			
Stools			
Table			
Other			
Other			

Bathroom(s)	Bath 1	Bath 2	Bath 1	Bath 2	
Dresser Tables					
Mirrors					
Shower Curtain					
Hamper					
Other					
Other					

Bedroom(s)	Bedroom 1	Bedroom 2	Bedroom 3	Bedroom 1	Bedroom 2	Bedroom 3	
Beds (single)							
Beds (double)							
Chairs							
Chests							
Dressing Tables							
Lamps							
Mirrors							
Night Tables							
Other							
Other							

Other Areas			
Bookcases			
Desks			
Pictures			
Other			
Other			

Landlord-Tenant Checklist completed on moving in on _____, 19_____, and approved by:

_____ and _____
Owner/Manager   Tenant

_____
Tenant

_____
Tenant

Landlord-Tenant Checklist completed on moving out on _____, 19_____, and approved by:

_____ and _____
Owner/Manager   Tenant

_____
Tenant

_____
Tenant

Lease

National Housing and Economic Development Law Project Form Lease (California)

1. Parties

The parties to this Agreement are _____, hereinafter called "Landlord," and _____, hereinafter called "Tenant." If Landlord is the agent of the owner of said property, the owner's name and address is _____
_____.

2. Property

Landlord hereby lets the following property to Tenant for the term of this Agreement: (a) the property located at _____ and (b) the following furniture and appliances on said property:_____
_____
_____ _____.

3. Term

The term of this Agreement shall be for _____ beginning on _____, 19____ and ending on _____, 19____.

4. Rent

The monthly rental for said property shall be $_____, due and payable on the first day of each month.

5. Utilities

Utilities shall be paid by the party indicated on the following chart:

	Landlord	Tenant
Electricity	_____	_____
Gas	_____	_____
Water	_____	_____
Garbage collection	_____	_____
Trash removal	_____	_____
Other	_____	_____

6. Use of Property

Tenant shall use the property only for residential purposes, except for incidental use in his trade or business (such as telephone solicitation of sales orders or arts and craft created for profit), so long as such incidental use does not violate local zoning laws or affect Landlord's ability to obtain fire or liability insurance.

7. Tenant's Duty to Maintain Premises

Tenant shall keep the dwelling unit in a clean and sanitary condition and shall otherwise comply with all state and local laws requiring tenants to maintain rented premises. If damage to the dwelling unit (other than normal wear and tear) is caused by acts or neglect of Tenant or others occupying the premises with his permission, Tenant may repair such damage at his own expense. Upon Tenant's failure to make such repairs, after reasonable notice by Landlord, Landlord may cause such repairs to be made and Tenant shall be liable to Landlord for any reasonable expense thereby incurred by Landlord.

8. Alterations

No substantial alteration, addition, or improvement shall be made by Tenant in or to the dwelling unit without the prior consent of Landlord in writing. Such consent shall not be unreasonably withheld, but may be conditioned upon Tenant's agreeing to restore the dwelling unit to its prior condition upon moving out.

9. Noise

Tenant agrees not to allow on his premises any excessive noise or other activity which disturbs the peace and quiet of other tenants in the building. Landlord agrees to prevent other tenants and other persons in the building or common areas from similarly disturbing Tenant's peace and quiet.

10. Inspection by Landlord

Unless Tenant has moved out, Landlord or his agent may enter the dwelling unit only for the following purposes: to deal with an emergency (such as fire); to make necessary or agreed repairs, decorations, alterations or improvements; to supply necessary or agreed services; or to show the unit to prospective or actual purchasers, mortgagees, tenants, workmen, or contractors. Unless there is an emergency, Landlord must give at least 24 hours prior written notice of his intent to enter and the date, time, and purpose of the intended entry. (In case of an emergency entry, Landlord shall, within 2 days thereafter, notify Tenant in writing of the date, time, and purpose of the entry.) Tenant shall have the right to refuse to allow any entry (except for an emergency) before 9 AM or after 5 PM. If Tenant objects to an intended entry between 9 AM and 5 PM, Landlord shall (where feasible) attempt to arrange a more convenient time for Tenant. Landlord's entries shall not be so frequent as to seriously disturb Tenant's peaceful enjoyment of the premises and shall not be used to harass Tenant.

11. Security Deposit

a) Upon signing this Agreement, Tenant shall deposit with Landlord the sum of $_____ as a security deposit. This deposit (with any interest accrued under the subparagraph (c) of this paragraph) may be applied by Landlord toward reimbursement for any costs reasonably necessary to repair any damage to the premises caused by Tenant, to clean the premises (where Tenant has not left the premises as clean as he found them), or for due and unpaid rent.

b) Landlord shall inspect the premises within one week prior to Tenant's vacating the premises and, before Tenant vacates, shall give Tenant a written statement of needed repairs and the estimate cost thereof.

c) Within two weeks after Tenant vacates the premises, Landlord shall return to Tenant the security deposit together with interest of one-half of one per cent for each month Landlord held the deposit, less any deductions Landlord is entitled to make under subparagraph (a) of this paragraph. If Landlord makes any such deductions, he shall, within two weeks after Tenant vacates the premises, give Tenant a written itemized statement of such deductions and explanations thereof.

12. Landlord's Obligation to Repair and Maintain Premises

a) Landlord shall maintain the building and grounds appurtenant to the dwelling unit in a decent, safe, and sanitary condition, and shall comply with all state and local laws, regulations, and ordinances concerning the condition of dwelling units.

b) Landlord shall take reasonable measures to maintain security on the premises and the building and grounds appurtenant thereto to protect Tenant and other occupants and guests of the premises from burglary, robbery, and other crimes. Tenant agrees to use reasonable care in utilizing such security measures.

c) If repairs are now needed to comply with this paragraph, Landlord specifically agrees to complete the following repairs by the following dates:

Repair	Date
_____	_____
_____	_____
_____	_____
_____	_____
_____	_____
_____	_____
_____	_____

d) If Landlord substantially fails to comply with any duty imposed by this paragraph, Tenant's duty to pay rent shall abate until such failure is remedied. This subparagraph shall apply to defects within Tenant's dwelling unit only if Tenant has notified Landlord or his agent of such defects. The remedy provided by this subparagraph shall not preclude Tenant from invoking any other remedy provided by law to Tenant for Landlord's violation of this Agreement.

13. Subleasing

Tenant shall not assign this Agreement or sublet the dwelling unit without the written consent of Landlord. Such consent shall not be withheld without good reason relating to the prospective tenant's ability to comply with the provisions of this Agreement. This paragraph shall not prevent Tenant from accommodating guests for reasonable periods.

14. Failure to Pay Rent

If Tenant is unable to pay rent when due, but on or before such due date he gives Landlord or his agent written notice that he is unable to pay said rent on time and the reasons therefor, Landlord shall attempt to work out with Tenant a procedure for paying such rent as soon as possible. If, after 10 days, Landlord and Tenant are unable to work out such a procedure, Landlord may serve a notice to pay rent or vacate within 3 days, as provided by California Code of Civil Procedure Section 1161.

15. Destruction of Premises

If the premises become partially or totally destroyed during the term of this Agreement, either party may thereupon terminate this Agreement upon reasonable notice.

16. Tenant's Termination for Good Cause

Upon 30 days' written notice, for good cause, Tenant may terminate this Agreement and vacate the premises. Said notice shall state good cause for termination. Good cause shall include, but not be limited to, entry into active duty with U.S. military services, employment in another community, and loss of the main source of income used to pay the rent.

17. Termination and Cleaning

Upon termination of this Agreement, Tenant shall vacate the premises, remove all personal property belonging to him, and leave the premises as clean as he found them (normal wear and tear excepted). If the property is located in an area covered by "just cause" for eviction regulations, Landlord must comply with these regulations in order to terminate or evict.

18. Lawsuits

If either party commences a lawsuit against the other to enforce any provision of this Agreement, the successful party shall be awarded court costs from the other. Landlord specifically waives any right to recover treble or other punitive damages pursuant to California Code of Civil Procedure Section 1174.

19. Notices

All notices and rent provided by this Agreement shall be in writing and shall be given to the other party as follows:

To the Tenant: at the premises.

To the Landlord: at _____.

20. Holdovers

If Tenant holds over upon termination of this Agreement and Landlord accepts Tenant's tender of the monthly rent provided by this Agreement, the Agreement shall continue to be binding on the parties as a month-to-month tenancy.

WHEREFORE We, the undersigned, do hereby execute and agree to this Lease.

LANDLORDS: TENANTS:

_____   _____
signature   signature

            _____   _____
            date of signature   date of signature

_____   _____
signature   signature

            _____   _____
            date of signature   date of signature

Rental Agreement

National Housing and Economic Development Law Project Form Lease (California)

1. Parties

The parties to this Agreement are _____, hereinafter called "Landlord," and _____, hereinafter called "Tenant." If Landlord is the agent of the owner of said property, the owner's name and address is _____
_____.

2. Property

Landlord hereby lets the following property to Tenant for the term of this Agreement: (a) the property located at _____ and (b) the following furniture and appliances on said property:_____
_____
_____.

3. Term

This Agreement shall run month-to-month, beginning on _____.

4. Rent

The monthly rental for said property shall be $_____, due and payable on the first day of each month.

5. Utilities

Utilities shall be paid by the party indicated on the following chart:

	Landlord	Tenant
Electricity	_____	_____
Gas	_____	_____
Water	_____	_____
Garbage collection	_____	_____
Trash removal	_____	_____
Other	_____	_____

6. Use of Property

Tenant shall use the property only for residential purposes, except for incidental use in his trade or business (such as telephone solicitation of sales orders or arts and craft created for profit), so long as such incidental use does not violate local zoning laws or affect Landlord's ability to obtain fire or liability insurance.

7. Tenant's Duty to Maintain Premises

Tenant shall keep the dwelling unit in a clean and sanitary condition and shall otherwise comply with all state and local laws requiring tenants to maintain rented premises. If damage to the dwelling unit (other than normal wear and tear) is caused by acts or neglect of Tenant or others occupying the premises with his permission, Tenant may repair such damage at his own expense. Upon Tenant's failure to make such repairs, after reasonable notice by Landlord, Landlord may cause such repairs to be made and Tenant shall be liable to Landlord for any reasonable expense thereby incurred by Landlord.

8. Alterations

No substantial alteration, addition, or improvement shall be made by Tenant in or to the dwelling unit without the prior consent of Landlord in writing. Such consent shall not be unreasonably withheld, but may be conditioned upon Tenant's agreeing to restore the dwelling unit to its prior condition upon moving out.

9. Noise

Tenant agrees not to allow on his premises any excessive noise or other activity which disturbs the peace and quiet of other tenants in the building. Landlord agrees to prevent other tenants and other persons in the building or common areas from similarly disturbing Tenant's peace and quiet.

10. Inspection by Landlord

Unless Tenant has moved out, Landlord or his agent may enter the dwelling unit only for the following purposes: to deal with an emergency (such as fire); to make necessary or agreed repairs, decorations, alterations or improvements; to supply necessary or agreed services; or to show the unit to prospective or actual purchasers, mortgagees, tenants, workmen, or contractors. Unless there is an emergency, Landlord must give at least 24 hours prior written notice of his intent to enter and the date, time, and purpose of the intended entry. (In case of an emergency entry, Landlord shall, within 2 days thereafter, notify Tenant in writing of the date, time, and purpose of the entry.) Tenant shall have the right to refuse to allow any entry (except for an emergency) before 9 AM or after 5 PM. If Tenant objects to an intended entry between 9 AM and 5 PM, Landlord shall (where feasible) attempt to arrange a more convenient time for Tenant. Landlord's entries shall not be so frequent as to seriously disturb Tenant's peaceful enjoyment of the premises and shall not be used to harass Tenant.

11. Security Deposit

a) Upon signing this Agreement, Tenant shall deposit with Landlord the sum of $_____ as a security deposit. This deposit (with any interest accrued under the subparagraph (c) of this paragraph) may be applied by Landlord toward reimbursement for any costs reasonably necessary to repair any damage to the premises caused by Tenant, to clean the premises (where Tenant has not left the premises as clean as he found them), or for due and unpaid rent.

b) Landlord shall inspect the premises within one week prior to Tenant's vacating the premises and, before Tenant vacates, shall give Tenant a written statement of needed repairs and the estimate cost thereof.

c) Within two weeks after Tenant vacates the premises, Landlord shall return to Tenant the security deposit together with interest of one-half of one per cent for each month Landlord held the deposit, less any deductions Landlord is entitled to make under subparagraph (a) of this paragraph. If Landlord makes any such deductions, he shall, within two weeks after Tenant vacates the premises, give Tenant a written itemized statement of such deductions and explanations thereof.

12. Landlord's Obligation to Repair and Maintain Premises

a) Landlord shall maintain the building and grounds appurtenant to the dwelling unit in a decent, safe, and sanitary condition, and shall comply with all state and local laws, regulations, and ordinances concerning the condition of dwelling units.

b) Landlord shall take reasonable measures to maintain security on the premises and the building and grounds appurtenant thereto to protect Tenant and other occupants and guests of the premises from burglary, robbery, and other crimes. Tenant agrees to use reasonable care in utilizing such security measures.

c) If repairs are now needed to comply with this paragraph, Landlord specifically agrees to complete the following repairs by the following dates:

Repair	Date
_____	_____
_____	_____
_____	_____
_____	_____
_____	_____
_____	_____

d) If Landlord substantially fails to comply with any duty imposed by this paragraph, Tenant's duty to pay rent shall abate until such failure is remedied. This subparagraph shall apply to defects within Tenant's dwelling unit only if Tenant has notified Landlord or his agent of such defects. The remedy provided by this subparagraph shall not preclude Tenant from invoking any other remedy provided by law to Tenant for Landlord's violation of this Agreement.

13. Subleasing

Tenant shall not assign this Agreement or sublet the dwelling unit without the written consent of Landlord. Such consent shall not be withheld without good reason relating to the prospective tenant's ability to comply with the provisions of this Agreement. This paragraph shall not prevent Tenant from accommodating guests for reasonable periods.

14. Failure to Pay Rent

If Tenant is unable to pay rent when due, but on or before such due date he gives Landlord or his agent written notice that he is unable to pay said rent on time and the reasons therefor, Landlord shall attempt to work out with Tenant a procedure for paying such rent as soon as possible. If, after 10 days, Landlord and Tenant are unable to work out such a procedure, Landlord may serve a notice to pay rent or vacate within 3 days, as provided by California Code of Civil Procedure Section 1161.

15. Destruction of Premises

If the premises become partially or totally destroyed during the term of this Agreement, either party may thereupon terminate this Agreement upon reasonable notice.

16. Notice of Termination

Tenant may terminate this Agreement upon 30 days' written notice thereof to Landlord. Landlord may terminate or change the terms of this Agreement upon 60 days' written notice thereof to Tenant unless the property is located in an area covered by "just cause" for eviction regulations, in which case those regulations control. No notice shall be valid, however, if the Landlord's dominant purpose in serving it is to retaliate against the Tenant because of Tenant's attempt to exercise or assert his rights under this Agreement or any law of the State of California, its governmental subdivisions, of the United States, or because of any other lawful act of

Tenant. Any such notice shall contain a statement of the reasons for termination or change of terms, and if such statement be controverted, Landlord shall have the burden of proving its truth. This paragraph shall not affect Landlord's right to terminate for cause after expiration of a 3-day notice given pursuant to California Code of Civil Procedure Section 1161.

17. Termination and Cleaning

Upon termination of this Agreement, Tenant shall vacate the premises, remove all personal property belonging to him, and leave the premises as clean as he found them (normal wear and tear excepted). If the property is located in an area covered by "just cause" for eviction regulations, Landlord must comply with these regulations in order to terminate or evict.

18. Lawsuits

If either party commences a lawsuit against the other to enforce any provision of this Agreement, the successful party shall be awarded court costs from the other. Landlord specifically waives any right to recover treble or other punitive damages pursuant to California Code of Civil Procedure Section 1174.

19. Notices

All notices and rent provided by this Agreement shall be in writing and shall be given to the other party as follows:

To the Tenant: at the premises.

To the Landlord: at ____ _____.

WHEREFORE We, the undersigned, do hereby execute and agree to this Rental Agreement.

LANDLORDS: TENANTS:

_____   _____
signature   signature

                    _____   _____
                    date of signature   date of signature

_____   _____
signature   signature

                    _____   _____
                    date of signature   date of signature

Notice to Repair

To _____, Landlord of the premises located at
_____.

NOTICE IS HEREBY GIVEN that unless certain defects on the premises are repaired within a reasonable time, the undersigned tenant shall exercise any and all rights accruing to him pursuant to law, including those granted by California Civil Code Sections 1941-1942.

The defects are the following:

_____
_____
_____
_____
_____
_____
_____
_____
_____
_____
_____

Dated: _____   _____
                                                          signature of tenant

Notice of Rent Withholding

To _____, Landlord of the premises located at
_____.

    NOTICE IS HEREBY GIVEN that because of your failure to comply with your implied warranty of habitability by refusing to repair defects on the premises, as previously demanded of you, the undersigned tenant has elected to withhold this month's rent in accordance with California law. Rent payments will be resumed in the future, as they become due, only after said defects have been properly repaired.

Dated: _____   _____
                                                          signature of tenant

Authority: *Green v. Superior Court*, 10 Cal.3d 616 (1974).

NOTICE: EVERYONE WHO LIVES IN THIS RENTAL UNIT MAY BE EVICTED BY COURT ORDER. READ THIS FORM IF YOU LIVE HERE AND IF YOUR NAME IS NOT ON THE ATTACHED SUMMONS AND COMPLAINT.

1. If you live here and you do not complete and submit this form within 10 days of the date of service shown on this form, you will be evicted without further hearing by the court along with the persons named in the Summons and Complaint.
2. If you file this form, your claim will be determined in the eviction action against the persons named in the Complaint.
3. If you do not file this form, you will be evicted without further hearing.

CLAIMANT OR CLAIMANT'S ATTORNEY (Name and Address):

TELEPHONE NO.:

FOR COURT USE ONLY

ATTORNEY FOR (Name):

NAME OF COURT:
STREET ADDRESS:
MAILING ADDRESS:
CITY AND ZIP CODE:
BRANCH NAME:

PLAINTIFF:

DEFENDANT:

PREJUDGMENT CLAIM OF RIGHT TO POSSESSION

CASE NUMBER:

Complete this form only if ALL of these statements are true:
1. You are NOT named in the accompanying Summons and Complaint.
2. You occupied the premises on or before the date the unlawful detainer (eviction) Complaint was filed.
3. You still occupy the premises.

(To be completed by the process server)
DATE OF SERVICE:

(Date that this form is served or delivered, and posted, and mailed by the officer or process server)

I DECLARE THE FOLLOWING UNDER PENALTY OF PERJURY:

1. My name is (specify):

2. I reside at (street address, unit No., city and ZIP code):

3. The address of "the premises" subject to this claim is (address):

4. On (insert date): _____, the landlord or the landlord's authorized agent filed a complaint to recover possession of the premises. (This date is the court filing date on the accompanying Summons and Complaint.)

5. I occupied the premises on the date the complaint was filed (the date in item 4). I have continued to occupy the premises ever since.

6. I was at least 18 years of age on the date the complaint was filed (the date in item 4).

7. I claim a right to possession of the premises because I occupied the premises on the date the complaint was filed (the date in item 4).

8. I was not named in the Summons and Complaint.

9. I understand that if I make this claim of right to possession, I will be added as a defendant to the unlawful detainer (eviction) action.

10. (Filing fee) I understand that I must go to the court and pay a filing fee of $_____ or file with the court the form "Application for Waiver of Court Fees and Costs." I understand that if I don't pay the filing fee or file with the court the form for waiver of court fees within 10 days from the date of service on this form (excluding court holidays), I will not be entitled to make a claim of right to possession.

(Continued on reverse)

CP10.5 [New January 1, 1991]

PREJUDGMENT CLAIM OF RIGHT TO POSSESSION

Code of Civil Procedure, §§ 415.46, 715.010, 715.020, 1174.25

CP10.5 [New January 1, 1991] **PREJUDGMENT CLAIM OF RIGHT TO POSSESSION** Page two

PLAINTIFF (Name):	CASE NUMBER:
DEFENDANT (Name):	

NOTICE: If you fail to file this claim, you will be evicted without further hearing.

11. (*Response required within five days after you file this form*) I understand that I will have *five days* (excluding court holidays) to file a response to the Summons and Complaint after I file this Prejudgment Claim of Right to Possession form.

12. **Rental agreement.** I have (*check all that apply to you*):
   a. ☐ an oral rental agreement with the landlord.
   b. ☐ a written rental agreement with the landlord.
   c. ☐ an oral rental agreement with a person other than the landlord.
   d. ☐ a written rental agreement with a person other than the landlord.
   e. ☐ other (*explain*):

I declare under penalty of perjury under the laws of the State of California that the foregoing is true and correct.

WARNING: Perjury is a felony punishable by imprisonment in the state prison.

Date:

....   ▶
(TYPE OR PRINT NAME)   (SIGNATURE OF CLAIMANT)

NOTICE: If you file this claim of right to possession, the unlawful detainer (eviction) action against you will be determined at trial. At trial, you may be found liable for rent, costs, and, in some cases, treble damages.

—**NOTICE TO OCCUPANTS**—

YOU MUST ACT AT ONCE if all the following are true:
1. You are NOT named in the accompanying Summons and Complaint.
2. You occupied the premises on or before the date the unlawful detainer (eviction) complaint was filed. (*The date is the court filing date on the accompanying Summons and Complaint.*)
3. You still occupy the premises.

(*Where to file this form*) You can complete and SUBMIT THIS CLAIM FORM WITHIN 10 DAYS from the date of service (on the reverse of this form) at the court where the unlawful detainer (eviction) complaint was filed.

(*What will happen if you do not file this form*) If you do not complete and submit this form (and pay a filing fee or file the form for proceeding in forma pauperis if you cannot pay the fee), **YOU WILL BE EVICTED.**

After this form is properly filed, you will be added as a defendant in the unlawful detainer (eviction) action and your right to occupy the premises will be decided by the court. If you do not file this claim, you will be evicted without a hearing.

PROOF OF SERVICE BY MAIL

I am a citizen of the United States and a resident of the county of _____. I am over the age of 18 years and not a party to the above action; my residence address is: _____

_____,

California.

On _____, 19___, I served the within

_____

document on the Plaintiffs in said action by placing a true copy thereof enclosed in a sealed envelope with postage fully prepaid, in the United States Post Office mail box at _____,

California, addressed as follows: _____

_____.

I, _____, certify under penalty of perjury that the foregoing is true and correct. Executed on

_____, 19___, at _____,

California.

_____

_____

_____
_____
_____
Defendant in Pro Per

IN THE MUNICIPAL COURT OF THE STATE OF CALIFORNIA

COUNTY OF _____, _____ DISTRICT

_____,)   No. _____
)
     Plaintiff(s),   )   DEMURRER OF
)   _____
     v.   )
_____,)   TO THE COMPLAINT OF
)
     Defendant(s).   )   _____

Defendant(s) demur to the Complaint on the following ground(s):

1. _____
_____
_____
_____

2. _____
_____
_____
_____

3. _____
_____
_____
_____

Dated: _____   _____

_____
_____
Defendant in Pro Per

IN THE MUNICIPAL COURT OF THE STATE OF CALIFORNIA

COUNTY OF _____, _____ DISTRICT

_____,) No. _____
)
            Plaintiff(s),   ) NOTICE OF HEARING ON DEMURRER OF
)
     v.   ) _____
)
_____,) TO THE COMPLAINT OF
)
            Defendant(s).   )
_____ _] _____

To:

_____

PLEASE TAKE NOTICE THAT on _____, 19____, at _____ in Department No. _____ of the above entitled court, located at _____ a hearing will be held on defendant's demurrer to the Complaint, a copy of which is served with this notice.

Dated:_____   _____

ATTORNEY OR PARTY WITHOUT ATTORNEY (NAME AND ADDRESS):	TELEPHONE:	FOR COURT USE ONLY
ATTORNEY FOR (NAME):		

Insert name of court, judicial district or branch court, if any, and post office and street address:

PLAINTIFF:

DEFENDANT:

ANSWER— Unlawful Detainer

CASE NUMBER:

---

1. This pleading including attachments and exhibits consists of the following number of pages: _____
2. Defendants *(name)*:

    answer the complaint as follows:
3. **Check ONLY ONE of the next two boxes:**
    a. ☐ Defendant generally denies each statement of the complaint. *(Do not check this box if the complaint demands more than $1,000.)*
    b. ☐ Defendant admits that all of the statements of the complaint are true EXCEPT:
        (1) Defendant claims the following statements of the complaint are false *(use paragraph numbers from the complaint or explain)*:

        ☐ Continued on Attachment 3.b.(1).
        (2) Defendant has no information or belief that the following statements of the complaint are true, so defendant denies them *(use paragraph numbers from the complaint or explain)*:

        ☐ Continued on Attachment 3.b.(2).
4. AFFIRMATIVE DEFENSES
    a. ☐ *(nonpayment of rent only)* Plaintiff has breached the warranty to provide habitable premises. *(Briefly state the facts below in item 4.k.)*
    b. ☐ Plaintiff waived, changed, or canceled the notice to quit. *(Briefly state the facts below in item 4.k.)*
    c. ☐ Plaintiff served defendant with the notice to quit or filed the complaint to retaliate against defendant. *(Briefly state the facts below in item 4.k.)*
    d. ☐ Plaintiff has failed to perform his obligations under the rental agreement. *(Briefly state the facts below in item 4.k.)*
    e. ☐ By serving defendant with the notice to quit or filing the complaint, plaintiff is arbitrarily discriminating against the defendant in violation of the constitution or laws of the United States or California. *(Briefly state the facts below in item 4.k.)*
    f. ☐ Plaintiff's demand for possession violates the local rent control or eviction control ordinance of *(city or county, title of ordinance, and date of passage)*:

        (Briefly state the facts showing violation of the ordinance in item 4.k.)

(Continued)

Form Approved by the
Judicial Council of California
Effective January 1, 1982
Rule 982.1(95)

ANSWER—Unlawful Detainer

CCP 425.12
Post Record Catalog # 982.1(95)

SHORT TITLE:	CASE NUMBER:

ANSWER—Unlawful Detainer

g. ☐ Plaintiff accepted rent from defendant to cover a period of time after the date stated in paragraph 8.b. of the complaint.

h. ☐ (nonpayment of rent only) On (date): _____ defendant offered the rent due but plaintiff would not accept it.

i. ☐ Defendant made needed repairs and properly deducted the cost from the rent, and plaintiff did not give proper credit.

j. ☐ Other affirmative defenses. (Briefly state below in item 4.k.)

k. FACTS SUPPORTING AFFIRMATIVE DEFENSES CHECKED ABOVE (Identify each item separately.)

☐ Continued on Attachment 4.k.

5. OTHER STATEMENTS

a. ☐ Defendant vacated the premises on (date):
b. ☐ Defendant claims a credit for deposits of $ _____
c. ☐ The fair rental value of the premises in item 12 of the complaint is excessive (explain):

d. ☐ Other (specify):

6. DEFENDANT REQUESTS

a. that plaintiff take nothing requested in the complaint.
b. costs incurred in this proceeding.
c. ☐ reasonable attorney fees
d. ☐ other (specify):

_____   _____
(Type or print name)   (Signature of defendant or attorney)

_____   _____
(Type or print name)   (Signature of defendant or attorney)

(Each defendant for whom this answer is filed must be named in item 2 **and** must sign this answer unless represented by an attorney.)

VERIFICATION

(Use a different verification form if the verification is by an attorney or for a corporation or partnership.)

I am the defendant in this proceeding and have read this answer. I declare under penalty of perjury under the laws of the State of California that this answer is true and correct.

Date: _____

_____   _____
(Type or print name)   (Signature of defendant)

Page two

_____
_____

Defendant in Pro Per

IN THE MUNICIPAL COURT OF THE STATE OF CALIFORNIA

COUNTY OF _____, _____ DISTRICT

_____,) No. _____
)
         Plaintiff(s),   ) REQUEST TO INSPECT AND FOR
) PRODUCTION OF DOCUMENTS
    v.   )
)
_____,) Code of civil Procedure Sec. 2031
)
         Defendant(s).   )

To _____, Plaintiff, and

_____, Plaintiff's attorney:

Defendant requests that you produce and permit the copying of the following documents: _____.

Defendant requests that you produce these documents at the following address: _____

at the following date and time: _____.

Defendant further requests permission to enter, inspect, and photograph the premises located at _____

at the following date and time: _____.

Dated: _____   _____

ATTORNEY OR PARTY WITHOUT ATTORNEY (Name and Address):	TELEPHONE NO.:
ATTORNEY FOR (Name):	

NAME OF COURT AND JUDICIAL DISTRICT AND BRANCH COURT, IF ANY:

SHORT TITLE OF CASE:

FORM INTERROGATORIES — UNLAWFUL DETAINER Asking Party: Answering Party: Set No.:	CASE NUMBER:

Sec. 1. Instructions to All Parties

(a) These are general instructions. *For time limitations, requirements for service on other parties, and other details, see Code of Civil Procedure section 2030 and the cases construing it.*

(b) These interrogatories do not change existing law relating to interrogatories nor do they affect an answering party's right to assert any privilege or objection.

Sec. 2. Instructions to the Asking Party

(a) These interrogatories are designed for optional use in unlawful detainer proceedings.

(b) There are restrictions that generally limit the number of interrogatories that may be asked and the form and use of the interrogatories. For details, read Code of Civil Procedure section 2030(c).

(c) In determining whether to use these or any interrogatories, you should be aware that abuse can be punished by sanctions, including fines and attorney fees. See Code of Civil Procedure section 128.5.

(d) Check the box next to each interrogatory that you want the answering party to answer. Use care in choosing those interrogatories that are applicable to the case.

(e) Additional interrogatories may be attached.

Sec. 3. Instructions to the Answering Party

(a) An answer or other appropriate response must be given to each interrogatory checked by the asking party. Failure to respond to these interrogatories properly can be punished by sanctions, including contempt preceedings, fine, attorneys fees, and the loss of your case. See Code of Civil Procedure sections 128.5 and 2030.

(b) As a general rule, within 30 days after you are served with these interrogatories, you must serve your responses on the asking party and serve copies of your responses on all other parties to the action who have appeared. See Code of Civil Procedure section 2030 for details.

(c) Each answer must be as complete and straightforward as the information reasonably available to you permits. If an interrogatory cannot be answered completely, answer it to the extent possible.

(d) If you do not have enough personal knowledge to fully answer an interrogatory, say so, but make a reasonable and good faith effort to get the information by asking other persons or organizations, unless the information is equally available to the asking party.

(e) Whenever an interrogatory may be answered by referring to a document, the document may be attached as an exhibit to the response and referred to in the response. If the document has more than one page, refer to the page and section where the answer to the interrogatory can be found.

(f) Whenever an address and telephone number for the same person are requested in more than one interrogatory, you are required to furnish them in answering only the first interrogatory asking for that information.

(g) Your answers to these interrogatories must be verified, dated, and signed. You may wish to use the following form *at the end of your answers:*

"I declare under penalty of perjury under the laws of the State of California that the foregoing answers are true and correct.

(DATE)   (SIGNATURE)

Sec. 4. Definitions

Words in **BOLDFACE CAPITALS** in these interrogatories are defined as follows:

(a) **PERSON** includes a natural person, firm, association, organization, partnership, business, trust, corporation, or public entity.

(b) **PLAINTIFF** includes any **PERSON** who seeks recovery of the **RENTAL UNIT** whether acting as an individual or on someone else's behalf and includes all such **PERSONS** if more than one.

(Continued)

(c) **LANDLORD** includes any **PERSON** who offered the **RENTAL UNIT** for rent and any **PERSON** on whose behalf the **RENTAL UNIT** was offered for rent and their successors in interest. **LANDLORD** includes all **PERSONS** who managed the **PROPERTY** while defendant was in possession.

(d) **RENTAL UNIT** is the premises **PLAINTIFF** seeks to recover.

(e) **PROPERTY** is the building or parcel (including common areas) of which the **RENTAL UNIT** is a part. (For example, if **PLAINTIFF** is seeking to recover possession of apartment number 12 of a 20-unit building, the building is the **PROPERTY** and apartment 12 is the **RENTAL UNIT**. If **PLAINTIFF** seeks possession of cottage number 3 in a five-cottage court or complex, the court or complex is the **PROPERTY** and cottage 3 is the **RENTAL UNIT**.)

(f) **DOCUMENT** means a writing, as defined in Evidence Code section 250, and includes the original or a copy of handwriting, typewriting, printing, photostating, photographing, and every other means of recording upon any tangible thing and form of communicating or representation, including letters, words, pictures, sounds, or symbols, or combinations of them.

(g) **NOTICE TO QUIT** includes the original or copy of any notice mentioned in Code of Civil Procedure section 1161 or Civil Code section 1946, including a 3-day notice to pay rent and quit the **RENTAL UNIT**, a 3-day notice to perform conditions or covenants or quit, a 3-day notice to quit, and a 30-day notice of termination.

(h) **ADDRESS** means the street address, including the city, state, and zip code.

Sec. 5. Interrogatories

The following interrogatories have been approved by the Judicial Council under section 2033.5 of the Code of Civil Procedure for use in unlawful detainer proceedings:

CONTENTS

70.0 General
71.0 Notice
72.0 Service
73.0 Malicious Holding Over
74.0 Rent Control and Eviction Control
75.0 Breach of Warranty to Provide Habitable Premises
76.0 Waiver, Change, Withdrawal, or Cancellation of Notice to Quit
77.0 Retaliation and Arbitrary Discrimination
78.0 Nonperformance of the Rental Agreement by Landlord
79.0 Offer of Rent by Defendant
80.0 Deduction from Rent for Necessary Repairs
81.0 Fair Market Rental Value

70.0 General

[Either party may ask any applicable question in this section.]

☐ 70.1 State the name, **ADDRESS**, telephone number, and relationship to you of each **PERSON** who prepared or assisted in the preparation of the responses to these interrogatories. (Do not identify anyone who simply typed or reproduced the responses.)

☐ 70.2 Is **PLAINTIFF** an owner of the **RENTAL UNIT**? If so, state:
 (a) the nature and percentage of ownership interest;
 (b) the date **PLAINTIFF** first acquired this ownership interest.

☐ 70.3 Does **PLAINTIFF** share ownership or lack ownership? If so, state the name, the **ADDRESS**, and the nature and percentage of ownership interest of each owner.

☐ 70.4 Does **PLAINTIFF** claim the right to possession other than as an owner of the **RENTAL UNIT**? If so, state the basis of the claim.

☐ 70.5 Has **PLAINTIFF'S** interest in the **RENTAL UNIT** changed since acquisition? If so, state the nature and dates of each change.

☐ 70.6 Are there other rental units on the **PROPERTY**? If so, state how many.

☐ 70.7 During the 12 months before this proceeding was filed, did **PLAINTIFF** possess a permit or certificate of occupancy for the **RENTAL UNIT**? If so, for each state:
 (a) the name and **ADDRESS** of each **PERSON** named on the permit or certificate;
 (b) the dates of issuance and expiration;
 (c) the permit or certificate number.

☐ 70.8 Has a last month's rent, security deposit, cleaning fee, rental agency fee, credit check fee, key deposit, or any other deposit been paid on the **RENTAL UNIT**? If so, for each item state:
 (a) the purpose of the payment;
 (b) the date paid;
 (c) the amount;
 (d) the form of payment;
 (e) the name of the **PERSON** paying;
 (f) the name of the **PERSON** to whom it was paid;
 (g) any **DOCUMENT** which evidences payment and the name, **ADDRESS**, and telephone number of each **PERSON** who has the **DOCUMENT**;
 (h) any adjustments or deductions including facts.

☐ 70.9 State the date defendant first took possession of the **RENTAL UNIT**.

☐ 70.10 State the date and all the terms of any rental agreement between defendant and the **PERSON** who rented to defendant.

☐ 70.11 For each agreement alleged in the pleadings:
 (a) identify all **DOCUMENTS** that are part of the agreement and for each state the name, **ADDRESS**, and telephone number of each **PERSON** who has the **DOCUMENT**;
 (b) state each part of the agreement not in writing, the name, **ADDRESS**, and telephone number of each **PERSON** agreeing to that provision, and the date that part of the agreement was made;
 (c) identify all **DOCUMENTS** that evidence each part of the agreement not in writing and for each state the name, **ADDRESS**, and telephone number of each **PERSON** who has the **DOCUMENT**;
 (d) identify all **DOCUMENTS** that are part of each modification to the agreement, and for each state

the name, **ADDRESS**, and telephone number of each **PERSON** who has the **DOCUMENT** (see also § 71.5);
(e) state each modification not in writing, the date, and the name, **ADDRESS**, and telephone number of the **PERSON** agreeing to the modification, and the date the modification was made (see also § 71.5);
(f) identify all **DOCUMENTS** that evidence each modification of the agreement not in writing and for each state the name, **ADDRESS**, and telephone number of each **PERSON** who has the **DOCUMENT** (see also § 71.5).

☐ 70.12 Has any **PERSON** acting on the **PLAINTIFF'S** behalf been responsible for any aspect of managing or maintaining the **RENTAL UNIT** or **PROPERTY**? If so, for each **PERSON** state:
(a) the name, **ADDRESS**, and telephone number;
(b) the dates the **PERSON** managed or maintained the **RENTAL UNIT** or **PROPERTY**;
(c) the **PERSON'S** responsibilities.

☐ 70.13 For each **PERSON** who occupies any part of the **RENTAL UNIT** (except occupants named in the complaint and occupants' children under 17) state:
(a) the name, **ADDRESS**, telephone number, and birthdate;
(b) the inclusive dates of occupancy;
(c) a description of the portion of the **RENTAL UNIT** occupied;
(d) the amount paid, the term for which it was paid, and the person to whom it was paid;
(e) the nature of the use of the **RENTAL UNIT**;
(f) the name, **ADDRESS**, and telephone number of the person who authorized occupancy;
(g) how occupancy was authorized, including failure of the **LANDLORD** or **PLAINTIFF** to protest after discovering the occupancy.

☐ 70.14 Have you or anyone acting on your behalf obtained any **DOCUMENT** concerning the tenancy between any occupant of the **RENTAL UNIT** and any **PERSON** with an ownership interest or managerial responsibility for the **RENTAL UNIT**? If so, for each **DOCUMENT** state:
(a) the name, **ADDRESS**, and telephone number of each individual from whom the **DOCUMENT** was obtained;
(b) the name, **ADDRESS**, and telephone number of each individual who obtained the **DOCUMENT**;
(c) the date the **DOCUMENT** was obtained;
(d) the name, **ADDRESS**, and telephone number of each **PERSON** who has the **DOCUMENT** (original or copy).

71.0 Notice

*[If a defense is based on allegations that the 3-day notice or 30-day **NOTICE TO QUIT** is **defective in form or content**, then either party may ask any applicable question in this section.]*

☐ 71.1 Was the **NOTICE TO QUIT** on which **PLAINTIFF** bases this proceeding attached to the complaint? If not, state the contents of this notice.

☐ 71.2 State all reasons that the **NOTICE TO QUIT** was served and for each reason:
(a) state all facts supporting **PLAINTIFF'S** decision to terminate defendant's tenancy;
(b) state the names, **ADDRESSES**, and telephone numbers of all **PERSONS** who have knowledge of the facts;
(c) identify all **DOCUMENTS** that support the facts and state the name, **ADDRESS**, and telephone number of each **PERSON** who has each **DOCUMENT**.

☐ 71.3 List all rent payments and rent credits made or claimed by or on behalf of defendant beginning 12 months before the **NOTICE TO QUIT** was served. For each payment or credit state:
(a) the amount;
(b) the date received;
(c) the form in which any payment was made;
(d) the services performed or other basis for which a credit is claimed;
(e) the period covered;
(f) the name of each **PERSON** making the payment or earning the credit;
(g) the identity of all **DOCUMENTS** evidencing the payment or credit and for each state the name, **ADDRESS**, and telephone number of each **PERSON** who has the **DOCUMENT**.

☐ 71.4 Did defendant ever fail to pay the rent on time? If so, for each late payment state:
(a) the date;
(b) the amount of any late charge;
(c) the identity of all **DOCUMENTS** recording the payment and for each state the name, **ADDRESS**, and telephone number of each **PERSON** who has the **DOCUMENT**.

☐ 71.5 Since the beginning of defendant's tenancy, has **PLAINTIFF** ever raised the rent? If so, for each rent increase state:
(a) the date the increase became effective;
(b) the amount;
(c) the reasons for the rent increase;
(d) how and when defendant was notified of the increase;
(e) the identity of all **DOCUMENTS** evidencing the increase and for each state the name, **ADDRESS**, and telephone number of each **PERSON** who has the **DOCUMENT**.

[See also section 70.11(d) – (f).]

☐ 71.6 During the 12 months before the **NOTICE TO QUIT** was served was there a period during which there was no permit or certificate of occupancy for the **RENTAL UNIT**? If so, for each period state:
(a) the inclusive dates;
(b) the reasons.

☐ 71.7 Has any **PERSON** ever reported any nuisance or disturbance at or destruction of the **RENTAL UNIT** or **PROPERTY** caused by defendant or other occupant of the **RENTAL UNIT** or their guests? If so, for each report state:
(a) a description of the disturbance or destruction;
(b) the date of the report;
(c) the name of the **PERSON** who reported;
(d) the name of the **PERSON** to whom the report was made;
(e) what action was taken as a result of the report;
(f) the identity of all **DOCUMENTS** evidencing the report and for each state the name, **ADDRESS**, and telephone number of each **PERSON** who has each **DOCUMENT**.

(Continued)

☐ 71.8 Does the complaint allege violation of a term of a rental agreement or lease (other than nonpayment of rent)? If so, for each covenant:
(a) identify the covenant breached;
(b) state the facts supporting the allegation of a breach;
(c) state the names, **ADDRESSES**, and telephone numbers of all **PERSONS** who have knowledge of the facts;
(d) identify all **DOCUMENTS** that support the facts and state the name, **ADDRESS**, and telephone number of each **PERSON** who has each **DOCUMENT**.

☐ 71.9 Does the complaint allege that the defendant has been using the **RENTAL UNIT** for an illegal purpose? If so, for each purpose:
(a) identify the illegal purpose;
(b) state the facts supporting the allegations of illegal use;
(c) state the names, **ADDRESSES**, and telephone numbers of all **PERSONS** who have knowledge of the facts;
(d) identify all **DOCUMENTS** that support the facts and state the name, **ADDRESS**, and telephone number of each **PERSON** who has each **DOCUMENT**.

[Additional interrogatories on this subject may be found in sections 75.0, 78.0, 79.0, and 80.0.]

72.0 Service

*[If a defense is based on allegations that the **NOTICE TO QUIT** was **defectively served**, then either party may ask any applicable question in this section.]*

☐ 72.1 Does defendant contend (or base a defense or make any allegations) that the **NOTICE TO QUIT** was defectively served? If the answer is "no," do not answer interrogatories 72.2 through 72.3.

☐ 72.2 Does **PLAINTIFF** contend that the **NOTICE TO QUIT** referred to in the complaint was served? If so, state:
(a) the kind of notice;
(b) the date and time of service;
(c) the manner of service;
(d) the name and **ADDRESS** of the person who served it:
(e) a description of any **DOCUMENT** or conversation between defendant and the person who served the notice.

☐ 72.3 Did any person receive the **NOTICE TO QUIT** referred to in the complaint? If so, for each copy of each notice state:
(a) the name of the person who received it;
(b) the kind of notice;
(c) how it was delivered;
(d) the date received;
(e) where it was delivered;
(f) the identity of all **DOCUMENTS** evidencing the notice and for each state the name, **ADDRESS**, and telephone number of each **PERSON** who has the **DOCUMENT**.

73.0 Malicious Holding Over

[If a defendant denies allegations that defendant's continued possession is malicious, then either party may ask any applicable question in this section. Additional questions in section 75.0 may also be applicable.]

☐ 73.1 If any rent called for by the rental agreement is unpaid, state the reasons and the facts upon which the reasons are based.

☐ 73.2 Has defendant made any attempts to secure other premises since the service of the **NOTICE TO QUIT** or since the service of the summons and complaint? If so, for each attempt:
(a) state all facts indicating the attempt to secure other premises;
(b) state the names, **ADDRESSES**, and telephone numbers of all **PERSONS** who have knowledge of the facts;
(c) identify all **DOCUMENTS** that support the facts and state the name, **ADDRESS**, and telephone number of each **PERSON** who has each **DOCUMENT**.

☐ 73.3 State the facts upon which **PLAINTIFF** bases the allegation of malice.

74.0 Rent Control and Eviction Control

☐ 74.1 Is there an ordinance or other local law in this jurisdiction which limits the right to evict tenants? If your answer is no, you need not answer sections 74.2 through 74.6.

☐ 74.2 For the ordinance or other local law limiting the right to evict tenants, state:
(a) the title or number of the law;
(b) the locality.

☐ 74.3 Do you contend that the **RENTAL UNIT** is exempt from the eviction provisions of the ordinance or other local law identified in section 74.2? If so, state the facts upon which you base your contention.

☐ 74.4 Is this proceeding based on allegations of a need to recover the **RENTAL UNIT** for use of the **LANDLORD** or the landlord's relative? If so, for each intended occupant state:
(a) the name;
(b) the residence **ADDRESSES** from three years ago to the present;
(c) the relationship to the **LANDLORD**;
(d) all the intended occupant's reasons for occupancy;
(e) all rental units on the **PROPERTY** that were vacated within 60 days before and after the date the **NOTICE TO QUIT** was served.

☐ 74.5 Is the proceeding based on an allegation that the **LANDLORD** wishes to remove the **RENTAL UNIT** from residential use temporarily or permanently (for example, to rehabilitate, demolish, renovate, or convert)? If so, state:
(a) each reason for removing the **RENTAL UNIT** from residential use;
(b) what physical changes and renovation will be made to the **RENTAL UNIT**;
(c) the date the work is to begin and end;
(d) the number, date, and type of each permit for the change or work;

(Continued)

(e) the identity of each **DOCUMENT** evidencing the intended activity (for example, blueprints, plans, applications for financing, construction contracts) and the name, **ADDRESS**, and telephone number of each **PERSON** who has each **DOCUMENT**.

☐ 74.6 Is the proceeding based on any ground other than those stated in sections 74.4 and 74.5? If so, for each:
(a) state each fact supporting or opposing the ground;
(b) state the names, **ADDRESSES**, and telephone numbers of all **PERSONS** who have knowledge of the facts;
(c) identify all **DOCUMENTS** evidencing the facts and state the name, **ADDRESS**, and telephone number of each **PERSON** who has each **DOCUMENT**.

75.0 Breach of Warranty to Provide Habitable Premises

[If plaintiff alleges nonpayment of rent and defendant bases his defense on allegations of implied or express breach of warranty to provide habitable residential premises, then either party may ask any applicable question in this section.]

☐ 75.1 Do you know of any conditions in violation of state or local building codes, housing codes, or health codes, conditions of dilapidation, or other conditions in need of repair in the **RENTAL UNIT** or on the **PROPERTY** that affected the **RENTAL UNIT** at any time defendant has been in possession? If so, state:
(a) the type of condition;
(b) the kind if corrections or repairs needed;
(c) how and when you learned of these conditions;
(d) how these conditions were caused;
(e) the name, **ADDRESS**, and telephone number of each **PERSON** who has caused these conditions.

☐ 75.2 Have any corrections, repairs, or improvements been made to the **RENTAL UNIT** since the **RENTAL UNIT** was rented to defendant? If so, for each correction, repair, or improvement state:
(a) a description giving the nature and location;
(b) the date;
(c) the name, **ADDRESS**, and telephone number of each **PERSON** who made the repairs or improvements;
(d) the cost;
(e) the identity of any **DOCUMENT** evidencing the repairs or improvements;
(f) if a building permit was issued, state the issuing agencies and the permit number of your copy.

☐ 75.3 Did defendant or any other **PERSON** during 36 months before the **NOTICE TO QUIT** was served or during defendant's possession of the **RENTAL UNIT** notify the **LANDLORD** or his agent or employee about the condition of the **RENTAL UNIT** or **PROPERTY**? If so, for each written or oral notice state:
(a) the substance;
(b) who made it;
(c) when and how it was made;
(d) the name and **ADDRESS** of each **PERSON** to whom it was made;
(e) the name and **ADDRESS** of each person who knows about it;
(f) the identity of each **DOCUMENT** evidencing the notice and the name, **ADDRESS**, and telephone number of each **PERSON** who has it;

(g) the response made to the notice;
(h) the efforts made to correct the conditions;
(i) whether the **PERSON** who gave notice was an occupant of the **PROPERTY** at the time of the complaint.

☐ 75.4 During the period beginning 36 months before the **NOTICE TO QUIT** was served to the present, was the **RENTAL UNIT** or **PROPERTY** (including other rental units) inspected for dilapidations or defective conditions by a representative of any governmental agency? If so, for each inspection state:
(a) the date;
(b) the reason;
(c) the name of the governmental agency;
(d) the name, **ADDRESS**, and telephone number of each inspector;
(e) the identity of each **DOCUMENT** evidencing each inspection and the name, **ADDRESS**, and telephone number of each **PERSON** who has it.

☐ 75.5 During the period beginning 36 months before the **NOTICE TO QUIT** was served to the present, did **PLAINTIFF** or **LANDLORD** receive a notice or other communication regarding the condition of the **RENTAL UNIT** or **PROPERTY** (including other rental units) from a governmental agency? If so, for each notice or communication state:
(a) the date received;
(b) the identity of all parties;
(c) the substance of the notice or communication;
(d) the identity of each **DOCUMENT** evidencing the notice or communication and the name, **ADDRESS**, and telephone number of each **PERSON** who has it.

☐ 75.6 Was there any corrective action taken in response to the inspection or notice or communication identified in sections 75.4 and 75.5? If so, for each:
(a) identify the notice or communication;
(b) identify the condition;
(c) describe the corrective action;
(d) identify of each **DOCUMENT** evidencing the corrective action and the name, **ADDRESS**, and telephone number of each **PERSON** who has it.

☐ 75.7 Has the **PROPERTY** been appraised for sale or loan during the period beginning 36 months before the **NOTICE TO QUIT** was served to the present? If so, for each appraisal state:
(a) the date;
(b) the name, **ADDRESS**, and telephone number of the appraiser;
(c) the purpose of the appraisal;
(d) the identity of each **DOCUMENT** evidencing the appraisal and the name, **ADDRESS**, and telephone number of each **PERSON** who has it.

☐ 75.8 Was any condition requiring repair or correction at the **PROPERTY** or **RENTAL UNIT** caused by defendant or other occupant of the **RENTAL UNIT** or their guests? If so, state:
(a) the type and location of condition;
(b) the kind of corrections or repairs needed;
(c) how and when you learned of these conditions;
(d) how and when these conditions were caused;
(e) the name, **ADDRESS**, and telephone number of each **PERSON** who caused these conditions;

(f) the identity of each **DOCUMENT** evidencing the repair (or correction) and the name, **ADDRESS**, and telephone number of each **PERSON** who has it.

[See also section 71.0 for additional questions.]

76.0 Waiver, Change, Withdrawal, or Cancellation of Notice to Quit

*[If a defense is based on waiver, change, withdrawal, or cancellation of the **NOTICE TO QUIT**, then either party may ask any applicable question in this section.]*

☐ 76.1 Did the **PLAINTIFF** or **LANDLORD** or anyone acting on his or her behalf do anything which is alleged to have been a waiver, change, withdrawal, or cancellation of the **NOTICE TO QUIT**? If so:
(a) state the facts supporting this allegation;
(b) state the names, **ADDRESSES**, and telephone numbers of all **PERSONS** who have knowledge of these facts;
(c) identify each **DOCUMENT** that supports the facts and state the name, **ADDRESS**, and telephone number of each **PERSON** who has it.

☐ 76.2 Did the **PLAINTIFF** or **LANDLORD** accept rent which covered a period after the date for vacating the **RENTAL UNIT** as specified in the **NOTICE TO QUIT**? If so:
(a) state the facts;
(b) state the names, **ADDRESSES**, and telephone numbers of all **PERSONS** who have knowledge of the facts;
(c) identify each **DOCUMENT** that supports the facts and state the name, **ADDRESS**, and telephone number of each **PERSON** who has it.

77.0 Retaliation and Arbitrary Discrimination

[If a defense is based on retaliation or arbitrary discrimination, then either party may ask any applicable question in this section.]

☐ 77.1 State all reasons that the **NOTICE TO QUIT** was served or that defendant's tenancy was not renewed and for each reason:
(a) state all facts supporting **PLAINTIFF'S** decision to terminate or not renew defendant's tenancy;
(b) state the names, **ADDRESSES**, and telephone numbers of all **PERSONS** who have knowledge of the facts;
(c) identify all **DOCUMENTS** that support the facts and state the name, **ADDRESS**, and telephone number of each **PERSON** who has it.

78.0 Nonperformance of the Rental Agreement by Landlord

*[If a defense is based on nonperformance of the rental agreement by the **LANDLORD** or someone acting on the **LANDLORD'S** behalf, then either party may ask any applicable question in this section.]*

☐ 78.1 Did the **LANDLORD** or anyone acting on the **LANDLORD'S** behalf agree to make repairs, alterations, or improvements at any time or provide services to the **PROPERTY** or **RENTAL UNIT**? If so, for each agreement state:
(a) the substance of the agreement;
(b) when it was made;
(c) whether it was written or oral;
(d) by whom and to whom;
(e) the name and **ADDRESS** of each person who knows about it;
(f) whether all promised repairs, alterations, or improvements were completed or services provided;
(g) the reasons for any failure to perform;
(h) the identity of each **DOCUMENT** evidencing the agreement or promise and the name, **ADDRESS**, and telephone number of each **PERSON** who has it.

☐ 78.2 Has **PLAINTIFF** or **LANDLORD** or any resident of the **PROPERTY** ever committed disturbances or interfered with the quiet enjoyment of the **RENTAL UNIT** (including, for example, noise, acts which threaten the loss of title to the property or loss of financing, etc.)? If so, for each disturbance or interference, state:
(a) a description of each act;
(b) the date of each act;
(c) the name, **ADDRESS**, and telephone number of each **PERSON** who acted;
(d) the name, **ADDRESS**, and telephone number of each **PERSON** who witnessed each act and any **DOCUMENTS** evidencing the person's knowledge;
(e) what action was taken by the **PLAINTIFF** or **LANDLORD** to end or lessen the disturbance or interference.

79.0 Offer of Rent by Defendant

[If a defense is based on an offer of rent by a defendant which was refused, then either party may ask any applicable question in this section.]

☐ 79.1 Has defendant or anyone acting on the defendant's behalf offered any payments to **PLAINTIFF** which **PLAINTIFF** refused to accept? If so, for each offer state:
(a) the amount;
(b) the date;
(c) purpose of offer;
(d) the manner of the offer;
(e) the identity of the person making the offer;
(f) the identity of the person refusing the offer;
(g) the date of the refusal;
(h) the reasons for the refusal.

80.0 Deduction from Rent for Necessary Repairs

[If a defense to payment of rent or damages is based on claim of retaliatory eviction, then either party may ask any applicable question in this section. Additional questions in section 75.0 may also be applicable.]

☐ 80.1 Does defendant claim to have deducted from rent any amount which was withheld to make repairs after communication to the **LANDLORD** of the need for the repairs? If the answer is "no," do not answer interrogatories 80.2 through 80.6.

☐ 80.2 For each condition in need of repair for which a deduction was made, state:
(a) the nature of the condition;
(b) the location;
(c) the date the condition was discovered by defendant;
(d) the date the condition was first known by **LANDLORD** or **PLAINTIFF**;

(Continued)

(e) the dates and methods of each notice to the **LANDLORD** or **PLAINTIFF** of the condition;
(f) the response or action taken by the **LANDLORD** or **PLAINTIFF** to each notification;
(g) the cost to remedy the condition and how the cost was determined;
(h) the identity of any bids obtained for the repairs and any **DOCUMENTS** evidencing the bids.

☐ 80.3 Did **LANDLORD** or **PLAINTIFF** fail to respond within a reasonable time after receiving a communication of a need for repair? If so, for each communication state:
(a) the date it was made;
(b) how it was made;
(c) the response and date;
(d) why the delay was unreasonable.

☐ 80.4 Was there an insufficient period specified or actually allowed between the time of notification and the time repairs were begun by defendant to allow **LANDLORD** or **PLAINTIFF** to make the repairs? If so, state all facts on which the claim of insufficiency is based.

☐ 80.5 Does **PLAINTIFF** contend that any of the items for which rent deductions were taken were not allowable under law? If so, for each item state all reasons and facts on which you base your contention.

☐ 80.6 Has defendant vacated or does defendant anticipate vacating the **RENTAL UNIT** because repairs were requested and not made within a reasonable time? If so, state all facts on which defendant justifies having vacated the **RENTAL UNIT** or anticipates vacating the rental unit.

81.0 Fair Market Rental Value

*[If defendant denies **PLAINTIFF** allegation on the fair market rental value of the **RENTAL UNIT**, then either party may ask any applicale question in this section. If defendant claims that the fair market rental value is less because of a breach of warranty to provide habitable premises, then either party may also ask any applicable question in section 75.0]*

☐ 81.1 Do you have an opinion on the fair market rental value of the **RENTAL UNIT**? If so, state:
(a) the substance of your opinion;
(b) the factors upon which the fair market rental value is based;
(c) the method used to calculate the fair market rental value.

☐ 81.2 Has any other **PERSON** ever expressed to you an opinion on the fair market rental value of the **RENTAL UNIT**? If so, for each **PERSON**:
(a) state the name, **ADDRESS**, and telephone number;
(b) state the substance of the **PERSON's** opinion;
(c) describe the conversation or identify all **DOCUMENTS** in which the **PERSON** expressed an opinion and state the name, **ADDRESS**, and telephone number of each **PERSON** who has each **DOCUMENT**.

☐ 81.3 Do you know of any current violations of state or local building codes, housing codes, or health codes, conditions of dilapidation or other conditions in need of repair in the **RENTAL UNIT** or common areas that have affected the **RENTAL UNIT** at any time defendant has been in possession? If so, state:
(a) the conditions in need of repair;
(b) the kind of repairs needed;
(c) the name, **ADDRESS**, and telephone number of each **PERSON** who caused these conditions.

SETTLEMENT AGREEMENT

1. _____ ("tenant") resides at the following premises: _____ ("premises").

2. _____ ("landlord") is the owner of the premises.

3. On _____, 19___ landlord caused a Summons and Complaint in unlawful detainer to be served on tenant. The Complaint was filed in the Municipal Court for the County of _____, _____ District, and carries the following civil number: _____.

4. Landlord and tenant agree that tenant shall vacate the premises on or before _____, 19___. In exchange for this agreement, and upon full performance by tenant, landlord agrees to file a voluntary dismissal with prejudice of the Complaint specified in clause #3.

5. Also in exchange for tenant's agreement to vacate the premises on or before the date specified in clause #4, landlord agrees to:

(choose one or more of the following)

[ ] Forgive all past due rent

[ ] Forgive past due rent in the following amount: $_____

[ ] Pay the tenant $_____ to cover tenant's moving expenses, new deposit requirements, and other incidentals related to the tenant moving out.

6. Any sum specified in clause #5 to be paid by the landlord shall be paid as follows:

(choose one of the following)

[ ] Upon tenant surrendering the keys to the premises

[ ] Upon the signing of this agreement

[ ] $_____ upon the signing of this agreement and
$_____ upon tenant surrendering the keys.

[ ] in the following manner:

7. The tenant's security deposit being held by landlord shall be handled as follows:

   [ ] restored in full to the tenant upon surrender of the keys
   [ ] treated according to law
   [ ] other:

8. Tenant and landlord also agree:

   a) to waive all claims and demands that each may have against the other for any transaction directly or indirectly arising from their landlord/tenant relationship;

   b) that this settlement agreement not be construed as reflecting on the merits of the dispute; and

   c) that landlord shall not make any negative representations to any credit reporting agency or to any other person or entity seeking information about whether tenant was a good or bad tenant.

9. Time is of the essence in this agreement. If tenant fails to timely comply with this agreement, landlord may immediately rescind this agreement in writing and proceed with his or her legal and equitable remedies.

10. This agreement was executed on _____, 19___ at
_____.

Signed:_____

Signed:_____

_____
_____

Defendant in Pro Per

IN THE MUNICIPAL COURT OF THE STATE OF CALIFORNIA

COUNTY OF _____, _____ DISTRICT

_____,) No. _____
)
        Plaintiff(s),   ) DEMAND FOR JURY TRIAL
)
    v.   )
)
_____,)
)
_____Defendant(s)._____)

To the clerk of the above-entitled court:

Defendant(s) hereby demand a jury trial in this action.

Date:_____   _____

```
_____
_____
_____
Defendant in Pro Per
```

IN THE MUNICIPAL COURT OF THE STATE OF CALIFORNIA

COUNTY OF _____, _____ DISTRICT

_____,)	No. _____	
Plaintiff(s),)	APPLICATION AND DECLARATION	
)	FOR RELIEF FROM EVICTION	
v.)		
)	Code of Civil Procedure	
_____,)	Secs. 1174(c), 1179	
)		
Defendant(s).)		

Defendant(s) _____

_____, hereby

apply for relief from eviction, after judgment for plaintiff in this action.

If defendants are evicted, they will suffer hardship in the following way(s): _____

_____.

Defendants are willing and able to pay all money they presently owe to Plaintiff, as a condition to this application being granted. Defendants are also willing and able to pay the rent as it comes due in the future.

I declare under penalty of perjury that the above statements are true and correct to the best of my knowledge.

Date:_____   _____

_____
_____
_____
Defendant in Pro Per

IN THE MUNICIPAL COURT OF THE STATE OF CALIFORNIA

COUNTY OF _____, _____ DISTRICT

_____,) No. _____
)
        Plaintiff(s),   ) APPLICATION AND DECLARATION
) FOR STAY OF EVICTION
   v.   )
)
_____,)
)
        Defendant(s).   )

   Defendant(s) _____,
hereby apply for stay of execution from any writ of restitution or
possession in this case, for the following period of time:
_____.

   Such a stay is appropriate in this case for the following reason(s):
_____
_____.

   I declare under penalty of perjury that the above statements are true
and correct to the best of my knowledge.

Date:_____   _____

_____
_____
_____

Defendant in Pro Per

IN THE MUNICIPAL COURT OF THE STATE OF CALIFORNIA

COUNTY OF _____, _____ DISTRICT

_____,) No. _____
)
      Plaintiff(s),   ) NOTICE OF APPEAL AND NOTICE
) <u>TO PREPARE CLERK'S TRANSCRIPT</u>
v.   )
)
_____,)

    Defendant(s) _____,

hereby appeal to the Appellate Department of the Superior Court.

    Defendant(s) hereby request that a Clerk's Transcript be prepared, and that this transcript include all documents filed in this action and all minute orders and other rulings and judgments issued by the court in this action.

    Date:_____   _____

Collective Bargaining Agreement

I. Parties

The parties to this Agreement are _____, hereinafter called "Landlord," and _____, hereinafter called "Organization."[1] The property covered by this Agreement is located at _____
_____.

II. Purpose

It is the general purpose of this Agreement to provide a better means of communication between Landlord and his tenants, through Organization, their bargaining agent, to assure a continuous harmonious relationship and an orderly method of resolving differences and grievances, which will result in a stable tenancy, reduced expenses through greater tenant concern, and a better community.

III. Dismissal of Pending Lawsuits

All lawsuits currently pending between Landlord and Organization or Landlord and any member of Organization shall be dismissed, including the following: _____
_____.

IV. Recognition of Tenants' Organization

Landlord recognizes Organization as the sole collective bargaining agent for its members who are tenants at the property covered by this Agreement on all matters relating to their tenancies, the building, and their dealings with Landlord in his capacity as owner.

V. Landlord Security

Landlord shall in no way discriminate against or take reprisals against any person because of his involvement or sympathy with Organization. Nor shall Landlord promise or give any benefits to any person conditioned on such person's quitting, failing to join, or refusing to assist Organization in any way.

VI. Tenant Responsibilities

Organization agrees and recognizes that each tenant has certain obligations and responsibilities, including the following, and Organization agrees to take no action to discourage tenants from complying with these obligations and responsibilities:

1. To pay rent promptly when due (except where provided otherwise by law, this Agreement, or agreement between Landlord and a tenant);
2. To pay for and correct any damage to the premises or Landlord's furnishings caused by any intentional or negligent act of a tenant or any person occupying the premises with his permission, excepting damage due to normal wear and tear;
3. To place his garbage and refuse inside the containers provided therefor;
4. To refrain from acts which unduly disturb his neighbors;
5. To obey all state and local laws and regulations relating to the occupancy of residential property;
6. To comply with his obligations under his lease or rental agreement.

---

[1] As noted, many groups will want to use the word "union" rather than "organization." Suit yourself, it makes no legal difference.

VII. Leases [or Rental Agreements]

A standard form Model Lease [or Model Rental Agreement] is attached to this Agreement and labelled "Exhibit A."

Within seven days of this Agreement, Landlord shall offer to sign such Model with each tenant who is a member of Organization. Landlord shall make the same offer to each new member of Organization within seven days of being notified of such membership by Organization.

The provisions of this Agreement shall be considered incorporated into and a part of each such Model signed.

VIII. Rents

1. Rents. The following monthly rentals shall apply to the following units:

Apartment (furn./unfurn.)	Rent	Apartment (furn./unfurn.)	Rent
_____	_____	_____	_____
_____	_____	_____	_____
_____	_____	_____	_____
_____	_____	_____	_____

2. Appliances. Landlord shall, without extra charge, furnish every apartment with a satisfactory stove and refrigerator, which he shall maintain in good working order.

3. Utilities. Landlord shall provide and pay for the following utilities, without adding to the monthly rent: gas, electricity, water, garbage collection, trash removal and sewer charges. [cross out those that do not apply]

4. Late Charges. No late charges or fines shall be imposed.

5. Rent Increases. There shall be no rent increases during the term of this Agreement.

6. Back Rents. Back rents in the amount of _____ now held by Organization shall be disposed of as follows: _____
_____.

IX. Repairs and Maintenance

1. Maintenance. Landlord shall maintain the building and grounds in a decent, safe and sanitary condition, and shall comply with all state and local laws, regulations and ordinances concerning the maintenance of residential property. In addition, as specific maintenance problems have arisen in the past, Landlord specifically agrees to provide the following maintenance services:

[Example: (a) check the coin-operated washing machine and dryer at least once a week to see that they are in good operating condition;

(b) repair broken mailboxes upon notice by affected tenants.]

2. Security. Landlord shall take reasonable measures to maintain security in the building and grounds to protect the tenants and their guests from burglary, robbery and other crimes.

3. Repairs. Landlord shall complete the following repairs by the following dates:

Repair	Date
_____	_____
_____	_____
_____	_____
_____	_____

4. Failure to Comply. Organization shall have the right to inspect the building at reasonable times to ensure compliance with this Section. If any repair is not completed by the date specified, or if Landlord fails to comply with any maintenance duty for seven days or longer, the tenants of the building may thereafter, until completion of repairs or resumption of maintenance, pay their rent into a bank account held by Organization. Organization shall use the money to make the repairs or perform the maintenance, remitting the balance to Landlord after repairs are completed and maintenance resumed. This remedy shall be in addition to any remedies provided by law or contract for tenants receiving inadequate maintenance or repair.

X. Grievance Procedure

1. The term "grievance" shall mean any dispute between Landlord and a tenant or between Landlord and Organization involving the interpretation, application, or coverage of this Agreement or any lease or rental agreement, except that any claim for personal injuries exceeding $500 shall not be considered a "grievance" subject to this procedure.

2. Any tenant having a grievance may present his grievance, by himself or through Organization, to Landlord or his agent.

3. If the grievance has not been resolved to the satisfaction of the tenant within ten days after being presented, a grievance meeting shall be held between the tenant, Organization and Landlord within the next five days, or as soon thereafter as the parties may agree. At such meeting, the parties shall attempt to resolve the grievance to everyone's satisfaction.

4. If Landlord has a grievance against any tenant, or against Organization, he may present such grievance to Organization, which shall attempt to resolve the grievance as soon as possible.

5. If Landlord's grievance has not been resolved to his satisfaction within ten days after it has been presented to Organization, the grievance meeting provisions subsection 3 above shall apply.

6. If the grievance meeting produces no resolution of the grievance, the aggrieved party may then file suit in any court of competent jurisdiction for final determination of the matter in dispute.[2]

XI. Enforcement

The provisions of this Agreement may be enforced through appropriate legal action by Landlord, Organization, or any affected person. As the amount of damages attributable to violation of any provision of this Agreement may be difficult to ascertain, the parties agree that these provisions may be specifically enforced by an appropriate court.

XII. Severability

In the event that any provision of this Agreement is deemed invalid by any court of law, such determination shall not affect any other provisions of this Agreement and the Agreement shall remain binding on all parties hereto.

XIII. Organization's Right to Information

In order to enable organization to maintain a continuing interest in the present and future condition of the building and to adequately represent the interests of the tenants, Landlord shall furnish Organization with

---

[2] For a grievance procedure containing a provision for arbitration by a neutral arbitrator before going to court, see the *Tenant Union Guide*, in Volume II of the *Handbook on Housing Law* (Prentice-Hall).

information and allow Organization to examine Landlord's records and books, upon reasonable notice by Organization, relating to the following matters:

1. Expenses of maintaining the building,

2. Income received from the building,

3. All other financial information relating to the building, including mortgages or deeds of trust on the building, and

4. All taxes affected by the building.

XIV. Duration

This Agreement shall remain in full force and effect from the date it is signed by both Landlord and Organization and until _____, 19_____.

On _____, 19_____, Landlord and Organization shall begin negotiations for a new agreement to go into effect at the expiration of this Agreement. Such negotiations shall continue in good faith until a new agreement is reached or this Agreement expires.

WHEREFORE, We, the undersigned, do hereby execute and agree to this Agreement.

FOR THE LANDLORD:

1. _____
   signature

   _____
   title

   _____
   date of signature

2. _____
   signature

   _____
   title

   _____
   date of signature

FOR THE ORGANIZATION:

1. _____
   signature

   _____
   title

   _____
   date of signature

1. _____
   signature

   _____
   title

   _____
   date of signature

A

Administration of rent control ordinances, 4/6. *See also* Rent control, chart
Advertising costs, and breaking lease, 9/5
Affirmative defense, 11/29, 11/32-34
Age, and discrimination, 5/2
Agreements
    between new tenant and old tenant, sample, 3/9
    between roommates, sample, 3/4
    with landlord, when moving out, sample, 9/6
American Arbitration Association, 1/12
Animals. *See* Pets
Annotated code, 1/10
Answer, to landlord's Complaint, 11/6, 11/13, 11/28-35
    sample, 11/30-31
Apartment locator service, 2/10
Appeal
    of eviction, 2/6, 11/50
    of eviction lawsuit, waiver of right to, in lease, 2/6
    of rent adjustment hearing decision, 4/13
Appellate districts, 1/10n
Application and Declaration for Relief from Eviction, 11/46-47
    sample, 11/47
Application and Declaration for Stay of Eviction, 11/48-49
    sample, 11/49
Arbitrary discrimination, 5/2, 5/3
Arbitration, 3/9. *See also* Mediation
Asbestos, 2/12
Assignment, 2/5, 9/2-3
Attorneys. *See* Lawyers
Avocations, discrimination against, 5/2, 5/3

B

Bankruptcy
    landlord, 1/2-3
    tenant, 11/6
Bar association referral panels, 1/8
Bargaining power, 2/15-16. *See also* Negotiations
Basement, 2/15
Bathroom, 2/13-14
Bathroom window, 2/14
Belongings left behind after moving, 9/8
Berkeley rent control ordinance, 4/5, 4/9, 4/15
    and affirmative defense, 11/29, 11/32
    and discrimination, 5/3
    and just cause for eviction, 3/5n, 4/8, 11/11-12
    and registration of property, 4/6, 4/7, 12/7
    and security deposits, 10/10
    and substandard housing, 12/9
    and vacancy decontrol, 3/7, 4/8
Beverly Hills rent control ordinance, 4/5, 4/10, 4/16
    and just cause for eviction, 4/8
    and vacancy decontrol, 4/7
"Bond" deposit, 2/9-10
Breach of promise, by landlord, 7/13
Building Inspection Department, 2/13, 2/15, 7/5-6, 12/8-9
Burglaries, and insurance, 13/1
Business hours, normal, and right of entry, 6/2, 6/3

C

California Department of Fair Employment and Housing, 5/7-8
California Eviction Defense Manual, 11/3
California Residential Landlord-Tenant Practice Book, 11/3
California State Housing Law, 2/12-13, 2/15, 7/5
California Supreme Court, 1/10n
Calls at work, by landlord, 6/7
Campbell rent control ordinance, 4/5, 4/17
Chain lock, and privacy, 6/6
Children
    born to tenant, and discrimination, 5/6-7
    families with, and discrimination, 3/2, 5/2-3, 5/5-7, 5/9
Cities with rent control, 4/5. *See also* names of specific cities
Civil Code (CC), 1/10
Claim of Right of Possession and Notice of Hearing, 11/13, 11/52-54
    sample, 11/53-54
Cleaning deposits, 10/2, 10/3-4
Coalition for Economic Survival, 12/6
Code of Civil Procedure (CCP), 1/10
Code violations, reporting, 7/5-7
Collective bargaining agreement, 12/2, 12/13
Combustible materials, 2/15
Community Board Program (San Francisco), 1/12, 3/9n, 10/6, 12/3, 12/12
Complaint, filing and service of, 11/5, 11/13
Complaints, to landlord, for failure to repair/maintain premises, 7/3-4
Condominium conversion, 14/2-3
Constructive eviction, doctrine of, 7/5
Contingency fee, 8/5
Co-signing leases, 2/20
Cotati rent control ordinance, 4/5, 4/9, 4/18
    and affirmative defense, 11/29, 11/32
    and registration of property, 4/6

and security deposits, 10/10
and vacancy decontrol, 4/8
Co-tenants. *See* Roommates
County recorder's office, and property ownership history, 12/7
Court reporter, and depositions, 11/39
Courts of Appeal, 1/10n
Credit bureaus, 2/11
Credit check fees, 2/10-11
Credit disclosure, 5/5
Credit rating, and stipulated judgment, 11/40
Credit reports, 2/11, 5/5

D

Damage
    by landlord, 6/5
    by tenant, 10/4
Damages, 2/6, 10/8-9
De novo hearing, 4/13
Deadbolt locks, 8/4
Declaration, 11/15, 11/16
    sample, 11/19
Deering's California Codes, 1/9
Default judgment, 11/15, 11/35
Demand for Jury Trial, 11/43-45
    sample, 11/44
Demand letter, for return of deposit, 10/6
Demurrer, to landlord's Complaint, 11/6, 11/13, 11/22-28
    sample, 11/23
Department of Housing and Urban Development (HUD), 5/8
Deposition, 11/39
Deposits, charged by landlord, 2/9-10, 10/2-11. *See also* names of specific deposits
Disabled tenants
    and discrimination, 5/2, 5/3, 5/9
    and dogs, 2/7, 5/3
Disclosures by landlord, 2/12
"Discounts," for early rent payment, 4/3
Discovery, 11/35-39
Discrimination, 5/2-9
    illegal, 5/2-4
    and lease, 2/7
    legal, 5/4-7
    legal recourse, 5/7-9
    and rent increases, 4/4

District attorney, and failure to return security deposits, 10/9
Doctrine of constructive eviction, 7/5
Doctrine of strict liability, 8/2
Dogs, and disabled, 2/7, 5/3
Domestic Violence Prevention Act, 3/9-10
Driveway, 2/15
Drug-dealing tenants, 7/12, 8/4-5, 11/11
Duplex rental, and discrimination, 5/5n
Duty of care, 8/2

E

Earthquake insurance, 13/1
Earthquakes, 8/6
East Palo Alto rent control ordinance, 4/5, 4/9, 10/10
    and affirmative defense, 11/29, 11/32
    and just cause for eviction, 4/8
    and registration of property, 4/6
    and vacancy decontrol, 4/8
Electricity, 2/14-15, 7/2
Emergencies, and landlord's right of entry, 6/2
Entire agreement clause, in lease, 2/7
Entry, right of, 6/2-6
Escrow account, and rent withholding, 7/9, 12/10
Ethnic background, and discrimination, 5/2
Eviction, 11/3-55. *See also* Rent control, chart
    appeal of, 2/6, 11/50
    and complaints about condition of premises, 7/4
    and just cause, 3/5n, 4/8, 11/5, 11/10, 11/11-12
    lawsuit, 11/13-46
    and nonpayment of rent, 4/2
    postponing, 11/48-49
    procedure, 11/5-7, 11/8-55
    relief from, 11/46-47
    retaliatory, 7/6, 7/8-9, 7/13, 11/4-5
    self-help, 11/3-4
    by sheriff, 11/50, 11/52
    stay of, 11/48-49
    stopping, 11/46-47
    timeline, 11/6-7
    trial, 11/6, 11/43-45
    wrongful, 11/32
Exceptions, to rent control ordinances, 4/6. *See also* Rent control, chart
Ex-managers, and information about landlord, 12/8

F

Fair Housing Act, 5/3-4
Fair Housing Amendments Act of 1988, 5/3
Fair market value, of property, 13/2
Families with children, and discrimination, 3/2, 5/2-3, 5/5-7, 5/9
Family member, of landlord, moving in, 11/11-12, 11/29, 11/32
Fees, charged by landlord, 2/9-10. *See also* names of specific fees and deposits
Fees, charged by lawyer. *See* Lawyers, fees
Filing fees, in responsive pleading, 11/14
"Finder's fees," 2/10
Fire Department, and housing violations, 2/13, 7/6
Fire safety, 2/15
Fixed-term lease, and eviction, 11/8
Floors, 7/2
"For Rent" and "For Sale" signs, 6/6
Forms, printed, 2/4-8. *See also* names of specific forms
Franchise Tax Board, and landlord deductions, 7/5n
Furnished, definition, 10/2
Furnished premises, 2/20, 10/2, 10/5
Furnishings, repair of, 2/20

G

Garages, 2/15
Garbage receptacles, 2/15, 2/20, 7/2
Gay couples, and living together, 3/2
    discrimination against, 5/2, 5/3, 5/9
Gossip, and landlords, 6/6-7
Guests, 2/7, 3/10, 6/7

H

Habitability, implied warranty of, 7/9-13, 11/45-46
Habitable, definition, 7/9
Hallways, 2/14, 2/15
Harassment, by landlord, 6/4-7, 11/3-4
Hayward rent control ordinance, 4/5, 4/9, 4/20
    and just cause for eviction, 4/8
    and security deposits, 10/10
    and vacancy decontrol, 4/7
Health Department, and housing violations, 2/13, 7/6, 12/9
Hearing officer, 4/12-13
Hearings, of rent control board, 4/10-13
Heating facilities, 2/14, 7/2
"Holding" deposit, 2/10-11

Home, sharing of, 3/2-10
"Homefinding services," 2/2
Hot water, 2/14, 7/2
Housing
    inspecting, 2/12-18, 2/19
    locating, 2/2
    renting, 2/2-20
Housing code inspection departments, 12/7
Housing code violations, 2/13, 7/5, 12/7, 12/8-9
    as public record, 7/6-7, 12/7
Housing conditions. *See* Living conditions
HUD, 5/8

I

Implied warranty of habitability, 7/9-13, 11/45-46
Income, and discrimination, 5/4-5
Income tax, and renters' credit, 1/5
Independent paralegals, 1/9
Individual adjustments, to rent, 4/7. *See also* Rent control, chart
Injuries
    and breach of implied warranty of habitability, 7/13
    and insurance, 13/1-2
    to others, by third parties, 8/3
    and substandard housing conditions, 8/2-5
Insects, 2/14
Inspection of premises
    checklist, 2/13-15
    landlord's right to, 2/6, 6/3
    pre-rental, 2/12-15
Installment payment of security deposit, 10/3
Insurance. *See* Earthquake insurance; Liability insurance; Renter's insurance
Interest, on security deposits, 10/4, 10/7, 10/10
International Conference of Building Officials, 2/12
Interpreter, in Small Claims Court, 10/7
Interrogatories, 11/38
Inventory, of condition of premises, 2/18, 2/19

J

Judge, disqualifying, 11/45
Judgment, in eviction trial, 11/45-46. *See also* Default judgment; Stipulated judgment; Summary judgment
Jury trial
    and eviction proceedings, 11/6, 11/43-45
    and payment to jurors, 11/43n
    waiver of right to, in lease, 2/6

Just cause for eviction, 3/5n, 4/8, 11/5, 11/10, 11/11-12. *See also* Rent control, chart

K
Key to premises, 6/2
Kitchen, 2/14

L
Landlord business, 1/4-5, 12/2-3
Landlord-occupied premises, and discrimination, 5/5
Landlord-tenant checklist, 2/18, 2/19
Landlords, 1/2-4
    and deposits, 2/9-10, 10/2-11
    and disclosure to tenants, 2/12
    and discrimination, 5/2-9
    and evictions, 11/2-55
    and improper entry, 6/4-6
    information about, 1/2, 12/6-8
    and leases, 9/2-8
    and liability for damages, 8/5-6, 13/2
    and liability for injuries, 8/2-5, 13/2
    and moving into premises, 11/11-12, 11/29, 11/32
    obnoxious, 6/2-7
    and privacy, 6/2-7
    and repairs and maintenance, 7/2-13
    and responsibility for damage or injury, 2/5
    and subletting, 2/5, 9/2-3
    and taxes, 1/4
    and tenants rights organizations, 12/2-13
Last month's rent, as deposit, 10/2, 10/10-11. *See also* Security deposits
Late charges, 2/6-7, 2/18, 4/2-3
Law libraries, 1/6, 1/9-10
Lawsuits. *See* Suits
Lawyer referral panels, 1/8
Lawyers, 1/5-9
    and consultation, 1/6
    fees, 1/5-6, 1/8, 2/6, 8/5, 10/6, 11/12
    and lawsuits, 1/7
    locating, 1/7-9
    and negotiation, 1/6
    and personal injury cases, 8/5
    and rent adjustment hearing, 4/11
    when needed, 1/6
Lease, 2/2, 2/3-9. *See also* Rental agreement
    addendum to, 2/17
    benefits of, 2/8-9
    breaking, 2/8-9, 9/3, 9/5-7
    changes in, 2/4
    compared to month-to-month agreement, 2/8-9
    compliance with, 2/18
    co-signing, 2/20
    expiration, 9/2
    fixed term, and eviction, 11/8
    and increase in security deposits, 10/5
    model, 2/9
    and notice to quit, 11/8-12
    and privacy, 6/2, 6/4
    renewal of, 9/2
    and rent increases, 4/4
    and repairs/maintenance, 7/3
    and retaliatory evictions, 7/6
    and roommates, 3/2-3, 3/6
Legal Aid offices, 1/7
Legal citations, 1/10-11, 11/3
Legal clinics, 1/8
Legal research, 1/9-11
Legal Services offices, 1/7
Legal typing services, 1/9
Letter
    demanding security deposit, sample, 10/6
    requesting landlord apply deposit to last month's rent, sample, 10/9
    suggesting prospective tenants, sample, 9/7
Liability insurance, 2/8, 13/2
Light, natural, 2/14
Lights, electrical, 2/14-15, 7/2
Liquidated damages, 2/8, 9/5
Living conditions, basic, 2/13-15, 7/2
Living together, 3/2-10
    and discrimination, 5/2, 5/3, 5/9
    legality of, 3/2
Lock box, 6/4
Locking out, of person, 3/9, 11/4
Locking up, of property, 3/9
Locks, 6/6, 8/4
Los Angeles rent control ordinance, 4/5, 4/10, 4/21-22
    and affirmative defense, 11/29, 11/32
    and discrimination, 5/3
    and just cause for eviction, 3/5n, 4/8, 11/11-12
    and landlord's relatives moving in, 11/11-12n
    and registration of property, 4/6
    and security deposit, 10/10
    and vacancy decontrol, 4/7, 4/8, 11/12n
Los Angeles Rent Escrow Account Program, 7/11
Los Gatos rent control ordinance, 4/5, 4/9, 4/23
    and just cause for eviction, 4/8
    and vacancy decontrol, 4/7

M

Mail, and filing papers, 11/20n
Maintenance, of premises, 7/2-13
Management corporations, 1/3
Manager, of apartment, 1/3, 12/8
    resident in building, 1/2n
Marital status, and discrimination, 5/2, 5/3, 5/9. *See also* Living together
Master tenant, 3/8
Material violation, of implied warranty of habitability, 7/9
Mediation, 1/12, 3/9n, 4/10, 10/6, 11/12, 12/8, 12/12
Memorandum of Points and Authorities, 11/15, 11/16, 11/24
    samples, 11/18, 11/25
Memorandum to Set for Trial, 11/43
Military bases, and rental of property nearby, 2/12
Mitigation of damages concept, 9/5
Model lease, 2/9
Model rental agreement, 2/9
Month-to-month agreement. *See* Rental agreement, written
Motion for Summary Judgment, 11/43
Motion to Quash Service of Summons, 11/6, 11/13, 11/14-20
Motion to Strike, 11/28
Moving in, with another, 3/5-10
Moving out, for failure to repair/maintain premises, 7/4-5, 7/7
Municipal Court, 9/7, 11/4
    and evictions, 11/13-46, 11/55

N

"Nail and mail" method of serving notice, 11/9
National Association for Independent Paralegals, 1/9
National origin, and discrimination, 5/2
Negotiations, between tenant(s) and landlord, 2/15-16, 11/12, 11/39-42, 12/12-13
Newspapers, and information about landlord, 12/7
Normal business hours, and right of entry, 6/2, 6/3
Notice of Appeal, 11/50, 11/51,
    sample, 11/51
Notice of Hearing on Demurrer, 11/22, 11/26
    sample, 11/27
Notice of Motion to Quash, 11/15
    sample, 11/17-18
Notice of rent increase, 4/4-5
Notice of rent withholding, sample, 7/10
Notice period, 2/3n, 2/5-6
Notice to quit, 11/5, 11/8-12. *See also* Thirty-day notice; Three-day notice
Notice to repair, sample, 7/8
Notice, waiver of right to, in lease, 2/5
"Nuisance," creating, 11/9

O

Oakland rent control ordinance, 4/5, 4/9, 4/24
    and just cause for eviction, 4/8
    and vacancy decontrol, 4/7
Occupants
    lease restrictions on, 2/7
    number of in rental premises, 3/3, 3/5
Occupations, discrimination against, 5/2, 5/3
Oral agreements, 2/16, 3/6
Oral rental agreement. *See* Rental agreement
"Overcrowding," 5/5-7
Owner-occupied rental unit, and discrimination, 5/5
Owner of property, information about, 1/2, 12/6-8

P

Palm Springs rent control ordinance, 4/5, 4/10, 4/25
    and affirmative defense, 11/29, 11/32
    and registration of property, 4/6
    and vacancy decontrol, 4/8
Pass key, 6/3
Peremptory challenge, 11/45
Personal injuries. *See* Injuries
Personal service, 11/14. *See also* Service
Petition for arbitration, 4/11
Petition for certification, 4/11
Petitioning, and tenant organizing, 12/8
Pets
    discrimination against, 5/3
    and restrictions in lease, 2/7
    and security deposit, 10/3
Photographs of premises
    and uninhabitable conditions, 7/11
    when moving in, 2/17
    when moving out, 10/5
Physically disabled. *See* Disabled
Picketing, and tenant organizing, 12/9-10
Plumbing, 2/13, 7/2
Possessions left behind after moving, 9/8
Prejudgment Claim of Right to Possession, 11/13, 11/52
Pre-paid legal plans, 1/7
Press conferences, 12/10

Printed forms, 2/4-8. *See also* names of specific forms
Privacy, right to, 6/2-7
Proof of Service by Mail, sample, 11/21
Property left behind after moving, 9/8
Property taxes, 12/6
Prospective tenants, letter suggesting, sample, 9/7
Public assistance, and discrimination, 5/3
Public housing, and rent increases, 4/4
Public Interest Clearinghouse, 12/6
Publicity, and tenant organizing, 12/9-10
Punitive damages, 10/8-9

R

Race, and discrimination, 5/2
Railings, 7/2
Real estate offices, and property owner, 12/7
Reasonable notice, and right of entry, 6/2, 6/3
Reasonable rent, and rent withholding, 7/9n, 7/11
Reasonable time, for repairs, 7/8
Receiver, to manage property, 7/13
Records and recordkeeping, 2/17, 2/18
Re-entry, right of, 2/6
Registration of rental units, 4/6-7. *See also* Rent control, chart
Relatives of landlord, moving in, 11/11-12, 11/29, 11/32
Religion, and discrimination, 5/2
Remodeling, and eviction, 11/11
Rent, 4/2-31. *See also* Rent control; Rent payments; etc.
Rent adjustment hearing, 4/10-13
Rent board. *See* Rent control, board
Rent control, 4/5-31, 12/2
    administration, 4/6
    and affirmative defenses, 11/29, 11/32
    board, 4/10-13, 12/7
    chart, 4/6-7, 4/14-31
    and eviction, 3/5n, 4/8, 11/5, 11/10, 11/11-12
    exceptions, 4/6
    and finder's fees, 2/10
    laws, 4/9-10
    registration, 4/6-7
    and rent adjustment hearings, 4/10-13
    and rent increases, 4/4, 4/6, 4/7, 4/8
    right to enact, 4/5n
    and security deposits, 10/5
    and subletting, 3/7
    and substandard housing, 12/9
    and vacancy decontrol, 3/7, 4/7-8
    violations, by landlord, 4/14

Rent Escrow Account Program (Los Angeles), 7/11
Rent formula, 4/7. *See also* Rent control, chart
Rent increases, 4/4-5
    notices of 4/4-5
    and rent control, 4/4, 4/6, 4/7, 4/8
Rent mediation laws, 4/10
Rent payments, 2/18, 4/2-3
    due date of, 2/18, 4/2
    early, and "discount," 4/3
    and late charges, 2/6-7, 2/18, 4/2-3
    partial, 4/3-4
    receipt for, 2/18
Rent reduction, and substandard housing, 12/9
Rent strikes, 12/10-11
Rent withholding, 4/2, 7/3, 7/9-12
    and cleaning deposit, 10/9-10
    and drug-dealing tenants, 8/4
Rental agencies, and discrimination, 5/7n
Rental agreement, 2/2-9
    addendum to, 2/17
    benefits of, 2/8-9
    changes in, 2/4
    compliance with, 2/18
    kinds of, 2/2-4
    and lawyers fees, 1/6
    model, 2/9
    oral, 2/2, 2/3, 10/7
    provisions of, 2/4-8
    and repairs/maintenance, 7/3, 7/8
    and retaliatory evictions, 7/8-9
    written, 2/2, 2/3-9
Rental management corporations, 1/3
Renter's insurance, 8/5, 13/1-2
Renters' tax credit, 1/5
Repair and deduct remedy, 2/5, 7/7-9, 12/11
Repairs, 2/15, 2/20, 7/2-13
    and eviction, 11/11
    and lease, 7/3
    remedies for lack of, 7/3-13
    and rental agreement, 7/3
    and right of entry, 6/3
    waiver of responsibility for, 2/5
Replacement value, of property, 13/2
Request for Inspection, 11/36-38
    sample, 11/37
Request to Admit, 11/39
Research, legal, 1/9-11
Residential hotels, and lock outs, 11/4
Response to eviction Complaint/Summons, 11/5-6
Responsive pleadings, 11/6

Retaliation, and rent increases, 4/4
Retaliatory eviction, 7/6, 7/8-9, 7/13, 11/4-5
Right of entry, 6/2-6
Right of re-entry, 2/6
Right to appeal eviction lawsuit, waiver of, in lease, 2/6
Right to inspect premises, 2/6, 6/3
Right to jury trial, waiver of, in lease, 2/6
Right to privacy, 6/2-7
Rodents, 2/13, 2/14, 7/2
Roommates, 3/2-10
    legal obligations to each other, 3/3-4, 3/8-10
    legal obligations to landlord, 3/2-3
    new, moving in, 3/5-10
    and security deposit, 10/4

S

Sale of premises
    and security deposit, 10/4-5
    and tenant's rights, 1/2-3
San Francisco Community Board Program, 1/12, 3/9n, 10/6, 12/3, 12/12
San Francisco rent control ordinance, 4/5, 4/26
    and discrimination, 5/3
    and just cause for eviction, 3/5n, 4/8, 11/11-12
    and moving in with another, 3/8
    and security deposits, 10/10
    and vacancy decontrol, 4/7
San Jose rent control ordinance, 4/5, 4/9, 4/27
    and just cause for eviction, 4/8
    and vacancy decontrol, 4/7
Santa Clara County, and discrimination, 5/3
Santa Cruz rent control ordinance, 10/10
Santa Monica rent control ordinance, 4/5, 4/9, 4/28
    and discrimination, 5/3
    and hearings, 4/10
    and just cause for eviction, 3/5n, 4/8, 11/11-12
    and registration of property, 4/6, 4/7, 12/7
    and security deposits, 10/10
    and substandard housing, 12/9
    and vacancy decontrol, 3/7
Secretary of State, and corporate ownership of property, 12/8
Section 8 housing
    and eviction, 11/10
    and rent increases, 4/4
Security deposits, 10/2-11
    amount, 10/2-3
    and co-tenants, 10/4
    duty to return, 10/4

    failure to return, 10/5-10
    increase in, 10/5
    installment payment of, 10/3
    interest on, 10/4, 10/7, 10/10
    problems in collecting, 10/5-10
    refundability, 10/3
    and rent withholding, 10/9-10
    and sale of premises, 10/4-5
    use of, 10/3-4
Security systems, broken, 8/4
Self-help evictions, 11/3-4
Senior citizen housing, 5/3n
Service
    of Answer, 11/34-35
    of Application and Declaration for Relief from Eviction, 11/46
    of Application and Declaration for Stay of Eviction, 11/48
    of Demand for Jury Trial, 11/45
    of Demurrer, 11/26
    of Interrogatories, 11/38
    of Motion to Quash, 11/20, 11/21
    of Notice of Appeal, 11/50
    of notice of rent increase, 4/4-5
    of Notice to Quit, 11/9, 11/11
    of Request for Inspection, 11/38
    of Summons and Complaint, 11/14
Services, decrease in, 4/10
Settlement, negotiating, 11/39-42
Settlement of Unlawful Detainer Action, sample, 11/41-42
Sex, and discrimination, 5/2, 5/9
Sexual harassment in housing, 5/9-10
Sexual orientation, and discrimination, 5/2, 5/3
Shared utility arrangements, 2/12
Sheriff, and eviction, 11/50, 11/52
Showing property, and right of entry, 6/3-4
Sickness, and breach of implied warranty of habitability, 7/13
Signs ("For Rent," "For Sale"), 6/6
Small Claims Court
    and breaking lease, 9/7
    and deposits, 10/6-9
    and finder's fees, 2/10
    and interpreter, 10/7
    and obnoxious tenants, 8/5
    and personal injury, 8/2
    and repairs, 7/5n, 7/13
    and trespass by landlord, 6/5
    and utility cut-off, 11/4
Smoke detectors, 2/15

Smokers, discrimination against, 5/3
Spanish translation, of lease/rental agreement, 2/4
Stairs, 2/14, 2/15, 7/2
Standards for decent housing, 2/13-15, 7/2, 7/9
 failure to meet, 8/2-5
State Housing Law, 2/12-13, 2/15, 7/5
Statement of Disputed and Undisputed Material Facts, 11/43
Stay, of eviction procedures, 11/48-49
Stipulated judgment, 11/40
Storage rooms, 2/15
Strangers, landlord providing information to, 6/6-7
"Strict liability," and landlords, 8/2, 8/5-6
Structure, of building, 2/13, 7/2
Students, discrimination against, 5/2, 5/3
Subdivision, definition, 14/2
Sublease agreement, sample, 9/4
Subleases and subletting, 2/5, 9/2-3. *See also* Roommates
Substandard housing, and rent reduction, 12/9
Substituted service, 11/14-15. *See also* Service
Suits, against landlord, 1/7, 12/11
 for discrimination, 5/8-9
 and drug-dealing tenants, 8/4-5
 for finder's fees, 2/10
 and implied warranty of habitability, 7/12-13
 for lack of repair/maintenance, 7/5n
 for malicious gossip, 6/7
 and obnoxious tenants, 8/5
 for return of deposit, 10/6-9
 for trespass, 6/5
 and wrongful eviction, 11/32
Suits, against tenant, for breaking lease, 9/7
Summary judgment, 11/43
Summons, filing and service of, 11/5, 11/13-14
Superior Court, 11/4, 11/50, 11/55

T

Tax assessor, and determining property owner, 12/6
Taxes
 and landlords, 1/4
 and tenants, 1/5
Tele-Lawyer, Inc., 1/8-9
Tenant screening agencies, 2/11
Tenants
 and drug-dealing, 7/12, 8/4-5, 11/11
 obnoxious, 8/5
 responsibilities of, 2/18, 2/20, 7/7
 rights of, 11/4-5

Tenants rights organizations, 1/7, 12/2-13
 setting up, 12/3-6
 tactics, 12/8-12
Tenants unions. *See* Tenants rights organizations
Tenants, former, and information about landlord, 12/8
Tenant-tenant problems, 12/3. *See also* Drug-dealing tenants
Termination of tenancy notices, 11/8-12. *See also* Notice to Quit; Thirty-day notice; Three-day notice
Termination period, of tenancy, 2/3n, 2/5-6
Thirty-day notice, 11/5, 11/10-12. *See also* Eviction
Thousand Oaks rent control ordinance, 4/5, 4/10, 4/29
 and affirmative defense, 11/29, 11/32
 and just cause for eviction, 4/8
 and registration of property, 4/6
 and vacancy decontrol, 4/7
Three-day notice, 4/2, 11/2, 11/5, 11/8-10, 11/12. *See also* Eviction
 service of, 11/9
 types, 11/8-9
Title insurance companies, and ownership of property, 12/7
Transcript of rent adjustment hearing, 4/13n
Translation of lease/rental agreement, 2/4
Translator, in Small Claims Court, 10/7
Trash receptacles, 7/2, 2/15, 2/20
Trespass by landlord, 6/4-6
Trial de novo, 11/55
Trial for eviction, 11/6, 11/43-45, 11/55. *See also* Eviction, procedure
Triplex rental, and discrimination, 5/5n
Typing services, 1/9

U

Unconditional Three-Day Notice to Quit, 11/9-10
Unfurnished premises, and security deposit, 10/2, 10/5
Uniform Housing Code, 2/12-13, 5/6
Unlawful detainer. *See* Eviction
Unmarried couples, and living together, 3/2
 and discrimination, 5/2, 5/3, 5/9
Unrelated persons, and living together, 3/2. *See also* Roommates; Subleases and subletting
Unruh Civil Rights Act, 5/3
Utilities, shared, 2/12
Utility cut-offs, and eviction, 11/3-4

V

Vacancy decontrol, 3/7, 4/6, 4/7-8. *See also* Rent control, chart
Value of property, and insurance, 13/2
Vermin, 2/14, 7/2
Violation of law provisions, in lease, 2/8
Visits at work, by landlord, 6/7

W

Walls, attachments to, 2/16-17
"Waste," committing, 11/9
Water-filled furniture, and lease, 2/8
Water supply, 2/14, 7/2
Waterbeds, 2/8, 6/3, 10/2
Waterproofing protection, 2/13, 7/2
Weatherproofing, 2/13, 7/2
Welfare recipients, discrimination against, 5/2, 5/3

West Hollywood rent control ordinance, 4/5, 4/9, 4/30
   and affirmative defenses, 11/29, 11/32
   and just cause for eviction, 4/8
   and registration of property, 4/6, 12/7
   and vacancy decontrol, 4/7
West's Annotated California Codes, 1/9
Westlake Village rent control ordinance, 4/31
Wiring, 2/14-15, 7/2
Writ of Possession, 11/6, 11/50, 11/52
Written agreements, 2/16-17
Written rental agreement. *See* Rental agreement
Wrongful eviction lawsuits, 11/32

Y

Yards, 2/15
Yellow pages, and locating a lawyer, 1/8

RECYCLE YOUR OUT-OF-DATE BOOKS AND GET 25% OFF YOUR NEXT PURCHASE

OUT - O F - DATE = DANGEROUS

Using an old edition can be dangerous if information in it is wrong. Unfortunately, laws and legal procedures change often. Generally speaking, any book more than two years old is of questionable value. Books more than four or five years old are a menace.

To help you keep up-to-date, we extend this offer:

If you cut out and deliver to us the title portion of the cover of any old Nolo book, we'll give you a 25% discount off the retail price of any new Nolo book. For example, if you have a copy of *Tenants' Rights*, 4th edition, and want to trade it for the latest *California Marriage and Divorce Law*, send us the *Tenants' Rights* cover and a check for the current price of *California Marriage and Divorce*, less a 25% discount.

Information on current prices and editions is listed in the back of this book and in the catalog in the *Nolo News* (see offer at the back of this book).

This offer is to individuals only.

NOLO PRESS

CATALOG OF SELF-HELP LAW BOOKS & SOFTWARE

ESTATE PLANNING & PROBATE

Plan Your Estate
Attorney Denis Clifford • National 2nd Ed.
This book covers every significant aspect of estate planning and gives detailed, specific instructions for preparing a living trust, a document that lets your family avoid expensive and lengthy probate court proceedings after your death. *Plan Your Estate* includes all the tear-out forms and step-by-step instructions to let you prepare an estate plan designed for your special needs.
$19.95/NEST

Make Your Own Living Trust
Attorney Denis Clifford • National 1st ed.
Find out how a living trust works, how to create one, and how to determine what kind of trust is right for you. Contains all the forms and instructions you need to prepare a: basic living trust to avoid probate, a marital life estate trust (A-B trust) to avoid probate and estate taxes, and a back-up will.
$19.95/LITR

Nolo's Simple Will Book
Attorney Denis Clifford • National 2nd Ed.
It's easy to write a legally valid will using this book. The instructions and forms enable people to draft a will for all needs, including naming a personal guardian for minor children, leaving property to minor children or young adults and updating a will when necessary. Good in all states except Louisiana.
$17.95/SWIL

The Conservatorship Book
Lisa Goldoftas & Attorney Carolyn Farren • California 1st Ed.
When someone becomes incapacitated due to illness or age, a conservator may need to take charge of their medical and financial affairs. *The Conservatorship Book* comes with complete instructions and all the forms necessary to file conservatorship documents, appear in court, be appointed conservator and end a conservatorship.
$24.95/CNSV

How to Probate an Estate
Julia Nissley • California 7th Ed.
If you find yourself responsible for winding up the legal and financial affairs of a deceased family member or friend, you can often save costly attorneys' fees by handling the probate process yourself. This book also explains the simple procedures you can use to transfer assets that don't require probate, including property held in joint tenancy or living trusts or as community property.
$34.95/PAE

Who Will Handle Your Finances If You Can't?
Attorneys Denis Clifford and Mary Randolph • National 1st Ed.
Contains all the forms and instructions necessary to create a durable power of attorney for finances. Creating this document means that you, not courts and lawyers, decide who will handle your financial affairs if illness or old age makes it impossible for you to handle them yourself. It also saves your family from going through painful conservatorship proceedings later.
$19.95/FINA

law form kits

Nolo's Law Form Kit: Wills
Attorney Denis Clifford and Lisa Goldoftas National 1st Ed.
Provides you with a legally valid will, quickly and easily. You can create a will that distributes your property according to your wishes, select beneficiaries, choose a guardian for your children, set up a children's trust and appoint an executor.
$14.95/KWL

audio cassette tapes

Write Your Will
Attorney Ralph Warner with Joanne Greene • National 1st ed. • 60 minutes
This tape answers the most frequently asked questions about writing a will and covers all key issues: What provisions the will must contain, how to provide for children and grandchildren, how to appoint a guardian, how to assign an executor, how to have the will signed and witnessed, when a living trust is useful and when a lawyer might be needed.
$14.95/TWYW

software

WillMaker
Nolo Press
Version 4.0
This easy-to-use software program lets you prepare and update a legal will—safely, privately and without the expense of a lawyer. Leading you step-by-step in a question-and-answer format, *WillMaker* builds a will around your answers, taking into account your state of residence. *WillMaker* comes with a 200-page legal manual which provides the legal background necessary to make sound choices. Good in all states except Louisiana.
IBM PC (3-1/2 & 5-1/4 disks included)
    $69.95/WI4
MACINTOSH $69.95/WM4

Nolo's Personal RecordKeeper
Carol Pladsen & Attorney Ralph Warner
Version 3.0
Nolo's Personal RecordKeeper lets you record the location of personal, financial and legal information in over 200 categories and subcategories. It also allows you to create lists of insured property, compute net worth, consolidate emergency information into one place and export to *Quicken®* home inventory and net worth reports. Includes a 320-page manual filled with practical and legal advice.
IBM PC (3-1/2 & 5-1/4 disks included)
    $49.95/FRI3
MACINTOSH $49.95/FRM3

Nolo's Living Trust
Attorney Mary Randolph
Version 1.0
A will is an indispensable part of any estate plan, but many people need a living trust as well. By putting certain assets into a trust, you save your heirs the headache, time and expense of probate. *Nolo's Living Trust* lets you set up an individual or shared marital trust, make your trust document legal, transfer your property to the trust, and change or revoke the trust at any time. The manual guides you through the process step-by-step, and legal help screens and an on-line glossary explain key legal terms and concepts. Good in all states except Louisiana.
MACINTOSH $79.95/LTM1

GOING TO COURT

Everybody's Guide to Municipal Court
Judge Roderic Duncan • California 1st Ed.
Explains how to prepare and defend the most common types of contract and personal injury law suits in California Municipal Court. Written by a California judge, the book provides step-by-step instructions for preparing and filing all necessary forms, gathering evidence and appearing in court.
$29.95/MUNI

Everybody's Guide to Small Claims Court
Attorney Ralph Warner
National 5th Ed. • California 11th Ed.
These books will help you decide if you should sue in Small Claims Court, show you how to file and serve papers, tell you what to bring to court and how to collect a judgment.
National $15.95/NSCC
California $16.95/CSCC

How to Win Your Personal Injury Claim
Attorney Joseph Matthews • National 1st Ed.
Armed with the right information anyone can handle a personal injury claim. This step-by-step guide will show you how to avoid insurance company run-arounds, evaluate what your claim is worth, obtain a full and fair settlement and save for yourself what you would pay a lawyer.
$24.95/PICL

Fight Your Ticket
Attorney David Brown • California 5th Ed.
Shows you how to fight an unfair traffic ticket—when you're stopped, at arraignment, at trial and on appeal.
$18.95/FYT

Collect Your Court Judgment
Gini Graham Scott, Attorney Stephen Elias & Lisa Goldoftas • California 2nd Ed.
Contains step-by-step instructions and all the forms you need to collect a court judgment from the debtor's bank accounts, wages, business receipts, real estate or other assets.
$19.95/JUDG

How to Change Your Name
Attorneys David Loeb & David Brown • California 5th Ed.
Explains how to change your name legally and provides all the necessary court forms with detailed instructions on how to fill them out.
$19.95/NAME

The Criminal Records Book
Attorney Warren Siegel • California 3rd Ed.
Shows you step-by-step how to seal criminal records, dismiss convictions, destroy marijuana records and reduce felony convictions.
$19.95/CRIM

audio cassette tapes

Winning in Small Claims Court
Attorney Ralph Warner with Joanne Greene • National 1st ed. • 60 minutes
This tape guides you through all the major issues involved in preparing and winning a small claims court case—deciding if there is a good case, assessing whether you can collect if you win, preparing your evidence, and arguing before the judge.
$14.95/TWIN

LEGAL REFORM

Legal Breakdown:
40 Ways to Fix Our Legal System
Nolo Press Editors and Staff • National 1st Ed.
Presents 40 common-sense proposals to make our legal system fairer, faster, cheaper and more accessible.
$8.95/LEG

BUSINESS/WORKPLACE

The Legal Guide for Starting & Running a Small Business
Attorney Fred S. Steingold • National 1st Ed.
An essential resource for every small business owner. Find out how to form a sole proprietorship, partnership or corporation, negotiate a favorable lease, hire and fire employees, write contracts and resolve disputes.
$19.95/RUNS

Sexual Harassment on the Job
Attorneys William Petrocelli & Barbara Kate Repa • National 1st Ed.
Describes what harassment is, what the laws are that make it illegal and how to put a stop to it. Invaluable both for employees experiencing harassment and for employers interested in creating a policy against sexual harassment and a procedure for handling complaints.
$14.95/HARS

Marketing Without Advertising
Michael Phillips & Salli Rasberry • National 1st Ed.
Outlines practical steps for building and expanding a small business without spending a lot of money on advertising.
$14.00/MWAD

Your Rights in the Workplace
Dan Lacey • National 1st Ed.
Here is the first comprehensive guide to workplace rights —from hiring to firing. Learn the legal rules about wages and overtime, maternity and parental leave, unemployment and disability insurance, worker's compensation, job safety, discrimination and illegal firings and layoffs.
$15.95/YRW

How to Write a Business Plan
Mike McKeever • National 4th Ed.
If you're thinking of starting a business or raising money to expand an existing one, this book will show you how to write the business plan and loan package necessary to finance your business and make it work.
$19.95/SBS

The Partnership Book
Attorneys Denis Clifford & Ralph Warner • National 4th Ed.
Shows you step-by-step how to write a solid partnership agreement that meets your needs. It covers initial contributions to the business, wages, profit-sharing, buyouts, death or retirement of a partner and disputes.
$24.95/PART

How to Form A Nonprofit Corporation
Attorney Anthony Mancuso • National 1st Ed.
Explains the legal formalities involved and provides detailed information on the differences in the law among all 50 states. It also contains forms for the Articles, Bylaws and Minutes you need, along with complete instructions for obtaining federal 501 (c) (3) tax exemptions and qualifying for public charity status.
$24.95/NNP

The California Nonprofit Corporation Handbook
Attorney Anthony Mancuso • California 6th Ed.
Shows you step-by-step how to form and operate a nonprofit corporation in California. It includes the latest corporate and tax law changes, and the forms for the Articles, Bylaws and Minutes.
$29.95/NON

How to Form Your Own Corporation
Attorney Anthony Mancuso
California 7th Ed. • New York 2nd Ed.
Texas 4th Ed. • Florida 3rd Ed.
These books contain the forms, instructions and tax information you need to incorporate a small business yourself and save hundreds of dollars in lawyers' fees.
California $29.95/CCOR
New York $24.95/NYCO
Texas $29.95/TCOR
Florida (with PC disk 3.5) $39.95/FLCO

The California Professional Corporation Handbook
Attorney Anthony Mancuso
California 4th Ed.
Health care professionals, lawyers, accountants and members of certain other professions must fulfill special requirements when forming a corporation in California. This book contains up-to-date tax information plus all the forms and instructions necessary to form a California professional corporation.
$34.95/PROF

The Independent Paralegal's Handbook
Attorney Ralph Warner • National 2nd Ed.
Provides legal and business guidelines for those who want to take routine legal work out of the law office and offer it for a reasonable fee in an independent business.
$24.95/PARA

audio cassette tapes

Getting Started as an Independent Paralegal
Attorney Ralph Warner • National 2nd ed. • Two tapes, approximately 2 hours
If you are interested in going into business as an Independent Paralegal—helping consumers prepare their own legal paperwork—you'll want to listen to these tapes. They will tell you everything you need to know about what legal tasks to handle, how much to charge and how to run a profitable business.
$44.95/GSIP

How to Start Your Own Business: Small Business Law
Attorney Ralph Warner with Joanne Greene • National 1st ed. • 60 minutes
This tape covers the basic issues facing the small business start-up: whether to organize as a sole proprietorship, partnership or corporation, how to protect the business name, what legal pitfalls to look out for when renting space, hiring employees and paying taxes.
$14.95/TBUS

software

Nolo's Partnership Maker
Attorney Anthony Mancuso & Mickael Radke • Version 1.0
Nolo's Partnership Maker prepares a legal partnership agreement for doing business in any state. You can select and assemble the standard partnership clauses provided or create your own customized agreement. And the agreement can be updated at any time. Includes on-line legal help screens, glossary and tutorial, and a manual that takes you through the process step-by-step.
IBM PC (3-1/2 & 5-1/4 disks included)
$129.95/PAGI1

California Incorporator
Attorney Anthony Mancuso
Version 1.0 (good only in CA)
Answer the questions on the screen and this software program will print out the 35-40 pages of documents you need to make your California corporation legal. Comes with a 200-page manual which explains the incorporation process.
IBM PC (3-1/2 & 5-1/4 disks included)
$129.00/INCI

books with disk

The California Nonprofit Corporation Handbook
(computer edition)
Attorney Anthony Mancuso • Version 1.0
This book/software package shows you step-by-step how to form and operate a nonprofit corporation in California. Included on disk are the forms for the Articles, Bylaws and Minutes.
IBM PC 5-1/4 $69.95/ NPI
IBM PC 3-1/2 $69.95/ NP3I
MACINTOSH $69.95/ NPM

How to Form Your Own New York Corporation & How to Form Your Own Texas Corporation
(computer editions)
Attorney Anthony Mancuso
These book/software packages contain the instructions and tax information and forms you need to incorporate a small business and save hundreds of dollars in lawyers' fees. All organizational forms are on disk. Both come with a 250-page manual.
New York 1st Ed.
IBM PC 5-1/4 $69.95/ NYCI
IBM PC 3-1/2 $69.95/ NYC3I
MACINTOSH $69.95/ NYCM

Texas 1st Ed.
IBM PC 5-1/4 $69.95/ TCI
IBM PC 3-1/2 $69.95/ TC3I
MACINTOSH $69.95/ TCM

THE NEIGHBORHOOD

Neighbor Law: Fences, Trees, Boundaries & Noise
Attorney Cora Jordan • National 1st Ed.
Answers common questions about the subjects that most often trigger disputes between neighbors: fences, trees, boundaries and noise. It explains how to find the law and resolve disputes without a nasty lawsuit.
$14.95/NEI

Dog Law
Attorney Mary Randolph • National 1st Ed.
A practical guide to the laws that affect dog owners and their neighbors. You'll find answers to common questions on such topics as biting, barking, veterinarians and more.
$12.95/DOG

MONEY MATTERS

Stand Up to the IRS
Attorney Fred Daily • National 1st Ed.
Gives detailed stategies on surviving an audit with the minimum amount of damage, appealing an audit decision, going to Tax Court and dealing with IRS collectors. It also discusses filing tax returns when you haven't done so in a while, tax crimes, concerns of small business people and getting help from the IRS ombudsman.
$19.95 / SIRS

Money Troubles: Legal Strategies to Cope With Your Debts
Attorney Robin Leonard • National 1st Ed.
Essential for anyone who is behind on your credit card bills or loan payments? It covers everything from knowing what your rights are, and asserting them, to helping you evaluate your individual situation. This practical, straightforward book is for anyone who needs help understanding and dealing with the complex and often scary topic of debts.
$16.95/MT

How to File for Bankruptcy
Attorneys Stephen Elias, Albin Renauer & Robin Leonard • National 4th Ed.
Trying to decide whether or not filing for bankruptcy makes sense? *How to File for Bankruptcy* contains an overview of the process and all the forms plus step-by-step instructions on the procedures to follow.
$25.95/HFB

Simple Contracts for Personal Use
Attorney Stephen Elias & Marcia Stewart • National 2nd Ed.
Contains clearly written legal form contracts to buy and sell property, borrow and lend money, store and lend personal property, release others from personal liability, or pay a contractor to do home repairs. Includes agreements to arrange childcare and other household help.
$16.95/CONT

law form kits

Nolo's Law Form Kit: Personal Bankruptcy
Attorneys Steve Elias, Albin Renauer & Robin Leonard and Lisa Goldoftas • National 1st Ed.
All the forms and instructions you need to file for Chapter 7 bankruptcy.
$14.95/KBNK

Nolo's Law Form Kit: Power of Attorney
Attorneys Denis Clifford & Mary Randolph and Lisa Goldoftas • National 1st Ed.
Assign someone you trust to take of your finances, business, real estate or children when you are away or unavailable. Easy, step-by step instructions show you how to fill out all forms, make all documents legal and binding and revoke a power of attorney when it is no longer necessary.
$14.95/KPA

Nolo's Law Forms Kit: Rebuild Your Credit
Attorney Robin Leonard • National 1st ed.
Provides strategies for dealing with debts and rebuilding your credit. Shows you how to negotiate with creditors and collection agencies, clean up your credit file, devise a spending plan and get credit in your name.
$14.95/KCRD

Nolo's Law Form Kit: Loan Agreements
Attorney Stephen Elias, Marcia Stewart & Lisa Goldoftas • National 1st ed.
Provides all the forms and instructions necessary to create a legal and effective promissory note. Shows how to decide on an interest rate, set a payment schedule and keep track of payments.
$14.95/KLOAN

Nolo's Law Form Kit: Buy and Sell Contracts
Attorney Stephen Elias, Marcia Stewart & Lisa Goldoftas • National 1st ed.
Step-by-step instructions and all the forms necessary for creating bills of sale for cars, boats, computers, electronic equipment, household appliances and other personal property.
$9.95/KCONT

FAMILY MATTERS

Divorce & Money
Violet Woodhouse & Victoria Felton-Collins with M.C. Blakeman • National 1st Ed.
Explains how to evaluate such major assets as family homes and businesses, investments, pensions, and how to arrive at a division of property that is fair to both sides.
$19.95/DIMO

The Living Together Kit
Attorneys Toni Ihara & Ralph Warner • National 6th Ed.
A detailed guide designed to help the increasing number of unmarried couples living together understand the laws that affect them. Sample agreements and instructions are included.
$17.95/LTK

How to Raise or Lower Child Support in California
Judge Roderic Duncan and Attorney Warren Siegal • California 1st ed.
Appropriate for parents on either side of the support issue. Because of recent law changes, many parents are entitled to a large increase. And those who have support obligations and have suffered a decrease in income are entitled to have their payments adjusted downwards. This book contains all the forms and instructions necessary to modify an existing child support order.
$16.95/CHLD

The Guardianship Book
Lisa Goldoftas & Attorney David Brown • California 1st Ed.
Provides step-by-step instructions and the forms needed to obtain a legal guardianship without a lawyer.
$19.95/GB

A Legal Guide for Lesbian and Gay Couples
Attorneys Hayden Curry & Denis Clifford • National 7th Ed.
Laws designed to regulate and protect married couples don't apply to lesbian and gay couples. This book shows you step-by-step how to write a living-together contract, plan for medical emergencies, and plan your estates. Includes forms, sample agreements and lists of both national lesbian and gay legal organizations and AIDS organizations.
$21.95/LG

How to Do Your Own Divorce
*Attorney Charles Sherman
(Texas Ed. by Sherman & Simons)
California 18th Ed. & Texas 4th Ed.*
These books contain all the forms and instructions you need to do your own uncontested divorce without a lawyer.
California $18.95/CDIV
Texas $17.95/TDIV

Practical Divorce Solutions
Attorney Charles Sherman • California 2nd Ed.
A valuable guide to the emotional aspects of divorce as well as an overview of the legal and financial decisions that must be made.
$12.95/PDS

California Marriage & Divorce Law
Attorneys Ralph Warner, Toni Ihara & Stephen Elias • California 11th Ed.
Explains community property, pre-nuptial contracts, foreign marriages, buying a house, getting a divorce, dividing property, and more.
$19.95/MARR

How to Adopt Your Stepchild in California
Frank Zagone & Attorney Mary Randolph • California 3rd Ed.
Provides sample forms and step-by-step instructions for completing a simple uncontested stepparent adoption in California.
$19.95/ADOP

JUST FOR FUN

Devil's Advocates: The Unnatural History of Lawyers
by Andrew & Jonathan Roth • National 1st Ed.
A painless and hilarious education, tracing the legal profession. Careful attention is given to the world's worst lawyers, most preposterous cases and most ludicrous courtroom strategies.
$12.95/DA

29 Reasons Not to Go to Law School
Attorneys Ralph Warner & Toni Ihara • National 3rd Ed.
Filled with humor and piercing observations, this book can save you three years, $70,000 and your sanity.
$9.95/29R

Poetic Justice: The Funniest, Meanest Things Ever Said About Lawyers
Edited by Jonathan & Andrew Roth • National 1st Ed.
A great gift for anyone in the legal profession who has managed to maintain a sense of humor.
$8.95/PJ

PATENT, COPYRIGHT & TRADEMARK

Trademark: How to Name Your Business & Product
Attorneys Kate McGrath and Stephen Elias, With Trademark Attorney Sarah Shena • National 1st Ed.
Every business owner needs to know how to protect names used to market services and products. This book shows how to: choose a name or logo that others can't copy, conduct a trademark search, register a trademark with the U.S. Patent and Trademark Office and protect and maintain the trademark.
$29.95 / TRD

Patent It Yourself
Attorney David Pressman • National 3rd Ed.
From the patent search to the actual application, this book covers everything including the use and licensing of patents, successful marketing and how to deal with infringement.
$36.95/PAT

The Inventor's Notebook
Fred Grissom & Attorney David Pressman • National 1st Ed.
Helps you document the process of successful independent inventing by providing forms, instructions, references to relevant areas of patent law, a bibliography of legal and non-legal aids and more.
$19.95/INOT

How to Copyright Software
Attorney M.J. Salone • National 3rd Ed.
This book tells you how to register your copyright for maximum protection and discusses who owns a copyright on software developed by more than one person.
$39.95/COPY

The Copyright Handbook
Attorney Stephen Fishman • National 1st Ed.
Provides forms and step-by-step instructions for protecting all types of written expression under U.S. and international copyright law. It contains detailed reference chapters on copyright infringement, fair use, works for hire and transfers of copyright ownership.
$24.95/COHA

LANDLORDS & TENANTS

The Landlord's Law Book, Vol. 1: Rights & Responsibilities
Attorneys David Brown & Ralph Warner • California 3rd Ed.
This book contains information on deposits, leases and rental agreements, inspections (tenants' privacy rights), habitability (rent withholding), ending a tenancy, liability and rent control.
$29.95/LBRT

The Landlord's Law Book, Vol. 2: Evictions
Attorney David Brown • California 4th Ed.
Updated for 1993, this book will show you step-by-step how to go to court and evict a tenant. Contains all the tear-out forms and necessary instructions.
$32.95/LBEV

Tenants' Rights
Attorneys Myron Moskovitz & Ralph Warner • California 11th Ed.
Explains how to handle your relationship with your landlord and understand your legal rights when you find yourself in disagreement. A special section on rent control cities is included.
$15.95/CTEN

HOMEOWNERS

How to Buy a House in California
Attorney Ralph Warner, Ira Serkes & George Devine • California 2nd Ed.
This book shows you how to find a house, work with a real estate agent, make an offer and negotiate intelligently. Includes information on all types of mortgages as well as private financing options.
$19.95/BHCA

For Sale By Owner
George Devine • California 2nd Ed.
Provides essential information about pricing your house, marketing it, writing a contract and going through escrow.
$24.95/FSBO

Homestead Your House
Attorneys Ralph Warner, Charles Sherman & Toni Ihara • California 8th Ed.
Shows you how to file a Declaration of Homestead and includes complete instructions and tear-out forms.
$9.95/HOME

The Deeds Book
Attorney Mary Randolph • California 2nd Ed.
If you own real estate, you'll need to sign a new deed when you transfer the property or put it in trust as part of your estate planning. This book shows you how to find the right kind of deed, complete the tear-out forms and record them in the county recorder's public records.
$15.95/DEED

OLDER AMERICANS

Elder Care: Choosing & Financing Long-Term Care
Attorney Joseph Matthews • National 1st Ed.
Guides you in choosing and paying for long-term care, alerting you to practical concerns and explaining laws that may affect your decisions.
$16.95/ELD

Social Security, Medicare & Pensions
Attorney Joseph Matthews with Dorothy Matthews Berman • National 5th Ed.
This book contains invaluable guidance through the current maze of rights and benefits for those 55 and over, including Medicare, Medicaid and Social Security retirement and disability benefits and age discrimination protections.
$15.95/SOA

REFERENCE

Legal Research: How to Find and Understand the Law
Attorneys Stephen Elias & Susan Levinkind • National 3rd Ed.
A valuable tool on its own or as a companion to just about every other Nolo book. Gives easy-to-use, step-by-step instructions on how to find legal information.
$19.95/LRES

Family Law Dictionary
Attorneys Robin Leonard & Stephen Elias • National 2nd Ed.
Here's help for anyone who has a question or problem involving family law—marriage, divorce, adoption or living together.
$13.95/FLD

Legal Research Made Easy: A Roadmap Through the Law Library Maze
2-1/2 hr. videotape and 40-page manual
Nolo Press/Legal Star Communications • National 1st Ed.
University of California law professor Bob Berring explains how to use all the basic legal research tools in your local law library with an easy-to-follow six-step research plan and a sense of humor.
$89.95/LRME

CONSUMER/REFERENCE

Nolo's Pocket Guide to California Law
Attorney Lisa Guerin and Nolo Press Editors • California 1st Ed.
Get quick clear answers to questions about child support, custody, consumer rights, employee rights, government benefits, divorce, bankruptcy, adoption, wills and much more.
$10.95/CLAW

Barbara Kaufman's Consumer Action Guide
Barbara Kaufman • California 1st Ed.
This practical handbook is filled with information on hundreds of consumer topics. Gives consumers access to their legal rights, providing addresses and phone numbers of where to complain when things go wrong, and providing resources if more help is necessary.
$14.95/CAG

VISIT OUR STORE

If you live in the Bay Area, be sure to visit the Nolo Press Bookstore on the corner of 9th & Parker Streets in west Berkeley. You'll find our complete line of books and software—new and "damaged"—all at a discount. We also have t-shirts, posters and a selection of business and legal self-help books from other publishers.

Monday to Friday 10 A.M. to 5 P.M.
Thursdays 10 A.M. to 6 P.M.
Saturdays 10 A.M. to 4:30 P.M.
Sundays 11 A.M. to 4 P.M.

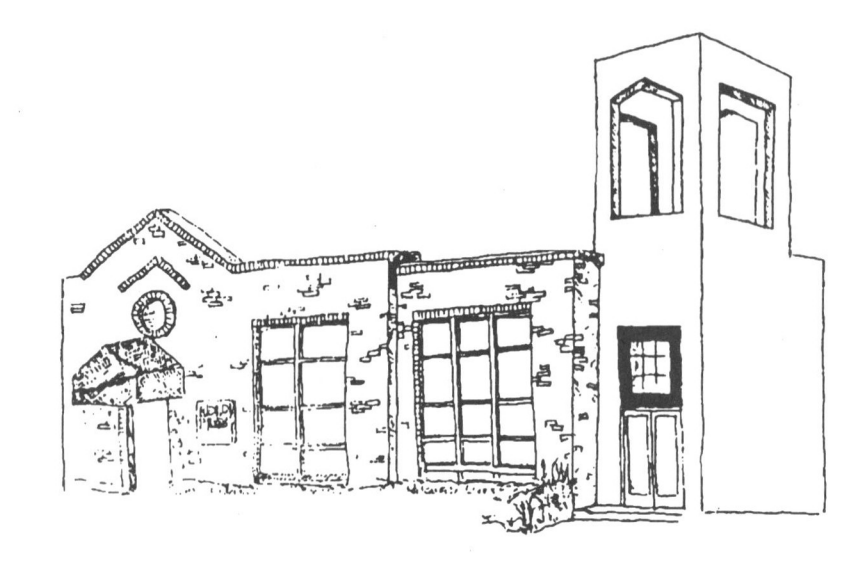

NOLO PRESS / 950 PARKER STREET / BERKELEY CA 94710

ORDER FORM

Name

Address (UPS to street address, Priority Mail to P.O. boxes)

Catalog Code	Quantity	Item	Unit price	Total
		Subtotal		
		Sales tax (California residents only)		
		Shipping & handling		
		2nd day UPS		
		TOTAL		

PRICES SUBJECT TO CHANGE

SALES TAX
California residents add your local tax

SHIPPING & HANDLING
$4.00 1 item
$5.00 2-3 items
+$.50 each additional item
Allow 2-3 weeks for delivery

IN A HURRY?
UPS 2nd day delivery is available:
Add $5.00 (contiguous states) or $8.00 (Alaska & Hawaii) to your regular shipping and handling charges

FOR FASTER SERVICE, USE YOUR CREDIT CARD AND OUR TOLL-FREE NUMBERS:
Monday-Friday, 7 a.m. to 5 p.m. Pacific Time
Order line   1 (800) 992-6656
General Information   1 (510) 549-1976
Fax us your order   1 (800) 645-0895

METHOD OF PAYMENT
☐ Check enclosed
☐ VISA ☐ Mastercard ☐ Discover Card ☐ American Express

Account #   Expiration Date

Signature Authorizing

Phone   CTEN 11

NOLO PRESS / 950 PARKER STREET / BERKELEY CA 94710

NOLO BOOKS ON DEFENDING YOUR RIGHTS IN COURT

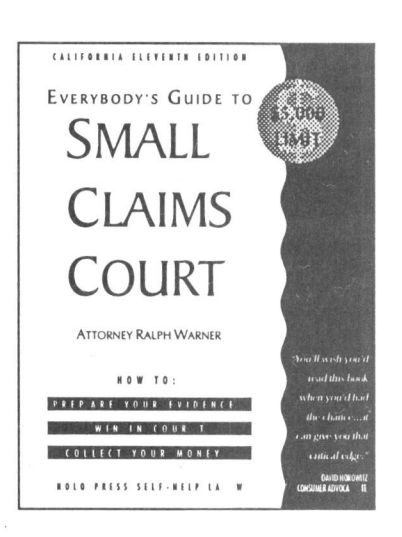

Everybody's Guide to Small Claims Court
by Attorney Ralph Warner

Everybody's Guide to Municipal Court
by Judge Roderic Duncan

Collect Your Court Judgment
by Gini Graham Scott, Attorney Stephen Elias & Lisa Goldoftas

Please see the preceding catalog pages for more information.

To order, please use order form in catalog or call 1-800-992-6656

NOLO BOOKS ON MONEY MATTERS

Money Troubles

by Attorney Robin Leonard

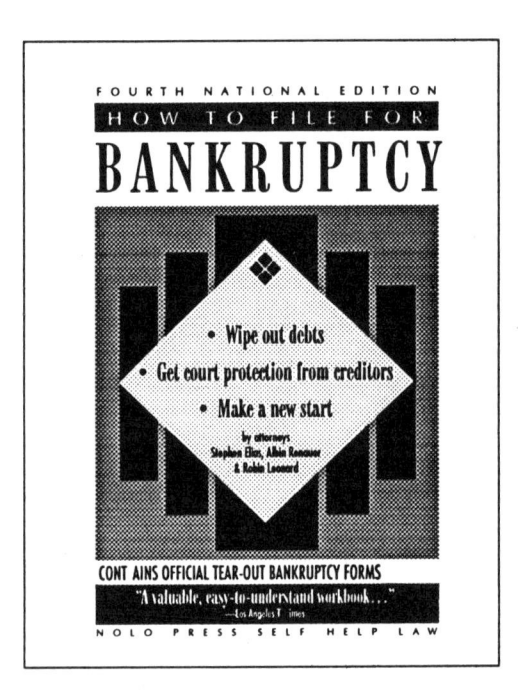

How to File For Bankruptcy

by Stephen Elias, Albin Renauer & Attorney Robin Leonard

Please see the preceding catalog pages for more information.

To order, please use order form in catalog or call 1-800-992-6656

FREE NOLO NEWS SUBSCRIPTION

When you register, we'll send you our quarterly newspaper, the *Nolo News,* free for two years. (U.S. addresses only.) Here's what you'll get in every issue:

INFORMATIVE ARTICLES

Written by Nolo editors, articles provide practical legal information on issues you encounter in everyday life: family law, wills, debts, consumer rights, and much more.

UPDATE SERVICE

The *Nolo News* keeps you informed of legal changes that affect any Nolo book and software program.

BOOK AND SOFTWARE REVIEWS

We're always looking for good legal and consumer books and software from other publishers. When we find them, we review them and offer them in our mail order catalog.

ANSWERS TO YOUR LEGAL QUESTIONS

Our readers are always challenging us with good questions on a variety of legal issues. So in each issue, "Auntie Nolo" gives sage advice and sound information.

COMPLETE NOLO PRESS CATALOG

The *Nolo News* contains an up-to-the-minute catalog of all Nolo books and software, which you can order using our toll-free "800" order line. And you can see at a glance if you're using an out-of-date version of a Nolo product.

LAWYER JOKES

Nolo's famous lawyer joke column continually gets the goat of the legal establishment. If we print a joke you send in, you'll get a $20 Nolo gift certificate.

We promise *never* to give your name and address to any other organization.

Your Registration Card

Complete and Mail Today

TENANTS' RIGHTS .... Registration Card

We'd like to know what you think! Please take a moment to fill out and return this postage paid card for a free two-year subscription to the *Nolo News.* If you already receive the *Nolo News,* we'll extend your subscription.

Name _____ Ph.( ) _____

Address _____

City _____ State _____ Zip _____

Where did you hear about this book? _____

For what purpose did you use this book? _____

Did you consult a lawyer?   Yes   No   Not Applicable

Was it easy for you to use this book? (very easy) 5 4 3 2 1 (very difficult)

Did you find this book helpful?   (very)   5 4 3 2 1 (not at all)

Comments _____

_____

_____

_____

_____

THANK YOU   CTEN 11.3

[Nolo books are]..."written in plain language, free of legal mumbo jumbo, and spiced with witty personal observations."

—ASSOCIATED PRESS

"Well-produced and slickly written, the [Nolo] books are designed to take the mystery out of seemingly involved procedures, carefully avoiding legalese and leading the reader step-by-step through such everyday legal problems as filling out forms, making up contracts, and even how to behave in court."

—SAN FRANCISCO EXAMINER

"...Nolo publications...guide people simply through the how, when, where and why of law."

—WASHINGTON POST

"Increasingly, people who are not lawyers are performing tasks usually regarded as legal work... And consumers, using books like Nolo's, do routine legal work themselves."

—NEW YORK TIMES

"...All of [Nolo's] books are easy-to-understand, are updated regularly, provide pull-out forms...and are often quite moving in their sense of compassion for the struggles of the lay reader."

—SAN FRANCISCO CHRONICLE

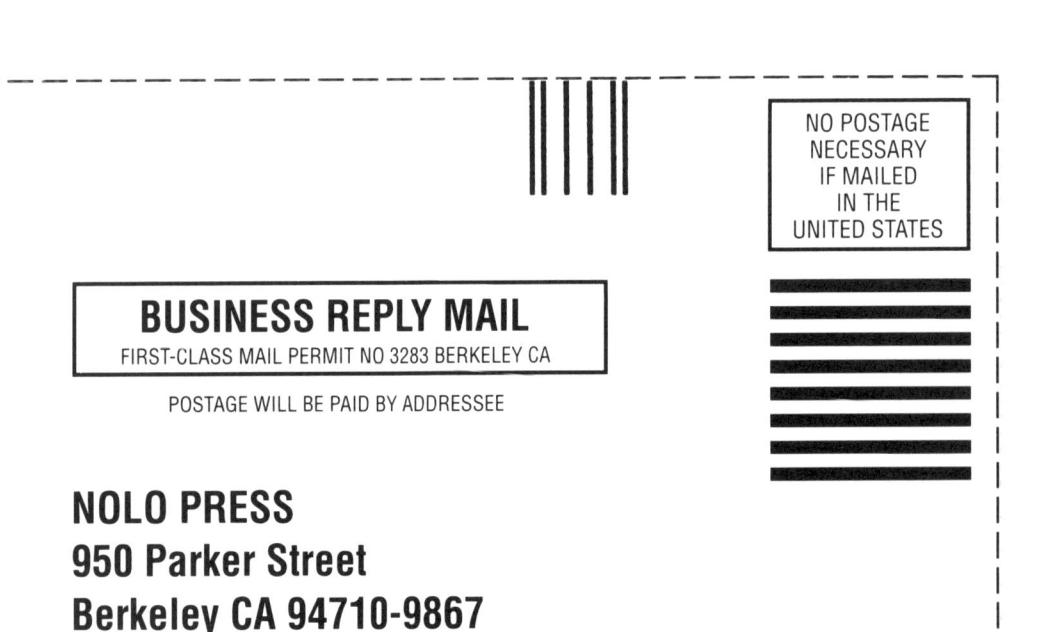

BUSINESS REPLY MAIL
FIRST-CLASS MAIL PERMIT NO 3283 BERKELEY CA

POSTAGE WILL BE PAID BY ADDRESSEE

NO POSTAGE
NECESSARY
IF MAILED
IN THE
UNITED STATES

NOLO PRESS
950 Parker Street
Berkeley CA 94710-9867